THE LAST OPERA

RUSSIAN MUSIC STUDIES

Simon A. Morrison and Peter Schmelz, *editors*

THE LAST OPERA

The Rake's Progress *in the Life of Stravinsky and Sung Drama*

Chandler Carter

INDIANA UNIVERSITY PRESS

This book is a publication of

Indiana University Press
Office of Scholarly Publishing
Herman B Wells Library 350
1320 East 10th Street
Bloomington, Indiana 47405 USA

iupress.indiana.edu

© 2019 by Lee Chandler Carter, II

All rights reserved

No part of this book may be reproduced or utilized in any form or by any means, electronic or mechanical, including photocopying and recording, or by any information storage and retrieval system, without permission in writing from the publisher. The paper used in this publication meets the minimum requirements of the American National Standard for Information Sciences—Permanence of Paper for Printed Library Materials, ANSI Z39.48-1992.

Library of Congress Cataloging-in-Publication Data

Names: Carter, Chandler, author.
Title: The last opera : the Rake's progress in the life of Stravinsky and sung drama / Chandler Carter.
Description: Bloomington, Indiana : Indiana University Press, [2019] | Series: Russian music studies | Includes bibliographical references and index.
Identifiers: LCCN 2018031197 (print) | LCCN 2018032316 (ebook) | ISBN 9780253041593 (e-book) | ISBN 9780253041579 (hardback : alk. paper) | ISBN 9780253041586 (pbk. : alk. paper)
Subjects: LCSH: Stravinsky, Igor, 1882-1971. Rake's progress. | Opera.
Classification: LCC ML410.S932 (ebook) | LCC ML410.S932 C53 2019 (print) | DDC 782.1—dc23
LC record available at https://lccn.loc.gov/2018031197

1 2 3 4 5 24 23 22 21 20 19

For Jane and Owen

CONTENTS

Acknowledgments ix

Part 1 The Cultural Moment

   Prelude 3

   1 A Convergence of Minds 19

Part 2 The Drama

   2 A Happy Collaboration 50

   3 Deeper Meanings 76

Part 3 The Music

   Introduction to Part 3 98

   4 Stravinsky's "Special Sense" 101

   5 Displacement, Text Setting, and Stravinsky's Evolving Aesthetic 123

   6 Stravinsky's Truths and Mozart's Lies—Music, Emotion, and Theatrical Distance 149

   7 The Structure of Scenes 172

   8 Ruin, Disaster, Saving Grace 196

Part 4 Performance

   9 Venice 237

   10 How *The Rake* Became a Masterpiece 268

Part 5 After *The Rake*

   11 "Good People, Just a Moment" 299

   Bibliography 327

   Index 337

ACKNOWLEDGMENTS

My research has been supported by numerous faculty research grants, a sabbatical leave from Hofstra University, and a generous fellowship from the Paul Sacher Foundation in Basel. I thank Dr. Heidy Zimmerman, Dr. Ulrich Mosch, and the staff of the Sacher Foundation for facilitating my study of Stravinsky's sketches and letters and especially Robert Piencikowski for his generous advice and encouragement over my many summer visits. I also thank the archivists and staffs of the Albert A. Berg Collection of English and American Literature at the New York Public Library; the Harry Ransom Center in Austin; the Royal Swedish Opera in Stockholm; the Glyndebourne Festival in Sussex, England; the Santa Fe Opera; and the Art Institute of Chicago, who allowed me access to important primary material.

For his countless insights, advice, and suggestions, I owe an enormous debt of gratitude to Joseph N. Straus, a model theorist and scholar who shares my love for this opera, who guided my research during my days as a doctoral student and aspiring Stravinskian, and who more recently read through the complete manuscript. I also greatly appreciate the valuable guidance from journal editors Joel Lester and Kate van Orden for earlier articles that formed important parts of the book. I thank my Basel colleague Natalia Braginskaya for pointing out Stravinsky's references to Russian music, and Polina Belimova and Rebecca Mitchell for their help in translating the Russian letters. And special thanks to my friends and colleagues Philip Stoecker, Mark Anson-Cartwright, and Brenda Elsey for helpful feedback and suggestions.

I am especially grateful for the constructive comments and criticism from the anonymous reviewers of this volume and indebted to my editors at Indiana University Press, Janice Frisch and Professors Peter Schmelz and Simon Morrison, for their careful reading and help in strengthening my work. Lastly, I thank my wife Jane Huber and son Owen for their forbearance and understanding. Both are passionate artists and thinkers in their own right who have inspired me in this and all my work. I dedicate this book to them.

Excerpts and images from Stravinsky's compositional sketches and personal correspondence are reprinted by permission of the Paul Sacher Foundation, Stravinsky Collection.

Excerpts from Auden's and Kallman's correspondence are reprinted by permission of the W. H. Auden Estate, the Chester Kallman Estate, and The Henry W. and Albert A. Berg Collection of English and American Literature, The New York Public Library, Astor, Lenox and Tilden Foundations.

Excerpts from *Doctor Faustus: The Life of the German Composer Adrian Leverkühn as told by a Friend* by Thomas Mann, translated by John E. Woods, translation copyright © 1997 by Penguin Random House LLC. Used by permission of Alfred A. Knopf, an imprint of the Knopf Doubleday Publishing Group, a division of Penguin Random House LLC. All rights reserved.

Excerpt from *Poetics of Music in the Form of Six Lessons* by Igor Stravinsky, translated by Arthur Knodel and Ingolf Dahl, Cambridge, MA: Harvard University Press, Copyright © 1942, 1947, 1970, 1975 by the President and Fellows of Harvard College.

Excerpts from the writings of Jörg Immendorff are used by permission, copyright © The Estate of Jörg Immendorff, Courtesy Galerie Michael Werner Märkisch Wilmersdorf, Köln & New York.

Excerpts from *Stravinsky: The Chronicle of a Friendship: 1948/1971* by Robert Craft, Nashville: Vanderbilt University Press, 1994, used by permission.

Excerpt from *Opera News* used by permission.

PART 1

THE CULTURAL MOMENT

PRELUDE

Composer Igor Stravinsky and poet W. H. Auden—two of the finest artists and most compelling minds of the twentieth century—collaborated from the fall of 1947 through the summer of 1951 on an opera, *The Rake's Progress*. At the time, their self-consciously conventional work seemed to appeal only to conservative audiences. Few perceived the creators were also confronting the central crisis of the modern age, for their story of a hapless eighteenth-century Everyman dramatizes the very limits of human will, a theme Auden insists underlies all Opera.

The story of their collaboration, the opera itself, and its subsequent reception also reveal each man's struggle to assert himself. Inner vision and outer forces especially drove the life and work of Stravinsky. He possessed perhaps the most distinctly individual voice in twentieth-century music, yet openly sought to be influenced and not just musically. Friends and colleagues he drew in close positively shaped his personal and professional choices, especially in his early and later years; those he kept at a distance did so negatively. The larger world of ideas and events, both great and terrible, likewise molded him. Revolution and world wars twice dislocated him from his home and loved ones, severing old ties and creating new ones; politics, in government and in the arts, stifled as well as kindled opportunities; competing ideologies established the terms we use to discuss his music and with which even the composer defined himself.

Probably more than any musician of his time, Stravinsky sought to control his circumstances, in part by shaping how the world perceived him and his work. Of the impact of Diaghilev and eighteenth-century classicism on his *Pulcinella*, he contended: "I created the possibility of the commission as much as it created me."[1] The Great Artist fascinates not just because he (the type is gendered) embodies the *Zeitgeist*, which is to say the cultural moment expresses itself through him. He also—and by contrast—exemplifies the very possibility of autonomy against the raging tempest of ideas, people, and events. In other words, Great Artists, we imagine, create the cultural moment. We exalt them as "unique creators irreducible to any condition or conditioning."[2] Indeed, their collective stories have defined the modern age. Postmodern scholars try to crack their seemingly freestanding facades, but the allure of the artist remains. Through him we project an ideal version of our collective self—at least, I confess, I so imagine Igor Stravinsky. If this brilliant, diminutive Russian émigré could somehow navigate the storms and stresses of his time and still assert artistic control, defy commercial pressures and still thrive, determine the nature and scope of his most ambitious work despite countless obstacles and entrenched resistance, then perhaps a vestige of autonomy remains.

To balance these competing perspectives *The Last Opera* will tell three stories, each framing but also interwoven with the next. The central, most detailed story explores Stravinsky's longest work and possibly richest collaboration. These chapters present a case study in the extent to which individuals and their work can encapsulate their time.[3] The second story fills out that time by positioning the opera as a focal point in the journeys of Stravinsky and those who helped him realize it—librettists Wystan H. Auden and Chester Kallman; his protégé Robert Craft; and his compatriot, fellow composer, and close friend, Nicolas Nabokov. By exploring the ominous cultural landscape in which these fascinating individuals lived and worked, the book extends well beyond a single opera and its nominal creators. It captures a pivotal twenty-five-year span (roughly 1945–70) during which modernists like Stravinsky and Auden confronted a tectonic shift in their world. This story in turn becomes swept up in the 400-year history of opera that both coincides with and marks the larger modern era. Observations about this seemingly waning genre frame the book and, thus, I begin.

The Last Opera?

My title is more conversation starter than definitive claim. Auden might have approved, though he would have thought of his collaboration with Stravinsky as a new first opera rather the last. Shortly after he delivered the completed libretto on March 31, 1948, the poet wrote for *Vogue* a light piece explaining the opera fanatic as he understood him:

> He is a conservative who does not welcome new opera; there are too many from the Golden Age which he has still to hear. That age is over: after Verdi and Wagner come Puccini and Strauss, but one can not listen to either without being conscious that this is the end of something. From Gluck until them the development of the form is continuous and organic, but there it stops. New operas may and, let us hope, will be written, but their composers can not carry on from where their predecessors left off, but must start anew from the beginning.[4]

Auden neither openly confessed to being such a fanatic nor did he mention his ongoing collaboration with the world's most famous living composer, though neither was a secret. (Lincoln Kirstein described the poet to Stravinsky: "He adores opera; he spends half his time playing records of Mozart and Verdi; for him opera is a ritual."[5]) The irony, or at least tension between these two conditions, was not lost on the librettist; rather, he was attempting, implicitly, to frame the creation of their new opera in light of that tension. How does one go about creating sung drama in the mid-twentieth century? If conventional opera doesn't interest you, then explore new creative paths. Yet, if you love Opera—as Stravinsky, Auden, and Kallman all professed—following that well-traveled road would seem, as the poet suggests, to lead to a dead end. And just how does one "start anew from the beginning"? These questions form a jumping off point for my exploration of *The Rake*, its creators, and its place in the operatic canon.

Artists and critics have been pronouncing the death of major art forms—painting, the novel, and ballet—for almost a century.[6] With the demise of old Europe, so the reasoning goes, came the demise of its cultured institutions. Like Auden, many date the end of opera to the last works of Puccini or Strauss. Pierre Boulez insisted, "No opera worth discussing has been composed since *Wozzeck* [1922] and *Lulu* [1935]."[7] Even Schoenberg's *Erwartung* (1909) has received a vote for this dubious distinction. The justification for such claims is that in the late modern and postmodern age opera functions anachronistically, as an elaborately preserved relic of a temporally distant cultural practice. "Whereas anthropologists have to travel to the primeval forests of South America and to the islands of the Pacific to find relics of ancient social rituals," writes philosopher Mladen Dolar, "we merely need to go to the opera."[8]

Dolar and coauthor Žižek associate the death of opera with the birth of psychoanalysis (hence, their vote for *Erwartung*). They claim that, in dramatizing ancient and modern myths, opera functioned to process and interpret the psychic underpinnings of modern man. Gary Tomlinson develops a similar thesis by tracing the "changing picture of envoiced subjectivity in the early modern and modern West" through the history of opera.[9] Rendered obsolete by the discoveries of Freud, Dolar argues, opera now occupies the hallowed halls of culture more as a preserved ritual than as a vital aesthetic force.

Auden makes essentially the same point, but being a true modernist he refused to surrender without a fight. His collaboration with Stravinsky only further whetted his appetite for this obsolete genre, which he compared favorably to the ancient tradition that first inspired it: "As a period of sustained creative activity in one medium, the seventy-five-odd years of Athenian drama . . . are surpassed by the hundred and twenty-five years between Gluck's *Orpheus* and Verdi's *Othello*, which comprise the golden age of European opera."[10] Indeed, for Auden the operatic voice expressed—and continues to express—the essential force driving the modern subject:

> The golden age of opera, from Mozart to Verdi, coincided with the golden age of liberal humanism, of unquestioning belief in freedom and progress. If good operas are rarer today [1951], this may be because, not only have we learned that we are less free than nineteenth-century humanism imagined, but also have become less certain that freedom is an unequivocal blessing, that the free are necessarily the good. To say that operas are more difficult to write does not mean that they are impossible. That would only follow if we should cease to believe in free-will and personality altogether. Every high C accurately struck utterly demolishes the theory that we are the irresponsible puppets of fate or chance.[11]

Auden meant the reference to high C literally and may have argued the same point when he talked Stravinsky into altering his original ending of Anne's act 1 Cabaletta, shown in example 0.1. In early 1949, during his annual winter trip to

a. Short score, dated Jan. 16, 1949.

b. Final version, altered after playthrough for Auden on Feb. 3, 1949.

Example 0.1. Comparison of original version (a) and final version (b) of the end of Anne's cabaletta (1.3).

New York, Stravinsky played through the completed first act for a group of close friends. Robert Craft describes the scene:

> We got to Sasha Schneider's for the *Rake*. Nabokov and Patricia [Blake] are already there, and Balanchine who, with Auden, follows the score over I. S.'s shoulder at the piano . . . Auden seems unaware that his violations of the strict rule of silence have irritated I. S. to an explosive degree. At the conclusion of the act, Auden asks him to change the soprano's final note to a high "C." The word is wrong, I. S. says, whereupon Auden, after much "uh-uh-uh"-ing and "now-let's-see"-ing, comes up with a new last ending in "heart."[12]

Auden described the play-through to his partner and colibrettist:

> I went off to the Ambassador Hotel to go through Act I. All your suggestions were conveyed and enthusiastically received; I wish you had been there to get the credit. I'm afraid you'll have to swallow my couplet for the Cabaletta
>
>> Time cannot alter
>> Thy loving heart
>>> Thy ever-loving heart.
>
> I was faced with fitting it into the music and it was the only thing I could think up that would fit.
>   The performance was from the piano score with the *maestro* at the piano: Bob Craft, Balanchine, self etc. screaming parts.[13]

That Stravinsky, even when irritated, was willing to make such a significant change attests to his respect for—and agreement with—Auden's reasoning. The poet was not asking for a merely conventional ending. On the contrary, for him the soprano's vocal feat, clichéd though it may be, attests to the possibility of individuation.

Enticed by opera's connection to deeper philosophical issues, Auden with Kallman would produce four more libretti: *Delia* (1952), which Stravinsky declined to set; *Elegy for Young Lovers* (1956) and *The Bassarids* (1961) for Hans Werner Henze; and *Love's Labour's Lost* (1973) for Nicolas Nabokov. *Elegy* has even clawed its way into the repertoire of European houses. Indeed, this expensive rite continues to attract leading composers—the late modernist masters who have indulged themselves (Stockhausen, Ligeti, Berio, Messiaen, even Elliot Carter) would seem to outnumber those who haven't—which may only testify to its lingering cachet. As with artists and performers, death seems to have enhanced Opera's reputation.

About Labels

> I believe "music drama" and "opera" to be very, very different things. My life work is a devotion to the latter.
>
> —Stravinsky, "Reflections on the *Rake*"

Born "from the spirit of humanism," the genre of opera, as we have come to label it, spans roughly 1600 to 1950 (granting, for the moment, the conceit of my title) and thus coincides with what Auden called the "age of liberal humanism."[14] Indeed, as much as painting and literature, opera helped define the modern era. What is usually meant when the label "modern" is applied to art and music—which I term twentieth-century modernism, or "modernist"—is better understood as the anxious final chapter of a much longer and more variegated period. The most extravagant expression of modern sensibility, Opera was also the most vulnerable when the shadow that fell across Europe and the world eclipsed the cultural landscape as well. The genre's demise thus signals the postmodern era, successor to not only the final modernist phase but also to the entire 400-year epoch. Yet, if Opera has died, she was the canary in the mineshaft of modern culture, and her singing echoes still.

Of course, this narrative assumes a narrow definition, something the evolving genre of sung dramas eluded throughout most of its history. Labels have always been loose. Seventeenth-century Italian composers wrote "tragedies," "fables," and "dramas" "in" or "through music"; the French court produced "tragédies lyriques" or "tragédies en musique"; the English wrote "masques" and "semi-operas." The term *opera seria* came to distinguish eighteenth-century serious works in Italian from various other nonserious or non-Italian categories, but only as the genre waned. Still, a consensus was forming. By the mid-nineteenth century, serious opera finally become "Opera"—except for the Italians, who continued to label their works "dramma lirico," "dramma tragico," "tragedia lirica," and "melodramma." Lawrence Kramer refers to Opera (big O) as arising "in the aftermath of the collapse of opera seria, . . . at the point of concurrence of two historical trends: the gradual replacement of aristocratic by bourgeois life as the paradigm of subjectivity and social presentation."[15] This Golden Age, though, only ripened the genre for a new round of reform by the next frustrated genius: thus, Wagner's "music drama" and the first of the obituary pronouncements: "With Rossini the real *life history of opera* comes to an end."[16]

Grounding the term in the broader cultural practice, Kramer paradoxically—but rightly—categorizes Wagner's and Strauss's music dramas as "best examples" of Opera. And thus nowadays, whether we're attending *Die Walküre*, *Carmen*, *Die Zauberflöte*, or *L'Orfeo*, we still say we go to the "opera." However, just because opera companies continue to stage new works doesn't mean *The Rake's Progress* isn't the end of a tradition. That we cling to the Italian term betrays the essential foreignness of the whole endeavor. The Italian and French artists who established its conventions begat a tradition that evolved naturally into various forms well into the twentieth century. German composers forged their own national tradition, reflected in their own set of conventions and labels. By contrast, the sung drama that grew from native English culture, beginning with *The Beggar's Opera* (1728), is musical theater. English audiences regarded "Opera" as pretentious, an attitude William Hogarth captures in the stodgy Handel-like figure playing through "The Rape of the Sabines, a New Opera" in, of all places, the second of his *Rake's Progress* series (1735) shown in figure 0.1.

Impetus behind *The Rake*

> *The Rake's Progress* is, emphatically, an opera, an opera of arias and recitatives, choruses and ensembles. Its musical structure, the conception of the use of these forms, even to the relations of tonalities, is in the line of the classical tradition.
>
> —Stravinsky, "Reflections on the *Rake*"

In his novel *Doctor Faustus*, Thomas Mann describes a proposed opera, the goal of which "was as Un-Wagnerian as possible, not even remotely akin to that mythic pathos and demonic natural world: a revival of opera buffa, in the spirit of artistic satire and as a satire on artificiality, a thing of the most playful preciosity, mocking both affected asceticism and the euphuistic fruit that classical studies bore in society."[17] Though he completed the novel before Stravinsky even began *The Rake*, the similarity between Mann's imagined opera and Stravinsky's real one is no coincidence. During the novel's gestation, Mann had read the composer's autobiography, "studied 'with the pencil,' that is to say, making underlinings for rereading."[18]

Stravinsky and Auden disclaimed any reformer's mission when, in November 1947, they set out to create *The Rake's Progress*. The composer explained their

Fig. 0.1. William Hogarth, *A Rake's Progress*, Plate II, "The Levee," June 1735, etching and engraving in black on ivory laid paper, 312 × 388 mm (images), Gift of Horace S. Oakley, 1921.339, The Art Institute of Chicago.

conservative impulse in notes for the first commercially released recording: "[Auden and I] knew very definitely what kind of opera we wanted to write . . . the type of Mozart-Italian opera that we both most admired."[19] Elsewhere he claimed to have previously "never written a 'real opera. By real,' Stravinsky says, 'I mean conventional.'"[20] True enough; his previous works for the theater avoid on principle most operatic conventions. Opera companies commonly stage three of them: *The Nightingale* (1908–14), *Mavra* (1923), and the opera-oratorio *Oedipus Rex* (1927), though only in *Mavra* are singers usually involved in the staging. *Les Noces* (1914–17), *Pulcinella* (1920), and *Perséphone* (1934), though both sung and danced (by different performers), are billed respectively as "choreographic scenes," "ballet," and "melodrama." From such idiosyncratic hybrids the conventional *Rake* stands apart.

In his initial invitation to Auden, Stravinsky indicates more clearly what the opera would not be (Wagnerian) than what it would. "Bear in mind," he wrote the poet in early October, "that I will compose *not* a musical drama, but just an opera with definitely separated numbers."[21] Even a decade after the premiere, Stravinsky continued to emphasize the distinction between his "number" opera and the "Daedalian examples of Alban Berg"; between his story "told . . . almost entirely in song—as distinguished from so-called speech-song, and Wagnerian continuous melody"; between himself and operatic reformers like "a Gluck, a Wagner or a Berg."[22] That *The Rake* was first an anti–music drama makes sense for a composer of Stravinsky's aesthetic proclivities and artistic stature; ambitious creative acts, *pace* Wagner, necessarily reject as well as embrace predecessors. Wagner's chief successor, Richard Strauss, was still alive in 1947 and Berg's two music dramas were already being accepted as modernist masterworks—that latter fact alone indicates a growing perception of conventional opera's irrelevance for living composers. If Stravinsky had any hope of countering this decline he had better act quickly.

From this initial negative impulse, composer and poet would forge a pointed critique. Auden later summarized:

> Our Tom Rakewell [tenor] is a man to whom the anticipation of experience is always exciting and its realization in actual fact always disappointing. . . .The real world from which he flies but can never forget is represented by Anne Trulove (soprano) with whom, when the curtain rises, he is singing a love duet in an idyllic garden [act 1, scene 1]; the instigator and director of his flight is personified in Nick Shadow (baritone), whom his first wish causes to appear with the news that an unknown uncle has left him a fortune. Rakewell engages Shadow as his servant and, at the latter's suggestion, promises to pay whatever shall seem a just wage at the end of a year and a day. Shadow is, of course, a Mephisto disguised as a Leporello, who brings into Rakewell's consciousness what is already latent there. He leads him to a brothel where he loses his innocence [1.2]. When Rakewell tires of pleasure and utters his second wish, Shadow suggests that he commit an absolutely gratuitous act, namely, marry Baba the Turk, a bearded lady from the circus [2.1]. . . . When this joke palls and Rakewell utters his third wish, Shadow enters with a fake machine for turning stones into bread [2.3]. . . . Ruined and hunted by those he has ruined, Rakewell is led by Shadow to a graveyard [3.2]. The year and a day are up. Shadow reveals himself and forces Rakewell to play a card game with the latter's soul as the stake. Thanks to the Devil's traditional overconfidence and the Divine intervention of Anne, Shadow loses his prey but before disappearing strikes Rakewell insane. The last scene takes place . . . in Bedlam [3.3]. Rakewell believes himself to be Adonis and Anne, who comes to see him, to be Venus. They sing a duet of forgiveness and he dies.[23]

Tellingly absent from Auden's synopsis is Anne's side of the story—that is, the stable reality from which Rakewell flees. The faithful girl determines to pursue her errant beloved in a classic *scena ed aria* (1.3). She arrives in dreary London just in time to encounter Tom and his new bride, Baba (2.2). Though betrayed and brokenhearted, Anne returns to search for the bankrupt rake when his property is auctioned off (3.1). Baba, now also abandoned but surprisingly empathetic, assures her former rival that "he still loves you."

Though secondary to Tom's tragicomic flight, Anne's tale of constancy represents Stravinsky and Auden's positive counter-message. In a sense, their archetypal soprano stands for Opera, both ideally and in practice (as example 0.1 demonstrates). In his lengthy essay for the 1953 recording, Robert Craft draws a more historically nuanced comparison between Opera and Music Drama than any implied by the terse statements published under Stravinsky's name. He applauds not only Stravinsky but also advocates for "long overdue" performances of Schoenberg's *Von Heute auf Morgen* and *Moses und Aron*—for him examples of Opera, not Music Drama (the young conductor was already undermining the Stravinsky/Schoenberg dualism). He exuberantly concludes: "The existence of the *Rake's Progress* today, . . . so perfectly rooted in the pure opera tradition, is little less than a miracle. It is a chief argument for a renaissance of opera."[24]

Chester Kallman describes a less partisan, more circumspect endeavor in his notes for the 1964 recording: "The over-all vocal thinking on the part of all three collaborators makes *The Rake's Progress* something much more than the polemical anti-Music-Drama it is too often hailed or dismissed as: it is a tribute to opera in much the same way that *Apollon musagète* is a tribute to the dance."[25] Even a tribute raised aesthetic concerns. What Craft would spin as "little less than a miracle," an Italian critic heard as "an act of birth and a certificate of death, a declaration of love and a sign of impotence, a miracle of open-mindedness and a triumph of conventionality . . . everything and nothing, everything that has for centuries existed within the orbit of melodrama, nothing that can stand comparison with all that those centuries have given us—nothing, that is, which might open up the hope of a substantial renewal of dramatic expression."[26]

Was Stravinsky seriously proposing a renewal of conventional opera or was his "opera created within the ruins of a finished tradition" by a composer for whom opera was dead?[27] Even appreciative critics seemed puzzled: "Despite the apparent clarity and simplicity, it is not easy to grasp this Proteus among modern composers. One must ask: has he masked only, does this work mean a subjective admission of debt to the once betrayed melody from the former revolutionary; or is it symptomatic of a turning away from new music altogether? Only time can provide the answer."[28]

Habitus and Field

Indeed, time would provide an answer. Stravinsky and Auden figure prominently in the story of modernism, but their opera seemed out of sync with its cultural moment. Conversely, their personal declines in the late 1960s mark the passing of the modern age at the very time it was gaining a footing. *The Rake's Progress*, in particular among Stravinsky's works and operas generally, exposes the uneasy distinction between the so-called "work itself" and its reception. The work itself—music and text—appears quintessentially neoclassical. Its reception—through interpreters who learned "not to treat the work as a frigid neoclassical pastiche"—has transformed it into something universal, even forward-looking.[29]

That thorny concept—the "music itself"—has been a special bone of contention between two titans of Stravinsky scholarship, musicologist Richard Taruskin and theorist Pieter van den Toorn. Their published exchanges over the issue cut to the heart of an ongoing tension—arguably a defining difference—between music historians and theorists. Van den Toorn makes the case for formal analysis as "an extension of the reflective process" that acts "to kindle and, if possible, intensify the aesthetic presence or 'presentness' of a given work.... Once individual works begin to prevail for what they are in and of themselves and not for what they represent, then context itself, as a reflection of this transcendence, becomes less dependent on matters of historical placement."[30] The musicologist counters that such closed reading "acts as a *cordon sanitaire*, a quarantine staking out a decontaminated space within which music can be composed, performed, and listened to in a cultural and historical vacuum." Furthermore, he traces "the music itself" as a concept back to Stravinsky's own efforts to redefine his musical legacy during his late serial period.[31]

While I value and practice the close reading van den Toorn defends, I share Taruskin's conviction that artist and work must be situated in historical context, both of the work's immediate creation and its subsequent reception. Both scholars recognize that myriad factors (including the academy) play a role in that reception and perhaps even creation, but neither is disposed to examine them systematically. Addressing cultural production more broadly, sociologist Pierre Bourdieu challenges the practice of close reading and even the importance of individual artists and works. His method instead involves surveying the field of "structural relations—invisible or visible only through their effects"—within which individuals and works operate as part of a decentered *habitus*. He defines the latter as a system of "durable, transposable dispositions, structuring structures predisposed to function ... as principles which generate and organize practices and representations." Habitus is not simply the passive backdrop to artistic creation but also is a subtly active force. It inheres in the formal and informal relationships—with other composers, artists, performers, patrons, publishers, producers, arts organizations, opera houses, festivals, media, critics, academia, and audiences—that condition a given work and determine its larger social meaning. It involves a practical sense, a "feel for the game" rather than a strict set of rules or conditions; it evolves over time, but at any given moment appears stable according to the established (but often unconscious) practices of the producers and institutions involved. Individuals can have an impact on their habitus, but only subtly and indirectly. Revolutionary works like *The Rite of Spring* or *Pierrot lunaire* appear to defy the system. However, viewed through the lens of habitus, they represent only a revolutionary disposition—a specific orientation of practice, or strategy, adopted by daring artists like Picasso and James Joyce—that in turn yields, perhaps unconsciously, to another strategic disposition. Hence, Stravinsky, Schoenberg, and Picasso each adopt neoclassicist attitudes in the decade after their revolutionary phases. Such a succession of dispositions constitutes a trajectory. Measured against conventional practice, Stravinsky's and

Schoenberg's defining masterworks seem unprecedented, but viewed as part of a habitus, they are typical. Bourdieu's theory thus entails "both a rejection of the direct relating of individual biography to the work of literature . . . and also to a rejection of internal analysis of an individual work or even of intertextual analysis. This is because what we have to do is all these things at the same time."[32]

The concepts of habitus and field add breadth to our understanding of artist and work, but they can take the wind out of our narrative sails (one reason Auden disliked sociologists; see note 40). Pronouncing *The Rite* "typical" spoils a wonderful story. Yet not investigating further the forces that structured those relationships leaves us with only a vague sense of what drove Stravinsky, especially after *The Rake*, when his career trajectory seems unclear—even to the composer himself. To address this confusion, I propose to analyze all these things—the cultural moment, the music and text, the work's afterlife, and the lives of its creators and facilitators—at the same time.

A thorough examination of the field of twentieth-century opera would require a sociological study, which this book is not. As a composer and music scholar, I fall uneasily within Stravinsky's habitus, "where the belief in the value of art and in the artist's power of valuable creation is continually produced and reproduced."[33] My task is to persuade, not to prove objective claims; I don't bother to suppress an admiration for my subject. Rather, I seek to better understand *The Rake's Progress*, its place in the trajectory of Stravinsky's life and work and in the field of opera generally. I ask in what ways does this work edify; for whom and why; and how so? By exploring the world surrounding a single work, I hope to expose a fascinating though often confused and hidden network of interrelationships, motivations, and influences that helps clarify the composer's sometimes unexpected choices. This task is imprecise, even somewhat arbitrary—writers with other perspectives, reading other documents, will construe other plausible narratives. Nonetheless, the effort is indispensable for understanding the creative act, for artist and work are not stable subject and object but enjoined ideas that, from one cultural moment to another, at one place or another, in the eyes of one observer or another continue to interact, shift, and evolve.

Part 1 and later part 5 explore the fluid cultural environment of the postwar decades and the interrelated efforts of individuals and institutions to create meaningful art in an unsettled time. The early chapters set the stage for the opera's creation and involve a constellation of friends and agents (for Stravinsky, the distinction is blurred)—Craft, Nabokov, choreographer George Balanchine, impresario Lincoln Kirstein, publisher Ralph Hawkes, and others—who attached themselves to the great composer out of love and admiration as well as to serve their own careers. This creative landscape was also shaped, albeit negatively, by those positioned against Stravinsky and his artistic orbit: Arnold Schoenberg, music theorist René Leibowitz, philosopher/sociologist Theodor Adorno and, to some extent, novelist Thomas Mann. The stories of these "friends and enemies" in turn interconnect through cultural milieux and institutions that seem to take us far afield—for example, postwar Paris, the subcultures of European émigrés and of opera queens, the Congress for Cultural Freedom, the Cold War—but that nonetheless condition, directly or not, the opera and its reception.

Parts 2 and 3 focus on the genesis and execution of *The Rake's Progress*. Even here, understanding the confluence of music, words, literary themes, and ideas requires cultivating a variety of disciplines, from biography, music analysis, and history to literary and dramatic criticism. To help the reader follow detailed discussions within these areas, I first introduce specific aspects of the opera—namely, dramatic and literary themes in part 2; musical language, dramaturgy, and formal structure in part 3—accruing as I go the background necessary for a broader interpretation.

In part 4, I consider the life of *The Rake* beyond its creators. The convoluted saga of the Venice premiere is a particularly fascinating case study in the struggle for artistic and financial control. And the story does not end there, for a living opera necessarily evolves as stage directors, singers, conductors, and even audiences subsequently embrace, reject, adjust, and remake it. In the case of *The Rake* this transformation has been especially felicitous for the opera's early reception presented a muddled image that Stravinsky's subsequent aesthetic shift would only further cloud.

The Great Artist Moves On

The Rake's reception inevitably overlaps with the seismic cultural shifts addressed in part 5. There we see the composer embark on a new and unexpected path prompted, he later admitted, by his work on the opera. "I have had to survive two crises as a composer," he recalled. "The first—the loss of Russia and its language not only of music but of words—affected every circumstance of my personal no less than my artistic life. . . . Crisis number two was brought on by the natural outgrowing of the special incubator in which I wrote *The Rake's Progress*."[34]

Thus Stravinsky explains the widely accepted division of his oeuvre into three distinct periods: the Russian, through the completion of *Les Noces* (1922); the neoclassical, the stirrings of which began in 1920, but—at least by Stravinsky's account—coalesced from *Oedipus Rex* (1927) through *The Rake's Progress*; and the serial, beginning in earnest with parts of *Agon* (1955–57) and *Canticum Sacrum* (1955). Some scholars downplay these stylistic contrasts by identifying connections between works from different periods.[35] But these links cannot offset two irrefutable truths: after 1922 Stravinsky decisively turned from Russian to European musical and literary sources; and after 1951 he gradually abandoned tonality in favor of a harmonic language he had previously rejected. In fact, immediately after finishing *The Rake* and well before he became comfortable with the twelve-tone method, Stravinsky was already moving toward a more controlled, ascetic style in his *Cantata* (1952).

Even the composer acknowledged the economic pressures that conditioned his neoclassical turn. The Bolshevik Revolution cut off his financial legacy and eventually compelled him to market his skills as pianist and conductor. Indeed, starting in 1923, the composer/performer presented himself and his music to concert audiences like hands in a pair of fitted gloves. But why did *The Rake* inspire such a crisis in Stravinsky's work? Did its sheer length and conservatism finally satisfy his appetite for the "lifeless" conventions of the past? Or had he "in fact wished to study dodecaphonic methods earlier and been embarrassed by the existence of a rival [Schoenberg] whose death [in 1951] alone could liberate him from this inhibition?"[36] The composer claimed he "was not aware of [a crisis] as such at the time, continuing as I did to move from work to work."[37]

The sociological perspective disregards such personal explanations, viewing Stravinsky's three periods only as strategies within an artistic trajectory. Such a view "differs from traditional biography in that it does not search . . . for some sort of 'original project' that determines and unifies all subsequent developments in a writer's life."[38] The composer's changing position within the field of contemporary music, rather than any personal crises or defining aesthetic, drives the shifts. While I do not wholeheartedly adopt this approach, by entertaining both perspectives I believe a fuller image of the composer and work can unfold.

Stravinsky well knew before he penciled a note of it that the young avantgarde detested neoclassicism and conventional opera. (The twenty-something Pierre Boulez scoffed to John Cage: "Have you heard *Rake's Progress*? What ugliness!"[39]) At the same time, Auden recognized that conservative audiences would never welcome new opera, neoclassical or not. The poet also claimed such works could not "carry on from where their predecessors left off," yet seemed as confused as the composer about what might constitute a new start. After all, he initially planned to satirize "some of our bugaboos like Twelve-toners, Sociologists etc." in the libretto he and Kallman wrote for Stravinsky immediately after *The Rake*.[40] Little did he suspect the "wise old" composer would himself become a twelve-toner.

Few artists expressed with such depth of understanding, clarity, and eloquence the anxiety of late modernism as did Wystan Auden. And though he had little affinity for the rootless age that followed, in his commentary for *Vogue* he entertained implicitly the hope that his planned opera would be, if not the start of something new, at least a new start to something old. He was more prescient than he imagined; for the postmodern spirit that delights in archaic practice, this self-consciously conservative poet and composer had crafted a ready-made relic. Would their "last opera" now occupy a spot among the reliquaries of operatic culture as the first "postopera"?

Yes and no. To read *The Rake's Progress* as proto-postmodern would be facile. First, it undervalues the opera's sheer conventionality, which entails both neoclassical detachment *and* a degree of sincere expression postmodernists typically disdain. In writing a Mozartian opera buffa, Stravinsky found himself immersed in the most warmly human of musical genres (the "incubator" referenced above). Its polar attraction toward stylization and expressiveness—Stravinsky described it precisely when he told Nicholas Nabokov he "will lace each aria into a tight corset"—no doubt contributes to the opera's enduring success, but it also made it difficult to repeat.[41]

The subtle tug between style and expressiveness exposes a second flaw in the postmodern label: much of the self-consciousness, self-referencing and self-parody we call "postmodern" permeates opera (as well as drama, art and literature) throughout the modern era. What exactly distinguishes modern from postmodern? Opera from postopera? This supposed "last opera" from the traditional operas written since 1951? And even if the distinction seems useful now, will it continue to be relevant? Will the label "postopera" be relegated, like Wagner's "music drama," to dusty academic texts?

Probably. However, for those who wish to appreciate better this subtle masterpiece and to understand the complex transitional moment in which it was created and its elusive position in the rich history of opera, these labels identify persistent ambiguities and tensions. Stravinsky summarized them succinctly when he asked: "Can a composer reuse the past and at the same time move in a forward direction?" He immediately directed "the listener to suspend the question . . . to try to discover the opera's own qualities."[42] My book addresses both his question and his directive: I heed the latter by exploring the opera's essential neoclassicism; I ponder the former by trying to understand how and why it resonates in a postmodern age.

Notes

1. Igor Stravinsky and Robert Craft, *Memories and Commentaries* (Garden City, NY: Doubleday, 1960), 86.

2. Pierre Bourdieu, *The Field of Cultural Production: Essays on Art and Literature*, ed. and introduced by Randal Johnson (Cambridge, MA: Polity Press, 1993), 29.

3. *Modernist Mysteries: Perséphone* is a precursor of what its author Tamara Levitz calls a "microhistory" of a single work; in her case, Stravinsky's collaboration with André Gide and dancer, actress, and patron Ida Rubenstein.

4. W. H. Auden, "Opera Addict: At the Root of the Addiction Is an Understanding of Willfulness," *Vogue* (July 1948), 65. See also Richard Taruskin, "The Death of Opera?" in *Oxford History of Western Music*, vol. 4 (New York: Oxford University Press, 2005), 547–49.

5. Letter of October 16, 1947 quoted in Vera Stravinsky and Robert Craft, *Stravinsky in Pictures and Documents* (New York: Simon and Schuster, 1978), 396; also Robert Craft, ed., *Stravinsky: Selected Correspondence*, vol. 1 (New York: Alfred A. Knopf, 1982), 269.

6. See ch. 11, note 74.

7. Pierre Boulez, "Blow Up the Opera Houses!" Interview in *Der Spiegel*, September 25, 1967.

8. Slavoj Žižek and Mladen Dolar, *Opera's Second Death* (New York: Routledge, 2002), 2, 4.

9. Gary Tomlinson, *Metaphysical Song: An Essay on Opera* (Princeton, NJ: Princeton University Press, 1999), 6.

10. Quoted in W. H. Auden and Chester Kallman, *Libretti and Other Dramatic Writings: 1939–1973*, ed. Edward Mendelson (London: Faber and Faber, 1993), xvi.

11. W. H. Auden, *The Dyer's Hand* (New York: Vintage International, 1989), 474.

12. Robert Craft, *Stravinsky: The Chronicle of a Friendship: 1948/1971* (Nashville: Vanderbilt University Press, 1994), 13–14.
13. Letter of February 21, 1949, Berg Collection. Stravinsky actually set "A loving heart,/ An ever-loving heart" rather than "*My* loving...." Auden's alteration has never been incorporated into the published libretto.
14. See F. W. Sternfeld, *The Birth of Opera* (New York: Oxford University Press, 1995).
15. Lawrence Kramer, *Opera and Modern Culture: Wagner and Strauss* (Berkeley: University of California Press, 2004), 6.
16. Richard Wagner, *Wagner on Music and Drama*, arr. Albert Goldman and Evert Sprinchon, trans. H. Ashton Ellis (New York: Da Capo, 1988), 106.
17. Thomas Mann, *Doctor Faustus: The Life of the German Composer Adrian Leverkühn, as Told by a Friend*, trans. John E. Woods (New York: Alfred A. Knopf, 1997), 174.
18. Thomas Mann, *The Story of a Novel* (New York: Alfred A. Knopf, 1961), 11 (also see chapter 1, note 68). The fictional opera is to be based on Shakespeare's *Love's Labour's Lost*, which, thirty years later, Auden and Kallman would adapt into a libretto for Nicolas Nabokov.
19. Robert Craft, "An Appreciation of the Music," in liner notes for *Igor Stravinsky: The Rake's Progress*. Columbia Records SL 125 (1953): 1.
20. V. Stravinsky and Craft, *Pictures and Documents*, 417.
21. Letter of October 6, 1947, in Craft, *Correspondence*, vol. 1, 299.
22. Igor Stravinsky, "The Composer's View," in Griffiths, *The Rake's Progress*, 2–4. Part I, "A programme note" originally published in liner notes, *Igor Stravinsky: The Rake's Progress*. Sony Classical SM2K 46 299 (1964), 2.
23. Auden and Kallman, *Libretti*, 617; originally published in *Harper's Bazaar*, February 1953.
24. Craft, "An Appreciation," 4. Craft later contradicts this glowing praise, which, given the context, one must take with a grain of salt (see chapter 2, note 3, and chapter 5, note 10). Of less interest to us here is his sincere opinion than the Stravinsky party line he was trumpeting.
25. Reprinted in Auden and Kallman, *Libretti*, 628.
26. Franco Abbiati, "La 'Carriera del libertino,'" quoted in Stephen Walsh, *Stravinsky—The Second Exile: France and America, 1934–1971* (New York: Alfred A. Knopf, 2006), 271.
27. Paul Griffiths, *Igor Stravinsky: The Rake's Progress* (New York: Cambridge University Press, 1982), 100.
28. H. Weiher-Waege, "'The Rake's Progress': The New Stravinsky Gleamingly Staged by Dr. Günther Rennert," *Hamburg Free Press*, November 15, 1951 (translated from German). Unless otherwise noted, all English translations are by the author.
29. Edward Mendelson, *Later Auden* (New York: Farrar, Straus and Giroux, 1999), 270.
30. Pieter C. Van den Toorn, *Music, Politics and the Academy* (Berkeley: University of California Press, 1995), 55, 196.
31. Richard Taruskin, "Stravinsky and the Subhuman—A Myth of the Twentieth Century: 'The Rite of Spring,' the Tradition of the New, and 'The Music Itself,'" in *Defining Russian Musically* (Princeton, NJ: Princeton University Press, 1997), 368; see also chapter 1, note 15. Taruskin first challenges narrow "professional discourse" about music in "Back to Whom? Neoclassicism as Ideology," *19th-Century Music* 16 (1992–3): 288–89.
32. Quoted in "Editor's Introduction," in Bourdieu, *Field of Cultural Production*, 5, 9. In *Art Worlds*, Howard Becker brings a similar sociological perspective, through which the creation of all art is seen as cooperative.
33. Bourdieu, *Field of Cultural Production*, 260. An example of such a study is part 1 of *Rules of Art* (47–173), where Bourdieu describes the field of French literature in the second half of the nineteenth century.

34. Igor Stravinsky and Robert Craft, *Themes and Episodes* (New York: Alfred A. Knopf, 1966), 23.

35. See Scott Messing, *Neoclassicism in Music: From the Genesis of the Concept through the Schoenberg/Stravinsky Polemic* (Ann Arbor, MI: University Microfilms International, 1988), 87–150; Andre Bouchourechliev, *Stravinsky*, trans. Martin Cooper (New York: Holmes and Meier, 1987); and William Austin, "Stravinsky's 'Fortunate Continuities' and 'Legitimate Accidents,' 1882–1982," in *Stravinsky Retrospectives*, eds. Ethan Haimo and Paul Johnson (Lincoln: University of Nebraska, 1987), 1–14.

36. Mikhail Drushkin, *Igor Stravinsky: His Personality, Works and Views*, trans. Martin Cooper (New York: Cambridge University Press, 1983), 141.

37. Igor Stravinsky, *Themes and Conclusions* (Berkeley: University of California Press, 1972), 33. Craft edited this version of "Change of Life" after Stravinsky died. Decades later he would describe a troubling personal episode indicating the composer acutely felt himself at a crisis point (see chapter 11, note 7).

38. Bourdieu, *Field of Cultural Production*, 18.

39. Letter of December 1951 in Jean-Jacques Nattiez, ed., *The Boulez-Cage Correspondence*, trans. and ed. Robert Samuels (New York: Cambridge University Press, 1993), 118.

40. Letter of December 24, 1951, in Auden and Kallman, *Libretti*, 630. See chapter 11, note 10 for longer excerpt.

41. Nicolas Nabokov, *Old Friends and New Music* (Boston: Little, Brown, 1951), 159.

42. I. Stravinsky and Craft, *Themes and Episodes*, 49.

1

A CONVERGENCE OF MINDS

"THE OPERA REVEALED ITSELF AS AN UNQUESTIONABLE MASTERPIECE," glowed Stravinsky's friend, "whose Mozartian dimensions and transparent beauty have not been matched by any other work for the lyric theater in the first half of our turbulent century. To many present it seemed they were hearing the most important work of the greatest living composer of our time."[1] Disinterested critics were more reserved. Indeed, Nicolas Nabokov was about as interested as a party could be in a work other than his own, and it testifies to his connections among journalists that he was able to place his openly biased reviews in the *Herald Tribune* and, two years later, in *Le Figaro littéraire*. Intimate friend to both composer and librettist, Nabokov had followed closely the work's conception and creation. He had pestered Stravinsky for photocopies of each completed act before the ink had barely dried and, on his own initiative, had served as Stravinsky's personal liaison and negotiator for the premiere. That Nabokov's review is also insightful—not surprising, given his understanding of the work and its creators—is almost beside the point.

Robert Craft described in his diary that determinedly high-class premiere of September 11, 1951, when Europe's *"ne plus ultra* of elegance" gathered at the Venice's Teatro La Fenice to witness the result of the collaboration between two of the greatest artists of the twentieth century:

> "*La Prima Assoluta.*" An afternoon and evening of stifling heat, the sirocco blowing like a bellows. The alleys near the theater have been roped off to keep the lower orders at bay, and hours before curtain time the Fourth Estate begins to line up along the wider streets. They have actually come to applaud the parade of the rich, most of whom, however, arrive in gondolas and motor launches and are deposited at the canal-side entrance; in Venice, 1789 is a long way in the future. Our own pedestrian party includes Nadia Boulanger, who carries I. S.'s valises, Auden and Kallman, both nervous in spite of liquid fortifications (a moat of martinis), . . . [Vera] is quickly besieged by old friends from Paris. Soldiers wearing tricorns and cross-webbing are positioned at the side entrances, and at the front they hold candelabras.
>
> La Fenice glitters and bouquets of roses, like debutantes' corsages, are pinned to each loge. The beauty of these hideouts is even less than skin deep, however, the red plush having suffered moth-pox and being badly in need of deodorants.

Another discomfort is that the seats are like European railroad compartments: the occupants on the side near the stage face in the wrong direction.... The audience is in formal dress, everyone except the *New York Times*'s Howard Taubman.

At 21:35, a prompt thirty-five minutes late, I. S. enters the pit and acknowledges the warm welcoming applause of both the ultra *mondaine* and the boisterous bravos in the top galleries. Expectancy is high: the last great master is presenting his largest-scale work.[2]

Though nearly every aspect of that first performance was shaky, the premiere justified a celebration. One image in particular from the postperformance party (shown in fig. 1.2) captures the spirit of the evening: a tired but spritely Stravinsky points at the camera as the trio of Nabokov, Vera, and Auden looks on, laughing. Along with Craft, also present, these three represent the larger—if sometimes uneasy—convergence of minds, energy, and ambition that made the occasion possible: Wystan Auden as literary genius, esteemed collaborator, and neglected junior partner; Vera as supportive wife, muse, and sounding board; Nika Nabokov as solicitous friend, networker, and emerging impresario; and young Bob Craft as welcomed interloper, navigator (literal and artistic), and, to some observers, Mephistopheles.

Stravinsky's close personal and professional associates merit more than a caption to a picture; they help us grasp the habitus of the mid-twentieth-century composer and the international cultural scene. Nabokov especially possessed that undefinable yet indispensable "feel" for discovering and creating opportunities for himself and his friends. An accomplished but not great composer, he intuitively understood the fluctuating field of postwar European musical culture. Of course, Stravinsky, Auden, and Chester Kallman directly determined the opera, but their story is not the whole story. On the contrary, their work tends to mask the invisible or forgotten network of interrelationships involving arts institutions, funders, publishers, media, government agencies, and ideological interests. Captivating on its own, Nabokov's story traverses this broad field and thus helps fill out the picture of the opera and Stravinsky's later life.

A Less Than Reliable Fly on the Wall

Well into the early morning hours, the giddy party guests entertained themselves by identifying musical reminiscences in Stravinsky's score: "V. thinks the Mourning Chorus begins like the *Volga Boat Song*," Craft recalls.[3] Although Auden claimed to hear echoes of Wagner and Strauss probably just to annoy the composer, according to one account he had previously privately expressed concerns about other "obvious resemblances, as for example between the first Bedlam aria ['Prepare yourselves'] and an aria in *Semele* ['Where e'er you walk']; between the *fandango* in the graveyard scene and, well, a *fandango*; and between 'Love that too quickly betrays,' 'Dear Father Truelove,' the whores' chorus, and three pieces in *Così*: 'Un aura amorosa,' 'Vorrei dir,' and 'Di scrivermi ogni giorno.'"[4] In his 1994 account, Craft admits, "I say that the Terzetto is Tchaikovskyan,

Fig. 1.1. Audience at La Fenice for the premiere of *The Rake's Progress*. (Photo by Cornell Capa, Life Picture Collection, Getty Images.)

Fig. 1.2. Postpremiere celebration at Taverna La Fenice: Stravinsky (*foreground*), Nicolas Nabokov (*left*), Vera Stravinsky, and W. H. Auden. (Igor Stravinsky Collection, Paul Sacher Foundation)

and the Epilogue a vaudeville or pasquinade, a la *Seraglio* or *L'Heure espagnole*."[5] However, in his earlier accounts, it is Auden who claims the Terzetto "is 'Tchaikovskyan,' and the Epilogue is modeled on *Don Giovanni*, to which I. S., who does not recognize or admit to any of the attributions, objects. 'The Epilogue is a vaudeville or pasquinade, the *Seraglio* or *L'Heure espagnole*. In fact, some of *The Rake* is close to Broadway, Baba's music especially.'"[6]

So, who heard Tchaikovsky in the Terzetto, Auden or Craft? And who connected the epilogue to Mozart and Ravel, the composer or scholar-conductor? Did Auden intend the epilogue as a reference to *Don Giovanni*? After all, he wrote the words. It is difficult to tell which diary entry is truthful and which "Crafted" (pun intended). If one assumes that the seemingly less abridged 1994 version is closer to Craft's original recollection, then it's unclear how Stravinsky reacted, if at all, to the game of tune detection. Did he actually claim some of *The Rake* is close to Broadway, or did he just acquiesce to the opinion of Craft (who also thought "the chord at the climax [of the Epilogue] would be less out of place in a Coca-Cola jingle")?[7] Exactly who said what may have made little difference to readers in 1963, 1972, or 1994 (or now, for that matter), but it apparently concerned Craft. Anyone researching Stravinsky's work after 1948 will necessarily turn to Craft's various and varying but informative and often fascinating accounts of the composer's life during that time, but as becomes increasingly clear, one should read carefully and critically.

Whether or not he admitted it to them that evening, the composer of *The Rake's Progress* would eventually confess to "a rare form of kleptomania" in his tendency to appropriate favorite snippets from older works. From the opening fanfare to the somber mourning chorus after Tom's death, nearly every moment recalls some musical-dramatic gesture culled from three and half centuries of operatic clichés. Indeed, conventional opera even influenced the way Stravinsky viewed the Hogarth paintings that first inspired him. "Five years ago, in Chicago, at an exhibition of English paintings," he recalled in his notes for the Venice premiere, "I was struck by the various Hogarth series as by a succession of operatic scenes."[8]

The English version of Stravinsky's original recollection did not appear in print until the American premiere in February 1953 and neglected to adjust for the number of years (*"cinque anni fa . . ."*) since he attended the exhibition, thus implying 1948 instead of 1946. Vera's reliable diary confirms that the couple viewed the "exhibit of Turner, Hogarth, and Constable" paintings on December 5, 1946.[9] Of the Hogarths, the museum catalogue lists the six paintings of the series *Marriage A-la-Mode* and six individual paintings; neither the *Rake's Progress* prints nor paintings were displayed. More contradictions creep into a later account of the genesis of the opera recorded in the second conversation book Stravinsky coauthored with Craft: "Hogarth's 'Rake's Progress' paintings, which I saw in 1947 on a chance visit to the Chicago Art Institute, immediately suggested a series of operatic scenes to me. I was, however, readily susceptible to such a suggestion, for I had wanted to compose an English-language opera ever since my arrival in the United States."[10]

Unpublished correspondence reveals that the composer discussed the idea for an English-language opera with his new publisher Ralph Hawkes as early as the winter of 1946–47. The following December, the *New York Times* reported "that Stravinsky and his publishers, Boosey & Hawkes, made an opera part of their joint plans when the composer signed an exclusive agreement with them a year ago."[11] That conversation probably took place in New York shortly after the December 1946 visit to the Chicago exhibit; however, Stravinsky's later account places the museum visit in 1947. Many years later in 1978, Craft reinforced the mistake by reporting the exact date as May 2, 1947, another time when the Stravinskys were traveling through Chicago.[12] The Art Institute in fact owns a set of Hogarth's *Rake's Progress* prints and well may have exhibited the set in May 1947, but there is no record of it now because exhibition records of the museum's regular holdings only go back to 1984. The recorded evidence from the time—Vera's diary (also edited by Craft) and the museum archive—confirms only the earlier December showing. In other words, no evidence can confirm that any version of *A Rake's Progress* was shown in Chicago in 1946 or 1947.

A second discrepancy in Stravinsky's conversation-book recollection refers to "Hogarth's 'Rake's Progress' *paintings*." In fact, Hogarth's original paintings are permanently housed in Sir John Soane's Museum in London and, by act of parliament, cannot be removed. Assuming, as later accounts assert, that Stravinsky viewed the *Rake's Progress* series, scholars have concluded he meant the prints, not the paintings. However, his first recollection of the visit—"I was struck by the *various* Hogarth series" (my emphasis)—quoted above, suggests that, subject aside, it may have been the six paintings of *Marriage A-la-Mode* that first impressed the composer. In other words, the mistake is not that Stravinsky viewed paintings—the exhibition consisted *only* of paintings—but that he viewed *A Rake's Progress*.

When, where, or even if Stravinsky saw Hogarth's *Rake's Progress* paintings or prints may make little difference. Having visited London numerous times before the war and being an avid museumgoer, he would have had several opportunities to view the originals before conceiving the opera. I explain these discrepancies not just to correct accounts of the opera's genesis but also to demonstrate just how slippery the published opinions and even factual information attributed to Stravinsky can be. Scholars question in particular the reliability of the Stravinsky-Craft "conversation" books: *Conversations with Igor Stravinsky* (1959), *Memories and Commentaries* (1960), *Expositions and Developments* (1962), *Dialogues and a Diary* (1963), *Themes and Episodes* (1966), and *Retrospectives and Conclusions* (1969). Craft openly admits his role extended beyond the bounds of mere interviewer, and after Stravinsky's death he further revised and edited the subsequent republications. Stephen Walsh and Charles Joseph also question the conductor-writer's role in selecting and shaping the three volumes of Stravinsky's correspondence, the several documentary "scrapbooks" he edited, and the lengthy portions of his own diaries (twice reedited and republished) and memoirs devoted to Stravinsky.[13]

Richard Taruskin is suspicious less of Craft than of the composer for distancing himself from, and even revising, previously recorded accounts, opinions, and ideas. In fact, Stravinsky admitted that correcting (as he put it) his previous books was a main motivation for publishing his conversations: "The chronology of the [autobiography] is not always reliable, I regret to say, which is one reason for the current tetralogy of my 'talk.' (Another reason is my wish to speak directly on a number of subjects.... My autobiography [1934] and *Poetics of Music* [1939], both written through other people, incidentally—Walter Nouvel and Roland-Manuel, respectively—are much less *like* me, in all my faults, than my conversations; or so I think.)"[14] Because copious evidence supports scholars' skepticism about these "corrections," one should read critically any statement attributed to Stravinsky and be wary of seemingly evident conclusions. As Taruskin warns, the authority of the colorful and provocative conversation books rests "only as *primary* source material on the mind of the Stravinsky who co-authored them."[15]

Yet, despite their contradictory claims and questionable authorships, at least the first four conversation texts bear the unmistakable tenor of Stravinsky's voice. A perceptive critic, Virgil Thomson described the author of *Themes and Episodes* as "a remarkably sharp musical observer. The latter personality let us call Craft-Igor, since it is a double one, in which the voice is the voice of Robert Craft, but the head is of Igor Fedorovich."[16] Assuming that time and possibly other motives inevitably distort, as the later accounts of Stravinsky's museum visit demonstrate, I will generally defer to earlier accounts, available correspondence, and other corroborating evidence as I explore the composer's motivations for creating his first and only conventional opera.

Plans for an English-Language Opera

By 1947 Stravinsky's personal and professional life seemed to have finally settled after a turbulent decade of family loss and dislocation. Peripatetic throughout most of the interwar years, he was now a US citizen and firmly committed to remaining in America. He enjoyed a stable domestic life and cherished the companionship of his second wife. Having just signed with a new publisher, he was busily revising and updating his old pieces in order to consolidate his work. As the world's most celebrated composer, he fielded countless offers to appear in public and conduct. Prospects for new commissions continued to present themselves while new and old friends and professional acquaintances constantly vied for his attention. In other ways, though, the years surrounding the composition of *The Rake's Progress* remained uncertain for Stravinsky. Lingering responsibilities for his children and grandchildren left him feeling financially insecure. Still wary of traveling abroad, he was nonetheless anxious to reestablish connections to Europe. Perhaps most troubling, he felt disconnected from the younger generation of composers, which made him increasingly insecure about his aesthetic choices.

Why would Stravinsky—or any modernist composer—want to write an opera? Disconnected from the genre's golden age, even a committed neoclassicist could expect to labor years on a full-length opera (as opposed to Rossini or Mozart, who could complete one in six weeks or less). That disconnection also made critical success all the more elusive. However adept a composer's skill and execution, half the critics were bound to disdain the result. Furthermore, opera has always been the genre least open to the composer's control. More musical forces, more theatrical apparatuses, more creative personalities, and much more money are required to realize an opera than any other project a composer might initiate. And more could go wrong.

The idea nonetheless germinated in Stravinsky's imagination. His earliest account is the most generous and perhaps most reliable: "For many years I have harbored the idea of writing an opera in English. By this I mean a music originated in the English prosody and worked out in my own way, as I did it before with Russian (*The Nightingale, Mavra, The Wedding*), French (*Persephone*) and Latin (*Oedipus Rex, Symphony of Psalms*) prosodies."[17]

Several factors conditioned his choice of the English language. First, such a project would force him to engage more seriously the language of his adopted country. Similar reasons would influence his invitation to Craft to be his assistant. "They were in transition from Russo-French to Anglo-American culture at the time," the conductor recalled, "and were trying to enlarge their English vocabularies by speaking, reading, and writing in English only."[18] Much as composing *Perséphone* had signaled his embrace of French language and culture, collaborating on an English opera would help cement Stravinsky's connection to a new circle of artists and a new culture.[19]

Second, an English-language opera could be financially lucrative. By the late 1940s, the number of important American and British opera companies was growing and English-language opera was beginning to be taken seriously again by international houses. Over 250 years had passed since Purcell's seminal masques and semi-operas, and a small but growing body of serious operas by British and American composers was emerging, most obviously Benjamin Britten's *Peter Grimes* (1945) and *The Rape of Lucretia* (1947). Eager to encourage this wave, Hawkes sent Stravinsky in April 1947 a prospectus of Britten's new English Opera Group, "just to keep you reminded that they are more than interested in your idea of a new piece." Hawkes was a member of the board of directors of the group, the mission of which was to "give annual seasons of contemporary opera in English and suitable classical works including those of Purcell." Later that fall, Hawkes even recommended that Stravinsky score for a specific ensemble of thirteen players ideally suited for the group.[20]

In June Stravinsky was taking his publisher's suggestions seriously enough to attend the West Coast premiere of Britten's *Lucretia*. However, by the time he first contacted Auden in October, his sights were set on the larger, though still modest, dimensions of a late eighteenth-century orchestra with thirty-five players and a small chorus. It soon became clear that, in spite of the composer's expressed intent, the new work would appeal to even larger houses. The same *New York Times* article that characterized the opera as part of "joint plans" between

Stravinsky and his publisher speculated that "because the publishers have a lease on Covent Garden in London, the premiere is likely to be there."[21] The article probably reflects Hawkes's wishful thinking, for in his letter to Stravinsky on September 23, 1948—in striking contrast to his modest initial advice—he reports that "Covent Garden are, of course, deeply interested in this work and there is but little doubt that we can place the premiere there either for the fall of 1950 or the spring of 1951."[22] Again, Stravinsky had in mind other ideas that would entail a confused, protracted, and highly contentious series of negotiations over the venue of the premiere (as described in chapter 9).

In every version of the story, Stravinsky makes clear that he had wanted to compose an opera in English ever since his arrival in the United States in 1939. His encounter with Hogarth's series aside, the crucial impetus to finally initiating this project was his formal agreement with Boosey & Hawkes, signed on January 1, 1947, in which the publisher guaranteed Stravinsky a minimum annual payment of royalties starting at $10,000 and eventually increasing to $12,000 a year. This financial arrangement enabled Stravinsky to forgo much of his usual concertizing and publicity touring in order to devote three years to composing the uncommissioned work. From the publisher's point of view, the short-term financial benefits alone, even if the opera were deemed unsuccessful, would easily repay the investment. Indeed, as soon as word of a planned opera got out, almost every major company in Europe clamored for the premiere. In essence, Boosey & Hawkes unofficially commissioned *The Rake's Progress* and, in fact, officially commissioned the libretto. Stravinsky might have never started the project without the publisher's financial investment.

Both Stravinsky's statements and his financial ties to an English publisher indicate the language of his planned opera was a primary determining factor, even before fundamental musical considerations. *The Rake's Progress* was English well before it was Mozartian or even fully sung. The composer revealed his initial intentions for musical structure and text setting in his first letter to Auden on October 6, 1947: "Bear in mind that I will compose *not* a musical drama, but just an opera with definitely separated numbers connected by spoken (not sung) words of the text, because I want to avoid the customary operatic recitative."[23]

Avoiding the seamless continuity of post-Wagnerian music drama would be obligatory for the neoclassicist Stravinsky. His intention to use spoken text also had precedents in *Perséphone*, *Oedipus*, and *Histoire du Soldat*, indicating a concern for clear narrative with typical Stravinskian artificiality. I imagine he had in mind something closer to the stiffly dramatized *Histoire* than the polished Mozartian opera buffa he would eventually compose. In "definitely" separating his musical numbers with spoken text, Stravinsky seems to have been planning an opera modeled on John Gay's *Beggar's Opera*, one of the examples of English text-setting he received from his publishers in late 1947 and early 1948 (others were by Handel, Byrd, and Purcell). The publisher's catalogue sent to Stravinsky the previous August even includes a reproduction of a ticket to an early performance of *The Beggar's Opera* etched by Hogarth.

At the same time that Stravinsky was requesting English-language settings, he was also urgently searching for vocal and orchestral scores and recordings for Mozart's major operas. The transformation, at least in Stravinsky's mind, of the proposed project from something like an early eighteenth-century ballad opera into a late eighteenth-century opera buffa took place around the time of his first face-to-face meetings with Auden in Hollywood from November 11–17, 1947. Though Auden certainly encouraged Stravinsky's movement toward Mozartian buffa—and therefore sung recitative—the composer had already come to regard Mozart's operas as "the source of inspiration for my future opera."[24] So he wrote to Ralph Hawkes on November 9—that is, before Auden's arrival. In that the conscious choice of a specific musical model was an integral part of Stravinsky's compositional process, his rather circuitous path to Mozart's operas is worth noting.

So, while he never strayed from an opera of "definitely separated" numbers, Stravinsky changed his mind about spoken dialogue. His initial thought may have been to follow the convention of English comic operas and operettas, though Craft suggests a more personal motivation: "He was very timid about setting English."[25] In any case, it is easy to imagine how Stravinsky would have been drawn to Mozart's Italian operas as models. Performing opera buffa in English translation was common in the 1940s (indeed, until the advent of supertitles in the 1990s). In fact, the composer and librettist attended a two-piano performance of *Così fan tutte* sung in English "in the parish hall of a Hollywood church" the very week that they met to develop the story.[26]

Progress and Return

Having settled on a broad model, the collaborators' first challenge was to shape Hogarth's vivid series into a convincing plot. I describe that process in detail in chapter 2 but offer a brief summary here. Rather than follow a self-propelled descent, Stravinsky and Auden introduced a Mephistophelean Villain—the "Shadow" of the rake's idle desires—to guide their un-named Hero to the brink of hell.[27] There the faithful Girl—the epitome of "Truelove"—helps save him, at least temporarily. The rake, whose name is found on documents in Hogarth's first two images, is thus a blank slate between forces struggling within his soul. Fully realized, the constant Anne symbolizes a return to tradition; Nick, who teaches "there is no return," represents the opposing tendency to press forward constantly.

This opposition between progress and return reflects more than the late history of sung drama that I address in my prelude: it critiques progressive modernism. Accordingly, Tom's "flight from reality" represents the ever-pressing search for new sounds, harmonies, rhythms, and textures that compelled modernists during the first decades of the twentieth century. In the middle-aged Stravinsky, this blind adventurism inspired "a sort of terror when, at the moment of setting to work," he found before him an infinitude of possibilities.[28] The conventions of musical tradition narrowed those options and thereby quelled the terror.

Stravinsky claimed not to be alone in seeking refuge in the classical past, asserting that Arnold Schoenberg, Alban Berg, and Anton Webern "now appear to have used musical form as I did, 'historically.' My use of it was overt, however, and theirs elaborately disguised."²⁹ *The Rake's Progress*, though, does more than "use" operatic conventions; it celebrates Opera, as Kallman suggests. Moreover, it dramatizes the modernist crisis to which neoclassicism responded. The story embodies the conflicting tendencies to at once run from and embrace the musical past. Stravinsky and Auden adopt operatic conventions not simply to charm discerning listeners (i.e., the tune-detectives at the postpremiere party); their archaic dramaturgy and music exemplify the dramatic conflict. By transforming the story into a moral victory, they establish dramatically what the composer intended all along: one can return to the past.

Still, how is one to hear a work that sounds so derivative? In paying tribute to an archaic form, Stravinsky parallels Tom's fixation on his beloved "Venus." By no coincidence do both composer and character drape themselves in timeless myth. A hallmark of neoclassicism, unlike the varied pursuits of the avant-garde, myths never change. But that stasis can also be a form of death. Tom's madness negates his moral triumph; the lovers' joyful reunion is a delusion. The opera thus warns against both reckless adventure and rigid convention, progress and return.

"Progressive" and "Reactionary"

Similarly opposed labels defined Stravinsky's "uniquely tangential relationship," as Craft described it, with his Austrian émigré neighbor, Arnold Schoenberg. The widely accepted picture of the two as reactionary and progressive intensified their already distinct artistic dispositions, prompting exaggerated reactions from both. Schoenberg famously memorialized his contempt for "kleine Modernsky" in "Vielseitigkeit" from his choral settings *Drei Satiren* (1925). For his part, Stravinsky professed to "despise all of modern music. I myself don't compose modern music at all nor do I write music of the future. I write for today. In this regard I don't want to quote names, but I could tell you about composers who spend all their time inventing a music of the future . . . I have listened to experiments of this kind. They sound like very ordinary music, or a little bit worse."³⁰ After Schoenberg died, he could dismiss this "popular notion" as "a nice parlor game, no more."³¹ However, in postwar Hollywood the rivals remained as wary—and aware—of each other as they had been in Europe between the wars, as Thomas Mann's diary attests: "Dining with the Schoenbergs in Brentwood . . . Talking with Sch. at length about music . . . Soirée at the Werfels' with Stravinsky; talked about Schoenberg."³²

This tension no doubt conditioned the choice to structure the plot of *The Rake's Progress* around the conflict between progress and return. Stravinsky-Craft's later attempts at revision notwithstanding, the consensus view of neoclassicism as a retreat from modernism—narrowly associated with atonality and serialism—framed the midcentury debate over the direction of new music.

That attitude confronted the composer the very week he penciled the first sketches of the opera in the person of René Leibowitz, who showed up on Stravinsky's Hollywood doorstep in December 1947 to interview him for the aptly named *Partisan Review*.

A year earlier, in a letter describing the turbulent politics of the postwar French musical scene, musicologist André Schaeffner had warned Stravinsky that this zealously pro-Schoenberg "stateless upstart" was armed against him.[33] He might have hoped for a more optimistic report. In early 1945, as the war wound down, Stravinsky's music, previously banned by the occupying Nazis, was made a cultural symbol for liberated France. Manuel Rosenthal and the National Orchestra programmed an ambitious survey of twenty-one Stravinsky works—including two French premieres—over a series of seven monthly concerts broadcast on French radio. Audiences and musicians generally welcomed the return of his music and even embraced the recent compositions. However, in February a claque of conservatory students from Olivier Messiaen's notorious harmony class—including the nineteen-year-old Pierre Boulez—disrupted the European premiere of *Danses concertantes* (1942) at a private Chamber Music Society concert. A month later the group staged a protest during Rosenthal's performance of the *Four Norwegian Moods* (1942). Critics and scholars have tended to exaggerate Boulez's role, conflating it with his subsequent embrace of serialism and later Cold War–era aesthetic debates (according to Craft, the folder of clippings and letters Stravinsky kept on the affair does not even mention Boulez).[34] In reality, the protests had more to do with the students' desire for a fresh new vision than a return of the old Stravinsky-Schoenberg debate. For his part, Leibowitz dismissed the scandal with damning indifference: "Given the scant attention Stravinsky pays to his scores today, I don't see why I should get worked up about them myself."[35] However, Boulez and others would soon defect from Messiaen's class to study twelve-tone music from this self-proclaimed apostle of Schoenberg.

Stravinsky had been inclined to dismiss the overblown reports of the protests, though the fact that he kept a dossier attests to his concern. After all, devotees like Poulenc and Nadia Boulanger continued to exalt him as the true bearer of "the light."[36] However, his once esteemed and still seemingly supportive friend Pierre Souvtchinsky was less sanguine. Around the time of his visit to the Chicago Art Institute exhibition, Stravinsky received the following update: "Lately in Paris (as everywhere, I suppose) there has emerged a youthful school of 'atonalists' which, with all its heresies, has unfortunately attracted a very talented circle of youngsters. I've got into a 'love-hate' relationship with this group, since I find that when it comes to culture these musical 'Trotskyites' are very interesting."[37]

Souvtchinsky does not mention Leibowitz by name, but he certainly had him in mind when the previous month he wrote, "The enemies of your music (our enemies) are unfortunately cleverer and more 'up-to-date' than some of our friends . . . and it's impossible not to worry about the damage to the new generation and necessary to help that generation find the right path once more."[38] Indeed, Leibowitz was proselytizing tirelessly about the historical inevitability of the twelve-tone method, denouncing any composer who refused to embrace "the entirely conscious and rigorous application of a thoroughgoing discipline, which has command of all the possibilities of chromatic polyphony."³⁹

Belying his feigned indifference to Stravinsky's new works, Leibowitz took his crusade to Hollywood in late 1947 under the pretext of interviewing the composer about his recent *Symphony in Three Movements*. Despite Schaeffner's warning, Stravinsky consented to meet, perhaps hoping his cooperation would be repaid with a degree of respect and sympathetic understanding. If so, he would be mistaken. The article for which Leibowitz, of course, also interviewed the venerated Schoenberg only reinscribed the already bold line dividing the two exiled masters:

> Schoenberg accepted the consequences of a tradition, developing it with lucidity and strength. But this cannot be said for Stravinsky. His approach to the same problems, bold as they may have sounded thirty-five years ago, today seems timorous and superficial. Originally attracted by new sounds and rhythmic devices, he failed to see really what they implied. His harmonic innovations (unlike Schoenberg's which are derived from a logical use of the twelve tones) are based on little more than notions.
>
> The sacrifice of arbitrary and hedonistic attitudes which Schoenberg demands is difficult for most musicians. Hence, many of them who want to be "modern" or "advanced" find it easier to follow Stravinsky.... But behind these frozen and sometimes readymade patterns (or rather, these petrified sound forms, put together with such diabolical skill) there is nothing except perhaps the illusion of music.⁴⁰

Nabokov defended his compatriot with an equally blindly partisan response that only further entrenched the debate along old nationalist lines:

> Atonality or Dodecatonalism as a system of musical composition is, as everyone knows, a product of Central Europe. As such it had from the outset the earmarks of a Messianic cult and a determinist religion....
>
> Only a small group of initiates led by Schoenberg adopted the twelve-tone technique in its entirety and by attempting to present it to the public as a "new" system, rather than a final step in a harmonic evolution, they created a strange kind of fetish, a hermetic cult, mechanistic in its technique and depressingly dull to the uninitiated listener. Now, twenty years later, the debate of atonality verses tonality is sporadically revived by the promoters of the Schoenbergian doctrine. This time the revival has taken place in France and in America. In France it is a part of a general infiltration of "Mittel-europa" ideas into the "core" of French civilization.⁴¹

Stravinsky told Nabokov his "answer to this twelve-tone obscurantism and to the impudent René Leibowitz is worthwhile," but he knew it would hardly counter the latter's impact.⁴² Souvtchinsky's warning that our "enemies ... are unfortunately cleverer and more 'up-to-date' than some of our friends," though probably referring to Nadia Boulanger, could as easily apply to Nabokov. It would not be the first time the younger Russian had stumbled in trying to ingratiate himself to his idolized compatriot. However, his contribution to Stravinsky's cause was just beginning.

Zelig

None other than Serge Diaghilev (1872–1929) introduced Stravinsky to the twenty-four-year-old Nabokov in 1927, seeking his opinion about the young Russian's music. The celebrity composer liked the cantata excerpts he had heard, which, as the ballet *Ode*, would share the program with *Apollon musagète* for the 1928 season premiere of Diaghilev's Ballets Russes.[43] More importantly, Stravinsky took a liking to the man. Cousin of the writer Vladimir Nabokov and distantly related to Diaghilev, Nicolas was handsome, intelligent, charming, as wellborn and cosmopolitan as Stravinsky and even more fluent in languages. Escaping Russia in 1919, his family settled first in Berlin, then Paris, where he earned a degree from the Sorbonne and his ambitious mother plotted to introduce him to the famous impresario. However, it was Nabokov's friendship with Prokofiev that would gain the ambitious youth entrée into Diaghilev's circle. Unfortunately, the starstruck composer soon fell from Stravinsky's good graces when, in a memorial tribute, he mistakenly attributed to Diaghilev the original ideas for *Petrushka* and *Les Noces*. Years passed before Stravinsky would even deign to answer his letters.[44]

Meanwhile, Nabokov continued to enjoy some artistic success and, more importantly, accumulate a list of friends that reads like a Who's Who of twentieth-century notables. In 1932, Dr. Albert Barnes invited him to lecture on modernist music and art at his foundation outside Philadelphia. Deciding to remain in America, Nabokov collaborated with the poet Archibald MacLeish on the first—quite popular—"American" ballet, *Union Pacific* (1934), for the reincarnated Ballets Russes de Monte Carlo. While a lecturer (alongside composer Elliot Carter) at St. John's College in Annapolis, the talkative Russian struck up a lifelong friendship with the brilliant writer, philosopher, British diplomat, and fellow Russian émigré Isaiah Berlin. During the war, he moonlighted for the Justice Department, translating newspaper articles from Nazi-occupied Russia. Nabokov's mastery of languages and talent for storytelling captured the attention of American diplomats Charles Bohlen and George Kennan, influential Russia experts who, as part of the so-called Wise Men, would help draft America's Cold War policy. Through Berlin, Nabokov would meet and befriend Auden (well before the latter's association with Stravinsky), who, in turn, suggested he join him to work for the United States Strategic Bombing Survey (USSBS) in Germany. Nabokov stayed on as a consultant to the Office of Military Government, United States (OMGUS), charged with aiding the process of de-Nazification and restoration of German cultural life.

Nabokov's memoirs, *Bagázh* (1975), describe a life of scattered experiences carried by the tumultuous currents of history in directions the subject seems never fully to control and only vaguely understand. (Whether one can entirely trust his accounts is another matter; Berlin affirmed that he could be a "fantasist."[45]) Zelig-like, Nabokov shows up in Paris during the twenties, in New York and Philadelphia in the thirties, in wartime Washington and postwar Germany, in Paris again in the fifties, and in Berlin once more at the height of the Cold War. And in every location, at every crucial historical moment, he somehow positioned himself near the highest echelons of political and cultural influence, cementing personal relationships with some of the most talented, important, and influential thinkers of the twentieth century. Precisely because he was a second-tier but still significant cultural figure, Nicolas Nabokov represents an informative comparison and contrast to the "great" Stravinsky. His significance belongs entirely to the cultural moment. The Cultural Cold War essentially created what we remember of him.

Nabokov was only a distant, if highly interested, bystander throughout the creation of *The Rake's Progress*. I introduce him because he played a crucial and mysterious role in negotiating the opera's premiere and, more importantly, in Stravinsky's lavish fee. Of more lasting significance would be his efforts over the subsequent fifteen years to reintroduce the seventy-year-old composer to Europe and the world. The "cultural generalissimo" (as Stravinsky dubbed him) would go on to arrange important commissions and lucrative guest appearances, all resulting from cultural and political contacts he forged during the 1940s, many of which remain shrouded in controversy. From 1950 to 1964, Nabokov helped transform Stravinsky's international profile (and earnings) almost as much as Robert Craft helped facilitate the composer's change in musical style. The fortunes of these three men would be inextricably linked.

The Modern Subject in Crisis

Stravinsky took a keen interest in philosophy and kept abreast of the distressing political situation in Europe and the Soviet Union, especially to the extent that it affected his family, his concert engagements, and his royalties (not always in that order). Though he considered the "expression" of feelings anathema to art, the composer was not indifferent to the world. Craft relays: "Stravinsky worried over the significance of each item of war news. He charted the fronts each day with pins and maps. The little *Norwegian Moods* is war-time homage. . . . But these pieces, however motivated, do not reflect Stravinsky's feelings about the wars. I think the finale of *Scènes de Ballet* does. At the end of the manuscript score Stravinsky added the words, 'Paris n'est plus aux allemands'; the whole jubilant apotheosis was written on the day of the liberation."[46]

Although perhaps less immediate, *The Rake's Progress* is no less inseparable from those momentous events and the tumult of ideas responding to them. Dominating philosophical and artistic discourse in America and Europe in the late 1940s was a diverse range of more or less leftist intellectuals, including Auden; philosophers Theodor Adorno, Walter Benjamin, and Jean-Paul Sartre; critic Clement Greenberg; and historian Arthur Schlesinger Jr., who saw the "twin tyrants" of consumerism and totalitarianism as threatening the very foundation of modern humanity: the autonomous individual. Their responses to this crisis were equally diverse—and hotly debated, as we shall see—but, in one way or another, each contributed to the cultural moment of Stravinsky's opera. Auden's libretto would parody Sartre's existential pessimism; Adorno's *Philosophy of Modern Music* (1949) would redefine the Stravinsky-Schoenberg debate in Marxist terms; and a group of mostly Anglo-Americans known collectively as the Non-Communist Left (NCL)—whose ideas Schlesinger encapsulated in a timely defense of liberal democracy, *The Vital Center* (1949)—would frame the Cold War debates about culture and society. How Nabokov came to play a leading role in those debates and use his position to help Stravinsky (and Stravinsky to help his position) figures prominently in the narrative of the composer's life from the completion of *The Rake* onward.

The "Middlebrow" Threat

> With *Life* you should really come to an agreement. It doesn't matter that asses read it; what is important is that not an ass would write about me.
>
> —Stravinsky to Nabokov[47]

Even in 1947 Nabokov's supportive role was neither tangential, nor was he driven solely to ingratiate himself to Stravinsky (though that was always lurking as a subtext). Like his compatriot, he paid only passing attention to politics until 1940, when he was drawn into the circle of State Department Russia experts. Tutored and encouraged by Charles Bohlen (a future ambassador to Russia) and Isaiah Berlin, Nabokov soon emerged as one of the few voices continuing to denounce Stalin's stranglehold on cultural life. In 1942, when, as new allies, Russian composers were being lionized in the West, he published a trio of articles on Shostakovich and Prokofiev in the *Atlantic Monthly* and *Harper's Bazaar* that challenged the prevailing sentiment.

Framing his criticism in aesthetic rather than political terms, Nabokov weaves "as a sort of motif" a "juxtaposition of the cosmopolitan with the provincial."[48] Ten years later, when he was organizing the inaugural festival *Masterpieces of the 20th Century* for the Congress for Cultural Freedom, "cosmopolitan" would mean any music the Soviets had denounced as rootless, decadent, or formalist: Stravinsky, Schoenberg, Bartók, Berg, even Shostakovich. However, in 1942 Nabokov used the terms more pointedly to expose what he regarded as the dull, trivial conformity of Shostakovich's and Prokofiev's recent music.

While his public writings adopt a facade of critical distance, Nabokov's private exchanges with Stravinsky vent a nasty elitism. In May 1944 he wrote, "I fear that in these latest works [Prokofiev] has begun to fall into a kind of bourgeois infantilism. And Shostakovich's Eighth Symphony is simply impossible to listen to. Such *merde* is imposed on the naively stupid, apathetic, and profoundly uncultivated American public by orchestra conductors who are themselves *canailles* [scoundrels] and who exploit the stupidest emotions of the people in this cultural desert."[49] He wasn't alone. Nearly all the émigré composers who heard the famous 1942 radio broadcast of Toscanini conducting Shostakovich's Seventh Symphony (the "Leningrad") "seem to have experienced a mass attack of envy and resentment."[50]

Nabokov attacks Shostakovich not so much for his politics—that is, as a composer of "Soviet" music—as for shamelessly appealing to a mass audience and, worse, succeeding. What separates the "dull" Soviet symphonies from *Petrushka*, *Oedipus Rex*, or his own *Union Pacific* is some vague notion of originality: "One would probably not object to [these common tunes] if they had been treated originally; for Haydn, Beethoven, Stravinsky often used tunes coming from the gutter."[51] Here Nabokov echoes Clement Greenberg, whose seminal 1939 essay, "Avant-Garde and Kitsch," sharply distinguishes the essentially self-critical expression of individuals from the ersatz culture aimed at the newly literate but uncritical masses. Essential to this distinction is the notion of authenticity, a concept also central for Sartre's midcentury existentialism. Modernity had increasingly rendered humans as beings for use: through mass consumerism to be both sold and sold to and through totalitarian government to be controlled and manipulated. "Authentic" individuals strive to "exist" beyond—even against—the role official institutions or markets assign them.

The rightist Spanish philosopher José Ortega y Gasset drew a similar but more explicitly elitist conclusion in his essay, "The Dehumanization of Art" (1925):

> Modern art . . . is essentially unpopular; moreover, it is antipopular. . . . Thus the work of art acts like a social agent which segregates from the shapeless mass of the many two different castes of men. . . .
>
> For a century and a half the masses have claimed to be the whole of society. Stravinsky's music or Pirandello's drama have the sociological effect of compelling the people to recognize itself for what it is: a component among others of the social structure, inert matter of the historical process, a secondary factor in the cosmos of spiritual life.[52]

The growing masses concerned not just critics of late modernity. Resistance to new and expanding modes of production has been a recurring trope since the earliest days of industrialization. An eighteenth-century German satirist and admirer of Hogarth observed, "Since the Universe has become subject to the book and picture market, thousands of writers and artists have grown blind to the direct light of Nature, but see quite satisfactorily if its beams are reflected from a sheet of paper."[53] The recurring presumption is that mass production somehow redirects or obstructs the creative "light" either of "Nature" (for the Enlightenment critic) or the "Individual" (for modernists)—hence, Walter Benjamin's claim that the artwork's "aura withers in the age of mechanical reproduction."[54] Yet, a prime example of an artist using mechanical production to reach middle-class consumers is Hogarth's *Rake's Progress* print series. No wonder Robert Craft presumed Stravinsky saw the original paintings. Reproduced copies could not have inspired a work of "high art."

Fig. 1.3. William Hogarth, *A Rake's Progress*, I. "The Heir," June 1735, etching and engraving in black on ivory laid paper, 319 × 387 mm (image), Gift of Horace S. Oakley, 1921.338, The Art Institute of Chicago.

Hogarth saw them differently, though—literally. Thinking like a printmaker, he created the paintings not as "ideal" or "authentic" works but as preparatory studies for his intended commodity: the set of engraved copperplates. Because the engraved images had to be reversed, Hogarth composed his paintings in reverse (the sole exception being *The Levée*). Aside from seemingly insignificant details, the reversal might seem to have no effect on the content. However, as with a text, viewers typically read an image from left to right. Thus, the eye moves quickly from the mostly empty left side of the first print, *The Heir* (shown in fig. 1.3), to the action on the right where Tom tries to pay off his formerly betrothed, Sarah Young, to her mother's great displeasure. The corresponding painting (shown in fig. 1.4) gives the story away at first glance, leaving the eye to wander aimlessly over the cluttered symbols lying about the apartment. Of course, Hogarth still sold the eight paintings for a fair sum (eighty-four guineas in 1745), but their real value—and intent—lay in the subscription sale of the series of prints for one and a half guineas each.[55] *A Rake's Progress* paintings hanging in Sir John Soane's Museum are thus a collection of

Fig. 1.4. William Hogarth, *A Rake's Progress*, I. "The Heir" painting, © Sir John Soane's Museum, London.

masterfully crafted by-products of an artistic enterprise designed expressly for a middle-class audience.

Indeed, the production and consumption of art have been ever changing since Gutenberg invented the printing press; such progressive change drove the modern era. What distinguishes the concerns of modernist critics and arguably defines twentieth-century modernism is the perceived threat to individuality. In their different ways, Greenberg, Sartre, and Ortega belong to a diverse range of intellectuals who saw consumerism and totalitarianism as threatening the very foundation of human freedom. Even as Auden lampoons Sartre's existential "*l'acte gratuit*" by having Nick council Tom to ignore the "twin tyrants of appetite and conscience," he also acknowledges the gigantic forces suffocating the autonomous subject. Auden doesn't disagree with the French philosopher's diagnosis, only with his nihilistic response.

Bourdieu takes a broader and opposing view, distinguishing highbrow classics from middlebrow commercial art not by artistic value but only by their "two modes of ageing." He observes, "The opposition is total between bestsellers with no tomorrow and the classics, lasting bestsellers which owe to the education system their consecration, hence their extended and durable market."[56] Elsewhere, he refers to the world of high art as "a sacred island systematically and ostentatiously opposed to the profane world of production, a sanctuary for gratuitous, disinterested activity in a universe given over to money and self-interest."[57] In this upside-down world of posed disinterestedness, economic and aesthetic values form a zero sum. A work judged aesthetically valuable must, by definition, be unmarketable; conversely, a marketable work is deemed of little aesthetic value. For Bourdieu, the shrill defense of "individual" or "true art" by elitists like Nabokov, Greenberg, and Ortega is just another form of cultural domination. Of course, Stravinsky's music elevated the glitterati attending *The Rake*'s premiere. That is its primary function. However, this perverse economy can sustain itself only to the extent that educated and, to a lesser degree (in America, to a much lesser degree), economic elites still value the cultural capital bestowed by the supposedly autonomous artist.

Accusations of middlebrow pandering—of which Stravinsky was both a source and target—would shape the Cold War cultural debate forming just as the composer took up *The Rake's Progress* in May 1948. The problem with Nabokov's response to Leibowitz was that, in trying to advocate for Stravinsky, he had to straddle the fault line between two cultural-historical tectonic plates. One was the old discourse pitting French "Civilization" against German "Culture"; Western against Central European; objective against subjective; Stravinsky against Schoenberg. The other was coalescing at that historical moment as the Cultural Cold War: West versus East; Democracy versus Communism; individual freedom versus social responsibility; Stravinsky versus Shostakovich. Nabokov's misstep in "The Atonal Trail" was less out of step than it was a last step from the ground of the Stravinsky-Schoenberg debate to that between Stravinsky and Shostakovich. He would stop opposing dodecaphonicism as an infiltration of "Mittel-Europa" ideas and recast his previous aesthetic critique of Shostakovich in overtly political terms. Thus, at the 1950 Berlin Congress for Cultural Freedom, he introduced himself as a "cosmopolitan musician . . . a citizen of the Republic of Art, in short, a man who loves complete creative freedom, who has a horror of all frontiers, geographical and spiritual barriers."[58]

Scholars tend to overlook Stravinsky's rivalry with Shostakovich. Their wary relationship would come to the fore in March 1949, when, in the midst of completing act 1, the Russian American pointedly and publically refused to welcome the Soviet composer to a Communist-sponsored "peace" conference in New York.[59] As a polarity, Stravinsky-Shostakovich frames a decidedly different narrative than Stravinsky-Schoenberg. The former positions him as an idiosyncratic but artistically free agent: the composer of *Les Noces*, the *Symphony of Psalms*, and *Mass*. In the latter, Stravinsky plays the popular sellout: the composer of *Histoire du Soldat*, the *Circus Polka*, and *Ebony Concerto*. Taken together, these framing narratives better capture the more complex image of Stravinsky in the 1940s and throughout his neoclassical period, navigating that precarious middle road—that is, the one Schoenberg asserts does not lead to Rome—between succumbing to commercial tastes and stubbornly preserving his individual vision.[60] In truth, the labels high, middle, and low only disguise the fluid continuum of engagement artists must negotiate with audiences. Where Stravinsky falls on that continuum, which musical and social factors condition his position for any given piece, and the extent to which he consciously chooses it at any given time, form a backdrop to the construction and reception of *The Rake's Progress*.

His Russian Circle

Stravinsky's reasons for bringing Nabokov back into his inner circle were, as usual for him, both personal and professional. He had welcomed his critique of the newly popular Soviet music—"It is gratifying to see that these American reviews take an interest in a mentality such as yours"—thinking he now had a strong advocate with access to a wide American readership.[61] Practically speaking, he appreciated an extra set of eyes and ears on the East Coast and in Europe; he also truly enjoyed Nabokov's company, as did most everyone. As both a compatriot and a composer, Stravinsky shared with Nabokov more life experiences than he did with any of his American friends. Nabokov also understood and embraced wholeheartedly his artistic vision. Writing from war-ravaged Germany, he reflected: "In the tragic world in which we live . . . only a few encouraging, reasonable, and beautiful things remain. One of these, and for me the most important, is your art, with all of its nobility, beauty, and intelligence." Stravinsky replied: "Come, come, we await you impatiently. . . . From the bottom of my heart, I hope for your return and your visit here. In this, the most *deaf* period we have ever suffered, it is good to see each other. After the few lines (concerning your experiences and observations) I declare with pleasure that we speak the same language—which I had doubted. So know that you are welcome, and do not forget to confirm your visit."[62]

To Stravinsky's disappointment, more than a year passed before his friend could get away for five days over Christmas 1947. In stark contrast to Leibowitz's visit the week before, Nabokov's would be an enthusiastic reunion with Stravinsky's "white Russian" inner circle. Arriving with him by train from New York was George Balanchine, who was rendezvousing with his twenty-two-year old third wife, the ballerina Maria Tallchief (the circle also included Stravinsky's neighbor, the artist and set designer Eugene Berman). Nabokov later memorialized the visit in a charmingly intimate portrait of the composer in the *Atlantic Monthly*.[63]

Nabokov was hesitant to stay at the Stravinskys' home, but his host insisted: "Yes, of course we will be expecting you for Christmas. You will stay right here with us. You will sleep on the sofa on which slept Nadia Boulanger, Olsen, Auden and others." Balanchine reassured him:

> Oh, no, . . . they love to have guests. He, in particular. Don't worry, he won't let you alone for a minute; he will talk to you day and night and ask you a million questions. They will drive you around Hollywood and take you to the best restaurants for dinner. In the morning you will have breakfast with him and his parrot and you will see him do his Hungarian calisthenics. . . . He jumps like a ball, walks on his head and does push-ups with the ease of a twenty-year-old. And besides . . . he will play you his scores: it will do you good to look at them carefully. Don't think of going to a hotel. You will offend him and he will never forgive you.[64]

Fig. 1.5. Christmas 1947 in Hollywood. *Clockwise from top*: Vera Stravinsky, Nicolas Nabokov, Igor Stravinsky, and George Balanchine. (Igor Stravinsky Collection, Paul Sacher Foundation)

One can imagine their excited conversations: about the forthcoming premiere of *Orpheus* by Balanchine's Ballet Society (the future New York City Ballet); the premiere in Boston of Nika's new orchestral piece, *The Return of Pushkin*; his soon-to-be third wife Patricia Blake (also twenty-two years old); Soviet cultural oppression and the growing political tensions in Europe; news from the New York and Paris arts scenes; gossip about friends and colleagues, both esteemed (the brilliant Auden and his questionable hygiene) and despised (the Nazi collaborator Serge Lifar). Stravinsky undoubtedly discussed his new opera, but Nabokov shared only a tidbit: "He was explaining how he intended to treat Auden's libretto: 'I will lace each aria into a tight corset.'"[65]

The Rake certainly occupied the composer's mind. With Auden back in New York busily drafting the libretto, Stravinsky was supposed to be completing the Credo and Sanctus of his interrupted *Mass*, begun three years earlier. Instead, on December 11, he began a short movement for string quartet, possibly intended to fulfill a commission from the Juilliard Quartet issued the previous summer, but more likely intended from the start as the prelude to the act 3 Graveyard scene (see chapters 4 and 7 for an analysis and explanation). He would finally complete the *Mass* just before traveling east where, on March 31 at the Hotel Raleigh in Washington, he met with Auden to discuss the completed libretto and with, for the first time in person, the twenty-four-year-old conductor Robert Craft. Upon his return to Hollywood, Stravinsky immediately set to work on act 1, scene 1, on May 8.

Understandably protective of the project to which he would devote the next three years, Stravinsky sought to draw his Russian friends into its creative orbit. He later advocated unsuccessfully for Berman to design the sets for both the

Venice and New York premieres. Deeply unsatisfied with Carl Ebert's staging at La Fenice, he would convince the Metropolitan Opera to entrust Balanchine with the American premiere (with hardly any better result). All Nabokov seemed to be able to contribute were flattering feature articles and a vigorous defense of his friend's music. He longed to make a greater impact and forge an even greater bond. Two years later he wrote:

> How would I like to have a lot of *gelds* [money] to fly to you and spend a week with you. I was so envious of both George and Craft . . . of the fact that they saw you and visited you. Just yesterday, Wystan and I talked about it in his room (which is a little less dirty than last year). . . . I caught a glimpse of the orchestration of the first scene of the opera. Igor Fedorovich, can I get it from somebody at least temporarily? How much have you written?[66]

By the time the opera was finished, Nabokov would make such an impact and forge such a bond.

Faust

The exchange in *Partisan Review* between Leibowitz and Nabokov captures some of the tension of the moment when Stravinsky settled down to compose *The Rake's Progress*, but neither article made a lasting contribution to understanding the composer.[67] Of greater significance would be Theodor Adorno's similarly polarizing but more penetrating (and often impenetrable) *Philosophy of Modern Music*. Adorno's binary framework, which was comprised of two separate essays, "Schoenberg and Progress" (1941) and "Stravinsky and Restoration" (1948), only reinforced the conventional opposition. Mann dramatizes their stances in the following conversation between the devil (He), modeled after Adorno, and the composer Leverkühn (I), who here adopts Stravinsky's aesthetic stance:

> HE: It is all up with conventions once considered prerequisite and compulsory, the guarantors of the game's freedom.
>
> I: One could know all that and yet recognize freedom again beyond any criticism. One could raise the game to a higher power by playing with forms from which, as one knows, life has vanished.
>
> HE: I know, I know. Parody. It might be merry if in its aristocratic nihilism it were not so woebegone. Do you think such tricks promise you much pleasure and greatness?[68]

Adorno's essay on Schoenberg goes well beyond Leibowitz's argument for the historical inevitability of twelve-tone composition, asserting that only such radical music, by alienating the audience subsumed by mass culture, can articulate the modern subject in crisis. He explains:

> The alienation present in the consistency of artistic technique forms the very substance of the work of art. The shocks of incomprehension, emitted by artistic

technique in the age of its meaninglessness, undergo a sudden change. They illuminate the meaningless world. Modern music sacrifices itself to this effort. It has taken upon itself all the darkness and the guilt of the world. Its fortune lies in the perception of misfortune; all of its beauty is in denying itself the illusion of beauty.... Modern music sees absolute oblivion as its goal. It is the surviving message of despair from the shipwrecked.[69]

Mann would seal this dour conclusion onto the bargain his devil strikes with Faust: "We want you cold, till scarcely the flames of production shall not be hot enough for you to warm yourself in them. You shall flee into them from the coldness of your life."[70]

In what is either a fascinating coincidence or an indirect influence, the German novelist created his own *Doctor Faustus* in Los Angeles in the years immediately preceding Stravinsky's work on *The Rake's Progress*. Furthermore, he appropriated Adorno's interpretation of modernist music as the central metaphor for the rise and catastrophic self-destruction of Nazi Germany. He later explained, "[Adorno's] rigorous manner of veneration, the tragically cerebral relentlessness of his criticism of the contemporary musical situation, was precisely what I needed. For what I could draw from it, and what I appropriated from it in order to portray the whole cultural crisis in addition to the crises of music, was the fundamental motif of my book: the closeness of sterility, the innate despair that prepares the ground for a pact with the devil."[71]

Mann's contemporary Faust, a theology student turned composer, symbolically sells (or imagines selling) his soul to the devil in return for twenty-four years of musical genius—a manifestation of which is his "discovery" of the twelve-tone technique—before succumbing to insanity. The story's narrator sets down his recollections in Germany during the years of the Second World War. Obviously, Mann based his hero in part on Schoenberg, though he drew the character's personality and tragic demise from the life of Friedrich Nietzsche. For his description of the twelve-tone technique and the devil's proposition, the novelist relied heavily on Adorno's essay on Schoenberg, the manuscript of which the philosopher, who was also a German refugee living in Los Angeles, shared with him. Mann, in turn, read aloud to Adorno chapters as he completed them, soliciting his response and advice as to how to describe his composer's increasingly esoteric music. Mann even went so far as to model his fictional musicologist Wendell Kretschmar, from whom the devil's persona later emerges, on his erudite musical consultant.

By incorporating Adorno's ideas, Mann presents a striking insight into the world of twentieth-century music: that the devil, the "tragically cerebral relentlessness" of whose criticism prods the composer in his artistic progress—who, in essence, confers success—is a philosopher-musicologist. The implications are deeply unsettling: the rise of musicology, itself emblematic of a historical self-consciousness, has functioned to goad composers and artists down the path toward aesthetic isolation.[72]

To Adorno, Stravinsky's attempts to accommodate his music to bourgeois tastes are not just futile but also a craven betrayal of the composer's duty to preserve at least the illusion of an individual voice in the face of totalizing forces. His radical judgment extends far beyond the merely elitist critiques of consumerism by Greenberg and Nabokov: "Since *Petrushka*, his scores prefigure gesture and step, this assuming a constantly increasing distance from empathy with the dramatic figure.... Subjectivity assumes the character of sacrifice, but—and this is where he sneers at the tradition of humanistic art—the music does not identify with the victim, but rather the destructive element. Through the liquidation of the victim it rids itself of all intentions—that is, of its own subjectivity."[73]

In the wake of Nazi atrocities, such criticism cuts to the bone, but it also shows little understanding of Stravinsky's true aesthetic stance. For their part, neither Schoenberg nor Stravinsky was open to viewing his own or any other artist's work in sociological terms. Schoenberg claimed to have "never been able to bear the fellow.... Now I know that he has clearly never liked my music.... It is disgusting, by the way, how he treats Stravinsky." Stravinsky, for once, was less sensitive. According to Craft, he "read a few pages before setting it aside, saying, indifferently, 'He doesn't like my music.'"[74]

Of Stravinsky's artistic circle, only Auden was positioned or inclined to engage Adorno's ideas. Versed in Marx and Freud, the poet may have shared Adorno's bleak diagnosis of modern society, as he did Sartre's, but again he prescribed a very different treatment. *Philosophy of Modern Music* had yet to be published when he and Kallman drafted *The Rake's Progress*, but Adorno's ideas, at least on the twelve-tone Schoenberg, were drifting, so to speak, in the southern California air. Nor would Auden have read Mann's *Doctor Faustus*, published in English translation in 1948, before completing the libretto. However, the poet had been a tangential member of Mann's family since 1935 when he married the novelist's daughter Erika, who was to be stripped of her German citizenship, so she could obtain a British passport. Though they never cohabitated as husband and wife, the two enjoyed a warm if contentious friendship.

As a result, Auden probably knew the subject and circumstances of *Doctor Faustus*, which in turn may have influenced his use of the Faust legend. However, the poet, who disfavored novels, also disapproved of political messages in works of art. His political disillusionment during the Spanish Civil War had led him to conclude it was "not the poet's duty to tell people what to do but to present them with ideas that enable them to make their own rational and moral choices." By contrast, under pressure to flee Nazi Germany, the Manns had taken increasingly activist roles. Thomas toured America in 1938 to rally support to fight Nazism; the passionate Erika organized aid for other refugee artists and even helped many escape through neutral Switzerland; and her brother Klaus founded the literary magazine *Decision: A Review of Free Culture* to press the argument for intellectuals to act. Given this very public disagreement—Auden and Klaus debated the "Function of the Writer in the Political Crisis" in a New York radio broadcast in March 1941—Auden's relatively light verse libretto may be read as an indirect response to Mann's dense and psychologically weighty novel.[75] Given this opposition, their similarities are all the more striking: both protagonists are stricken with insanity in climactic scenes—namely, Mann's chapter 47 soirée and Stravinsky's graveyard encounter—and suffer syphilitic deaths. Another connection between opera and novel was Mann's relationship to Schoenberg and Stravinsky: Leverkühn's plan for *Love's Labor's Lost* describes a Stravinskian opera buffa, making Mann's fictional composer a composite of both.[76]

* * *

Whether from the Marxist left, the vital center, or the elitist right, midcentury intellectuals somehow agreed that modernist art stood alone in preserving at least a sense of the individual voice in the face of totalizing mass culture. Aside from Adorno, this group perceived Stravinsky's music as a guiding "light" in the encroaching darkness. Their shrill attacks on consumerist culture have not aged well, but Stravinsky's music has. The walls separating "high," "middle," and "low" seemed to be collapsing at the time of the great composer's death in 1971, yet his old-fashioned opera flourishes. How has a work that in 1951 seemed stillborn managed to thrive, even as its defenders have been dismissed with the bygone age?

The question would have baffled the postpremiere party guests at Taverna La Fenice. For them, *The Rake* represented the high-water mark—though, in retrospect, the last hurrah—of neoclassicism. Assembled were all the major and minor players: Stravinsky at center, Auden at his side, defender and facilitator Nicolas Nabokov to toast the occasion, and Nadia Boulanger to carry the composer's valise. For the time being, the opera's accessible classicism would be its greatest asset and most crippling impediment. As time moved on, so would *The Rake*.

Notes

1. Nicolas Nabokov, "Stravinsky's 'Rake' Has Its Surprises," *New York Herald Tribune*, November 30, 1951.

2. Robert Craft, *Stravinsky: The Chronicle of a Friendship: 1948/1971* (Nashville: Vanderbilt University Press, 1994), 62–63. This account first appeared as "*The Rake's Progress: 'La Prima Assoluta*'" in Igor Stravinsky and Robert Craft, *Themes and Episodes* (New York: Alfred A. Knopf, 1966), 51–54, under Vera's name, omitting the jibes aimed at the upper class but elaborating on those aimed at the *Times* critic. A comparison of the two versions gives a sense of how Craft and the Stravinskys conformed the tone of their written voices and opinions and serves as an indication of their unusual personal symbiosis and as an alert to read critically.

Viewing the scene through the eyes of an inveterate networker, Nabokov described "an exceptionally distinguished audience of conductors, opera managers, modern-music addicts, composers and publishers who mingled with the most elegant and snobbish set of international café society and titled owners of Venetian palaces" ("Stravinsky's 'Rake'").

3. Igor Stravinsky and Robert Craft, *Dialogues and a Diary* (Garden City, NY: Doubleday, 1963), 110; slightly altered in Robert Craft, *Stravinsky: The Chronicle of a Friendship: 1948/1971* (New York: Vintage Books, 1972), 29.

4. Craft, *Chronicle* (1972), 26; omitted from the otherwise more detailed *Chronicle* (1994).

5. Ibid., *Chronicle* (1994), 63.

6. I. Stravinsky and Craft, *Dialogues and a Diary*, 110.

7. Craft, *Chronicle* (1994), 46.

8. Igor Stravinsky, "About *The Rake's Progress*," English typescript published in Italian translation as "Como ho composto *The Rake's Progress*" in *La Biennale di Venezia* (1951): 8. The following reworded version appears in Liner notes (1953): "The various Hogarth 'progresses' suggested themselves as operatic tableaux."

9. Robert Craft, ed., *Dearest Bubushkin: The Correspondence of Vera and Igor Stravinsky, 1921–1954, with Excerpts from Vera Stravinsky's Diaries, 1922–1971* (London: Thames and Hudson, 1985),138. Full entry reads: "Chicago. To the exhibit of Turner, Hogarth, and Constable at the Museum. Also Chagall." According to the institute's catalogue, "Masterpieces of English Painting: William Hogarth, John Constable, J. M. W. Turner" ran from October 15 to December 15, 1946.

10. Igor Stravinsky and Robert Craft, *Memories and Commentaries* (Garden City, NY: Doubleday, 1962), 144.

11. Ross Parmenter, "The World of Music: Stravinsky Plans Opera," *New York Times*, December 7, 1947. In June 1947 Hawkes wrote, "Mr. Benjamin Britten, whose new opera group is now functioning in England has a great interest in your doing a piece for them along the lines we discussed last winter" (Paul Sacher Foundation; see also note 20).

12. Vera Stravinsky and Robert Craft, *Stravinsky in Pictures and Documents* (New York: Simon and Schuster, 1978), 396. (Vera's diary records nothing for May 2, 1947.)

13. Robert Craft, "On a Misunderstood Collaboration: Assisting Stravinsky," *Atlantic Monthly* (December 1982): 68, 70–74. Taruskin (*Russian Traditions*, 12–13n) and Walsh (*Second Exile*, 421–22) observe the increasing dominance of Craft's authorial voice in the later books, especially *Themes and Episodes* and *Retrospectives*, written and compiled when the composer's health and mental acuity were declining.

Having reviewed drafts of the conversation books and published correspondence, Charles Joseph attests: "The differences between the composer's original drafts and the published versions sometimes amount to more than simple copyediting. Many pages of the original typescripts exhibit Stravinsky's corrections and deletions suggesting that he studied his responses and refined them after Craft had transcribed his remarks (an example of such a draft page from *Memories* appears in *Themes and Conclusions*, 18). Yet there are just as many instances demonstrating that, rather than reproducing Stravinsky's own thoughts verbatim, the original responses were initially Craft's. It seems that Craft sometimes answered his own questions, then later Stravinsky was asked to revise them" (*Stravinsky Inside Out*, 260).

14. Igor Stravinsky and Robert Craft, *Expositions and Developments* (Garden City, NY: Doubleday, 1962), 153n; reprint (Berkeley, CA: University of California Press, 1981), 134n. [Citations refer to both editions.]

15. Richard Taruskin, *Stravinsky and the Russian Traditions* (Berkeley: University of California Press, 1996), 12. On Walter Nouvel's contribution to the autobiography, see Stephen Walsh, *Stravinsky—A Creative Spring: Russia and France, 1882–1934* (New York: Alfred A. Knopf, 1999), 514 and *Stravinsky—The Second Exile: France and America, 1934–1971* (New York: Alfred A. Knopf, 2006), 3. See also Robert Craft, "Roland-Manuel and the *Poetics of Music*," *Perspectives of New Music* 21, no. 1–2 (1982–83): 487–505. Souvtchinsky helped with the initial Russian draft of *Poetics* and essentially wrote the fifth lecture on Russian music (Walsh, *Second Exile*, 94–95). Taruskin claims "the voice that speaks to us from the Stravinsky/Craft books . . . was in an indirect but important sense as much the creation of Pierre Souvtchinsky as the voice that had spoken two decades earlier out of the *Poetic Musicale*" (*Russian Traditions*, 4).

16. Virgil Thomson, *The Virgil Thomson Reader* (Boston: Houghton Mifflin, 1981), 417.

17. Igor Stravinsky, "Reflections on the *Rake*," *Opera News* 9 (February 1953): 8.
18. Robert Craft, *Stravinsky: Glimpses of a Life* (New York: St. Martin's Press, 1992), 53.
19. Walsh, *Creative Spring*, 537.
20. Prospectus and letters of April 24, 1947, and September 30, 1947, Paul Sacher Foundation. Composer Benjamin Britten, producer Eric Crozier, and designer John Piper founded the group after their successful collaboration on *The Rape of Lucretia*.
21. Parmenter, "Stravinsky Plans Opera."
22. Letter of September 23, 1948, Paul Sacher Foundation.
23. Robert Craft, ed., *Stravinsky: Selected Correspondence,* vol. 1 (New York: Alfred A. Knopf, 1982), 299.
24. V. Stravinsky and Craft, *Pictures and Documents*, 397.
25. Outtake from interview for Tony Palmer's *Aspects of Stravinsky*, vol. 1, 93, Paul Sacher Foundation. I examine his idiosyncratic text settings in chapter 5.
26. V. Stravinsky and Craft, *Pictures and Documents*, 397.
27. The outline is reproduced in I. Stravinsky and Craft, *Memories and Commentaries*, 156–67, and W. H. Auden and Chester Kallman, *Libretti and Other Dramatic Writings: 1939–1973*, ed. Edward Mendelson (London: Faber and Faber, 1993), 581–89. In Robert Craft, "A Note on the Sketches and Two Versions of the Libretto," 20, 27, Craft describes the version in *Memories* as "inaccurate and incomplete," in that it fails to include Kallman's detailed outline of the duet with chorus in act 3, scene 1 (see fig. 8.2). However, that diagram was obviously not part of Stravinsky and Auden's original conception.
28. Igor Stravinsky, *Poetics of Music*, trans. Arthur Knodel and Ingolf Dahl (Cambridge, MA: Harvard University Press, 1970), 63.
29. Igor Stravinsky and Robert Craft, *Conversations with Stravinsky* (Garden City, NY: Doubleday, 1959), 145. Many scholars agree; see Joseph N. Straus, *Remaking the Past* (Cambridge, MA: Harvard University Press, 1992). Others have continued to emphasize Stravinsky's reliance on tonal conventions; see Alan Lessem, "Schoenberg, Stravinsky, and Neoclassicism," *Musical Quarterly* 68 (1982): 532–33, while Taruskin questions the sincerity of Stravinsky's retroactively professed affinity with the Viennese School (see *Russian Traditions*, 4).
30. Quoted in Leonard Stein, "Schoenberg and 'Kleine Modernsky,'" in *Confronting Stravinsky: Man, Musician, and Modernist*, ed. Jann Pasler (Berkeley: University of California Press, 1988), 322.
31. I. Stravinsky and Craft, *Dialogues and a Diary*, 58.
32. Thomas Mann, *Story of a Novel* (New York: Alfred A. Knopf, 1961), 51–52.
33. "Not much is known about the Judeo-Austro-Russian origins of this cram-packed German musician. This stateless upstart shoves himself everywhere" (letter of September 1, 1946, Paul Sacher Foundation; translated from French).
34. Robert Craft, *Stravinsky: Selected Correspondence*, vol. 2 (New York: Alfred A. Knopf, 1982), 347.
35. Quoted in Leslie A. Sprouts, "The 1945 Stravinsky Debates: Nigg, Messiaen, and the Early Cold War in France," *Journal of Musicology* 26, no. 1 (2009): 119.
36. Poulenc: "At any rate, be assured that I am one of those for whom you carry the light" (letter of December 28, 1945, in Robert Craft, ed., *Stravinsky: Selected Correspondence*, vol. 3 (New York: Alfred A. Knopf, 1985), 212; Boulanger: "Those who matter among the young musicians [know] perfectly well whence comes the light" (letter of October 11, 1946, Paul Sacher Foundation; translated from French).
37. Letter of December 1946, quoted in Walsh, *Second Exile*, 200. Souvchinsky regarded the young protesters (some of whom were political leftists) as poser "revolutionaries."

38. Letter of October 1946, quoted in Walsh, *Second Exile*, 199.

39. René Leibowitz, "Béla Bartók, ou la possibilité du compromise dans la musique contemporaine," *Les Temps Modernes* 3, no. 25 (1947): 729. Leibowitz wrote numerous other articles and a book, *Schoenberg and His School*.

40. René Leibowitz, "Music Chronicle—Two Composers: A Letter from Hollywood," *Partisan Review* 15, no. 3 (1948): 362, 364.

41. Nicolas Nabokov, "The Atonal Trail: A Communication," *Partisan Review* 15 (1948): 580–81. A veiled anti-Semitism underlies Nabokov's article and the whole debate about "dodecatonalism"—"a Messianic cult and deterministic religion" from "Mittel-europa." See also Schaeffner's attack on the "Judeo-Austro-Russian upstart" Leibowitz (note 33).

42. Letter of September 23, 1948, Craft, *Correspondence*, vol. 2, 374–75.

43. Despite a chaotic rehearsal process, described in *Bagázh* (150–59), the ballet was well received at the company's Paris season premiere, thanks to Diaghilev's intervention.

44. Craft summarizes the ups and down of their long relationship in *Correspondence*, vol. 2, 364ff.

45. Ian Wellens, *Music on the Frontline: Nicolas Nabokov's Struggle against Communism and Middlebrow Culture* (Burlington, VT: Ashgate, 2002), 3.

46. Robert Craft, "A Personal Preface," *Score* 20 (1957): 9–10.

47. Undated letter (ca. 1948) of Stravinsky to Nabokov, Paul Sacher Foundation.

48. Wellens, *Music on the Frontline*, 18. See "Music under Dictatorship," "Sergei Prokofiev," and "The Case of Dmitri Shostakovich." The latter two are incorporated as chapters in Nicolas Nabokov, *Old Friends and New Music* (Boston: Little, Brown, 1951).

49. Craft, *Correspondence*, vol. 2, 376n.

50. Alex Ross, *The Rest Is Noise: Listening to the Twentieth Century* (New York: Picador, 2007), 327. Nabokov doesn't identify specific works by Prokofiev but in earlier articles criticizes the ballet *Romeo and Juliet* and Second Violin Concerto, both composed in 1935. Bartók went so far as to parody Shostakovich's "invasion" theme in the fourth movement of his *Concerto for Orchestra* (1945).

51. Nabokov, *Old Friends*, 207.

52. José Ortega y Gasset, *"The Dehumanization of Art" and Other Writings on Art and Culture* (Garden City, NY: Doubleday, 1956), 5–7.

53. Christopher Lichtenberg quoted in David Bindman, *Hogarth and His Times* (Berkeley: University of California Press, 1997), 29.

54. Walter Benjamin, "The Work of Art in the Age of Mechanical Reproduction," in *Illuminations*, ed. Hannah Arendt (New York: Schocken Books, 1968), 221.

55. Christina Scull, *The Soane Hogarths* (London: Sir John Soane's Museum, 1991), 16, 20.

56. Pierre Bourdieu, *Rules of Art: Genesis and Structure of the Literary Field*, trans. Susan Emanuel (Stanford, CA: Stanford University Press, 1995), 147.

57. Pierre Bourdieu, *Outline of a Theory of Practice*, trans. Richard Nice (New York: Cambridge University Press, 1977), 197. Bourdieu derives his insights from the study of French literary publishers and art galleries.

58. Quoted in Wellens, *Music on the Frontline*, 35–36.

59. Craft, *Correspondence*, vol. 1, 358. See chapter 9 for more details.

60. "I want to attack all those who seek their personal salvation by taking the middle road. For the middle road is the only one that does not lead to Rome" in Arnold Schoenberg, *A Schoenberg Reader, Documents of a Life*, ed. Joseph Auner (New Haven, CT: Yale University Press, 2003), 186.

61. Letter of September 8, 1943, in Craft, *Correspondence*, vol. 2, 368–69.

62. Letters of June 1, 1956, and April 1, 1946, in Craft, *Correspondence*, vol. 2, 372.
63. Nicolas Nabokov, "Igor Stravinsky," *Atlantic Monthly*, November 1949, 21–27.
64. Nabokov, *Old Friends*, 139, 142.
65. Ibid., 159.
66. Letter of December 10, 1949, Paul Sacher Foundation (translated from Russian).
67. Boulez would later reject Leibowitz's influence: "Leibowitz, for serial music, was the worst academicism; [he was] much more dangerous for serial music than tonal academicism had ever been for tonal music" (quoted in Sprouts, "The 1945 Stravinsky Debates," 119).
68. Thomas Mann, *Doctor Faustus: The Life of the German Composer Adrian Leverkühn, as Told by a Friend*, trans. John E. Woods (New York: Alfred A. Knopf, 1997), 257; cf. prelude, note 18.
69. Theodor W. Adorno, *Philosophy of Modern Music*, trans. Anne G. Mitchell and Wesley V. Blomster (New York: Seaburg, 1973), 133.
70. Mann, *Doctor Faustus*, 265.
71. Thomas Mann, *The Story of a Novel* (New York: Alfred A. Knopf, 1961), 63–64; Mann describes the importance of Adorno's essay on pages 42–48.
72. See Bourdieu's similar conclusion in *Rules of Art* (note 56).
73. Adorno, *Philosophy of Modern Music*, 142–43.
74. Letter of December 5, 1949, to H. L. Stuckenschmidt quoted in Schoenberg, *A Schoenberg Reader*, 335; Robert Craft, "Robert Craft on Stephen Walsh's *Stravinsky: The Second Exile*," Naxos.com (2006).
75. Sherill Tippins, *February House* (New York: Houghton Mifflin, 2005), 145, 282.
76. See prelude in Craft, *Stravinsky: Glimpses of a Life*.

PART 2

THE DRAMA

Je ne suis au plus que l'intermédiare qui a combine heureusement le rencontre de ces deux éminentes lesbiennes Musique et Poésie dont le collage, depuis trente siècles est si notoire.

I am no more than the intermediary who happily arranged the meeting of these two eminent lesbians, Music and Poetry, whose bonding for thirty centuries is so well known.

—Aldous Huxley (as relayed by Robert Craft)[1]

2

A HAPPY COLLABORATION

After the four ballets he created with George Balanchine (*Apollo, Jeu de Cartes, Orpheus,* and *Agon*), Stravinsky's collaboration with W. H. Auden on *The Rake's Progress* was probably the most fulfilling and mutually edifying of his career. Before he had even completed the opera, the composer eagerly sought the poet's suggestions for further settings from his then new anthology of English poetry. Within three months of the premiere, the two were planning a new collaboration and, though *Delia* would not pan out as an opera, they remained close until Stravinsky's death. They readily celebrated one another in print and media broadcasts; Stravinsky asked Auden to write the text for his memorial tribute to President Kennedy, and the poet was one of the few close friends to frequent his New York residence during the composer's fragile last years. Throughout his life, Stravinsky collaborated with several literary figures, but none maintained his respect and affection as did Wystan Auden.

The creation of *The Rake's Progress* libretto is one of the more interesting and well documented in the history of opera. Appropriating themes from classic literature and mythology, composer and poet fashioned from Hogarth's series a detailed scenario into which Auden and (initially unbeknown to Stravinsky) his companion Chester Kallman further wove important themes. The result is one of the most richly literary—but to some, confusing and unsatisfying—librettos ever written. Craft's 1953 liner notes mount an energetic defense: "The composer of pure opera . . . inherits its clichés and formulas and he thrives and delights in its limitations. Least of all is he concerned with the creation of credible situations (Shadow's 'asides' to the audience would be 'incredible' to a music-dramatist). Fantasy is an important element (the fact that Baba—muffled by her husband's wig and seated motionless in an armchair for several months—should be auctioned off as an 'unknown object,' is a delightful fantasy)."[2]

Forty years later, Craft would confess what he really thought: "The plot is creaky, even by operatic standards. . . . The characters . . . are dimensionless, devoid of anything remotely like a psychological makeup."[3] This unsympathetic assessment may seem surprising given Craft's familiarity with the libretto. Not only did he repeat aloud each section to Stravinsky (see chapter 5), but also he conducted the opera dozens of times and enjoyed a respectful rapport with Auden

Fig. 2.1. Stravinsky and Auden. (Igor Stravinsky Collection, Paul Sacher Foundation)

and Kallman. Certainly his relationship to Stravinsky precluded any public—and probably little private—criticism of either the music or libretto; his program notes function more as publicist's copy than criticism. Yet, as we have seen, Craft's assessments often either evolved or became less tempered and generally more antipathetic as the years passed. Whatever the case, the young musician's essay displays greater insight and appreciation than the experienced conductor's review. Even the grain of truth in his later critique is misapplied: Nick and, to a lesser degree, Anne lack psychological depth by design, while Tom and even Baba display an emotional range unprecedented in characters from a fable.

Craft is not alone, though, in missing crucial points. *The Rake*'s libretto has vexed even admiring critics, Joseph Kerman so much so that he suggested, "For future productions, and there will be many, the authors ought to be prevailed upon to think through the conclusion again, and redo this last scene, if not the Epilogue. Piercing as it would be to lose any of the present music, the present ending causes even more dismay; some sacrifice is certainly necessary for a final relevance, and a greater beauty."[4] Given such mixed feelings, disagreements, and outright confusion, it will be helpful to separate the artistic, literary, and mythic themes that comprise Auden and Kallman's text in order to elucidate its obscure references, finer points, and overall design. Tracing the creators' attraction to these sources also provides some insight into their process. Strong aesthetic and philosophical convictions conditioned their seemingly peculiar choices and help explain their meaning.

"Happily Arranged"

Since his earliest successes with the Ballets Russes, Stravinsky generally conceived his own dramatic projects and chose his collaborators accordingly. Unfamiliar with English poets, he sought from his neighbor Aldous Huxley, whom he consulted "as if he were a mobile encyclopedia," suggestions for a librettist.[5] The composer admitted, "At that time all I knew of [Auden's] work was the commentary for the film 'Night Train [*sic* Night Mail].' When I described to Huxley the kind of verse opera I wished to write, he assured me Auden was the poet with whom I could write it."[6] The accessible verse he wrote for this documentary displays the mastery of verbal rhythms and variety of poetic meters Stravinsky desired:

> This is the night mail crossing the Border,
> Bringing the cheque and the postal order,
> Letters for the rich, letters for the poor,
> The shop at the corner, the girl next door . . .

The seemingly modest ending also hints at a deeper significance:

> And none will hear the postman's knock
> Without a quickening of the heart,
> For who can bear to feel himself forgotten?

Stravinsky recalled his choice in a 1965 BBC documentary on Auden:

> I chose Wystan Auden as librettist for my opera because of his special gift for versification; I have never been able to compose music to prose, even poetic prose. That he was a great poet others had assured me—I felt as much, but was too new to English to judge for myself—yet my first requisite was more modest and more specific.... What I required was a versifier with whom I could collaborate in writing songs, an unusual starting point for an opera, I hardly need to add, as most composers begin with a search for qualities of dramatic construction and dramatic sensation. I had no knowledge of Wystan's dramatic gifts or even whether he was sensible to operatic stagecraft. I simply gave all priority to verse, hoping that we could evolve the theatrical form together....
>
> ... As soon as we began to work together I discovered that we shared the same views not only about opera, but also on the nature of the Beautiful and the Good. Thus, our opera is indeed, and in the highest sense, a collaboration.[7]

Only after he met Kallman in 1939 did Auden really discover opera, but he found the delay advantageous. "I am eternally grateful to the musical fashion of my youth which prevented me from listening to Italian Opera until I was over thirty," he admitted, "by which age I was capable of really appreciating a world so beautiful and so challenging to my own cultural heritage."[8] During the 1930s, the young activist had sought to engage a larger public through socially conscious verse plays: the farcical *Dance of Death* (1933), *The Dog beneath the Skin* (1935), and *The Ascent of F6* (1937), the latter two in collaboration with Christopher Isherwood. He even worked with Bertolt Brecht on an adaptation of John Webster's *The Duchess of Malfi* (1944–46) for Broadway. Auden, though, found spoken drama conducive only to either intimate, naturalistic settings that ill-suited him or flattened public pronouncements, à la Brecht, that to him rang false.

His disillusionment with the Spanish Popular Front and Stalin and his despair at the encroaching war with the Nazis led Auden to reconsider the artist's political and social role, an issue he hotly debated with his brother-in-law and sometime Brooklyn housemate, Klaus Mann. Whereas in the 1930s, Auden, like Brecht, actively engaged the troubled world through stylized populism, in the 1940s he would seek a more elevated plane by enshrouding his work in period language and settings and in myth (he even framed his contemporary *Age of Anxiety* as a "Baroque eclogue").[9] Correspondingly, his moral concerns shifted from the material suffering wrought by class, corruption, and prejudice to the existential suffering pervading all modern life. Not in the language of the street or office or public stage but through the refined power of the operatic voice would Auden now confront the modernist crisis.

Opera allows, even demands, both the conscious artifice and immediate expression that vitalize formal poetic language. Operatic singing heightens human expression while preserving its emotional immediacy; indeed, it intensifies both. Auden explains:

> A verbal art like poetry is reflective; it stops to think. Music is immediate, it goes on to become....

> If music in general is an imitation of history, opera in particular is an imitation of human willfulness; it is rooted in the fact that we not only have feelings but insist upon having them at whatever cost to ourselves. The moment a person starts to sing, he becomes a monomaniac. Opera, therefore, cannot present character in the novelist's sense of the word, namely, people who are potentially good and bad, active and passive, for music is immediate actuality and neither potentiality nor passivity can live in its presence.[10]

Auden modeled his first attempt at a libretto, for Britten's *Paul Bunyan* (1939–41) about mythic early America, on Dryden's text for Purcell's semi-opera *King Arthur* (1691) about mythic early Britain. He "may have been motivated in part by his sense of his and Britten's place in literary and musical history. *King Arthur* was the first and still only libretto written by a major English poet for a major English composer. *Paul Bunyan* would be the second."[11] Critics apparently missed the connection, and despite high hopes the work was dropped after the premiere production (by students) and never staged again during the librettist's lifetime. (Lincoln Kirstein and Balanchine tried and failed to mount a Broadway production, just as they would attempt with *The Rake's Progress* a decade later.) Though he was not the poet to capture the spirit of Paul Bunyan—"Auden's characters were American in the same way that the characters in *The Mikado* are Japanese," writes Edward Mendelson—Auden was not wrong in anticipating a renewal of English-language opera led by his friend.[12] Between 1935 and 1942, he and Britten collaborated on several projects: documentary films like *Night Mail*, incidental settings for Auden's plays, cabaret songs and the choral *Hymn to St. Cecilia*. They even resided for a time in the same untidy "February house" in Brooklyn Heights. However, growing resentful of the opinionated and domineering poet, the shy composer ended their professional relationship when he declined to set Auden's Christmas Oratorio, *For the Time Being* (1942). His reasons were similar to Stravinsky's in refusing *Delia* ten years later. Without consulting the composer, the poet had written a beautiful text that was too long and literary for musical setting; Britten was also growing artistically in a different direction that would take him back to England and to a different kind of opera, *Peter Grimes* (1945). Auden tried to maintain contact, but by the early 1950s Britten had withdrawn almost completely.

Given these dashed ambitions, one can understand why the celebrated poet felt "being asked to work with Stravinsky was the greatest honor he had ever received." Scarcely could he have imagined that his chance to revitalize the tradition of English-language opera would be in collaboration with a Russian expatriate living in Hollywood. Auden's aesthetic temperament, though, perfectly suited that of the composer. Stravinsky later recalled their weeklong visit in November 1947:

> Auden fascinated and delighted me more every day. When we were not working, he would explain verse forms to me, and, almost as quickly as he could write, compose examples—I still have a specimen sestina and some light verse that he scribbled off for my wife—and any technical question, of versification, for example, put him in a passion; he was even eloquent on such matters.

The making of poetry he seemed to regard as a game, albeit played in a magic circle.... Auden's task, as he considered it, was to redefine and be the custodian of its rules. All his conversation about Art was, so to speak, *sub specie ludi*.[13]

Like Stravinsky, Auden played with a wide range of styles, from high Baroque to clever cabaret to low doggerel. The opera afforded ample opportunity to indulge in such stylized play and, judging from the scenario, the creators imagined even more. In their outline of the opening scene, the villain forecasts the futures of the hero and girl "in the manner of a Baroque Delphic Oracle."[14] Upon his return to New York, Auden almost immediately altered it to Nick's story about Tom's "unloved and forgotten" uncle, but one can imagine the type of ceremonial pronouncement they originally had in mind. Sellem's auction and Shadow's card-guessing game would create a similar ritual atmosphere. The idea finds its fullest expression, though, in the perverse "catechism" in the Brothel, the first stop of Tom's progress:

SHADOW: So tell my Lady-Bishop of the game
          What I did vow and promise in thy name.

RAKEWELL: "One aim in all things to pursue:
          My duty to myself to do."

SHADOW, *to Mother Goose*: Is he not apt?

MOTHER GOOSE: And handsome, too.

SHADOW: What is thy duty to thyself?

RAKEWELL: "To shut my ears to prude and preacher
          And follow Nature as my teacher."

MOTHER GOOSE: What is the secret Nature knows?

RAKEWELL: "What Beauty is and where it grows." (1.2)

Auden later commented, "The trouble with the Brothel scene is that they will try to make it sexy and dirty, which it shouldn't be. They should behave like people in a nursery—really a more perverse thing, like playing doctor and patient ... their actual behavior must be either very childish or religious. It's a mixture of the two."[15]

In making room for such artificial set pieces, composer and librettist eschew what they regarded as trivial naturalism in favor of rarefied art. Their tastes did not always coincide, though. Auden's love for Wagner and Strauss seemed to betray the cool facade of his poetry (he granted himself greater emotional latitude as a listener than as a writer). However, what Stravinsky asserted bluntly—that is, "Music is, by its very nature, essentially powerless to express anything, whether a feeling, an attitude of mind, a psychological mood, a phenomenon of nature, etc."—Auden states more subtly and empathetically: "A work of art is not *about* this or that kind of life; it *has* life, drawn, certainly, from human experience but transmuted, as a tree transmutes water and sunlight into treehood, into its own unique being. Every encounter with a work of art is a personal encounter; what it *says* is not information but a revelation of ourselves."[16] The former defines itself against Wagnerian music drama; the latter embraces almost all forms of opera.

The personal affects of composer and poet also differed profoundly. Craft's first face-to-face meeting with Stravinsky coincided with a working session between the composer and Auden in Washington, DC. The twenty-four-year-old took it all in:

> The dinner in the restaurant of the Raleigh Hotel was memorable mainly as a study in contrasts, not only in culture, temperament, and mind, but also in appearance, for the shabby, dandruff-speckled, and slightly peculiar-smelling poet (attributes easily offset by his purity of spirit and intellectual punctiliousness) could not have been more unlike the neat, sartorially perfect, and faintly eau-de-cologned composer....
>
> These habits illustrate an essential difference between the two men. While with Auden the senses seemed to be of negligible importance, with Stravinsky the affective faculties were virtual instruments of thought. And whatever the acuteness of his aural sense, the idea of music appealed to him more than music itself, music with words—opera and Anglican hymns—more than Haydn quartets and Beethoven symphonies. That the music of Auden's poetry is not its strongest feature, therefore, should hardly surprise us. A conceptualizer in quest of intellectual order, he was above all a social, moral, and spiritual diagnostician....
>
> Both were religious men, equally keen on dogmas, ritual, faith in the redemptive death; but the poet had evidently arrived at his beliefs through theology, the composer through "mystical experience."[17]

Auden recognized opera ultimately expressed itself through music, not words. "They have their moment of glory," he admitted, "in which they suggest to [the composer] a certain melody; once that is over, they are as disposable as infantry to a Chinese general."[18] Nonetheless, his far-ranging intellectual interests compelled him to interweave, indirectly or through parody, an unwieldy number of literary themes and concepts. From Hogarth, he and Stravinsky assumed the libertine's descent into madness; from Kierkegaard, he countered with a pilgrim's ascent from existential aimlessness to Christian redemption. From the Faust myth, he and Kallman introduced the bargain with the devil; from Freud, the struggle between the id and superego; and from Jung, the encounter with shadow and anima. From ancient mythology, they imposed the cycle of seasons and the Venus-Adonis symbolism.

Peter Yates, cofounder of the "Evenings on the Roof" concerts of contemporary music in Los Angeles, offers a thoughtful critique:

> Auden the poet ... put together a libretto that is very nearly a model for beginners, and few if any librettists these days are other than beginners. It fails as a libretto at the point where it begins aspiring to serve as something more than a framework for dramatic music, just at the point, you may say, where Auden as a poet usually fails, where he steps out of the parody manner, of which he is a master, and tries to go it on his own as a conceptual artist.... Auden is an interesting conceptual

thinker; his thought like his art depends upon a parodic restatement of existing concepts. He fails when he tries to merge the thinker with the artist, to become creative. He loses altitude just at the level where Richard Wagner, who had trouble getting off the ground as a poet, began rushing like a ram-jet through the thinnest atmosphere.[19]

To grasp Auden's ambitious conceptual framework requires unpacking his libretto and considering its component sources, themes, and ideas on their own. I begin with the work that gave the opera its name, subject, and setting.

The Hogarths

The eight images of *A Rake's Progress* trace the degeneration of a profligate libertine:

1. "The Heir": Tom Rakewell comes into his inheritance on the death of his father and is visited by Sarah Young, a town girl he has seduced, together with her mother.
2. "The Levee": Tom is seen with various professors in the gentlemanly arts.
3. "The Orgy": he rollicks with whores in a low tavern.
4. "The Arrest": he is about to be apprehended for debt, but Sarah arrives with her savings to redeem him.
5. "The Marriage": he makes a marriage of convenience to an elderly and ill-favored rich lady, while Sarah, carrying his child in her arms, is excluded from the ceremony.
6. "The Gaming House": he loses his second fortune.
7. "The Prison": he is committed to the Fleet for debt.
8. "The Madhouse": he is removed to an asylum, where the ever-faithful Sarah continues to visit him.[20]

As I noted in chapter 1, Stravinsky's attraction to this pictorial series as the basis for an opera reflected his preference for stylized drama. Hogarth's chaotic scenes, broad character types, and exaggerated emotions evoke comic theater; their period setting and clear emotional trajectory are ideal for conventional opera. The artist's defining legacy, though, is his moralizing stories. Auden describes: "'The Rake's Progress' as depicted by Hogarth, is a bourgeois cautionary tale; its twin is the story of The Virtuous Apprentice who is never late for work, saves his pennies and finally marries the master's daughter. Wine, Women and Cards are to be avoided, not because debauchery is wrong in itself but because it lowers the bank balance; Chastity is the child of Economic Abstinence."[21]

Hogarth pioneered the satirical series in *A Harlot's Progress* (1732) and continued to exploit it in *Marriage A-la-Mode* (1745), which Stravinsky viewed in Chicago, and *Idleness and Industry* (1747). He tailored these "bourgeois cautionary tales" to what Jürgen Habermas calls the "Bourgeois Public Sphere" then emerging in London. The English aristocracy was giving way to a politically and economically robust mercantile class anxious for the status afforded by literature and the arts. Modestly affluent consumers could now support artists and writers just as the latter's dependency on the court and aristocracy was diminishing. This new audience in turn conditioned both Hogarth's choice of medium—namely, reproducible prints—and his didactic message. Artist and audience, medium and message together helped set off the tectonic cultural shift that would so alarm Benjamin and Greenberg two hundred years later.[22]

Although didactic art was hardly new to the eighteenth century, Hogarth's Modern Moral Subjects, as he called them, are quite different from the mythic heroes of the Renaissance and Baroque periods. In fact, Hogarth parodies those old masters, whom he detested, with his narrative candor and wit. In contrast to their ideal figures, his characters display human behavior at its weakest and most ridiculous. Sean Shesgren writes:

> Under Charles II, the arts embodied aristocratic values like cosmopolitanism, cynicism (especially in matters of religion), sexual freedom and love of leisure and amusement. Hogarth's *A Rake's Progress* is a frank summary of these values from a middle-class viewpoint; Tom Rakewell affects taste, conspicuously neglects religion, drinks, gambles, seduces women and marries for money rather than love. Such values were directly opposed to the qualities of character which were necessary to the survival of the bourgeoisie as a class.... Their commitment was to such concepts as thrift, work, temperance, ... sentimentalism, religion, nationalism (i.e., hatred of the French) and humanitarianism.[23]

It is worth noting that Hogarth's forthright social and moral agenda, contemporary setting, and seedy characters correspond more closely to the dramas of Bertolt Brecht, who based his *Dreigroschenoper* (1928) on Gay's *Beggar's Opera*, than to Stravinsky's *Rake*. Hogarth's setting was contemporary; his message direct and, in the printed series, underscored by versed captions; and his symbols—such as the mischief-maker who sets fire to a map of the world in figure 2.2—obvious. Stravinsky's opera, by contrast, is a period piece: its stylized setting matches its stylized music and text, its allegorical meaning complicated and deeply embedded. Lacking the moral immediacy of Hogarth's images, its Hogarthian moral—"For idle hands and hearts and minds, the Devil finds a work to do"—rings hollow. In short, Stravinsky and Auden's archaic medium speaks not to the middle class but to the cultural elite.

Auden and Kallman still adopt Hogarth's satirical tone, though for them his seedy underside of the "Age of Reason" inspired not an admonition to potential idlers but biting parodies of "enlightened" thought. Like the idle apprentice (another of Hogarth's ne'er-do-wells) from the series *Idleness and Industry*, Tom justifies laziness—"Have not grave doctors assured us that good works are of no avail...?" (1.1)—with a determinism reminiscent of Pangloss's "best of all possible worlds" from Voltaire's *Candide* (1756). Equally ridiculous is Sellem's pseudo-Darwinian rationale for profiting from the loss of others: "Truly there is a divine balance in Nature; a thousand lose that a thousand may gain; and you who are the fortunate are ... Nature's missionaries. You are her instruments for the restoration of that

Fig. 2.2. William Hogarth, *A Rake's Progress*, III, "The Orgy," June 1735, etching and engraving in black on ivory laid paper, 315 × 390 mm (image), Gift of Horace S. Oakley, 1921.339, The Art Institute of Chicago.

order we all so worship" (3.1). The most "rational" of all, Nick Shadow, steers his master into actions both gratuitous (the marriage to Baba) and foolish (investing in the bread machine). Tom's wild optimism about the machine—a device derived from Ben Jonson's *The Alchemist*—lampoons blind faith in progress:[24]

> Omnipotent when armed with this,
> In secular abundant bliss
>   He shall ascend the Chain
> Of Being to its top to win
> The throne of Nature and begin
>   His everlasting reign. (2.3)

Knowing Stravinsky viewed *Marriage A-la-Mode* at the Chicago exhibition, one is struck by the resemblance between "The Tête à Tête" (shown in fig. 2.3) and Baba's aria in act 2, scene 3 (fig. 2.4). The image depicts a breakfast scene shortly after the arranged marriage of Viscount Squanderfield and his wealthy bourgeois bride. The cluttered array of tasteless art objects on the mantel attests

Fig. 2.3. William Hogarth, *Marriage A-la-Mode*, II. "The Tête à Tête." (National Gallery, London)

Fig. 2.4. Baba (Marina de Gabarain) and Tom (Richard Lewis), act 2, scene 3 (1954). (Guy Gravett/Glyndebourne Productions Ltd/ArenaPAL)

to her gauche extravagance and anticipates Baba's gaudy souvenir collection. Like Tom, the profligate Viscount, "collapsed in a chair, having returned from a night on the town," ignores his self-satisfied wife. A faithful dog sniffs at "the lady's bonnet protruding from his pocket (his wife is wearing *her* bonnet)."[25] Neither Stravinsky nor Auden mention *Marriage A-la-Mode* by name, but the composer initially professed being "struck by the various Hogarth *series*," not just *A Rake's Progress*. This image more readily suggests an operatic scene than the rake's marriage to the old lady in the fifth image of *A Rake's Progress*.

While his satirical undercurrent adds a delightfully cynical dimension to the libretto, Hogarth's discrete tableaux nonetheless required considerable adaptation and fleshing out before an evening-long drama could take shape. Years later Auden commented, "Certainly the Hogarths are an interesting series about eighteenth-century life, but there's no plot. . . . In each picture, there's the Rake with a completely new set of people. And our problem was: Could we make a story out of this?"[26]

The November Scenario

Stravinsky asked his publisher to initiate contact with Auden about a libretto commission. The composer followed up on October 6, 1947:

> The first thing is that you prepare a general outline of *The Rake's Progress*. I think at the moment of two acts, maybe five scenes (five [sic, i.e., three] for the first act and two for the second act). I also plan to incorporate a Choreographic Divertissement in the first act's finale. Chamber music orchestra of which dimension not yet established. Mr. Hawkes suggested about ten characters, but I believe seven soloists a good number.
>
> After the outline is completed, I suggest you prepare a free verse preliminary for the characters (arias, duets, trios, etc.), also for the small chorus. Bear in mind that I will compose *not* a musical drama, but just an opera with definitely separated numbers. Please, do feel absolutely free in your creative work on the chosen theme. Of course, there is a sort of limitation as to form in view of Hogarth's style and period. Yet make it as contemporary as I treated Pergolesi in my *Pulcinella*. As the end of any work is of importance, I think that the hero's end in an asylum scratching a fiddle would make a meritorious conclusion to his stormy life. Don't you think so?[27]

Auden responded immediately:

> Dear Mr. Stravinsky,
>
> As a) you have thought about the Rake's Progress for some time and b) it is the librettist's job to satisfy the composer not the other way round, I should be most grateful if you could let me have any ideas you may have formed about characters, plot, etc.
>
> I think the Asylum finale sounds excellent, but, for instance, if he is to play the fiddle then, do you want the fiddle to run through the story?
>
> You speak of a "free verse preliminary." Do you want the arias and ensembles to be finally written in free verse or only as a basis for discussing the actual

form they should take? If they were spoken, the eighteenth-century style would of course demand rhyme, but I know how different this is when the words are set.

I have an idea, which may be ridiculous, that between the two acts, there should be a choric parabasis as in Aristophanes.

I need hardly say that the chance of working with you is the greatest honor of my life.

In addition to Aldous Huxley, I think we have another mutual friend, Nicholas Nabakov [sic].[28]

Meanwhile, the excited poet fretted to his secretary, Alan Ansen:

Boosey & Hawkes called up and asked me if I wanted to do it. It's a great honor. It will be given at the Metropolitan.... Boosey & Hawkes pay him $25,000 [sic] a year. I hope they'll pay me to fly out to the coast and confer with him sometime in January. It will be done before April. It's to be on Hogarth's *Rake's Progress*. Evidently Stravinsky's been thinking about it a long time.

I hope he had some idea about the plot because before I can do any work on it, I'll have to have a plot.

Yet, apparently not wanting for ideas, he proceeded to share the details of an allegory he had in mind:

There are to be seven characters—three men and three women, in addition to the hero. I think I'd like to connect it with the Seven Deadly Sins. The hero, of course, will represent Pride, the young girl Lust, I think. The rich old woman will be Avarice, the false friend Anger, the servant Envy and so on. Instead of the gambling scene I'd like to have a cockfight, but I don't know whether I can get away with it. Perhaps the crowd could be standing round concealing the cocks from view and the orchestra could imitate the noises they would make in fighting. Or perhaps we could use marionettes. I don't know. The final scene in the madhouse where the hero is crowned as Lucifer I'd like to treat as a coronation service. He ought to be anointed with a chamber pot, but I don't know whether people would stand for that. But piss is the only proper chrism. It has to be done eighteenth-century style.

Oh yes, there will be prose passages. The standard meter will have to be heroic couplets. In the choruses, where the words aren't so important, I can fool around with fancier meters. The girl turns up in the final scenes. I don't know what I'm going to do with her. The duets ought to be got out of the way earlier. In the last scene I want the hero to stand alone. But what *am* I going to do with the plot? Stravinsky's supposed to be very easy to work with. It will be a wonderful experience. I'm so excited about it. No, I don't think there will be any friction. He'll tell me where he wants long lines for his music, and I can let him know when a scene seems insufficiently dramatic.[29]

Eager to have a completed libretto before Auden left for Italy and realizing little progress could be made without a face-to-face discussion, Stravinsky finally offered to fly the poet to Los Angeles at his own expense after his publishers declined to pay. Auden "shame-facedly" accepted (then "anxiously consulted Nabokov as to whether he should take a dinner-jacket, and if he ought to kiss hands with his Russian hosts").[30] Arriving late on the night of November 11, "this big, blonde, intellectual" but "very gentle and lovable bloodhound" settled down to sleep on the Stravinskys' too-short studio couch with "his feet, covered by a blanket pinioned with books, on a nearby chair, like the victim of a more humane and reasonable Procrustes. Early the next morning, primed by whisky and coffee," the two set out to make a story of Hogarth's paintings over the course of the next seven days. Stravinsky recalled, "We followed Hogarth closely at first... until our own story began to assume a different significance."[31]

Kallman, who was not involved at this point, later explained the rationale behind the three central characters:

> The subject itself suggested a picaresque treatment.... However, if, with a variety of incident, there needed to be a corresponding change in the principal character (the Rake), both that character and the incidents in which he took part might, by the very fact of their moving together, cancel each other's effectiveness.
>
> This meant that we had to place both against a fairly constant background. Our subject made this scenically impossible, so our constancy of background had to be supplied by other characters. This led us, on one side to Anne Trulove, the Rake's ever-faithful sweetheart and, on the other side, to Shadow, his man-servant and evil familiar. And with two characters of such obviously symbolic nature on our hands, it became clear that our picaresque was, further, to be a fable.[32]

Of all Hogarth's images, the scene of the rake in the madhouse, shown in figure 2.5, immediately captured Stravinsky's imagination. But the image he relayed in his initial letter to Auden was that of "the hero's end in an asylum scratching a fiddle"—a fusion of Hogarth and his own *Histoire du Soldat* in which the violin symbolizes the protagonist's soul.[33] In the libretto, Auden references Hogarth by having a member of the chorus portray "a blind man with a broken fiddle," but that Stravinsky initially fixed upon a Faustian symbol hints at the theme the librettists would later develop.

Much of Stravinsky and Auden's task was simply editing Hogarth's numerous characters, a task largely accomplished by eliminating the episodes in pictures two, four, and seven. In addition to Tom's whoring and loveless marriage—for which Auden would invent Mother Goose and Baba the Turk—they had the villain introduce a "fantastic apparatus for making gold out of sea water," thus completing the framework for the hero's three-staged progress. Each step was to be initiated by the hero's yawn—indicative of his idleness and boredom—followed by the arrival of the whistling villain.

Although some of the outlined scenes are suggested by Hogarth (the brothel, the rake's marriage, and the madhouse), Stravinsky and Auden entirely invented others (the gold-producing apparatus and auction). Somewhere in between is the hero and villain's dice-playing in the graveyard, which seems vaguely derived from Hogarth's sixth image, "The Gaming House." While the idea of guessing cards was yet to come, the collaborators clearly wanted the hero's fate to be decided in the form of a game during which the offstage heroine would play a decisive role. Herein lies another telling difference between the opera and the print series. The self-indulgence of Hogarth's rake is mundane—that is, he gambles away his

Fig. 2.5. William Hogarth, *A Rake's Progress*, VIII. "The Mad House," June 1735, etching and engraving in black on ivory laid paper, 315 × 387 mm (image), Gift of Horace S. Oakley, 1921.345, The Art Institute of Chicago.

fortune—but Stravinsky and Auden elevate theirs to a universal condition: he gambles for his soul.

Though similar, the outline version of the Graveyard scene differs in significant details from the final libretto, particularly in the suspension of time just before midnight. Stravinsky and Auden already establish Time as a symbol in the Brothel scene by specifying the inscription "Tempus fugit" (not included in the final libretto) on the cuckoo clock the villain turns back. Later in the graveyard, in quizzing the hero as to his next desire, the villain recapitulates the steps of his progress: "'Qu'est-ce que vous désirez maintenant? Le plaisir?'... 'La gloire?'... 'La puissance?'"[34] Displaying a quality of reflectiveness completely foreign to Hogarth's rake, the hero rejects these desires and answers: "Le passé." And when the clock begins to strike twelve, presumably the hour of his death, it is the hero, empowered by his love for the girl, and not the villain who stops the clock:

A clock begins to strike twelve.

VILLAIN: C'est trop tard.

HERO: J'arrête le temps. Ecoute.
The clock stops in the middle of its striking.

The final libretto reverses this exchange. There it is Tom who exclaims, "Too late," and Nick responds, "No, wait" (3.2).

Stravinsky and Auden further develop the theme of time at the end of the Graveyard scene when the clock resumes and the hero declares: "Let it strike. Time no longer frightens me. For love there is no past or future, there is only the present. Lover and loved, I am Adonis, forever young."[35] Thus, in the outline, the villain does not condemn the hero to insanity for his sins, as in the completed opera. Rather, the hero willingly embraces a state of mind in which he is no longer driven by temporal desires. Nick's vengeful curse may make for better theater, but it is crucial to understand Tom's insanity as a blissful state in which he finally embraces that timeless, if illusionary, Golden Age from which he ran in the opening scene.

The hero's embrace of madness completely alters the trajectory and meaning of Stravinsky and Auden's progress, the subject of the following chapter. Before pondering this new meaning, though, we should first consider the contribution of that other collaborator.

Wystan and Chester

> Stravvy... was very anxious to get you back... to discuss his idea [for a new collaboration]. You have, I'm happy to say, made a terrific hit with the old boy, and he said "You are a team and must stick together."
>
> —Auden to Kallman[36]

Stravinsky was not exactly pleased when, upon receiving the completed first act of the libretto, he read the following enclosed note: "As you will see, I have taken in a collaborator, an old friend of mine in whose talents I have the greatest confidence. We are in the middle of Act II now, which I will send as soon as it is done."[37] When they met in Washington, DC, in late March, Auden sought to "smooth over the question of dual authorship," assuring Stravinsky "that 'Mr. Kallman is a better librettist that I am,' that 'the scenes which Mr. Kallman wrote are at least as good as mine,' and that 'Mr. Kallman's talents have not been more widely recognized only because of his friendship with me.'"[38] He exaggerated, but only a little.

In due time, "Stravvy" would discover Chester Kallman was far more than an old friend; he was the poet's great love, his life companion, and, despite his youth, Auden's guide into the world of opera and an invaluable contributor to the libretto. Of their first meeting in New York on April 5, 1948, Craft observes: "The composer was quickly won by Chester Kallman's intelligence and sense of humor. Furthermore, Kallman was easier to understand than Auden, and could bring out the poet's sometimes dormant affability, as well as subdue his tempers...

Bluntly stated, the Stravinskys were happier with Auden when Chester Kallman was present. On the trip from Washington to New York, Stravinsky had read the opera's final act and hence could give his blessings to the partnership, telling the librettists how delighted he was with *their* work." Whether or not Craft is right to conclude "the older poet could never have written libretti without his younger colleague," Kallman was certainly an ideal complement to Auden, both socially and artistically.[39] More than competent, his writing is at times inspired and he possessed a practical sense of the theater his partner often neglected. Unburdened by any artistic or philosophical "vision," he willingly accommodated whatever poetic style Stravinsky and Auden required.

As important as his contribution appears in retrospect, Kallman's involvement was apparently unplanned. In notes for the 1964 recording he recalls:

> When Auden returned from California with the outline that he and Stravinsky had constructed for the opera, he showed it to me; and I made some slight criticisms. . . . They were not well received. Auden's "Don't just point out little flaws if you have no idea what to put in their place," was said more in anger than sorrow. But it did impel me to more active thinking, and the days of discussion and argument that followed, during which stray lines for possible arias came to my mind unsummoned, led us into actually starting to work on the libretto together.[40]

Thus began a twenty-five-year partnership writing and translating texts for the genre that had brought them and, as it turned out, would keep them together. Auden later sent Craft a detailed account of who wrote what:

> Though of course two librettists are not two people but a composite personality, I have been amused at the way in which critics, trying to decide who wrote what, have guessed wrong. The actual facts are:
>
> Act I: Scene 1. Down to the end of Tom's aria . . . "This beggar should ride." W.H.A.
>
>   From here to the end of scene. C.K.
>
> Scene 2. W.H.A.
>
> Scene 3. C.K.
>
> Act II: Scene 1. Down to end of Tom's aria . . . "in my heart the dark." C.K.
>
>   From there to end of scene. W.H.A.
>
> Scene 2. C.K.
>
> Scene 3. W.H.A.
>
> Act III: Scene 1. C.K. (except for the lyrics sung offstage by Tom and Shadow).
>
> Scene 2. Baba's [sic] verses at beginning and end of scene. W.H.A.
>
>   Middle (card-guessing game). C.K.
>
> Scene 3 and Epilogue. W.H.A.[41]

Not surprisingly, Auden composed most of the verses with psychological or philosophical implications: Tom's "Here I stand" (1.1); the Brothel catechism; Nick's recitative and aria (2.1); the Bread machine episode (2.3); and the Bedlam scene. The only exception is the climactic card-guessing game (3.2). Otherwise, Kallman tended to write the more conventional expressions of longing (Anne's aria, 1.3) and remorse (Tom's aria, 1.2), and complex ensembles: the closing quartet (1.1), the duet and trio (2.2), and the auction scene (3.1).

Auden was particularly sensitive to critics' tendency to overlook Kallman's contribution. When his partner was unable to attend the second performance in Venice, Craft observed Auden quietly leave the theater before the end, "not wishing to risk having to bow alone and receive credit that ought to be shared with his friend."[42] Responding to an otherwise "critically acute" analysis of their libretto that failed to acknowledge Kallman's contribution, Auden dictated his secretary's letter correcting the oversight:

> Having had the privilege of preparing a typescript of the libretto for Mr. Stravinsky's attention, I feel peculiarly authorized to make a protest against the unscholarly carelessness with which the author has failed to take note of Mr. Chester Kallman's contribution to the text.
> Though the scheme of the work was largely Mr. Auden's, its execution was in equal measure his responsibility and that of Mr. Kallman.
> . . . Mr. McFadden's judgment that "the lyrics" are "of a simple and classic beauty which it would be hard to match in modern English verse" must redound as much to the credit of Mr. Kallman as to that of Mr. Auden.[43]

Though Auden deferred to his companion's expertise in opera and jealously defended his reputation as a poet, the latter's shortcomings become apparent when one compares their contributions. The older poet's verses possess a more naturally musical quality. He especially excels in groups of rhymed lyric verses: the Brothel choruses (1.2), the Ballad verses (3.1, 3.2), Anne's Lullaby (3.3), and the epilogue. Among these, the childish, nonsensical rhymes of "Lanterloo" (analyzed in chapter 5) and the original Ballad verse (quoted below) most closely resemble the strict verse forms with which he delighted Stravinsky and Vera:

> If boys had wings and girls had stings
> And gold fell from the sky,
> If new-laid eggs wore wooden legs
> I should not laugh or cry. (3.1)

Auden preserves the musical flow even for important dialogue. The following tense exchange from the Graveyard scene follows the same iambic meter as the earlier trivial verse:

> SHADOW: Behold your waiting grave, behold
> Steel, halter, poison, gun.
>
> Make no excuse, your exit choose:
> Tom Rakewell's race is run.

RAKEWELL: Oh let the wild hills cover me
          Or the abounding wave.

SHADOW: The sins you did may not be hid.
          Think not your soul to save.

RAKEWELL: Oh why did an uncle I never knew
          Select me for his heir?

SHADOW: It pleases well the damned in Hell
          To bring another there.

          Midnight is come: by rope or gun
              Or medicine or knife,

          On the stroke of twelve you shall slay yourself
              For forfeit is your life. (3.2)

Even at his lyric best, Kallman tends to obscure the tonic accent with long, complicated sentences. The convoluted first verse of Anne's aria conveys only a vague sense of meaning:

Quietly, night, O find him and caress,
    And may thou quiet find
His heart, although it be unkind,
    Nor may its beat confess,
Although I weep, it knows of loneliness. (1.3)

Kallman himself later admitted, "Distracted by the sheer invariable goodness of her simple soul, I found verbalizing her a task approaching penance. My solution was to imagine the most conventional elementary soprano gesture that might serve in the situation, and then write words that could justify and perhaps illuminate that gesture."[44] By contrast, his poignant "Vary the song" perfectly matches the emotional arc Auden established in Tom's equally heartfelt cavatina from act 1, scene 2:

Vary the song, O London, change!
Disband your notes and let them range;
Let rumor scream, let folly purr.
Let Tone desert the flatterer.
Let Harmony no more obey
The strident choristers of prey;
Yet all your music cannot fill
The gap that in my heart—is still. (1.2)

In establishing plot and introducing characters in the earlier scenes, the librettists often resort to terse—or, in Kallman's case, wordy—prose suited for secco or orchestral recitative. Tom's address to Father Trulove is particularly awkward: "And when she arrives, all London shall be at her feet, for all London shall be mine, and what is mine must of needs at least adore what I must with all my being worship" (1.1).

Stravinsky summarizes the dramaturgical structure: "In the earlier scenes the mold is to some extent pre-Gluck in that it tends to crowd the story into the secco recitatives, reserving the arias for the reflective poetry, but then, as the opera warms up, the story is told, enacted, contained almost entirely in song."[45] By rendering even plot-driven dialogue in rhymed verse, the librettists contribute to the greater musical continuity of the final two acts. After abandoning an entire first draft of the auction scene, Kallman adroitly handled a tricky interchange involving the chorus and several principals:

[responding to Tom and Nick's mocking street-cry from offstage]

Recitative

CROWD: Now what was that?

BABA:　　　　　　　　The pigs of plunder!

ANNE: Was that his voice?

CROWD:　　　　　　　　What next, I wonder?

BABA: The milk-maid haunts me.

ANNE:　　　　　　　　Gone!

BABA:　　　　　　　　　　　　All I possessed

　　Seems gone. Well, well. (*to Anne*) My dear!

ANNE:　　　　　　　　　　　　His wife!

BABA:　　　　　　　　　　　　　　His jest—

　　No matter now. Come here, my child, to Baba.

SELLEM: Ladies, the sale, if you could go out.

BABA:　　　　　　　　　　　Robber.

　　Don't interrupt.

CROWD:　　　　　　Don't interrupt or rail;

A SOLO VOICE: A scene like this is better than a sale. (3.1)

Kallman had contributed more than a modest literary talent and dramatic sense to the libretto. Despite his youth, he had also played a crucial role in introducing his esteemed partner to the genre that cemented their relationship.

Opera Camp

Auden and Kallman met in April 1939, when the eighteen-year-old undergraduate at Brooklyn College determined to interview the celebrity poet for his school literary magazine. At the time Auden was rooming with Isherwood, but he soon fell in love with the clever, highly literate, and handsome American, fourteen years his junior. From the start, their love of opera, rather than sexual passion, would draw them together. By autumn they were regularly attending performances at the Metropolitan Opera—"my chief luxury," Auden wrote to a friend in England.⁴⁶ This enthusiasm continued to light up his personal correspondence: "We had a nice birthday party, quite small; we went all through *Figaro*"; "I have bought *Falstaff*"; "Have bought *Rosenkavalier* . . . Also *The Bartered Bride* . . ."; "Went to *Rosenkavalier* in Philadelphia . . ."; "The Koehler's gave me four records from the *Drei Groschen Opera* [sic] for my birthday, so I've been kvelling in nostalgia."⁴⁷ Shortly after Stravinsky invited him to collaborate, Lincoln Kirstein would report, "Wystan spent the evening with me talking about *The Rake's Progress*. He has wonderful ideas. . . . He adores opera; he spends half his time playing records of Mozart and Verdi; for him opera is a ritual."⁴⁸

In truth, Kallman had done more than share his passion for opera; he had introduced his lover to the highly cultured world of gay opera fanatics, so-called opera queens. Despite its importance, especially in America and England, both as an expression of gay identity and for opera culture in general, few serious commentators openly addressed this phenomenon until Wayne Koestenbaum published *The Queen's Throat* (1993), a loose and entertaining part memoir, part cultural critique, and part kitsch scrapbook. In his insightful commentary, Paul Robinson explains: "In its strong sense . . . 'opera queen' denotes a particular kind of devotion to opera, one not only excessive but also involving a fetishisation of opera. . . . The initial difficulty I face in writing about 'the opera queen' is that the category is both unstable and ideologically loaded. In the most encompassing sense, it can stand for the general affinity between gays and opera."⁴⁹

For all his seemingly stereotypical devotion, Auden recognized this tendency of opera queens to fetishize their objects of devotion—for example, divas, recordings, magazines, photos—which made them generally unreceptive to new work. His 1948 article "Opera Addict" addresses precisely this issue; however, without acknowledging the essentially controlling nature of the attachment (or that those "addicts" were mostly homosexual men), his philosophical explanation for the addiction does not quite convince. Over time Auden and even Kallman grew ambivalent about such gay cliques. Having been what Edmund Wilson described as "homosexual to an almost fanatical degree," Auden by the late 1940s became disenchanted with the group of chauvinists he now sarcastically referred to as the "Homintern"—not unlike his earlier disillusionment with the Comintern that his term parodies.⁵⁰

Auden's unreciprocated commitment to Kallman also alienated him from this world. He felt he would never have "a place which I can call home," as he confided to Elizabeth Mayer, or "a person with whom I shall be one flesh."⁵¹ Having wholeheartedly embraced his "marriage"—he even wore a wedding ring for a time—Auden could not bring himself to accept his companion's open promiscuity. They stopped cohabitating in 1942, and for a time Auden fancied himself as "*Die alte Marschallin. Ja, Ja, Die Zeit fliesst unaufhaltsam.*"⁵² Kallman may have had a less flattering association in mind when, in a column he wrote as opera reviewer for *The Commonweal*, he "described Hans Sachs as a tired old man, 'bitter about his age, disappointed in love, unsatisfied with his art ... a recluse trying to be one of the boys.'"[53]

The character with which Auden most identified, though, is his own Anne Trulove. Concealed within *The Rake*'s public allegory, Mendelson reads "a private allegory about Kallman's relations with Auden, for the rake's self-destructive choices correspond to Kallman's erotic ones. Tom Rakewell, Auden wrote, 'is a manic-depressive, elated by the prospect of the future and then disgusted by the remembrances of the recent past.'"[54] His letters from Fire Island likewise describe the character he would soon create: "Chester ... hit a trough in his manic depressive cycle. Now he is riding the wave and J ... R ... is here for two days"; "We had one crisis when we nearly parted for ever, but that passed off. The truth is, the bar here is a little too much for him. I call it Klingsor's Magic Garden"; "Chester came out on Saturday completely exhausted and slept with only slight intervals from noon on Saturday till noon on Sunday. He's through with that matelot."[55]

Depressed and feeling alone, in 1946 Auden sought to alter this cycle of jealousy and hurt by allowing himself, to everyone's surprise, an emotionally gratifying affair with Rhoda Jaffe, a former classmate of Kallman's at Brooklyn College and the model in part for the character of Rosetta in *The Age of Anxiety*. He would bring their relationship to an amicable end by early 1948, around the time he invited Kallman to collaborate on *The Rake's Progress* libretto.

Consciously or not, each colibrettist picked his opposite role to write. Thus, the faithful Auden penned Tom's opening aria "Here I stand" and his first pangs of conscience in the cavatina:

> Love, too frequently betrayed
> For some plausible desire
> Or the world's enchanted fire,
> Still thy traitor in his sleep
> Renews the vow he did not keep,
>   Weeping, weeping, ... (1.2)

And the promiscuous Kallman authored Anne's anthem to constancy:

> I go to him
> Love cannot falter,
> Cannot desert;
> Though it be shunned
> Or be forgotten,
> Though it be hurt
> If love be love
> It will not alter.
> O should I see
> My love in need
> It shall not matter
> What he may be. (1.1)

(The principle exception to this role switching is Kallman's text for Tom's "Vary the song" in act 1, scene 2.)

Expressing each other's feelings, if only through operatic characters, helped Auden and Kallman come to terms with their relationship. Richard Davenport-Hines concludes, "For Auden personally the most important feature of his work as a librettist was the happiness it brought him with Kallman.... Their collaboration in *The Rake's Progress* revivified—perhaps even saved from destruction—Auden's relations with Kallman."[56] Indeed, the two poets would spend that and every summer thereafter together in either Ischia or Kirchstetten, Austria; the following year they shared a Greenwich Village apartment. From Ischia, Auden announced to Rhoda, "To my great delight (praise be to S.[alve] R.[egina]) I find myself completely untroubled by sex; Chester, too, is quite changed, and in consequence our relationship is, for the first time, a really happy one."[57]

Ever explaining himself in relation to dramatic characters, the great poet clarified for his life companion—and, happily, for posterity—his feelings in a letter written on his forty-second birthday: "If I am anxious for you to approve of [my lover] W, it's not because you are the Beatrice for whom I cherish a grotesque passion, but because you [are] the one comrade, my non-sexual life cannot do without. Expressions like 'bowing out' and 'disappear' are turns of the knife which, as you know only too well, you beast, hurt. Still, I adore you as I suppose you must deserve it."[58]

Notes

1. Quoted in Robert Craft, *Stravinsky: Chronicle of a Friendship: 1948/1971* (New York: Vintage Books, 1972); revised and expanded (Nashville: Vanderbilt University Press, 1994). Used courtesy of Vanderbilt University Press.

2. Robert Craft, "An Appreciation of the Music," in liner notes for *Igor Stravinsky: The Rake's Progress*, Columbia Records SL 125 (1953): 4.

3. Robert Craft, "Words for Music Perhaps," review of *The Complete Works of W. H. Auden: Libretti and Other Dramatic Writings (1939–1973)*. *The New York Review of Books* 41, no. 18 (1994): 56.

4. Joseph Kerman, "Opera à la mode," *Hudson Review* (Winter 1954): 577.

5. Vera Stravinsky and Robert Craft, *Stravinsky in Pictures and Documents* (New York: Simon and Schuster, 1978), 392.

6. Igor Stravinsky and Robert Craft, *Memories and Commentaries* (Garden City, NY: Doubleday, 1960), 144.

7. Igor Stravinsky and Robert Craft, *Themes and Episodes* (New York: Alfred A. Knopf, 1966), 96.

8. W. H. Auden, *The Dyer's Hand* (New York: Vintage International, 1989), 40.

9. Auden's shift of disposition recalls the "double rejection" of both bourgeois and social or useful art by the French "art-for-art's sake" movement; see Pierre Bourdieu, *The Rules of Art, Genesis and Structure of the Literary Field*, trans. Susan Emanuel (Stanford, CA: Stanford University Press, 1995), 77.

10. Auden, *Dyer's Hand*, 466, 470 (also see prelude, note 11). Auden is indebted to Kierkegaard's notion of "sensuous genius" [*Genialitet*], here translated as "elemental originality": "The most abstract idea conceivable is the sensuous in its elemental originality. But through which medium can it be presented? Only through music"; see Søren Kierkegaard, *Either/Or*, part 1, ed. and trans. Howard V. Hong and Edna H. Hong (Princeton, NJ: Princeton University Press, 1987), 56. The philosopher's ideal expression of "sensuous genius" is Mozart's *Don Giovanni* (see chapter 3, note 27).

11. Edward Mendelson, ed., "Editor's Introduction," in *Libretti and Other Dramatic Writings: 1939–1973*, W. H. Auden and Chester Kallman (London: Faber and Faber, 1993), xvii.

12. Edward Mendelson, *Later Auden* (New York: Farrar, Straus and Giroux, 1999), 97. Auden's Drydenesque "Anthem for St. Cecilia's Day" (1940), set by Britten for chorus, is a worthier successor to that tradition.

13. I. Stravinsky and Craft, *Memories*, 146–47. See Robert Craft, ed., *Stravinsky: Selected Correspondence*, vol. 1 (New York: Alfred A. Knopf, 1982), 301, note 3 for the sestina he composed for Vera.

14. I. Stravinsky and Craft, *Memories*, 157; W. H. Auden and Chester Kallman, *Libretti and Other Dramatic Writings: 1939–1973*, ed. Edward Mendelson (London: Faber and Faber, 1993), 581.

15. Glenn Loney, "Elegy for a Bacchic Rake," *Opera Monthly* 4, no. 11 (1992): 13.

16. Igor Stravinsky, *An Autobiography* (New York: Norton, 1962), 53; Auden, *Dyer's Hand*, 482. Maureen Carr traces the idea that music is independent from thought and expression indirectly to Nietzsche and Schopenhauer through Stravinsky's longtime Swiss friend, Charles-Albert Cingria in *Multiple Masks: Neoclassicism in Stravinsky's Works on Greek Subjects* (Lincoln: University of Nebraska Press, 2002), xxii, 195–99. Craft records a telling anecdote about Auden's teasing affection for Wagner in Craft, *Chronicle* (1972), 40; see also chapter 1, note 4.

17. V. Stravinsky and Craft, *Pictures and Documents*, 399–400. Of Auden's hygiene Stravinsky would remark, "He is the dirtiest man I have ever liked," quoted in Edmund Wilson, *The Fifties: From Notebooks and Diaries of the Period* (New York: Farrar, Straus and Giroux, 1986), 292. In the years to come, Craft and the Stravinskys would come to celebrate the anniversary of this first meeting.

18. Auden, *Dyer's Hand*, 473.

19. Peter Yates, "The Rake's Progress," *Arts and Architecture* (June 1953): 38.

20. Paul Griffiths, *Igor Stravinsky: The Rake's Progress* (New York: Cambridge University Press, 1982), 8.

21. Auden and Kallman, *Libretti*, 617.

22. David Bindman, *Hogarth and His Times* (Berkeley, CA: University of California Press, 1997), 29. See also Jürgen Habermas, *The Structural Transformation of the Public Sphere: An Inquiry into a Category of Bourgeois Society* (Cambridge, MA: MIT Press, 1989); Walter Benjamin, "The Work of Art in the Age of Mechanical Reproduction," in *Illuminations*, ed. Hannah Arendt (New York: Schocken Books, 1968); and Clement Greenberg, "Avant Garde and Kitsch," *Partisan Review* 6, no. 5 (1939): 34–49.

23. Sean Shesgren, ed., *Engravings by Hogarth* (New York: Dover, 1973), xiii.

24. Loney, "Elegy," 11.

25. Christina Scull, *The Soane Hogarths* (London: Sir John Soane's Museum, 1991), 22. Like the painting in figure 1.4, figure 2.3 is composed in reverse. In the subsequent print, the Viscount sits on the far left and is therefore the first character the viewer scans.

26. Loney, "Elegy," 11.

27. Craft, *Correspondence*, vol. 1, 299; Auden and Kallman, *Libretti*, 578. Boosey & Hawkes paid Auden a $3,000 advance against future royalties (he asked for $5,000), which he split with Kallman.

28. Craft, *Correspondence*, vol. 1, 299–300; Auden and Kallman, *Libretti*, 579.

29. Alan Ansen, *The Table Talk of W. H. Auden* (Princeton, NJ: Ontario Review, 1990), 76–77; entry dated October 20, 1947.

30. Humphrey Carpenter, *W. H. Auden: A Biography* (Boston: Houghton Mifflin, 1981), 350.

31. I. Stravinsky and Craft, *Memories*, 146.

32. Auden and Kallman, *Libretti*, 619.

33. Craft, *Correspondence*, vol. 1, 299.

34. The fragmentary dialogue of the outline alternates arbitrarily between French and English. Of his week with the composer Auden recalled, "We kept talking a tutti frutti language, from English to German to French—"*C'est* the end, *nicht wahr?*" (Alan Ansen, unpublished journal entry of November 21, 1947, Berg Collection).

35. I. Stravinsky and Craft, *Memories*, 164; Auden and Kallman, *Libretti*, 587 (translated from French).

36. Courtesy W. H. Auden Estate and the Henry W. and Albert A. Berg Collection of English and American Literature, The New York Public Library, Astor, Lenox and Tilden Foundations.

37. Letter of January 16, 1948 in I. Stravinsky and Craft, *Memories*, 150.

38. V. Stravinsky and Craft, *Pictures and Documents*, 398.

39. Ibid., 401, 414. Craft notes: "On first reading the libretto Stravinsky was exasperated by Shadow's philosophical asides in the Graveyard scene—'The positive appalls him,' and 'the simpler the trick.' By the time Stravinsky reached this point in the composition, however, he treasured every word of the libretto and cut or changed very few of them"; see Robert Craft, "A Note on the Sketches and Two Versions of the Libretto," in Paul Griffiths, *Igor Stravinsky: The Rake's Progress* (New York: Cambridge University Press, 1982), 19.

40. Auden and Kallman, *Libretti*, 626.

41. Quoted in V. Stravinsky and Craft, *Pictures and Documents*, 650, note 90. Craft mistranscribes "*Ballad* verses" as "*Baba's* verses" at the beginning and end of act 3, scene 2. Griffiths's citation of the same letter mistakenly attributes act 1, scene 2, to C.K. and act I, scene 3 to W.H.A (Griffiths, *The Rake's Progress*, 14). Craft also misattributes act 1, scene 2, in I. Stravinsky and Craft, *Memories*, 150, note 3.

42. V. Stravinsky and Craft, *Pictures and Documents*, 413–14.

43. Reproduced in Auden and Kallman, *Libretti*, 574–75.

44. Auden and Kallman, *Libretti*, 627.

45. Igor Stravinsky, "The Composer's View," in Griffiths, *The Rake's Progress*, 2.

46. Quoted in Auden and Kallman, *Libretti*, xvi.

47. Excerpts of letters to Elizabeth Mayer from February 23, 1942, to March 1, 1943, Berg Collection.

48. Letter of October 16, 1947, in Craft, *Correspondence*, vol. 1, 269.

49. Paul Robinson, "The Opera Queen: A Voice from the Closet," *Cambridge Opera Journal* 6, no. 3 (1994): 290.

50. Quoted in Edward Mendelson, *Early Auden* (New York: Farrar, Straus and Giroux, 1981), 267.

51. Letter of February 20, 1943, Berg Collection.

52. Letter to Elizabeth Mayer of November 3, 1942, Berg Collection.

53. Quoted in Mendelson, *Later Auden*, 269.

54. Ibid., 272; quotations from Auden reprinted in Auden and Kallman, *Libretti*, 617. Craft would concur: "Auden's devotion to Chester Kallman was the most important fact of the poet's personal life, as well the real subject of the libretto (the fidelity of true love)" (V. Stravinsky and Craft, *Pictures and Documents*, 413).

55. Various letters to Rhoda Jaffe from August 1946 and June 1947, Berg Collection. In July he would report, "Work has been rather difficult since Chester came but I think he's settling down now into a more regular life. The triple situation, of being sexually jealous, like a wife, anxious like a momma and competitive like a brother is not easy for my kind of temperament. Still, it's my bed and I must lie in it" (Berg Collection).

56. Richard Davenport-Hines, *Auden* (New York: Pantheon, 1995), 254–55.

57. Letter of May 17, 1949, quoted in Mendelson, *Later Auden*, 273.

58. Letter of February 21, 1949, Berg Collection.

3

DEEPER MEANINGS

Interjecting what Craft would call his "Brooklyn common sense," Kallman questioned the scenario's call for the hero to prompt the villain's entrances by yawning. "'In an opera house, people in the top balconies are going to think he's just trying to sing, and they can't hear him,'" he pointed out. "I don't think that's very operatic. So we talked about it, and the idea of the three wishes came up."[1] Auden gave the following philosophical rationale:

> Mr Kallman and I were faced with two problems: how to make Tom Rakewell a singing being, and how to make him a dramatic being with a coherent life story and a sustained involvement with others. Our Tom Rakewell is a man to whom the anticipation of experience is always exciting and its realization in actual fact always disappointing; temperamentally, therefore, he is a manic-depressive, elated by the prospect of the future and then disgusted by the remembrance of the recent past. To define and differentiate the stages of his flight from reality, we have employed the familiar fairy-story device of the three wishes (which are spoken, not sung); these, in his case, are, successively, to be rich, to be happy and to make the world a utopia.[2]

Auden weights every scene—indeed, nearly every action—with such philosophical and psychological meaning. In this chapter, I uncover these deeper meanings to explain some of the more puzzling turns in the story, the foremost being Tom's nonsensical decision to marry Baba.

Hedonistic desires drive the progress of Hogarth's rake as well as the hero of the November scenario—the villain recapitulates its stages when in the graveyard he asks, "What do you desire now? Pleasure? Glory? Power?" To the first draft of act 2 Auden appended a note justifying changing the rich Ugly Duchess into the exotic Baba the Turk and the machine for making gold into a machine for making bread:

> Have made a few slight alterations in our original plot in order to make each step of the Rake's Progress unique, i.e.:
> Bordel.—Le Plaisir
> Baba.—L'acte gratuite.
> La Machine.—Il désire devenir Dieu.[3]

Tom now signals the beginning of each episode not by yawning but by declaring: "I wish I had money" (1.1); "I wish I were happy" (2.1); and "I wish it were true" (2.3)—each of which Stravinsky would punctuate with a distinctive harpsichord flourish.

Critics like Craft have found these unmotivated and unfulfilling changes dramatically unconvincing, yet the librettists went out of their way to make them so. Auden informed Stravinsky of his first change soon after returning from Hollywood: "I think it will be better if it is an unknown uncle of the hero instead of his father who dies, because then, wealth is quite unexpected, and the pastoral tone is not interrupted by sadness, but only by the presence of the sinister villain."[4] By structuring their plot around Tom's conscious wishes rather than his idle boredom, Auden and Kallman dramatize the futility of faithless acts. In failing to fulfill Tom's desire, each episode only fuels a new one.

The librettists devised their most convoluted scheme in response to Tom's second wish—to be happy. In having Nick persuade him to marry a carnival freak, they parody the existentialist notion of the "gratuitous act." After Kallman's heartfelt opening aria, Auden took over writing the scene at Shadow's entrance:

SHADOW: Do you desire her?

RAKEWELL: Like the gout or the falling sickness.

SHADOW: Are you obliged to her?

RAKEWELL: Heaven forbid.

SHADOW: Then marry her.

RAKEWELL: Have you taken leave of your senses?

SHADOW: I was never saner. Come. Master, observe the host of mankind. How are they? Wretched. Why? Because they are not free. Why? Because the giddy multitude are driven by the unpredictable Must of their pleasures and the sober few are bound by the inflexible Ought of their duty, between which slaveries there is nothing to choose. Would you be happy? Then learn to act freely. Would you act freely? Then learn to ignore those twin tyrants of appetite and conscience. Therefore I counsel you, master,—Take Baba the Turk to wife. (2.1)

Representative of a widespread confusion, Craft asks in his review of the collected libretti, "But do irrational and emotionally indifferent acts hurtful to innocent others bring happiness to those who commit them?"[5] Of course not; Tom's senseless marriage naturally makes him unhappy. That message was perhaps more obvious to critics in postwar Europe (though apparently not to Craft), when Sartre's existential philosophy was in vogue, than it is now. A review of the 1951 Hamburg premiere—the headline of which reads, "Stravinsky contra Sartre"—concludes, "Thus [is the opera] a protest against existentialism by the

Catholic Stravinsky.... [Stage director Günther] Rennert underlines this point at the end by erecting a (Greek Orthodox) cross."[6]

Kierkegaard's Christian existentialism had come to replace Freudian psychology in the forefront of Auden's moral/aesthetic thinking. During long conversations with Nabokov in Bad Homburg, Germany, in June 1945, Auden claimed, "Kierkegaard was the only nineteenth-century thinker, next to Nietzsche, worth talking about." He shared his plan to write a "longish essay" that eventually became the preface to his selection of the Danish theologian's writings. He even presented "Nicky" with "a plump volume of *Either/Or* and read parts of it aloud" and may have done the same for Stravinsky during their November meeting.[7] Shortly thereafter, the composer reported reading "Lev Shestov's wonderful book on Kierkegaard" and, echoing Auden, commented: "When one thinks about what Sartre did with Existentialism, one cannot help recalling the anecdote about the peasant woman who saw a camel for the first time in Soviet Moscow ... 'Look what the Bolsheviks have done to horses!'"[8]

One likewise detects Auden's philosophical pessimism in Nabokov's general impression of postwar Europe, expressed in his long letter of December 1950: "But on the whole ... alas ... it smells of degeneration and a certain unbearable *fin-de-siecle, mittel-Europaisches, Reisebureau*. It smells of feet or else of shit, or simply of decay. Over all this half-alive body of Europe prevails a fear and terror in the face of future, unending hopelessness and a certain loathsome Sartre's slush of the soul."[9] Auden dramatizes that "unending hopelessness" in Tom's graveyard crisis that, coincidentally, the composer was just completing when Nabokov's letter arrived. However, as Rennert's Hamburg production would realize, the final scene presents a Christian existential response.

Tom actually declares "I wish" four times, but his final "I wish for nothing else" in the graveyard is a renunciation of idle desires. The libretto originally read "Wishful chance, farewell," before the double entendre was introduced.[10] This detail is significant, for Nick always appears to grant Tom's wishes; but when Tom stops wishing, he disappears into the fire and ice of Hell.

Faust and Contemporary Psychology

> To be quite frank I was not happy with Wystan Auden's libretto
> for *The Rake's Progress*.... My chief objection was that I thought
> he had combined unsuccessfully two quite different themes,
> the first that of Hogarth and the second that of the
> traditional contract with the devil.
>
> —T. S. Eliot to Stravinsky[11]

Freudian Inner Dialogue

Though implied in the initial scenario, the Faustian narrative was not fully articulated until Auden and Kallman fleshed out the libretto. Kallman "found the placing of Shadow as a character too vague," prompting them to cast the hero and villain as master and servant.[12] Auden would examine the implications of such a relationship in an essay, "Balaam and His Ass." Because a master gives the orders and his servant obeys, Auden finds their relationship "peculiarly suitable as an expression of the inner life, so much of which is carried on in imperatives."[13] Following Freud's model of the psyche, he demonstrates his point in an amusing inner dialogue over a minor ethical dilemma:

> If a large lady carelessly, but not intentionally, treads on my corn during a subway rush hour, what goes on in my mind can be expressed dramatically as follows:
>
> SELF: "Care for my anger! Do something about it!"
>
> COGNITIVE EGO: "You are angry because of the pain caused by this large lady who, carelessly but not intentionally, has trodden on your corn. If you decide to relieve your feelings, you can give her a sharp kick on the ankle without being noticed."
>
> SELF: "Kick her." . . .
>
> SUPER-EGO: "Smile! Say 'Not at all, Madam.'"
>
> VOLITIONAL EGO (*to the appropriate voluntary muscles*): *either* "Kick her!" *or* "Smile! Say 'Not at all, Madam!'"[14]

This episode typifies Auden's strategy of opposing polar attributes that need to be held in balance. John Blair observes: "Auden's schematic habit of imagination leads very easily to the practice of allegory. . . . When the subject is the nature of a human being, the schematic imagination leads directly to the separation and allegorization of human faculties or emotion."

In constructing such allegories, Auden often "borrows the categories and concepts of an existing intellectual framework, be it Freudian (as in *The Orators*), Kierkegaardian (as in 'New Year Letter'), or Jungian (as in the four-sided analysis of man in *The Age of Anxiety*)."[15] For his 1943 seminar, "Romanticism from Rousseau to Hitler," at Swarthmore College, the poet went so far as to diagram the complex scheme of his poem "The Sea and the Mirror," parts of which (reproduced in tables 3.1 and 3.3 seem to inform his thinking in *The Rake's Progress*.

One finds in the little drama quoted above a framework similar to the relationship between Tom, Nick, and Anne. Self-centered Tom corresponds to Auden's SELF/id, the literal expression of which is his three wishes. Anne, who in the epilogue sings, "Not every man is given an Anne to take the place of Duty," corresponds to Auden's SUPER-EGO. Were he a neutral agent, Nick would ostensibly function as the COGNITIVE EGO, ever apprising the master of his options, and as his VOLITIONAL EGO, which is "a servant in relation to either my self or my super-ego."[16] But Tom, as he declares in "Here I stand" (1.1), refuses to exercise his volition out of sheer principle, preferring to throw himself to the winds of Fate:

> Since it is not by merit We rise or we fall,
> But the favor of Fortune That governs us all,

> Why should I labour For what in the end
> She will give me for nothing if she be my friend? (1.1)

Coached by Nick, he tries to shed his SUPER-EGO, declaring, "One aim in all things to pursue: My duty to myself to do" (1.2). By shutting "his ears to prude and preacher," Tom allows his SELF/id to go unchecked. And Nick, who only masquerades as an obedient servant, abuses his role as COGNITIVE EGO and ever misinforms his gullible master.

To this end, Nick proposes that Tom ignore both "twin tyrants of appetite [SELF/id] and conscience [SUPER-EGO]" (2.1; see full text above). By circumventing his inner voices, so Nick's "logic" goes, Tom can rely solely on his cognitive and volitional egos to determine action and is thereby free to exercise his own will. In other words, the "servant" (the VOLITIONAL EGO) becomes the "master" (of the SELF/id and SUPER-EGO) because the master has relinquished his role.

Jungian Individuation

In striking contrast to Kallman's practical explanation is Auden's psychological rationale for Anne and Nick: "The first thing then: what were we to do with the Rake . . . ? Well, we began by splitting him in two—himself and his malevolent alter ego or shadow. The shadow could then propose various things, initiate actions to which he could respond. . . . On the other side of the shadow is the Good Angel—Anne—the soprano . . . who would be an awful bore at dinner but she just has to sing very beautifully."[17]

In naming his villain after the Jungian dark self, Auden makes explicit his Mephistophelean character. According to Jung, aspects of our collective unconscious become manifest in dreams, in projections onto other persons, and through figures of art and literature in the form of collective images, or *archetypes*. He writes: "The character that summarizes a person's uncontrolled emotional manifestations consists, in the first place, of his inferior qualities or peculiarities . . . I have called the inferior and less commendable part of a person the *shadow*. We have met with this figure in literature; for instance, Faust and his shadow Mephistopheles."[18] Auden explains that in the modern age, the objects of our desires—our idols—dissipate so quickly in favor of other objects that "our real idolatry . . . is an idolatry of possibility. And in such an age the Devil appears in the form of Mephisto, in the form, that is, of an actor."[19] The opera's most contrived character, Shadow alone directly addresses the audience. He even retains his identity in the epilogue: "Many insist I do not exist. At times I wish I didn't." Thus, Nick is at once Tom's personified dark side—that is, without his own identity—and the most real figure in the opera. He is, indeed, an actor. When the other singers, now referring to their characters in third person, step in front of the curtain for the epilogue, they simply join Nick in the theatrical space he has occupied all along.

At a level deeper within the Jungian collective unconscious lies the more elusive contrasexual side of the psyche: the *anima* for men and *animus* for women. This mysterious figure represents all that is unknown to the subject and, unlike the SUPER-EGO/conscience in Auden's Freudian anecdote, is therefore "characterized by an extraordinary many-sidedness."[20] Marie-Louise von Franz describes: "The anima appears in crude, childish form in men's erotic fantasies.... A still more subtle manifestation of a negative anima appears ... in the form of a princess who asks her suitors to answer a series of riddles.... If they cannot give the answers ... they must die."[21]

Auden stages a similar scene in Tom's perverse catechism; as Mother Goose afterward leads him off to the bedchamber, Nick remarks cryptically, "Sweet dreams, my master. Dreams may lie, / But dream. For when you wake, you die" (1.2). From this stumbling start, the opera's female figures represent increasingly elevated aspects of Tom's anima: Mother Goose is a cartoonish fusion of mother and whore; Baba the Turk is exotic, mysterious, and appalling; Anne, its most complete manifestation, is his betrothed "better half"; and the imagined "Venus" is the exalted Queen of Heaven. As we shall see, this Jungian interpretation neatly conforms to the Kierkegaardian ascent from existential aimlessness to Christian redemption.

Anne and Baba, though, function as more than archetypal projections. Each possesses her own sense of self and embarks upon a progress (and, in Baba's case, a return) of her own. Anne makes a character-defining choice by bravely rousing herself to follow Tom to London. Her classic response (recitative, aria, and cabaletta) to a classic dilemma (abandonment) forms a counterpoint to Tom's passive embrace of "Destiny" and arbitrary act of "Free Will." Anne and Baba may even be viewed as each other's shadow, particularly for the latter ("The milkmaid haunts me," 3.1). One is "young, demure, delightful," domestic, feminine, and innocent; the other is older, worldly, ugly, masculine, but belatedly wise. Yet their encounter in the auction scene culminates in an unexpected exchange, crucial for Anne's pivotal appearance in the card game: Baba's revelation that "he still loves you."

Jung defines the encounters with the shadow and anima as progressive stages in the individual's process of self-realization, or *individuation*. He writes:

> The anima can appear also as an angel of light, a psychopomp who points the way to the highest meaning, as we know from *Faust*. . . . If the encounter with the shadow is the "apprentice-piece" in the individual's development, then that with the anima is the "master-piece." The relation with the anima is again a test of courage, an ordeal by fire for the spiritual and moral forces of man.... The first encounter with her usually leads one to infer anything rather than wisdom.... [Only] when this hard task has been faced, does he come to realize more and more that behind all her cruel sporting with human fate there lies something like a hidden purpose which seems to reflect a superior knowledge of life's laws. It is just the most unexpected, the most terrifyingly chaotic things which reveal a deeper meaning. And the more this meaning is recognized, the more the anima loses her impetuous and compulsive character. Gradually breakwaters are built against the surging of chaos, and the meaningful divides itself from the meaningless.[22]

The initial stage of this process of self-discovery is often marked by a sense of emptiness and boredom and symbolized by "the run-down interior of a decayed aristocrat's castle."[23] Of his life without Anne, Tom sings:

> I walk
> An endless hall of chandeliers
> In light that blinds, in light that sears,
> Reflected from a million smiles
> All empty as the country miles
> Of silly wood and senseless park;
> And only in my heart—the dark. (2.1)

In Tom's misguided journey to the graveyard and Anne's mysterious appearance during the card-guessing game, Auden and Kallman dramatize this process of self-discovery. Here, the struggle between the forces of Progress (shadow) and Return (anima) within Tom's soul finally plays out. Nick, having well taught his master "that there is no return," plants the Queen of Hearts for a second time in the third and final play. But the forbidden words "Return" and "Love," which belong to the purview of Anne, fix in his mind. The key phrase from her C-minor arioso, "A love that is sworn before Thee can plunder Hell of its prey" (2.2), resounds from her disembodied voice into Tom's unconscious.[24] By renouncing idle desires ("I wish for nothing else") and embracing immutable Love, Tom saves his soul and attains a new awareness.

> Love, first and last, assume eternal reign;
> Renew my life, O Queen of Hearts, again. (3.2)

Don Giovanni

Up to this point, the dramatic trajectory of *The Rake's Progress* resembles Goethe's *Faust*, the hero of which is redeemed by Gretchen's love. But if *Faust* influenced its shape, Mozart's *Don Giovanni* (1787) at least colors the drama and some of the music. Stravinsky, who readily admitted his debt to *Così*, also attended three performances of *Don Giovanni* during the years he labored on *The Rake*. He even commented cryptically on the connection in a joint interview with Auden for the *Los Angeles Times* during their first meeting in 1947, when he claimed their new opera "will be tragic only in the sense that *Don Giovanni* is tragic."[25] Yet, in a letter to the same newspaper fifteen years later, Stravinsky corrected the reviewer of a recent production: "The final ensemble, he says, 'borrows a page from *Don Giovanni*.' It does no such thing."[26]

The composer's denials aside, many observers have noticed links: the protagonists' licentious behavior, the conspicuous graveyard scenes, the theatrical descents into Hell, and their moralizing epilogues. What Tom does not share with Mozart's legendary rake is his primal drive. In Don Giovanni, Kierkegaard memorably claims, "desire is absolutely qualified as desire . . . The issue here is not desire in a particular individual but desire as principle, qualified by spirit as that which spirit excludes. This is the idea of the elemental originality of the sensuous [sensuous genius]."[27] Auden recognized that Hogarth's rake "is not a demonically passionate man like Don Giovanni but a self-indulgent one who yields to the temptations of the immediate moment. Consequently in the engravings, the décor is more significant than the protagonist." The poet concluded he would have to lend his operatic rake some of the Don's willfulness, for "the mere fact that they sing is such an assertion of will that you simply cannot deal with a passive character."[28]

Thus, Auden and Kallman bestow upon Tom precisely what Don Giovanni and Hogarth's rake lack: a conscience. As the epilogue says, "Not every man is given an Anne to take the place of Duty." Though, to be accurate, those two eighteenth-century libertines each have a version of Anne—Donna Elvira and Sarah Young, respectively—but remain unmoved by them. By contrast, passive Tom is ever moved by his memory of Anne but cannot bring himself to respond decisively until the last second. Were he to follow Nick's advice and ignore "the inflexible Ought" of duty, Tom would be deaf to Anne's saving message and, like Mozart's demonic hero, perish in hell. But he is not a single-minded force; he is a simple "Everyman," subject to the pull of both desire and conscience. As Kerman observes, "Auden made a decisive departure from the eighteenth-century view when he pitied the Rake and set about analyzing him."[29]

But despite his resemblance to Goethe's Faust, Tom still originated from Hogarth. And though they dispensed with most of his details, Stravinsky and Auden derive their concluding scene from the image that compelled the composer from the beginning: the rake's demise in the madhouse. Thus, as a final gesture before his fiery descent, Nick, empowered by Tom's sins, strikes his former master with insanity.

Here emerges a subtle but significant difference between the Jungian and Freudian underpinnings of the libretto. Stated simplistically, the Freudian view of the opera amounts to a battle between Tom's id (egged on by the devil Nick) and his superego (the angelic voice of duty, Anne). Tom's (and Anne's) victory in the card game would seem to resolve the conflict. However, the Jungian conception of shadow and anima is not so black and white. Identified with the impulses to progress and return, these two complexes each possess positive and negative aspects. Even the spiritual dimension of the anima can receive too much attention. "If the ego adopts the standpoint of the anima," Jung observes, "the subject is fully adopted to the collective unconscious but has no adaptation to reality."[30] The process of individuation stagnates and the subject becomes delusional—hence, Tom's fixation upon Anne as an imaginary "Venus."

The balancing aspect of individuation ideally suits Auden's proclivity for defining extremes and promotes a more subtle understanding of Tom's demise.[31] Though no evidence suggests Stravinsky was aware of this psychological dimension, he certainly understood the Faustian implications of the libretto. He also understood that the idle wishes and pangs of conscience of his rakish "Everyman" mirrored a universally human experience.

"Adonis" and "Venus"

> Reverence forbids me from describing in detail Adrian's condition when he came to after the twelve hours of unconsciousness into which his paralytic stroke at the piano had plunged him. He did not come to himself, but rather to an alien self that was only the burned-out shell of his personality.... Originally, the word "dementia" simply meant this deviation from one's own ego, this alienation from oneself.
>
> —*Doctor Faustus*, Epilogue[32]

Tom is consigned to neither heaven nor hell but to earthly insanity, which is arguably both. Ever searching for a dramatic model, Stravinsky and Auden as early as their November scenario recast their insane hero as Adonis. According to the classical myth, the beautiful but arrogant youth, adored by Venus, pursued the wild boar despite her warnings. When Adonis is killed, the distraught goddess sprinkled nectar onto his blood, whence flowers now bloom each spring. The myth thus celebrates the annual death and rebirth of nature.

"Adonis" and "Venus" dominate the Bedlam scene, the outline of which includes more detailed dialogue than any other. Auden had only to translate and expand the original French and compose lines for the chorus/minuet, Anne's lullaby, and the duettino. Stravinsky and Auden even contemplated introducing the myth in Tom and Anne's opening duet of act 1, scene 1, the outline of which reads: "Pastoral, *comme* Theocritus, of love, youth, country, etc. (Perhaps mention Adonis here?)"[33] In the end, the librettists peppered their text with oblique references, which inspired some of Kallman's finest imagery:

> Up, Nature, up, the hunt is on; thy pack is in full cry. They smell the blood upon the bracing air. On, on, on, through every street and mansion, for every candle in this capital of light attends thy appetizing progress and burns in honor at thy shrine. (2.1)

Unlike Hogarth's morality tale or the Faust legend, the tragedy of Adonis is unmitigated by idleness or hubris. Adonis's only fault is that he heeds the call of Nature to chase the wild boar, symbolic of his need to separate from the anima. Auden brings the myth to a touching closure:

Tom: In a foolish dream, in a gloomy labyrinth

I hunted shadows, disdaining thy true love...

Anne: Kiss me Adonis: the wild boar is vanquished. (3.3)

According to George McFadden, the boar specifically represents Tom's self-will, "the same boar that brought [Adonis] to birth by ripping open the tree into which his mother, Smyrna, had been transformed by the gods." By contrast, Anne offers "the love of Aphrodite (i.e., Venus) Urania, or Aphrodite Pandemos; that is, the love which unites husband wife and family, and therefore, the generations and the whole community, in its bond."[34] Aphrodite Urania and Aphrodite Pandemos refer to a twofold conception of the goddess of love; the former represents the spiritual or heavenly, the latter the sensual or earthly. Aphrodite Pandemos implies a further dualism between erotic love and the procreative love to which McFadden alludes. Over the course of the opera, Auden manages to reference all three aspects of the goddess:

1. the Pastoral queen of Tom's opening line presides over spring festivities:
   Now is the season when the Cyprian Queen
   With genial charm translates our mortal scene,
   When swains their nymphs in fervent arms enfold
   And with a kiss restore the Age of Gold. (1.1)
2. the Roaring Boys and Whores praise the Erotic goddess in the Brothel chorus:
   A toast to our commanders then
     From their Irregulars;
   A toast, ladies and gentlemen:
     To VENUS and MARS! (1.2)
3. "Adonis" imagines the Heavenly queen (Aphrodite Urania) in Bedlam:[35]
   Prepare yourselves, heroic shades. Wash you and make you clean. Anoint your limbs with oil, put on your wedding garments and crown your heads with flowers. Let music strike. Venus, queen of love, will visit her unworthy Adonis. (3.3)

In fact, part of Auden's detailed diagram for "The Sea and the Mirror," shown in table 3.1, directly refers to these three manifestations.[36] First, an explanation of its general organization: Auden's left and right columns represent opposing conceptions of Hell resulting from the search for Salvation: the left by finding refuge in Nature; the right by finding release from Nature. The center column represents "This World." Within the center box for the category labeled "Requiredness" he writes on the left edge "Venere Vulgare" (Earthly Venus or *Aphrodite Pandemos*), just above "Blind Eros"; on the right edge he writes "Venere Celeste" (Heavenly Venus or *Aphrodite Urania*) above "Seeing Anteros" (the god of requited love). In the center he names the ideal balance: Subjective; Grace (from which the name "Anne" is derived); and Agape, for the unconditional love between subjects (as opposed to objectified bodies) that is the basis for family and community. Similarly, Auden positions the real Anne (Grace) between the vulgar Mother Goose and the imagined "Venus."

Another attraction of the Adonis story is its seasonal theme, only vaguely implied in the November outline, where act 1, scene 1, is set on a "Fine spring afternoon" and act 1, scene 3, on a "Winter night" (changed to "Summer" in

Table 3.1. "Requiredness" category from Auden's diagram for "The Sea and the Mirror" for Swarthmore College seminar (1943).

	HELL Of The Pure Deed Power without Purpose		THIS WORLD Dualism of Experience Knowledge of Good and Evil Existential Being		HELL Of The Pure Word Knowledge without Power
Requiredness	Objective Determined	Instinctive	Venere Vulgare Blind Eros	Subjective Venere Celeste Grace Agape Seeing Anteros	Conscious lack of requiredness The void of Indecision or Self-Reflection

Search for Salvation by finding refuge in Nature →

Search for Salvation by finding release from Nature ←

the libretto and finally "Autumn" in Stravinsky's score). In the classical myth, the handsome mortal spends autumn and winter in the underworld with Persephone, whose story Stravinsky and Gide recreated in their 1934 melodrama, and spring and summer on earth with Venus.[37] The theme of seasonal return counters the progressive desires of a Faust or Don Juan and casts in a new light Tom's transformation after the card-guessing game. As fervently as he fled the Arcadian garden (and Anne), the victorious Tom now returns full circle "a year and a day hence."

In viewing Tom's insanity as a retreat from his disastrous Progress, we seemingly invert the allegory of Progress and Return. Anne is now the one who moves on, which is puzzling, given her courageous devotion to Tom earlier in the opera. Kerman asks,

> What is the significance of having Anne save him in the graveyard, only to betray him now? . . . Aphrodite did not leave Adonis to die in anguish. And in so specifically Faustian a tale, we want to know which way Tom goes when he dies—a matter treated squarely by Marlowe and Goethe and Thomas Mann, who, like Auden, brings his hero to insanity before death. In his madness, Tom's ravings cannot properly reflect his feelings about salvation, Purgatory, Anne's departure, or the meaning of his ordeal. Anne is extinguished. Neither of them touches the theme of redemption or half-redemption on which the opera promised to culminate.[38]

Yet, could one really expect Stravinsky, or even Auden, to bow to such a romantic (not to mention Wagnerian) convention as redemption through love? But if reuniting the lovers within the story, as Kerman seems to suggest, would betray its deeper message, then what does Tom's lonely end mean?

Before tackling this question, let us reestablish two points: first, Tom is at least half-redeemed. Like Goethe's Faust, his soul is saved and Anne even allows that they may be reunited in an afterlife—only "in this *earthly* city we shall not meet again" (3.3). Yet despite all his pursuing, Tom never finds true fulfillment. At the beginning he is too immature to appreciate his beloved, and in the end he is too deluded to know she isn't real. Like the mythic Adonis, he swings from a winter of rakishness to a spring of blind devotion. Against this gullible and obsessive Tom is poised Anne, who is neither foolishly desirous nor blindly devoted. Her departure is not a betrayal; when Tom's love becomes an obsession she knows it cannot be realized, at least in this world. Myths cannot replace life. In leaving her insane lover, Anne, not Tom, demonstrates a deeper awareness.

Second, the choice of Hogarth's rake as subject entails his downfall; yet, because their protagonist never completely renounces his conscience (Anne), Stravinsky and Auden can imbue their final tableau with a greater depth of passion than that of Hogarth. The latter's eighteenth-century moral sensibilities required the rake to suffer, whereas Goethe allowed his romantic hero a saving grace. Mozart's Don Giovanni straddles the two eras. Stravinsky and Auden's twentieth-century rake belongs wholly to neither tradition. Imposing neither self-righteous punishment nor a *lieto fine*, they subject their modernist hero to a subtler judgment.

Kierkegaardian Progress

Kerman perceives Tom's progress as one of growing awareness rather than degeneration.[39] Even if based on trickery, each of his wishes reflects a distinct stage in a developing consciousness: from idle greed to disillusionment with material things, to a prideful sense of virtue, and finally to the renunciation of idle desires. Responding to Kerman, McFadden was the first critic to recognize in Tom's madness not the Devil's vengeful punishment or a traumatized hero's withdrawal from reality but a Kierkegaardian "leap into the absurd." He sees Tom's transformation as a dramatization of the Christian saint, the literary model of which, for Auden, is Don Quixote:

> Auden's intention seems unmistakable in the light of an article of his which appeared in *Horizon* (August, 1949), shortly after he had delivered his libretto to Stravinsky. I quote two sentences: "Suddenly [Don Quixote] goes mad, i.e., he sets out to become what he admires. Aesthetically this looks like pride; in fact, religiously, it is a conversion, an act of faith, a taking up of his cross." Tom's insanity is willed; Nick's curse (presented as a magic trick) is superfluous except to explain what is happening to Tom. Further, "each has to believe by himself," Auden declares in the same article. That is why Anne leaves Tom, not because of stern country morality (as Mr. Kerman fears). For, of course, each must bear his own share of suffering. It would seem, then, that Auden regards *The Rake's Progress* as a drama involving not the Christian tragic hero (for he, as in the case of Othello, is damned), but a comedy with a "saint" for hero—only since the saint can hardly be made aesthetically interesting as he is, repetitive as his existence must be, Auden follows Cervantes in giving his hero the spectacular trait of madness.[40]

Whereas Hogarth, in another series, would counter the rake's sinful Idleness with virtuous Industry, Stravinsky and Auden oppose it with a leap of Faith—for Kierkegaard, the only meaningful gratuitous act. Nick's vengeful curse disguises the voluntary nature of Tom's madness, but in the November scenario (published for the first time only in 1960) Stravinsky and Auden made it explicit. No card-guessing game, no reference to return; only a cessation of time—according to Kierkegaard, a fundamental condition for the Christian existential experience—brings the hero's progress to an end. Auden explains in the following quotation from the essay he had been pondering for years:

> If I take away from my sense of existence all that can become an object of my consciousness, what is left?
>
> 1) An awareness that my existence is not self-derived . . .
>
> 2) An awareness that I am free to make choices . . .

3) An awareness of being *with* time, i.e., experiencing time as an eternal present to which past and future refer, instead of my knowledge of my feelings and of the outer world as moving or changing *in* time.

4) A state of anxiety (or dread), pride (in the theological sense), despair or faith.[41]

Auden published these ideas the year after *The Rake* premiered, but he had already dramatized them in the character of Tom. He parodies the first two points in the radically deterministic "Here I stand" (1.1) and failed "*l'acte gratuite*" (2.1). Tom experiences the emotions of the fourth in the bread-machine episode (pride) and the graveyard (dread, despair, and faith). We can infer the third point in the ecstatic duet between "Adonis" and "Venus" in Bedlam:

> Rejoice, beloved: in these fields of Elysium
> Space cannot alter, nor Time our love abate;
> Here has no words for absence or estrangement
> Nor Now a notion of Almost or Too Late. (3.3)

The outline version of the hero's transformation in the graveyard, though, expresses almost verbatim the existential experience of time. Auden and Kallman abandoned that language in favor of the dramatically more convincing card game. However, Stravinsky, true to the original scenario, realizes Tom's metamorphosis by constructing a musical sense of timelessness at the scene's conclusion (see chap. 8).

Building on McFadden's observations, Geoffrey Chew has demonstrated how the opera is much more than a *rake's* progress; by the second act Tom has grown bored with sins of the flesh. "It is a 'progress' in the fullest, religious sense," he writes, "ultimately closer to Bunyan's *Pilgrim's Progress* than to Hogarth's moral allegory."[42] Auden maps that progress onto Kierkegaard's three categories of living: the aesthetic, ethical, and religious, shown in table 3.2.

"The aesthetic hero," Auden tells us, "is glorious but not responsible for his successes or his failures."[43] Hence, Tom's "it is not by merit we rise or we fall / But the favor of Fortune that governs us all" (1.1). Passion drives the aesthetic man. As we know from Kierkegaard, its exemplar is Mozart's Don Giovanni, its ideal medium is music. Tom's consciousness begins to emerge when, instead of reciting his prepared catechism for Mother Goose—and thus renouncing Love, like Alberich in *Das Rheingold*—he discovers his true feelings for Anne:

> Love, too frequently betrayed
> For some plausible desire
> Or the world's enchanted fire,
> Still thy traitor in his sleep
> Renews the vows he did not keep,
> > Weeping, weeping,
> He kneels before thy wounded shade. (1.2)

Table 3.2. Kierkegaard's three categories and their projection in *The Rake's Progress* (from Chew).

1. Aesthetic Religion (the Greek Gods)
    Tom's "baptism" in Mother Goose's Brothel, with Whores and Roaring Boys
2. Ethical Religion (the god of Greek Philosophy)
    Tom's "marriage" to Baba the Turk to demonstrate his freedom
3. Revealed Religion (Judaism and Christianity)
    Tom's "death" to sanity in the game of chance in the graveyard

In the equally heartfelt "Vary the song" that opens act 2—the counter to Don Giovanni's soulless "Fin ch'han del vino"—Tom denounces the aesthetic life, thereby parting ways with Hogarth's rake and setting up his next step. Auden knew he was on secure footing in dramatizing the first stage, for operatic characters ideally are aesthetic beings. The trick would be redirecting Tom's passion, for "the ethical hero is not a man of power, the man who does, but the philosopher, the man who knows."[44] He wisely leaves the philosophizing to Nick—Stravinsky would later realize "Shadow is a preacher as well as a Devil."[45] Still, Kallman admitted "that placing our tenor between Shadow, who rather triggers the wishes he too wickedly grants, and Anne, the voice of Good Pursuant, neat as the pattern is, leaves this protagonist almost as passive as his Hogarth original."[46] No longer invested emotionally, Tom stumbles along. His blustery enthusiasm to marry Baba ("My tale shall be told / Both by young and by old") and for the bread-machine ("Thanks to this excellent device / Man shall re-enter Paradise") dissipates instantly. His one moment of sincere expression at this ethical stage is his prayer of thanks for the bread turned from stone: "O miracle! / O may I not, forgiven all my past / For one good deed, deserve dear Anne at last?" (2.3). Stravinsky highlights the connection by setting these words to the music of Anne's prayer in act 1, scene 3.

As McFadden first observed, Tom's dramatic leap of faith—the turning point of the opera—marks his transition to the final religious stage. Earlier I described this moment as the end of his aimless pursuit of idle desires and a return to immutable Love. But this Faustian redemption convinces only in so far as Tom and Anne reunite either in this life or in the afterlife. The rake's madness undercuts that theme, leaving us confused. A Jungian interpretation suggests "Adonis" has swerved too far to his anima side, a conclusion supported by Auden's opposition of "Venere vulgare" and "Venere celeste" (table 3.1). However, the poet's reading of Kierkegaard, which postdates his diagram for "The Sea and the Mirror," may have caused him to reconsider.

In his above-quoted article, Auden categorized Don Quixote as a Comic or Ironic Hero (along with Dostoyevsky's Idiot and Lewis Carroll's Alice), positioned at the center of his 1943 diagram of Hero types, shown in table 3.3. By 1949, though, Auden had come to regard Cervantes's leading man as a portrait of a Christian saint rather than a comic hero and, through him, sought to define a

Table 3.3. "Hero" category of Auden's diagram for "The Sea and the Mirror" (1943).

	Search for Salvation by finding refuge in Nature ⟷		Search for Salvation by finding release from Nature ⟷
Hero	HELL Of The Pure Deed Power without Purpose The Tragic Hero-Outlaw With S[ex] A[ppeal] Flying Dutchman Vamp	THIS WORLD Dualism of Experience Knowledge of Good and Evil Existential Being The Comic or Ironic Hero Don Quixote Bryon's The Beggar Don Juan The Idiot (Dost.) The Child (Alice) Marx Bros. Detectives (Holmes)	HELL Of The Pure Word Knowledge without Power The Demonic Villain Without natural S[ex] A[ppeal] Iago Stavrogin The Grand Inquisitor Depraved or Cissy Master-Crooks

separate category for the "Ironic Hero."⁴⁷ Kierkegaard's Christian existentialism, particularly his understanding of faith and despair, informs Auden's reading:

MADNESS AND FAITH

To have faith in something or someone means:

a) that the latter is not manifest . . .

b) The relation of faith between subject and object is unique in every case . . .

Don Quixote exemplifies both. *a*) He never sees things that aren't there (delusion) but sees them differently. . . . *b*) He is the only individual who see them thus.

FAITH AND DESPAIR

People are tempted to lose faith *a*) when it fails to bring worldly success, *b*) when the evidence of their senses and feelings seem against it.⁴⁸

"Adonis" worships "Venus" just as Cervantes's "Don Quixote" (his real name is Alonso Quixano) worships "Dulcinea," in the manner of a knight errant. Their madness and faith are inseparable. As to whether we should pity the Ironic Hero, Auden explains, "For the tragic hero suffering is real and destructive; for the comic hero it is unreal or temporary or curative; for both it is a sign that they are not in the truth. . . . The saint, on the other hand, is ironically related to suffering; it is real, nevertheless he understands that it is a blessing, a sign that he is in the truth. 'I say pain but ought to say solace.'"⁴⁹

Auden's article may also shed light on the bread-machine scheme, the least developed of Tom's three wishes. Explained as Tom's attempt "*devenir Dieu*," the point seems to be to parody the poet's conception of the Christian tragic hero, who "is as responsible for the manifest sins he commits as he is for the invisible sin of pride which produced them. . . . Pride means a defiant attempt to *become* a god, when you secretly know you are a mortal creature."⁵⁰

I summarize the various and sometimes conflicting dramatic trajectories of *The Rake's Progress* in table 3.4. Level A shows the uninterrupted and unredeemed catabasis of Hogarth's rake. The Faust narrative promises at least a half-redemption but stagnates in Tom's fixation with "Venus." The seasonal cycle would seem to imply a positive return, with the imaginary "Venus" substituting for the Cyprian Queen of the opening duet. But again, this *volte face* lacks a dramatic motivation. Only when one recognizes the Kierkegaardian anabasis unfolding in counterpoint to the Hogarthian catabasis does the destination of Tom's progress become clear. The Jungian narrative, which is still for me the most dramatically convincing interpretation, in effect combines these progressions, its turning point being the moment they intersect in the climactic encounter in the graveyard.

Eliot was probably right to question the imposition of a Faustian half-redemption onto Hogarth's unsubtle degeneration. Few are able or willing to follow Auden when he imagines his divinely mad rake as a Christian saint. Kerman

Table 3.4. Four Dramatic Trajectories in *The Rake's Progress*.

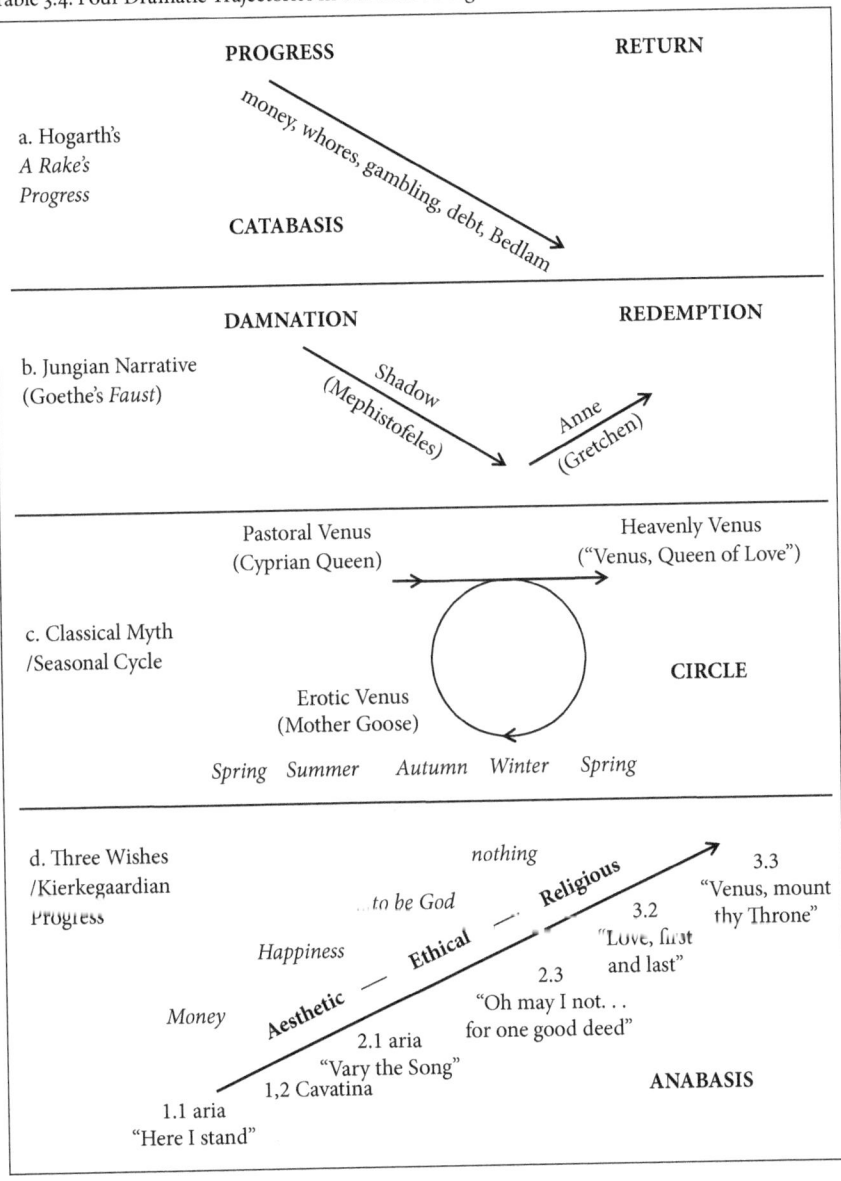

put it succinctly: "The destination of the Rake's progress is not clear."[51] The same might be said, though, of Don Giovanni's fate. Nineteenth-century interpreters like Kierkegaard and E. T. A. Hoffman have made him a Tragic Hero, his demise a tribute to human willfulness—just as Auden saw all of opera. Perhaps the destination of the modern hero—whether a Faust or a Don Giovanni—must remain uncertain. Kerman misses this point when he questions madness as dramatically unviable. On the contrary, madness may be the only fate for modernist heroes like Wozzeck, Adrian Leverkühn, and Tom Rakewell.

At its heart, *The Rake's Progress* is not a tragedy but a love story; not the conventional "romantic idolization of the fair woman," but the love Auden discovered in Cervantes's great ironic hero, whose "language is the language of Eros, . . . but its real meaning is the Christian agape."[52] Auden recognized this spiritual love—with or without its Christian imagery—as a recurring theme in classical literature and myth, yet desperately missing from modernism's bleak worldview. Perhaps during their week together in November 1947, in between demonstrations of Baroque verse, Biblical exegeses, and fervent talk of Kierkegaard, he and Stravinsky discussed how their opera might attempt to fill that spiritual void.

Auden conceived Tom's catabasis as a flight from existential reality—where one experiences time "as an eternal present"—as well as a pursuit of idle desires. The nadir of that downward spiral comes in the graveyard. Forced to guess cards to save his soul, Tom must live in the anguished moment, the only condition in which existentialists, from Kierkegaard to Sartre, agree man can act freely. His progress leads to both an existential crisis and existential salvation, thus, the true moral of *The Rake's Progress*.

Auden probably recognized that any opera requiring a diagram for comprehension is too complicated, but he could not help himself. Furthermore, he trusted Stravinsky to navigate his libretto's intersecting dramatic trajectories and realize its deepest meanings. His trust would be rewarded, as I demonstrate in part 3.

Notes

1. Glenn Loney, "Elegy for a Bacchic Rake," *Opera Monthly* 4, no. 11 (1992): 11.

2. W. H. Auden and Chester Kallman, *Libretti and Other Dramatic Writings 1939-1973*, ed. Edward Mendelson (London: Faber and Faber, 1993), 617. See prelude, note 23, for his full summary.

3. Igor Stravinsky and Robert Craft, *Memories and Commentaries* (Garden City, NY: Doubleday, 1960), 151.

4. Letter of November 20, 1947; Robert Craft, ed., *Stravinsky: Selected Correspondence*, vol. 1 (New York: Alfred A. Knopf, 1982), 303; author's translation from the original French.

5. Robert Craft, "Words for Music Perhaps," review of *The Complete Works of W. H. Auden: Libretti and other Dramatic Writings (1939-1973)*. *The New York Review of Books* 41, no. 18 (1994), 55.

6. Heinz Joachim, "Stravinskij contra Sartre—Der respektvolle 'Wüstling,'" *Die Welt* (Hamburg), November 15, 1951 (translated from German).

7. Nicolas Nabokov, *Bagázh: Memoirs of a Russian Cosmopolitan* (New York: Atheneum, 1975), 222.

8. Letter of January 2, 1948, Craft, *Correspondence*, vol. 2, 374. See W. H. Auden, *The Living Thoughts of Kierkegaard* (Bloomington: Indiana University Press, 1952) and Lev Shestov, *Kierkegaard et la philosophie existentielle* (Paris: Librarie J. Vrin, 1936).

9. Letter of December 23, 1950, Paul Sacher Foundation (translated from Russian). McFadden senses that Auden addressed *The Rake's Progress* to "a society so desperately lacking in any bond of love that its members seem to resemble atoms in a void. His task is to enable us to find a subjective bond with Tom, to see ourselves in him, despite the sense of isolation which is the mark of modern man"; see George McFadden, "*The Rake's Progress*: A Note on the Libretto," *Hudson Review* 8, no. 1 (1955): 106.

10. Craft, *Correspondence*, vol. 3, 510.

11. Letter of March 19, 1959, from T. S. Eliot to Stravinsky, Paul Sacher Foundation.

12. Auden and Kallman, *Libretti*, 626.

13. W. H. Auden, *The Dyer's Hand* (New York: Vintage International, 1989), 111.

14. Ibid., 111–12. Auden's SELF corresponds to what Freud terms the *id*.

15. John G. Blair, *The Poetic Art of W. H. Auden* (Princeton, NJ: Princeton University Press, 1965), 74, 75.

16. Auden, *Dyer's Hand*, 112.

17. Auden and Kallman, *Libretti*, 621. See chapter 2, note 32, for Kallman's justification.

18. Carl S. Jung, *The Collected Works of C. G. Jung*, trans. R. F. C. Hull (Princeton: Princeton University Press, 1969), 9/I, 20.

19. Auden, *Dyer's Hand*, 118 (cf. note 2 above).

20. Carl S. Jung, *The Portable Jung*, ed. Joseph Campbell (New York: Penguin Books, 1971), 174.

21. Marie-Louise von Franz, "The Process of Individuation," in *Man and His Symbols*, ed. C. G. Jung (Garden City, NY: Laurel, 1964), 181, 179.

22. Jung, *Collected Works*, 9/I, 29–31.

23. Von Franz, "Process of Individuation," 167.

24. "Whenever a man's logical mind is incapable of discerning facts that are hidden in his unconscious, the anima helps him dig them out" (ibid., 180). Pamina represents another memorable image of this relationship as guide for Tamino's trials by fire and water in *The Magic Flute*.

25. Craft, *Correspondence*, vol. 1, 303.

26. Igor Stravinsky and Robert Craft, *Themes and Episodes* (New York: Alfred A. Knopf, 1966), 83; see also chapter 1, note 6.

27. Søren Kierkegaard, *Either/Or* part 1, ed. and trans. Howard V. Hong and Edna H. Hong (Princeton, NJ: Princeton University Press, 1987), 85; see also chapter 2, note 10.

28. Auden and Kallman, *Libretti*, 617, 621. For connections to *Don Giovanni*, see Joseph Kerman, *Opera as Drama* (Berkeley: University of California Press, 1988) 191; Joseph N. Straus, *Remaking the Past* (Cambridge, MA: Harvard University Press, 1992), 155–61; Peter Conrad, "The Libertine's Progress," in *Don Giovanni: Myths of Seduction and Betrayal*, ed. Jonathan Miller (New York: Schocken Books, 1990), 89; and Colin Mason, "Stravinsky's Opera," *Music and Letters* 33 (1952): 8–9.

29. Kerman, *Opera as Drama*, 201.

30. Jung, *Collected Works* 7, 304. Elsewhere Jung writes, "Conscious and unconscious do not make a whole when one of them is suppressed.... It is the old game of hammer and anvil: between them the patient iron is forged into an indestructible whole, an 'individual'" (ibid., 9/1, 288).

31. Auden's revised ending for a 1945 production of *The Ascent of F6* at Swarthmore College also represents "the climax of a Jungian quest for self-realization"; see Edward Mendelson, *Early Auden* (New York: Farrar, Straus and Giroux, 1981), 286.

32. Excerpt(s) from *Doctor Faustus: The Life of the German Composer Adrian Leverkuhn as Told by a Friend* by Thomas Mann, translated by John E. Woods, translation copyright ©

1997 by Penguin Random House LLC. Used by permission of Alfred A. Knopf, an imprint of the Knopf Doubleday Publishing Group, a division of Penguin Random House LLC. All rights reserved. For the digital rights of Thomas Mann: All rights reserved S. Fischer Verlag GmbH, Frankfurt am Main.

33. I. Stravinsky and Craft, *Memories*, 156; Auden and Kallman, *Libretti*, 581.

34. McFadden, "A Note on the Libretto," 112.

35. Blair, *Poetic Art*, 183.

36. The complete diagram is reproduced in Mendelson, *Later Auden*, 240.

37. In contrast to his easy agreement with the Catholic Auden over the theme of Christian redemption in *The Rake*, Stravinsky's Christian interpretation of Persephone's rebirth and return conflicted sharply with that of Gide. See Tamara Levitz's chapter, "The Promise of Irreconcilable Difference" in *Modernist Mysteries: Perséphone* (New York: Oxford University Press, 2012).

38. Kerman, *Opera as Drama*, 201.

39. Ibid., 196.

40. McFadden, "A Note on the Libretto," 109–10; quotations from W. H. Auden, "The Ironic Hero: Some Reflections on Don Quixote," *Horizon* 20 (1949): 86–94.

41. *Living Thoughts*, 7; see chapter 2, note 35, for relevant passage from the November scenario.

42. Geoffrey Chew, "Pastoral and Neoclassicism: A Reinterpretation of Auden's and Stravinsky's *Rake's Progress*," *Cambridge Opera Journal* 5 (1993): 241; my table 3.2 is based on Chew's table 1, 244.

43. Auden, *Living Thoughts*, 10.

44. Ibid., 12.

45. Igor Stravinsky and Robert Craft, *Themes and Episodes* (New York: Alfred A. Knopf, 1966), 50.

46. Auden and Kallman, *Libretti*, 627.

47. Chew summarizes Auden's four categories of Hero: Epic (*Gilgamesh, Odysseus*); Tragic (*Oedipus, Flying Dutchman, Othello*); Comic (*Figaro, Papageno*); and Ironic (*Don Quixote, The Idiot, Alice*) in Chew, "Pastoral and Neoclassicism," 246.

48. Auden, "The Ironic Hero," 90–91.

49. Ibid., 89.

50. Ibid., 87.

51. Kerman, *Opera as Drama*, 191.

52. Auden, "The Ironic Hero," 92.

PART 3

THE MUSIC

Don Giovanni reflected in a Coney Island mirror.
—Balanchine's description of the music as relayed by Auden[1]

INTRODUCTION TO PART 3

"Tonality is not a language which the music breathes," Paul Griffiths concludes his informative handbook on the opera, "but rather a means of creating directional pulls which it may go along with, resist or change without warning. And it is the same here as it is in the use of operatic references, that the work returns to past conventions not to inhabit them but to use them in ways of its own. . . . *The Rake's Progress* is an opera created within the ruins of a finished tradition."[2]

That insight nicely sets up the premise of my book's title but requires elaboration. Exactly how is the experience of Stravinsky's formal clichés fundamentally different from that of Mozart's? His arias, classical textures, secco recitatives, and even his simple songs, many of which reference specific works while others are just generically familiar, differ from the originals. But the distinction is not solely musical; it also depends on the listener's disposition. The ontological condition of this (and all) music extends beyond hermetic structure through performers to the audience. The nature of that connection is what distinguishes Mozart from Stravinsky, not just the "music itself."

To Bourdieu, strictly internal readings serve to fetishize the aesthetic experience—the literary and aural equivalents of the "pure gaze" that nineteenth-century critics cultivated to imbue objects with an aura of "high art"—that in turn functions to inscribe class identity. In *Distinction* (1979), his analysis of French culture of the 1960s, Bourdieu argues that aesthetic disposition—that is, taste—"unites and separates. Being the product of the conditionings associated with a particular class of conditions of existence, it unites all those who are the product of similar conditions while distinguishing them from all others."[3] How ironic that this statement echoes the elitist Ortega y Gasset, who lionized modernists like Stravinsky as cultural saviors, whereas Bourdieu rejects outright any essential value ascribed to "great artists" and "masterworks."

What do these observations imply for the music analyst? I agree that internal readings actively construct rather than passively describe aesthetic value, but that value does more than imbue social status. A 2010 Belgian study confirms Bourdieu's observation that musical taste correlates to education level, but the authors report finding no "effect of income on music consumption—neither on concert attendance nor on listening at home—contrary to Bourdieu's findings on arts consumption in France in the '60s."[4] Patrons of the arts still display themselves at season premieres and pose for photographers at fund-raisers. However, sociological evidence no longer confirms a correlation between the consumption of high culture and economic or political power, if it ever did. (Economic and political power expresses itself culturally—at least in the United States—far more conspicuously in luxury boxes of a sporting arena than in the loges of an opera house.) Cultural practice in late modern France may have supported Bourdieu's conclusions, but it seems less applicable to the United States and postmodern culture in general. Even when taste strongly correlates to education level, I question whether signaling social status—and, by implication, power—is its ultimate purpose.

Judging from his postscript to *The Rules of Art*, published in 1992, Bourdieu's attitude at least to the autonomy of the artist-intellectual seems to have evolved. Even as he deconstructs the "free artist" as a disposition, he also recognizes the role free-thinking intellectuals (despite their inextricable ties to habitus) play in opposing what Auden might call the "twin tyrants" of corporate and state control.[5] In midcentury Europe these oppressors bore down in the form of consumerism and totalitarianism; in *The Rake* they are "Appetite" and "Conscience." All threaten to snuff out freedom of thought and action. Inescapable, they define the modern condition.

In reaction, postmodern culture addresses a fundamentally different human subject, decentered and devalued (like the creators that produce that culture). What is the symbolic value of highbrow art if it no longer provides entrée into elite society, political influence, or access to important people and a lucrative career? The metaphysical questions of philosophy and psychology may better address this elusive question than a sociological study.

Cultural acts, which include not just the creation but also the performance and appreciation of art, do not simply confirm a subject's class or social status; they fundamentally define the human subject. Economic and social class, religious, ethnic, and even national identities may align to create the impression of stable, even rigid, identities. Yet postmodern culture seems to have loosened the restraints that bind individuals to identity. A subject who wishes to project independence, that is, to be "different," will break, often consciously, against cultural type. Bourdieu is reluctant to acknowledge these mismatches, ascribing the educated elite's indulgence in low culture as self-ironic "slumming." Conversely, a common worker who takes an interest in opera must be pretentious. Cannot both be sincere?

At a time when identity seems increasingly rootless, Bourdieu's insights still help clarify the basic, identity-forming function of culture. Certain groups (say, opera queens) or institutions (say, the Junior League) continue to fetishize or co-opt culture to attain status. However, human subjects create, attend, observe, and listen not just to attach themselves to a group. We imagine cultural acts as asserting, first and foremost, our individual existence, illusory though it may be. In a state of despair—the true existential state—we express ourselves all the more vehemently, arbitrarily if need be, simply to show we can. This condition drove modernists like Auden and Stravinsky. They even made it the central message of their opera.

On Analysis

Having in part 1 explored the broad but subtly interconnected world of late modernism, I risk getting lost in the forest of internal readings by now focusing on Stravinsky's music. Keeping in mind the sociological factors underlying all cultural acts—namely, creative, performative, and attentive—I offer two justifications. First, formal analysis establishes a relatively stable object to which listeners can affix their intentions; otherwise meaningful discourse is impossible. Where and how the analyst fixes that point is, of course, subject to debate and evolves over time, but a persuasive analysis at least anchors the work. (Pedantic analysis, by contrast, ossifies—even Schoenberg understood Leibowitz's rigidity did not serve his music.) Imaginative and informed analysis entails subjective interpretation. The analyst in turn helps mediate between the composer, the work, and other listener-performers and is attuned to all three.

Second, analysis exposes important potential relationships to which, consciously or not, listeners of varying experience and inclination respond in a variety of ways. Understanding its structure cannot explain everything about an opera, but it can reveal what the composer may have intended and how a listener may react. It also exposes a level of craftsmanship that, besides disclosing accomplished practices, establishes the work's symbolic capital. Keeping these principles in mind, I turn now to musical structure.

4

STRAVINSKY'S "SPECIAL SENSE"

> "Let us return to old times,
> and that will be progress."
> —Stravinsky quoting Verdi, *Poetics of Music*

CONVENTIONAL TONALITY PERMEATES THE CHARMING TEXTURES AND stylistic references of Stravinsky's neoclassic works like a familiar scent. It greets the listener in the form of diatonic melodies and scales, tertian harmonies, and surface progressions and even exerts a subtle pull in passages laden with chromatic harmonies and abstruse voice leading. As compositional craft, such conventions ground the work in centuries-old practice, similar to linear perspective and shading for the visual artist; as an artistic disposition, it engages a ready-made audience. These benefits, though, pose a challenge for the modernist. What conservative operagoers find "very easy to listen to" (as Stravinsky assured his publisher) the young avant-garde might call "ugliness."[6] Neoclassicism facilitated Stravinsky's transition into the European musical scene after the Russian Revolution cut him off from his homeland. But it demanded new musical models and a subtler handling of his material. In this chapter I assess the various ways tonal conventions function within the broader scope of Stravinsky's posttonal language.

Tonality as Rhetorical Gesture

Neither reactionary nor nostalgic, Stravinsky's handling of tonal conventions reflects his "special sense of the 'past,'" as distinguished from Schoenberg's "no less special sense of 'immediate tradition.'" Donald Mitchell claims Stravinsky's "music was 'about' the past, not an attempt to revive it or extend it or transform it; nor to touch up a pre-existent style with classical 'features.' The past, in fact for Stravinsky, enjoys the status as an 'object.'"[7] Stravinsky invokes and shapes tonality to simulate an anachronistic world of fanfares and arias, classical textures and florid melismas.

Alan Lessem suggests Stravinsky's overt use of historical forms reflects "an esthetic posture less characteristic of European Neo-Classicists than of the Russian Formalists."[8] For Hindemith or Bartok, whose music tends to blur the tonal and posttonal, movements stand as more or less organic wholes. By contrast, Stravinsky's music bristles rhetorically; one hears the broken phrase, the discords, the displaced voice leading or rhythm as broken, distorted, and displaced. Using and misusing tonal conventions in varying degrees, his numbers suggest heads, torsos, and limbs from different bodies imposed onto single figures.

Such stylistic incongruities, however, represent a challenge for music analysts, who tend to search for (and usually discover) unity and coherence. When a conventional gesture—for example, a sequential progression, a symmetrical phrase—sounds in a modernist context, contradictory forces interact. For these gestures to stand out, Stravinsky must conserve certain salient features. An experienced listener indeed may perceive such music as a distinct "object," as Mitchell suggests, but maintaining that delicate status poses an aesthetic challenge, to which I will return in chapter 6.

In Stravinsky's rhetorical use of tonality, Glenn Watkins discerns a more radical "instinct to recompose," which he ties to modernism's broader attraction to collage. His view, in turn, suggests a more pluralistic approach to analysis. "Rather than promoting a disorienting, incoherent jumble of contradictions," Watkins writes, "collage has exhibited a vigorous capacity to enlighten through juxtaposition, to forego resolution, to sponsor pluralistic conclusions, and to promote understanding of an order that eludes all edicts."[9]

With such an approach in mind, I consider four relatively short numbers: Anne's Lullaby, the Graveyard prelude, Anne's B-minor aria, and Anne and Father Trulove's Duettino. Responding to their diverse and often contradictory musical surfaces, I view each piece from multiple perspectives. By analyzing tonal and posttonal voice leading, complex harmonies, and chromatic motives, I expose seemingly irreconcilable differences that potentially mediate between the divergent styles. This pluralistic approach allows for the stylistic conflict and interplay that distinguishes Stravinsky's music without reducing it to an ancillary or exceptional status.

Tonal and Nontonal Conventions

THE TONAL LULLABY

What does it mean to label music tonal? To the extent that Stravinsky conserves tonal conventions, I apply the term conservatively, referring to the functional tension and release implied by chords or tones directed toward a tonal goal. Although every number of *The Rake's Progress* adheres to a tonic of some sort, few passages closely conform to tonal conventions. The label "tonal" therefore describes a range of musical events, as grounded as a prolonged tonic and linear descent to $\hat{1}$ or as superficial as an ostinato or fleeting cadence.

a. *The Rake's Progress*, Anne's lullaby (3.3)

b. Verdi, *Otello*, act 4, "Willow Song"

c. Rimsky-Korsakov, *Sadko*, scene 7, Volkhova's lullaby

Example 4.1. Possible models for Anne's lullaby.

Anne's consoling Lullaby from act 3, scene 3, is the opera's most conventionally tonal number. Accompanied by only two flutes, she sings her idyllic song three times unaltered, each followed by increasingly anxious choral responses from the inhabitants of Bedlam. The musical structure entails a motion from I to V in A♭ major, with subsidiary motion to III (C minor). Aside from a few "wrong notes" (discussed below), the counterpoint is mostly consonant and the harmonies typical of a romanticized folk melody.

As example 4.1 shows, Auden's threefold repetitions of "Glide," "Falls," and "Sways" (a) suggest a possible model in Desdemona's "Willow Song" from *Otello* (b). Indeed, Stravinsky seems to borrow Verdi's haunting falling thirds, though he may also have had in mind his teacher Rimsky-Korsakov's equally memorable refrain *"Bayu bai"* ("bye bye") in Volkhova's Lullaby from *Sadko* (c).[10] Both in style—sentimentally romantic rather than Mozartian classic—and conservativeness, the Lullaby stands out within the Bedlam scene and the opera in general.

THE NONTONAL GRAVEYARD PRELUDE

Conversely, nontonal means the functional relationships of tonal music play little or no part. In *The Rake*, only the prelude to the Graveyard scene (3.2) seems devoid of any tonal relations. Dated "11 December 1947"—less than a month after Stravinsky and Auden worked out the scenario and weeks before the librettists would deliver a word of the libretto—the summary sketch is the first music Stravinsky composed for the opera. (Example 4.7a–c represents a diplomatic transcription of sketches scattered across two 28.5 cm × 45 cm sheets; a facsimile of the first page is reproduced in figure 7.1.) Although his eagerness underscores the importance of the scene—in the scenario, the Graveyard opens the two-scene final act—this passage nonetheless stands alone in its general avoidance of stylistic allusions. Economically scored for string quartet, the quiet, dark prelude projects no overt clichés or tonal references until an F-major chord emerges from the unrelenting chromaticism in the final measure. Its tonal and stylistic austerity aptly evokes the frightening and alienated world to which Nick Shadow has led Tom. Indeed, the graveyard is the end of Tom's progress and, therefore, an extreme point in the opera, both dramatically and musically.

As with any nontonal work, context determines if and what specific pitches, chords, or intervals govern the choice of harmony. Example 4.2 highlights several dyads and chords (see Explanation of Terminology given in the example) that Stravinsky emphasizes through repetition. Noteworthy is the consistency with which he builds and maintains harmonic density. Beginning with a solo cello, he gradually thickens the texture, first as double stops and then by introducing the viola in measures (mm.) 2–8. Once he establishes a three-note texture in m. 4, Stravinsky rarely returns to dyads, even when only two instruments are playing. With the entrance of the two violins in m. 9, the harmonic density increases to five pitches (with no doublings), where it remains until m. 13. There the texture "lightens" to four notes (with some pentachords and an occasional trichord) until the last measure, where it quickly and unexpectedly thins to a single dyad (F/A). The resolution to F major is almost as striking for its sparseness as for its anomalous tonal reference.

This gradual increase in harmonic density provides a growing sense of Stravinsky's harmonic language. Interval classes (ic's) 3, 5, and 1 in mm. 1–3 grow into set classes 014, 015, 016, and 027 (among other singly occurring trichords) in mm. 4–8. These trichords contribute to the general consistency of the four- and five-note texture after R159—x, y, and z identify most frequently used trichords, 014, 015, and 016—especially in the recurring tetrachords in mm. 15–17. For example, (C–D♭–E–F) 0145 sounds three separate times and contains two 014's (F–F–D♭ and C–D♭–E) and two 015's (F–E–C and C–D♭–F).

Understanding a composer's harmonic vocabulary is important, but focusing solely on chord structure fails to consider harmonic movement and voice leading. When Stravinsky "progresses" from one version of a chord to another, the transformation can help us conceptualize voice leading, as example 4.3 demonstrates. The D♭/G/G♭ in m. 6 forms an 016 trichord. The same D♭/G forms another 016 in m. 7, this time with D. Mediated by the consistent intervals, G♭ can therefore be heard as "leading" to D over the sustained D♭/G. Any two pitches suffice to define a given operation; my choice reflects what I regard as the most salient change. In mm. 6–7, the cello's motion from G♭ leads to D under the sustained D♭/G and most clearly expresses the transformation of 016.

A more significant transformation occurs between the emphasized 01469s in m. 9, except for the final F major, the longest-sounding chord of the prelude, and

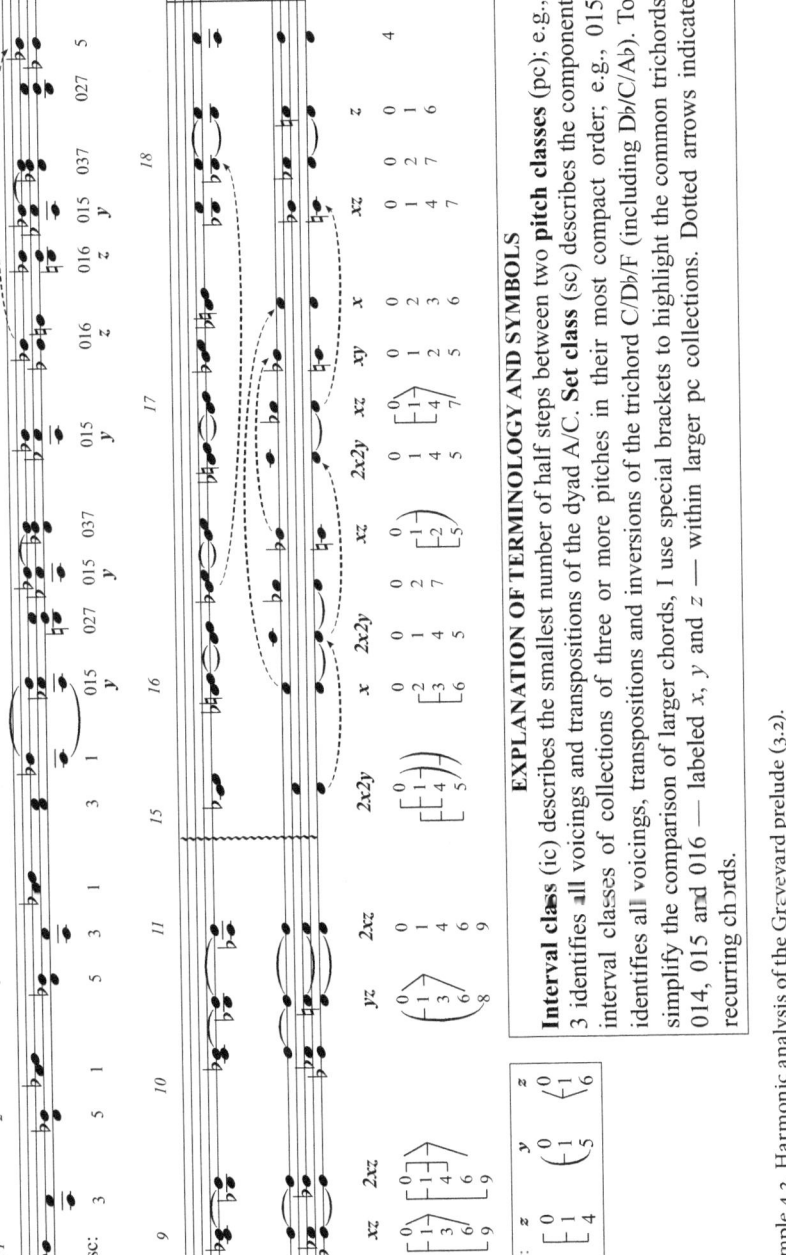

Example 4.2. Harmonic analysis of the Graveyard prelude (3.2).

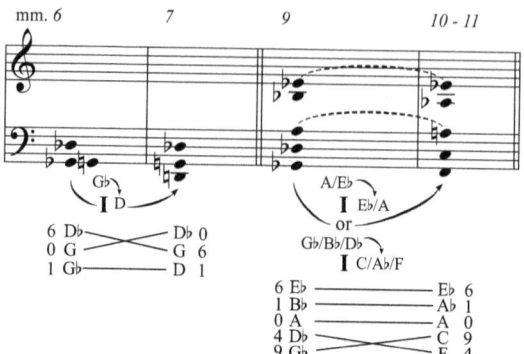

Example 4.3. Chord transformations in the Graveyard prelude.

m. 10 (E♭–B♭–A–D♭–G♭) and the 01469s in m. 11 (E♭–A–A♭–C–F). The inversion may be heard in two ways: (1) as preserving the A/E♭ dyad (the key-defining tritone in B♭ minor?); or (2) as leading G♭–B♭–D♭ (G♭ major?) to C–A♭–F (F minor?). I show both in example 4.3.

Other forms of nontonal voice leading permeate the prelude. The B–A–C–H motive in m. 3 (B♭–A–C–B) may allude to eighteenth-century music but is not conventionally tonal. Stravinsky seamlessly interweaves this chromatic cambiata figure into the prelude's "crab-like movement" and "sluggish, dark, slipping harmony."[11] B–A–C–H is but one of nine instances where Stravinsky chromatically fills in a minor third, but only twice does he do so in consecutive semitones (in the violin II and viola in m. 12). The other times he chooses one of three distinct motivic shapes, <+1,–3,+1>, <+1,+2,–1> or <+2,–3,+2>, as shown in example 4.4.

Common to all of these shapes is the single three-note motive (+1,–2) and its possible transformations: <+1,–2>, <–1,+2>, <+2,–1>, and <–2,+1>.[12] Like the original B–A–C–H, the chromatic (+1,–2) can function tonally under special circumstances, such as modulation or mode mixture. Otherwise its numerous occurrences in the prelude undermine any sense of a tonal goal. Stravinsky introduces the motive in both tonal and posttonal contexts throughout the opera, often at dramatically pivotal moments. In fact, (+1,–2) is often the fulcrum around which both the music and drama pivot.

Example 4.4. Motivic analysis of the Graveyard prelude.

Posttonal Anomalies

Certain anomalous features in Anne's Lullaby and the Graveyard prelude elude these single-perspective analyses. Recurring harmonies and motivic structure cannot explain the prelude's unambiguous conclusion on F major. Isolated voices in the conventional Lullaby, reproduced in example 4.5, refuse to lead conventionally. The flute II's dissonant D♭'s in mm. 2 and 3, the bass of V$^{4/2}$, instead of descending to C as part of an expected I^6, ascend to E♭ and D♮. Rhythmic displacement also subtly undermines harmonic clarity. The chords in m. 5 seem to progress from C^6 (beats 1–2) to B♭$^{6/5}$ (beat 3) to E♭ (beat 4), but the bass D

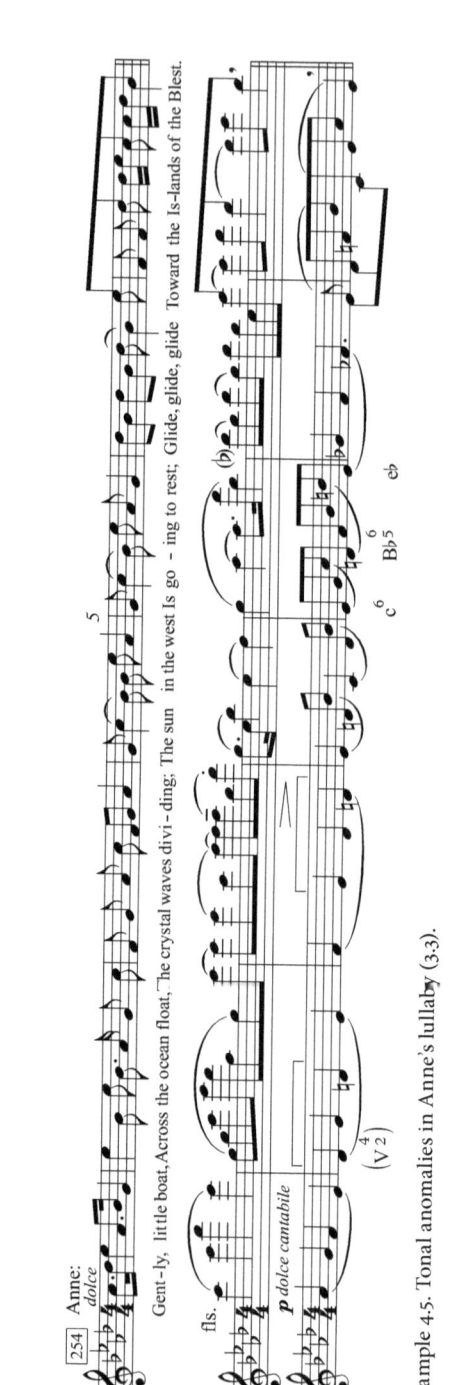

Example 4.5. Tonal anomalies in Anne's lullaby (3.3).

Example 4.6. Three stages (a–c) of sketches for Anne's lullaby, m. 7.

appears one eighth too soon, creating a syncopated harmonic rhythm.[13] A similarly early entrance of the C in m. 7 results in a brief clash with the D♭'s in the voice and flute I. These displacements seem to serve a larger purpose though, for all three voices, beginning on the last eighth of m. 6, follow the same basic voice leading: E♭–D♭–C (the flute I D♭—part of an augmentation of the singer's escape tone figure—skips over its expected C to B♭). By anticipating the resolution to C in flute II and skipping over C altogether in flute I, Stravinsky misaligns the three voices and thereby disguises the heterophony. (Though not directly related to harmonic syntax, Stravinsky's setting of the text here involves similar rhythmic displacement, which I discuss at length in chapter 5.)

Stravinsky's sketches for m. 7, reproduced in example 4.6, reveal this process of displacement as it unfolded in the early stages of composition. (The displaced progressions in mm. 4–5 and 7 are in fact the only measures he bothered to revise.) His first attempt (a) shows a simple doubling of the D♭–C discussed above. The flute I replicates the soprano voice, without the escape tones, while the lowest voice ascends to C. Below (and presumably sketched after) his second—and ultimate—version (b), Stravinsky toys with skipping over the flute's D♭ (c).

These subtle displacements are typical of Stravinsky's compositional process for *The Rake*. Joseph Straus observes: "The initial sketches tend to be rhythmically square and harmonically rudimentary. They often have the appearance of a simple, classical prototype. As musical ideas are brought to a more final state, the sketches often become increasingly free rhythmically and increasingly remote from classical tonal norms harmonically. A significant aspect of Stravinsky's compositional process . . . involves the explicit transformation of relatively traditional tonal prototypes. . . . The 'classical' often comes first chronologically, and the 'neo' emerges as the compositional process unfolds."[14]

The absence of the leading tone at the cadence (notice its inclusion in example 4.6a), the peculiar path of D♭ to C, and the rhythmic and harmonic ambiguity in mm. 5 and 7 all subtly undermine the conventionality of the Lullaby. While the pastoral text and simple scoring conform to that idyllic prototype, these subtle anomalies imply that Anne's soothing verses may be as illusory as Tom's idealized vision of Venus.

How typical of Stravinsky that even—perhaps especially—in an obviously tonal piece, he refuses to cadence in a conventional fashion, and how ironic the contrast with the intensely motivic graveyard prelude, the cadence of which is its only unambiguously tonal feature. In both cases, he subverts expectations. We can better gauge the play between tonal and nontonal impulses by investigating these anomalous features from different analytical perspectives.

THE TONAL GRAVEYARD PRELUDE

Meandering chromatically from tone to tone, the three-note motive (+1,−2) that pervades the prelude contrasts starkly with the directed voice leading associated with normative tonal practice. It encapsulates the final, as yet unsettled, stage of Tom's progress, where each step is tenuous and the goal unclear. Close listening, though, uncovers a voice-leading path even through these slippery tones. The graph in example 4.7 shows the initial B♭ leading through the double neighbor B–A–C–H to A in m. 4. The upper voice of the cello continues to snake its way down the chromatic scale to G♭ in m. 8, to the "leading tone" E in m. 12, and finally to "tonic" F in m. 18. The pull of tonality is not so much absent as elaborately disguised. For example, realigning the delayed C–F in mm. 1–3 (example 4.7a) transforms the dyads C/A and F/B♭ into a conventional V7-I in F (example 4.7b).

Stravinsky's first sketch for the prelude—indeed, for the entire opera—shown in example 4.8a, begins with a similarly circuitous descent to F♯ (the G♭ in m. 8). Its elemental voice leading presents itself from the start: B–A–C–H in m. 2 and interlocking (+1,−2)s in mm. 4–5 (A♭–G–A; G–F–F♯). In the subsequent stages (b and c) the thorough composer explores seemingly every possible chromatic variant of this initial span.

Furthermore, the voice leading E to F (in viola and cello) and B♭ to A (in violin II) that forms the resolution to F major in m. 18 recurs throughout the dense chords of mm. 10–17 (see example 4.2), though never in a concerted fashion. Are these various E–F's and B♭–A's part of the buried tonal motion? Do the cello's repeated leaps from C to F in mm. 1–7 anticipate the final cadence? That Stravinsky forms his harmonies from 014, 015, and 016 trichords does not necessarily negate the subtle pull of tonality beneath the murky surface. Although not explicit, the progression to F major at least alludes to functional harmony and voice leading. Example 4.7c offers an idea of what this background tonal movement might look like.

Heard as potentially tonal, those murky surface harmonies take on a new significance. Seven of the viola's nine D♭'s in mm. 2–8 sound against C in the cello, thus highlighting pitches important to the background tonal structure but in a manner consistent with the dissonant foreground. Returning to the sketches, notice how Stravinsky at each successive stage introduces more neighboring D♭–C–D♭'s. At first, the viola's solitary C♯/D♭ merits little notice (Stravinsky wrote the two measures to the immediate right of the first sketch in example 4.8a for insertion in a later stage, shown in example 4.8c). However, by the bottom of the first page (example 4.8b), more and more D♭'s begin to appear, almost every one carefully aligned against a cello C. Straus suggests this C–D♭ idea—made explicit in Anne's opening C–C♯ motive (see example 5.1)—will serve a structuring role in the opera, an idea I return to in chapter 7.[15] Similarly striking are the three 0145's in mm. 15–16. Just as he first coupled D♭/C, Stravinsky now repeatedly aligns E, F, D♭, and C—tones central to the underlying VII°7–I in F, but sounding together on the tonally murky surface. The melody and bass voices exchange E's and F's in mm. 16–17 not to prolong a single harmony, like a tonal voice exchange, but to extend the dissonance. Both voices actually share the same voice leading—structural E embellished by a neighboring F. Similar to his treatment of D♭–C in Anne's Lullaby (cf. example 4.5, m. 7), Stravinsky disguises the redundant voice leading by misaligning every return to E in one voice with a neighboring motion to F in the other. In so doing, he embeds the strongest tonal voices within his most rigorously motivic chords (as example 4.2 confirms). Like the displaced I–V7–I in mm. 1–3, Stravinsky is here fracturing and reassembling a normative tonal model.

For all the dense counterpoint preceding it, the voice leading of the cadence is rather mundane, with three voices resolving from E to F at different points and different structural levels (again, cf. the redundant D♭–C in example 4.5). The violin and cello are clearly misaligned, but the viola's cadence merits closer attention. That persistent D♭ from mm. 2–8 appears ready to resolve finally to C in m. 17, but Stravinsky instead diverts it up to E♭ and E, creating, with the preceding D, the familiar <−1,+2,+1>. Even as it reaches a tonal goal, the viola voice refuses to follow its expected tonal path, yet another awkward step as Tom nears the end of his progress.

THE MOTIVIC LULLABY

The viola's slippery D–D♭–E♭ is echoed in, of all places, Anne's Lullaby. Besides denying an expected resolution to C, the flute II in m. 2 (D♭–E♭–D) and m. 3 (E♭–D♭–D) also replicates the (+1,−2) motive that underpins much of the voice leading in the prelude. In fact, the flute in m. 3 plays a near retrograde of the viola's cadence (cf. example 4.5 and example 4.7, mm. 17–18).

The resistance of D♭ to resolve to C and the motive by which it is diverted (+1,−2) form a surprisingly strong connection between this "dark, sluggish"

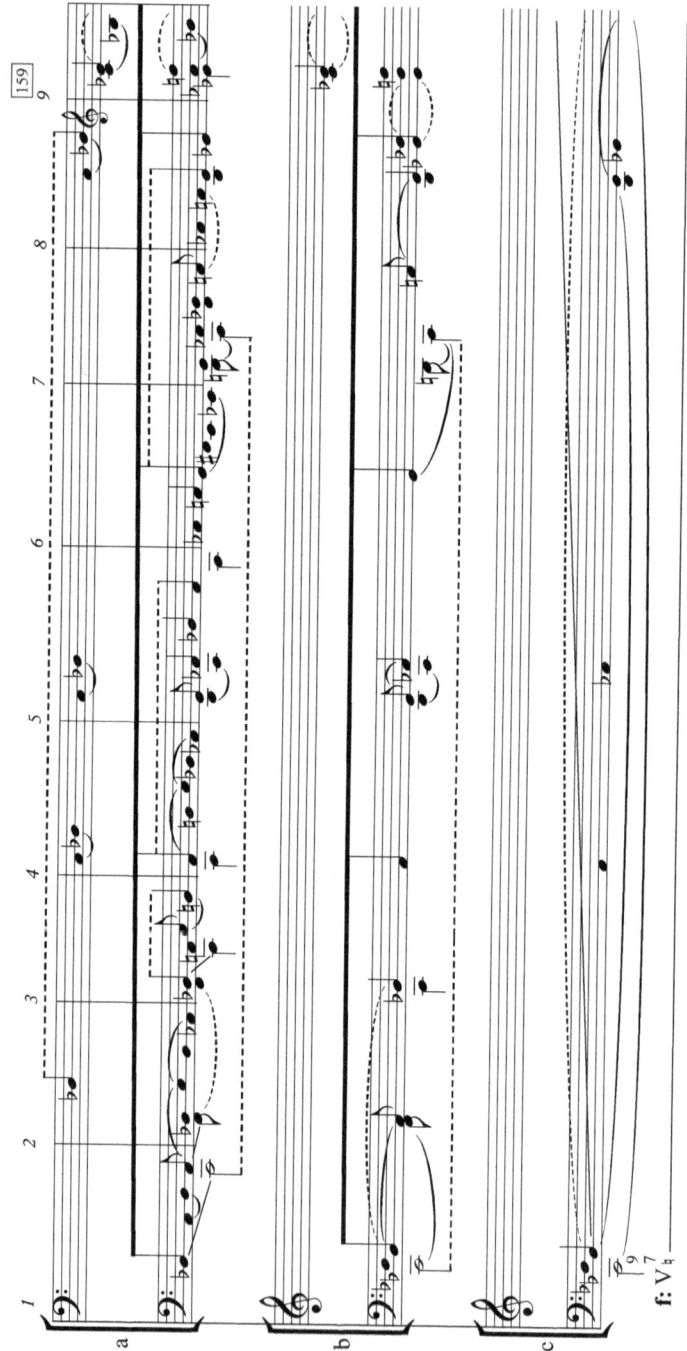

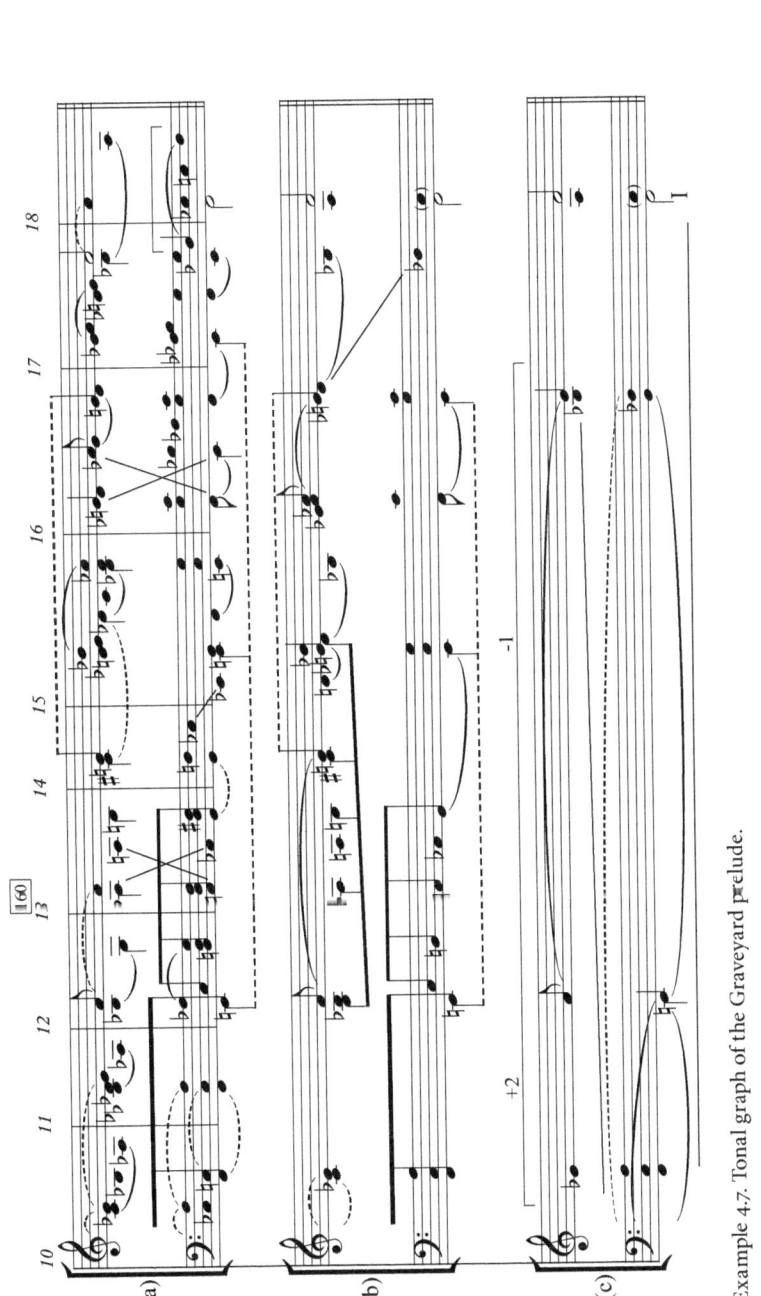

Example 4.7. Tonal graph of the Graveyard prelude.

Example 4.8a. Diplomatic transcription of sketches for Graveyard prelude, top of the first page (reproduced in fig. 7.1).

Example 4.8b. Diplomatic transcription of sketches for Graveyard prelude, bottom of the first page (no key signature).

Example 4.8c. Diplomatic transcription of sketches for Graveyard prelude, second page.

prelude and simple, innocent Lullaby. At first hearing, these passages sound a world apart, but their seemingly anomalous features turn out to be hidden links.

Posttonal Middle Ground—Anne's Aria

Most of *The Rake's Progress* and Stravinsky's neoclassical oeuvre in general display a more obviously diverse surface than the Lullaby and Graveyard prelude. Tonal and nontonal elements typically coexist side by side and even simultaneously at different structural levels. Griffiths observes that often "the key of a passage is not inherent in the music but exists instead as a background perspective, established by means of a pedal or an arpeggio ostinato, against which the more foreground features are placed, or rather displaced."[16] This phenomenon raises a particularly challenging theoretical issue, for a single musical event may be interpreted as nontonal at one structural level and tonal at another.

Consider the opening of Anne's B-minor aria near the end of act 1. Having heard nothing from Tom since he left for London the previous spring, the troubled Anne looks to the autumn moon for guidance and reassurance. Even as the opening phrase progresses conventionally from I to V7, a persistent E♯ ($\hat{4}$) agitates the string accompaniment. Anne anticipates this sonority in the wide-ranging final pitches of her recitative, B–D–E♯–F♯, shown in example 4.9a. By compressing her melody, Stravinsky forges a "home" sonority with potentially strong tonal and posttonal implications: both the "I+$^{\sharp 4}$" of example 4.9b and the 0147 of example 4.9c.

Anne's lyrical melody ultimately follows a conventional tonal descent (F♯ to B) with supporting bass. However, between her opening phrase and concluding cadence, the melody and harmony veer sharply from B minor. The ambiguous D^7 after R184 can be heard as an inversion of the "tonic" 0147 around E♯/F♯, shown in example 4.9c. The bass continues on to F♯ at R184+4, supporting motion to V. The vocal phrase, though, ends ambiguously on C♯ over an even more peculiar E^{o7} (R185). Embedded in this chord is yet another 0147—C/D♭/E/G—transposed so that the soprano's previous F leads to C. Only then does the melody return to F♯ and descend conventionally to B and the original I+$^{\sharp 4}$. By imposing E♯ onto his tonic harmony, Stravinsky paints more than an agitated surface; he establishes a posttonal middle ground that captures his character's deepest concerns.

Posttonal Background—Duettino

Having analyzed more or less stable tonal backgrounds, I now consider a number built on structural conflict: Anne and Trulove's bitonal Duettino from the Bedlam scene. Having bid farewell to the insane Tom, Anne and her father draw the lesson of his demise in a stoic G-major dirge, shown in example 4.10, level a, sounding over a repeating $\hat{5}$ to $\hat{1}$ in B♭, shown in level b. The juxtaposition of

Example 4.9. Tonal and posttonal structure of Anne's B-minor aria (1.3).

these specific keys is significant. Straus describes G as "the musical emblem of departure from the Garden," while B♭ has "come to symbolize [Tom's] apotheosis, his transformation into the mythic Adonis."[17] In Bedlam, B♭ and its related keys—E♭ major in Tom's Arioso (R239), A♭ major in Anne's Lullaby—signal his belief that he and "Venus" are reunited. The key of G, both minor (R243) and major (R261), serves to foil this illusion. (I explore the musical and dramatic conflict between illusion and reality in chapter 8, especially example 8.13 and fig. 8.4.)

The preceding recitative prepares the Duettino's tonal conflict. The third and final choral response to Anne's Lullaby (R258) progresses to B♭. Father Trulove interrupts at R260 to declare an end to the tale over V$^{6/5}$ of G. Such stark disjunctions are typical of Stravinsky's harmonic/melodic practice from his early Russian period. Separating the discrete sections into tonally unified strata (a and b) highlights both the continuity within and discontinuity between them.[18] Anne echoes her father's descending B to E (R260+2); but in turning to Tom, she slips into E♭ major, her upper voice E♭ recalling the opening structural tone of her preceding Lullaby. Stravinsky thus juxtaposes horizontally in the recitative the tonal regions he will superimpose vertically in the Duettino.

Separating strata, though, only addresses tonal conflict. Example 4.10c identifies posttonal features that either link or belong to neither of the two conflicting keys. For example, the continuous bass line of the recitative follows an octatonic scale from F♯ to D♭. This rare appearance in *The Rake* of what is otherwise a favored resource for Stravinsky points to a more fundamental connection with the 014 trichord, as it occurs twice within each four-note segment of the scale.[19] The familiar <+2,–1> motive in the bass—E♭♭–F♭–E♭—lends a tone of regret to Anne's last "goodbye."

Example 4.10c also shows how 014-related chords (indicated by vertical brackets) connect the juxtaposed strata of the Duettino: first at R261+2, when the bass F♮ sounding against F♯/A in the upper voices ascends to B♭ sounding against B♮/D (this succession recurs in the following measures). Another pair of 014's is embedded in chords after R263 leading to the return of the "tonic" B♭/B/D. This same progression underscores the singers' final cadence and leads to the return of the introductory material at R265. By emphasizing the bass A♭ (as opposed to A♮), Stravinsky anticipates the ultimate resolution down to G.

If the B♭ bass dramatizes Anne's lingering attachment to Tom, its conclusive resolution to G confirms her decision to leave. The final cadence, though, is not as obviously tonal as it first appears. The foreground voice leading depends less on harmonic function (the middle ground VII^{o7} to I) than on the coincidence of G, B, and G via separate (+1,–2) motives. In fact, comparing example 4.10c and example 4.3 reveals a strong resemblance between the Duettino's bass and the Graveyard prelude, both in its serpentine journey and its unambiguous conclusion. Recurring twelve times in the bass alone, (+1,–2) comes to dominate the foreground of the Duettino from R263 to the end in yet another instance where tonal and nontonal impulses operate at separate structural levels. The multivalent perspective of example 4.10 shows the conflicting tonal strata receding (levels a and b) as more intensely chromatic voice leading emerges into the foreground (level c).

In three of the passages I analyzed in this chapter, conventional tonality signals a dramatic illusion that posttonal dissonance serves to dispel. Rhythmic displacement and the (+1,–2) motive subtly betray the innocent vison of Anne's Lullaby; the dissonant morass of the Graveyard prelude foreshadows Tom's frightening encounter with the "real" Nick Shadow; and finally, creeping (+1,–2)'s choke off the tonal world of Tom's illusion in the Duettino. As we will see, the (+1,–2) motive and chromaticism in general similarly underscore deeper truths throughout the opera.

Having introduced Stravinsky's rhetorical treatment of tonality, I turn now to his manipulation of text, where he just as rigorously applies the now familiar technique of rhythmic displacement.

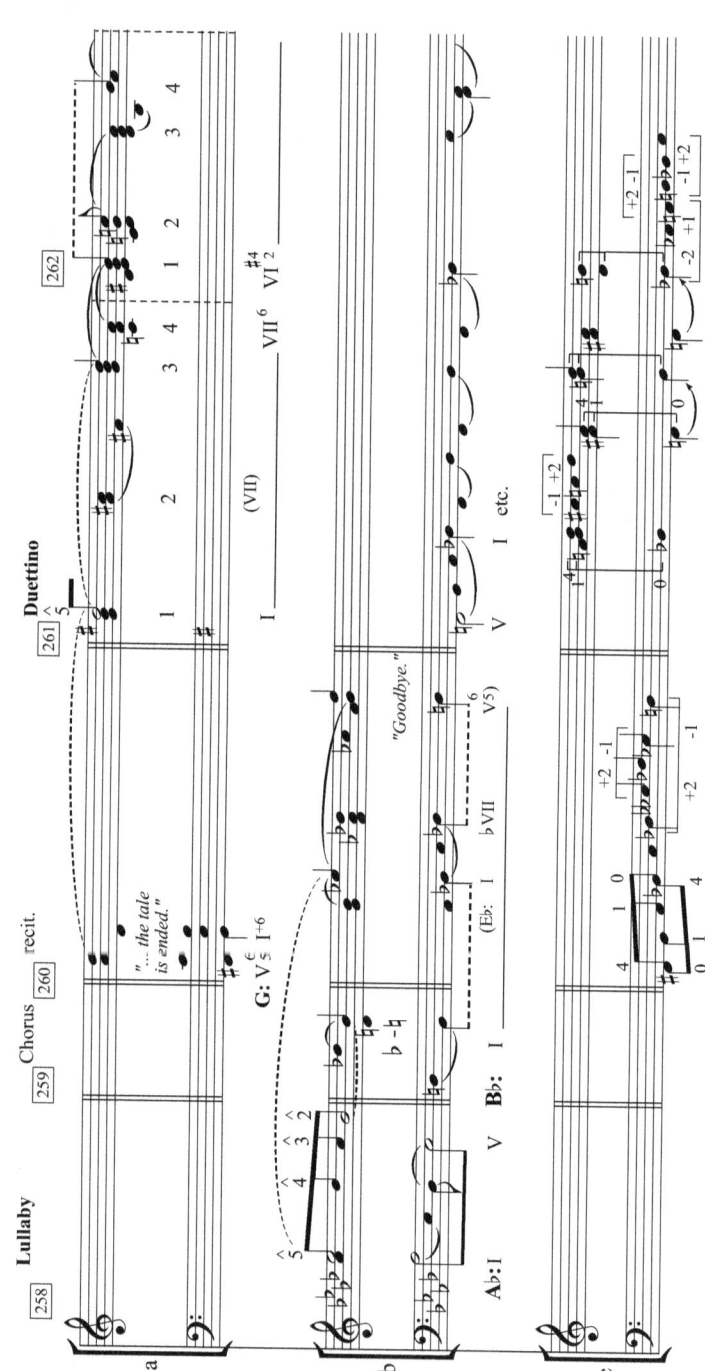

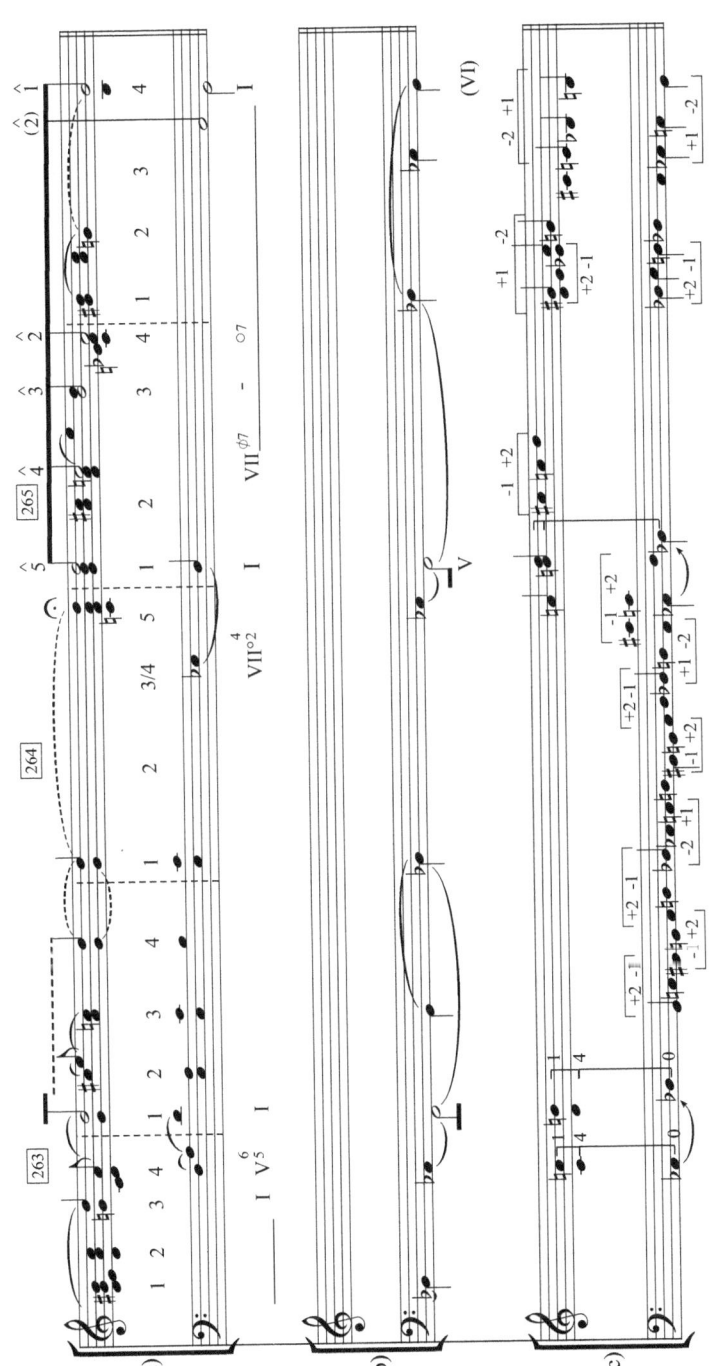

Example 4.10. Background structural conflict in act 3, scene 3.

Notes

1. Courtesy W. H. Auden Estate and the Henry W. and Albert A. Berg Collection of English and American Literature, The New York Public Library, Astor, Lenox and Tilden Foundations.
2. Paul Griffiths, *Igor Stravinsky: The Rake's Progress* (New York: Cambridge University Press, 1982), 100.
3. Pierre Bourdieu, *Distinction: A Social Critique of the Judgment of Taste*, trans. Richard Nice (Cambridge, MA: Harvard University Press, 1984), 56.
4. Henk Roose and Alexander Vander Stichele, "Living Room vs. Concert Hall: Patterns of Music Consumption in Flanders," *Social Forces* 89, no. 1 (2010): 199.
5. Pierre Bourdieu, *The Rules of Art: Genesis and Structure of the Literary Field*, trans. Susan Emanuel (Stanford, CA: Stanford University Press, 1995), 344–45.
6. Vera Stravinsky and Robert Craft, *Stravinsky in Pictures and Documents* (New York: Simon and Schuster, 1978), 401; see also prelude, note 39.
7. Donald Mitchell, *The Language of Modern Music* (London: Faber and Faber, 1963), 105–6. For a broader discussion of the analytical implications of such stylistic varied music, see my "Stravinsky's 'Special Sense': The Rhetorical Use of Tonality in *The Rake's Progress*," *Music Theory Spectrum* 19, no. 1 (1997): 55–80.
8. Alan Lessem, "Schoenberg, Stravinsky and Neo-Classicism," *Musical Quarterly* 68 (1982): 534–35.
9. Glenn Watkins, *Pyramids at the Louvre: Music, Culture and Collage from Stravinsky to the Postmodernists* (Cambridge, MA: Harvard University Press, 1994), 2.
10. I thank Natalia Braginskaya for pointing out the connection to *Sadko*.
11. Griffiths, *The Rake's Progress*, 77; see also Mary Hunter, "Igor and Tom: History and Destiny in *The Rake's Progress*," *Opera Quarterly* 7, no. 4 (1990/91): 38–39. Contrapunctus XIX from Bach's *Art of the Fugue* is the source of this often used motive.
12. The unordered notation (+1,−2) refers collectively to all four versions.
13. Lynne Rogers observes a similar procedure, which she calls *phrase staggering*, in her analysis of Stravinsky's *Violin Concerto* in "Stravinsky's Alternate Approach to Counterpoint," PhD diss., Princeton University, 1989.
14. Joseph N. Straus, "The Progress of a Motive in Stravinsky's *The Rake's Progress*," *Journal of Musicology* 9, no. 2 (1991): 165–66; see also Volker Scherliess, "Inspiration und fabrication: Beobachten zu Igor Strawinsky's Arbeit an 'The Rake's Progress,'" in *Quellen Studien II: Zwölf Komponisten des 20. Jahrhunderts*, ed. Felix Meyer (Winterthur: Amadeus Verlag, 1993).
15. Straus, "The Progress of a Motive," 172.
16. Griffiths, *The Rake's Progress*, 99.
17. Straus, "Progress of a Motive," 179, 182. Griffiths initially associates G major with Tom himself and B♭ major with "his longings" (*Rake's Progress*, 34, 37). See table 7.1 for my summary of the dramatic significance of keys throughout the opera.
18. I model this technique after Edward Cone's analyses of stratification in "Stravinsky: The Progress of a Method," *Perspectives of New Music* 1, no. 1 (1962): 18–26.
19. Pieter C. Van den Toorn cites only one instance of the octatonic collection in the opera: act 2, scene 3; R189–93 in *The Music of Igor Stravinsky* (New Haven, CT: Yale University Press, 1983), 45–46.

5

DISPLACEMENT, TEXT SETTING, AND STRAVINSKY'S EVOLVING AESTHETIC

Reaching out to the greatest living composers and programming their music was an audacious strategy for the ambitious young conductor from Kingston, New York. Erudite to a fault, the spectacled Juilliard graduate cofounded and managed the "bogus" (his own description) Chamber Art Society to showcase himself and his musical interests, which leaned decidedly toward early Baroque and modernist—that is, the repertory least represented on more established (and popular) concert programs. From 1947 to 1950, Robert Craft and his partners mustered enough funds and interest to present twelve concerts in respectable New York venues, including Carnegie Hall. What he lacked in experience and financial backing he made up for in sheer chutzpah and good timing. When in August 1947 he wrote the composer about procuring the score and parts for the neglected *Symphonies of Wind Instruments* (1921), Stravinsky, dissatisfied with his existing version (which was unavailable anyway), was already contemplating a revision. Later that year he even volunteered to conduct for free the *Symphonies* and *Danses Concertantes* to help, as he explained to his irritated publisher, "that young and gifted Robert Craft and by the way to hear myself how it sounds."[1]

The immediate upshot of this surprising support was that the starstruck musician would get to meet his idol and Madame Stravinsky at the Hotel Raleigh in Washington, DC, in March 1948. The couple immediately took to Craft, who remained that week to accompany the composer to rehearsals at the National Symphony, concerts, parties, and a press interview. That was only the beginning. They then settled in New York City for another four weeks, "the most exciting in my life," Craft described to a friend: "I was with Stravinsky every day, early morning to late night, at rehearsals for *Orpheus* as well as for our concert. I absorbed his talk with Balanchine, Kirstein and others; accompanied him to the theater and to parties, went with him and Nicholas and Patricia Nabokov to a debate . . . , ate multiple-decker sandwiches with the composer at Reuben's, but, chiefly, basked in the man himself, whose energy, alertness, and vivacity left everyone else behind."[2]

Craft seems to have stepped instantly into the role he would serve for the rest of the Stravinskys' lives. They invited him to visit Hollywood that summer. He would return in 1949 and eventually relocate permanently. As years turned into decades, he evolved from librarian, reader, gofer, and secretary into musical consultant, travel companion, assistant conductor, ghost writer, and spokesman; musical mentor, interpreter, writer/confessor, and, especially to Vera, surrogate child. By the end, he was Stravinsky's gatekeeper and her executor and heir.[3]

Craft remained committed to the Chamber Art Society for another two years before moving to Los Angeles. The young conductor had made the most of his series—too much, in that his programs were "too long and almost impossibly difficult to prepare."[4] However, by presenting major works like the *Symphony in C*, *Les Noces*, *Pulcinella*, and *Perséphone*, among other Stravinsky pieces; Schoenberg's *Pierrot lunaire*, *Suite* op. 29, and *Serenade*; plus works by Webern, Berg, and Bartók; the conductor, still in his mid-twenties, had built a serious reputation, if not before the larger public, at least among the most important composers in America. He would build on that experience: first through the "Evenings on the Roof" concert series in Los Angeles and later as guest conductor for international orchestras and opera houses. His most lasting legacy would be his series of comprehensive, critically admired recordings of Stravinsky, Schoenberg, Webern, and Varèse. That most readers know the name Robert Craft not for these prodigious accomplishments but as the amanuensis to a great artist is the price of his own Faustian bargain. He almost certainly could not have achieved so much had he not tied his star to that of Igor Stravinsky.

Becoming Acquainted

Whatever other factors motivated him, we know well what pressing compositional concern drove Stravinsky to reach out to Craft that summer of 1948: he needed his assistance with questions about the English text of the opera. Upon arriving in Hollywood, "my first task was to sort manuscripts," Craft recalls. "I was also to do various jobs connected with *The Rake's Progress*. The most important of these required, quite simply, that I pronounce and repeat the lines of the libretto."[5]

Stravinsky had begun to work in earnest on the opera in May. When Craft visited in early August, the composer asked him to "read aloud, over and over and at varying speeds, the lines of whichever aria, recitative, or ensemble he was about to set to music."[6] The following detailed recollection is particularly revealing: "Stravinsky began these numbers in accordance with a strict procedure, first adding scansion marks (as well as, occasionally, the musical meter), then memorizing the lines while pacing up and down repeating them aloud. Finally he timed each number according to a tempo that he had decided would be most suitable for the words. The last is puzzling, for how could he know the duration of a passage of unwritten music? Yet the musical speed does appear to have been predetermined from these verbal recitations."[7]

These accounts describe a composer who not only absorbed but also based fundamental musical choices on the sound of the spoken words. This is not to say Stravinsky always adheres to so-called "natural" declamation. In an early commentary Craft explains: "Stravinsky is a 'music first' composer . . . which means that for him words must serve the musical use he finds for them, whether or not this use violates the common practice with regard to stresses, syllable groupings, metrics, etc." He nonetheless concludes, "*The Rake's Progress* is very much more full of natural than of shifted stresses, but what is amazing is the amount of invention Stravinsky's feeling for English rhythms and sounds brings forth."[8]

Auden, who best understood the intended function of the words, wrote for himself and Kallman:

> Though, as lovers of opera, we both knew that musical and spoken rhythmical values cannot be identical, we were afraid, particularly since Stravinsky had never set English before, that he might distort our words to the point of unintelligibility. But, from the moment we started working with him, we discovered that our fears were groundless. Going through our text, he asked for, and marked into his copy, the spoken rhythmical value of every word. In one instance, only one, did he make a mistake. He thought that in the word "sedan-chair," the accent fell on the first syllable of "sedan." When we pointed this out to him, he immediately altered his score. In one number in the opera, the Auctioneer's aria . . . , it is dramatically essential that the sung rhythms conform pretty closely to the spoken. They do. In the rest of the work, whatever occasional liberties he took, none of them struck our English and literary ears as impermissible.[9]

One might question the candor of Auden's tribute on the occasion of Stravinsky's death; of Craft's disingenuousness, there can be little doubt. Again, he would wait forty years to share what he really thought about the settings he helped facilitate: "It is nonsense to pretend . . . that there is method in I. S.'s stresses on prepositions and conjunctions, the truth being that his settings of them are hit and miss."[10]

Craft's private skepticism is neither surprising, considering his reservations about the libretto, nor unique. Reviewers of the British and American premieres agreed that English was "obviously an acquired language with him. Far too often the sensitive English ear winces at the proofs the composer is giving us of this."[11] Craft, though, was reacting specifically to Virgil Thomson, who, uniquely for the time, perceived a method in Stravinsky's sometimes maddening settings:

> When read on the musical page, with bar lines jumping to the eye, much of this musical declamation seems mannered, even clumsy, full of false accents, arbitrary as to word groupings, and often, as to vowel placements, vocally inept. Heard in the theater, it falls into place. The accents, which almost never hit bar lines, are right enough for clarity; and the vowel extensions are amazingly subtle as expressions of passion or of tenderness.
>
> . . . I have not, previous to *The Rake*, heard employed in any language such a high degree of verbal freedom against so rigidly measured an accompaniment. . . . Let it

be an example to us all . . . of the value of a rational method sensitively applied to the troubling problem that is English declamation today.[12]

Anne's opening line, "The woods are green," shown in example 5.1a, illustrates Thomson's point. Walsh accuses Stravinsky of twisting Auden's iambs into trochees by stressing the elongated "The" and auxiliary verb "are."[13] But Thomson rightly directs us away from the notated score to the more subtle aural affect. By displacing both "woods" and "green," Stravinsky effectively shifts our sense of the start of the phrase. (A sensitive singer may as easily phrase her melody in a flowing 6/8—suggested above example 5.1a—as in the awkward 2/4.) Example 5.1b–e shows four successive drafts of the setting in which the composer tries positioning Anne's entrance at different points in relation to the accompaniment. Note that in no draft did he alter the vocal rhythm or place "woods" on a downbeat, but he did reduce the metronome marking from 84 to 76 and remove the *Allegretto* (example 5.1c). (Throughout the opera, Stravinsky generally marks only tempo relationships—"*L'istesso tempo, piu mosso, molto meno,*" and so on—avoiding subjective or expressive terms like *Allegretto*.)

Only after completing the Duet did Stravinsky compose the instrumental introduction, at which point he considered anticipating Anne's entrance with vamping sixteenths (stages d and e). In the end he opted for a clean break, thus exposing for the first time the all-important C–C♯ motive and underscoring "woods" on beat two. The shifted stresses subtly deemphasize the 2/4 meter (similar to the way persistent C♯s in the bass deemphasize the tonic A major). These sketches show Stravinsky striving to make Anne's entrance eminently subtle, as Virgil Thomson suggests, not perversely awkward, as Walsh assumes.

Though perhaps Thomson's first exposure to such free settings, *The Rake's Progress* is hardly the first piece in which Stravinsky plays with verbal accents. According to Taruskin,

> Ignoring punctuation was nothing new to Stravinsky by the time he wrote *The Rake's Progress*. The Russian settings abound with examples, and so, of course, do Russian folk songs. . . . For Stravinsky . . . the accents of spoken language were merely there to be manipulated like any other musical parameter, for the sake of musical enjoyment. . . . Though it may discomfit us that he saw fit to set the poetry of Auden or of Gide as if it were a Russian limerick, that is what he did, and seriously. To fail to take this aspect of his art seriously is to fail at a very basic level to understand it.[14]

Taruskin's groundbreaking article validates Thomson's judgment and forms the foundation for a subtler understanding of Stravinsky's approach to text. However, his assertion that the later settings are equally rooted in Russian folk practice is misleading. The neoclassical works show a much more varied practice than the Russian settings. Rather than arbitrarily playing with words, Stravinsky could now embrace more varied conventions for setting them. His models would lead him toward a more expressive style, culminating in the heightened settings of *The Rake*. From the fragmented syllables of *Les Noces* (1917) and wild melismas

Example 5.1. Anne's entrance (1.1): final version (a) and four stages of drafts (b–e).

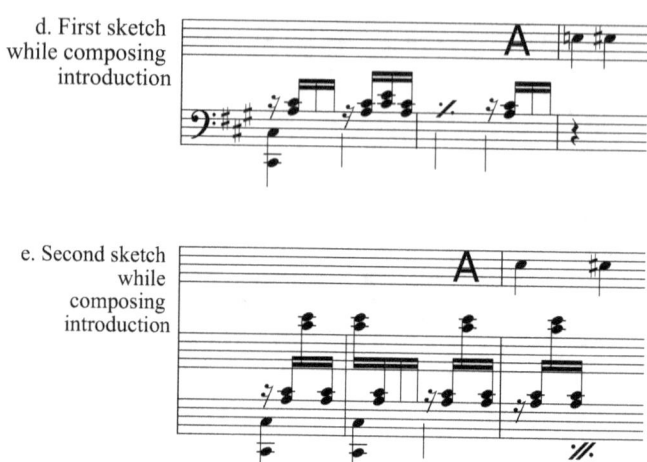

Example 5.1. (*Continued*)

of *Oedipus* (1927), the opera stands out not just for its general fidelity to the English words but also for its expressive range. Certain intimate moments reveal an expressivity to which the composer of the cartoonish *Histoire du Soldat* (1918) and masked *Oedipus* was supposedly averse. The farcical characters of *Renard* (1917) become in *The Rake* emotionally flexible; the nameless subjects of *Les Noces* acquire human dimension.

The Classical Attitude and the Expressive *Rake*

By his own admission, Stravinsky strove to make *Les Noces* (and arguably all his late Russian-period works) "perfectly homogenous, perfectly impersonal, and perfectly mechanical."[15] Those goals seemed to change when Diaghilev's commission for *Pulcinella* prompted him to turn from archaic Russia to classical Europe for his musical models. Predictably, many former admirers now condemned him as a sellout. However, Ortega y Gasset saw the turn to neoclassicism as a positive development in the modernist aesthetic:

> The imperative of unmitigated realism that dominated the artistic sensibility of the last century must be put down as a freak in aesthetic evolution. It thus appears that the new inspiration, extravagant though it seems, is merely returning . . . to the royal road in art. For this road is called "will to style." But to stylize means to deform reality, to derealize; style involves de-humanization. . . . Whereas realism, exhorting the artist faithfully to follow reality, exhorts him to abandon style. . . . The eighteenth century, on the other hand, . . . was a past master of style.[16]

Stravinsky's embrace of archaic models—be it Russian folk ritual or classical Greek drama—manifests Ortega's "will to style." He will not be diverted from the "royal road" by realism.

Though he defined the nineteenth-century attitude differently than Ortega, the English literary critic T. E. Hulme anticipated his argument in "Romanticism and Classicism" (ca. 1911–12), an essay that explicitly champions the classical attitude:

> Here is the root of all romanticism: that man, the individual, is an infinite reservoir of possibilities: and if you can so rearrange society by the destruction of oppressive order then these possibilities will have a chance and you will get Progress.
> One can define the classical quite clearly as the exact opposite to this. Man is an extraordinarily fixed and limited animal whose nature is absolutely constant. It is only by tradition and organization that anything decent can be got out of him.[17]

Hulme is of particular interest here for the fact that Taruskin recognizes in this duality the essence of Stravinsky's approach to setting text and by inference his artistry in general. He even cited the following passage as a perfect description of "the whole matter of text declamation as Stravinsky came to practice it."[18] Hulme writes:

> I always think that the fundamental process at the back of all the arts might be represented by the following metaphor. You know what I call architect's curves—flat pieces of wood with all different kinds of curvature. By a suitable selection from these you can draw approximately any curve you like. The artist I take to be the man who simply can't bear the idea of that "approximately." He will get the exact curve of what he sees whether it be an object or an idea in the mind.... Suppose that instead of your curved pieces of wood you have a springy piece of steel.... Now the state of tension or concentration of mind, if he is doing anything really good in this struggle against the ingrained habit of the technique, may be represented by a man employing all his fingers to bend the steel out of its own curve and into the exact curve which you want. Something different to what it would assume naturally.[19]

Taruskin's recognition that this struggle against the "natural" curve precisely describes Stravinsky's struggle against natural declamation is, to my mind, even more important for understanding the composer's artistry than knowing of his "rejoicing discovery" of Russian folk verse. Understood as a manifestation of the classical ideals espoused by Hulme and Ortega, Stravinsky's Russian-period settings are not so different from his later works, but not because his work remained essentially Russian. At heart, Stravinskian modernism, including the earlier Russian works, expresses this "classical" attitude. Indeed, among composers, Stravinsky was its standard-bearer.

Nonetheless, several of his neoclassical works—especially vocal settings like *Perséphone* and *The Rake*, but also the ballets *Apollo* (1928) and *Orpheus* (1947) and the Violin Concerto (1931)—even as they retain some of the stasis and displacement of his earlier period, convey an expressive warmth that seems to betray his classical attitude. And even among these "expressive" works, *The Rake's Progress* stands out; his discerning wife judged its final scene "the most touching music he ever wrote."[20] Not only is the opera Stravinsky's first serious attempt at setting English, it adheres most closely to its classical models. Whereas *Oedipus* and *Perséphone* are contrived hybrids, *The Rake* is conventional: singer-actors embody their characters with no narration and little commentary, like *Mavra* but less farcical. Several musical factors contribute to this emotional effect: harmony, tempo, meter, melodic contour, and rhythm. Because the composer based many of these choices on the text, a close study of his settings helps elucidate his expressivity.

A Variety of Settings

Despite Stravinsky's "rejoicing discovery" of Russian folk songs and his shaky grasp of spoken English, Auden's appreciative comments about *The Rake* hold true. As his working methods imply, the composer generally adheres to conventional accents and pacing. Translation into other languages especially concerned him, as he insisted to Boulanger (who was promoting French-language productions): "the whole work—its musical prosody—is calculated to display Wystan Auden's magnificent English text."[21] What brought about his change in attitude? Was Stravinsky reverting to the naturalism of his settings prior to 1914? Hardly. As critic John Briggs put it, he "set the English words with as much solicitude as Handel or Purcell"—that is, he privileges text in the recitatives and music in the set pieces.[22] When striving for clarity of speech, Stravinsky avoids displaced accents, vocal embellishments, and sustained melody. Such naturalism, though, forces him "faithfully to follow reality," as Ortega would put it. So, while he may not have set Auden's verse "as if it were a Russian limerick" (at least not much of it), Stravinsky still refracts the text through some stylistic prism, be it a Mozartian ensemble, Purcellian recitative, bel canto ornamentation, Stravinskian displacement, or some combination thereof. The librettists surely imagined as much when they wrote the words.

Stravinsky's sketches for any given setting reflect its musical/dramatic function. He left hardly any for the recitatives but drafted numerous versions of expressive passages like Anne's B-minor aria (examples 5.10–5.12). There we see Stravinsky bending, as Hulme would describe, the steel "into the exact curve" that he wants. The artifice a bel canto composer follows as a matter of convention Stravinsky must consciously impose.

The variety of settings demonstrates how Stravinsky adapts to changing dramaturgical demands. He takes three basic approaches: (1) for the recitatives, ariosos, and even certain arias he follows natural declamation; (2) for highly stylized language or nonsensical verses he subverts natural declamation; and (3) for especially expressive moments he heightens and intensifies declamation.

Natural Declamation—Sellem's Aria (3.3)

For secco recitatives, which are little more than inflected speeches, Stravinsky made virtually no sketches prior to the short score. A more involved process is

Example 5.2. Draft and final version of Nick's "Let wish be thought" (3.2).

evident in the accompanied recitatives, such as Sellem's entrance in act 3, scene 1 (R43), and numbers where the flow of words demand the pacing and clarity of speech: Nick's "Come, master, observe the host of mankind" in act 2, scene 1 (R29); the first half of Baba's aria in act 2, scene 3 (R157); and Tom and Nick's duet in act 3, scene 2 (R187+7). Because the conventions of speech drive these settings, Stravinsky usually works out proper pacing and accents first. As in the patter songs of comic opera, he makes ample use of repeated pitches and often sketches only the rhythm.[23]

Nonetheless, the composer periodically imposes his artistry upon these accompanied settings. The change may be an arbitrary elongation for comic effect, for example, a sudden pause for reflection amid Baba's patter or an eccentric point of emphasis by Sellem. One of his more striking revisions is Nick's "Let wish be thought and think on one to name" (3.2, R187), shown in example 5.2. The initial dotted rhythms resemble Shadow's martial pronouncements throughout the scene (a). In the final version, though, he adopts Tom's turning embellishments, giving the previously cold command a mock-consoling quality (b). The elaborate turns slow the natural flow of the sentence and slightly obscure the words, but the subtle characterization more than compensates for the minor compromise in prosody.

The only other formal number for which Stravinsky first sketched the rhythm is the first phrase of Sellem's aria, shown in example 5.3, which is not surprising, given the librettists felt it "dramatically essential that the sung rhythms conform pretty closely to the spoken" (see note 9 above). Nonetheless, this would not be a patter aria like that of Baba, for even in the first sketch melodic contour is as important as rhythm.

Figure 5.1 reproduces a subsequent draft. Because the verses share a similar number of syllables and parallel stresses (underlined below), Stravinsky sketched most of the second-verse text in red pencil either above or below the setting of verse 1, superimposing rhythmic and melodic adjustments as needed:

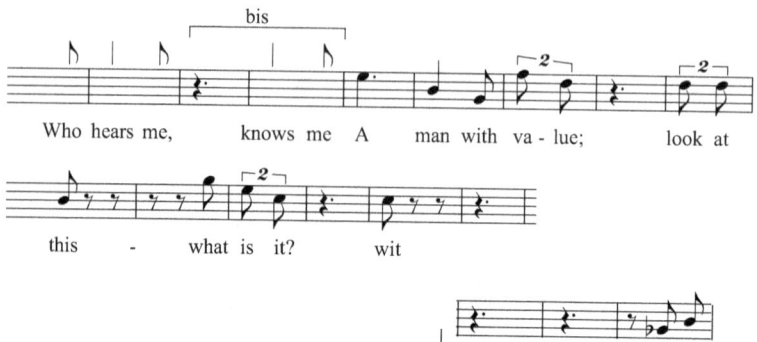

Example 5.3. First sketch for verse 1 of Sellem's aria (3.1).

Verse 1
Who hears me, knows me; knows me
A man of value; look at this—
What is it?—Wit
And Profit: no one, no one
Could fail to conquer, fail to charm,
Who had it by
To watch. And who could not be
A nimble planner, having this
Before him?

Verse 2
Behold it, Roman, moral,
The man who has it, has it
Forever—yes!
And holy, holy, curing
The Body, soul and spirit;
A gift of—God's!
And not to mention this or
The other, more and more and—
So help me—more!

Stravinsky's adjustments—both in this draft and in the final score—demonstrate, if anything, his sensitivity to the subtle differences between the verses. In the opening line of verse 1 he elides "Who hears, knows me" and places a measure break before the second "knows me." In verse 2, he shifts the measure break so that it comes after "Behold it," thus setting off "Roman, moral." The alteration

Displacement, Text Setting, and Stravinsky's Evolving Aesthetic | 133

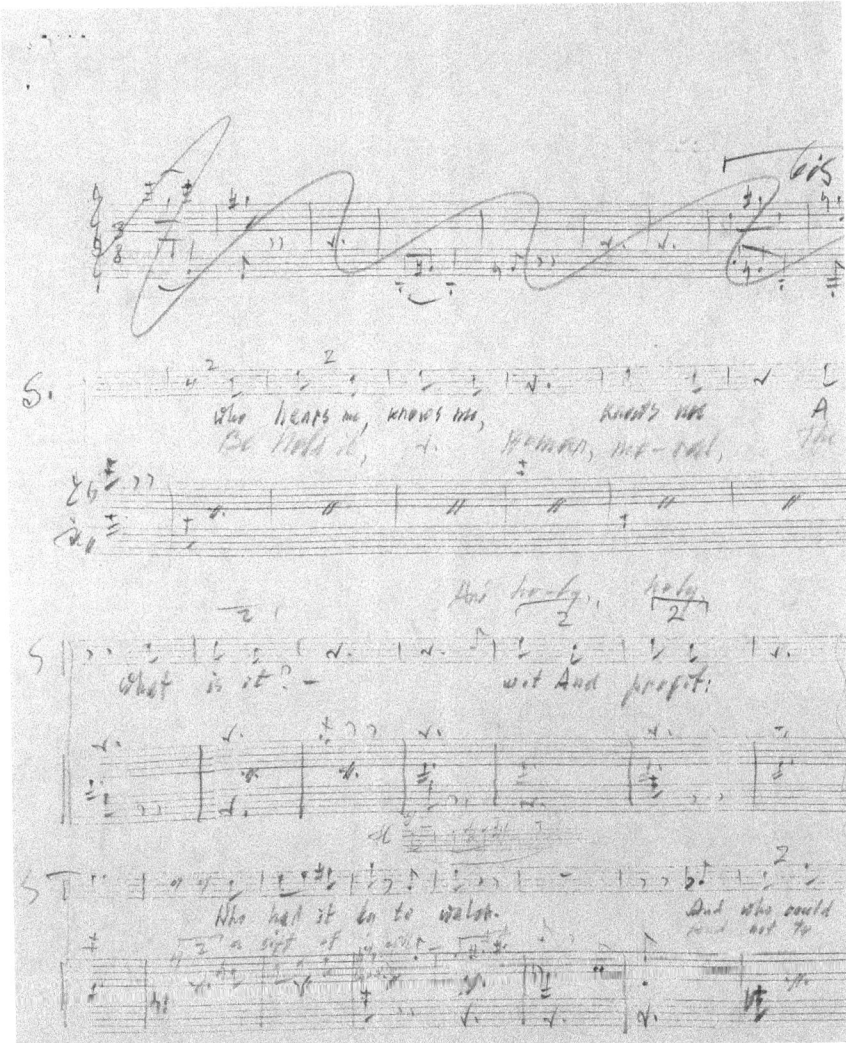

Fig. 5.1. Facsimile of first complete draft of verses 1 and 2 of Sellem's aria. (Igor Stravinsky Collection, Paul Sacher Foundation)

helps clarify the meaning, these last two words being attributes of the marble bust that Sellem asks us to behold. Stravinsky does not even attempt to overlay the completion of the enjambed third line, "has it Forever," shown in example 5.4.

Similarly, Stravinsky paces the second tercets of the two verses differently to accommodate the different punctuation. "Wit and Profit:" of the first verse— another enjambment—is set off grammatically by a semicolon and musically by a measure of rest. The corresponding tercet of the second verse ("And holy, holy, curing the body . . .") contains no such punctuation until the semicolon after

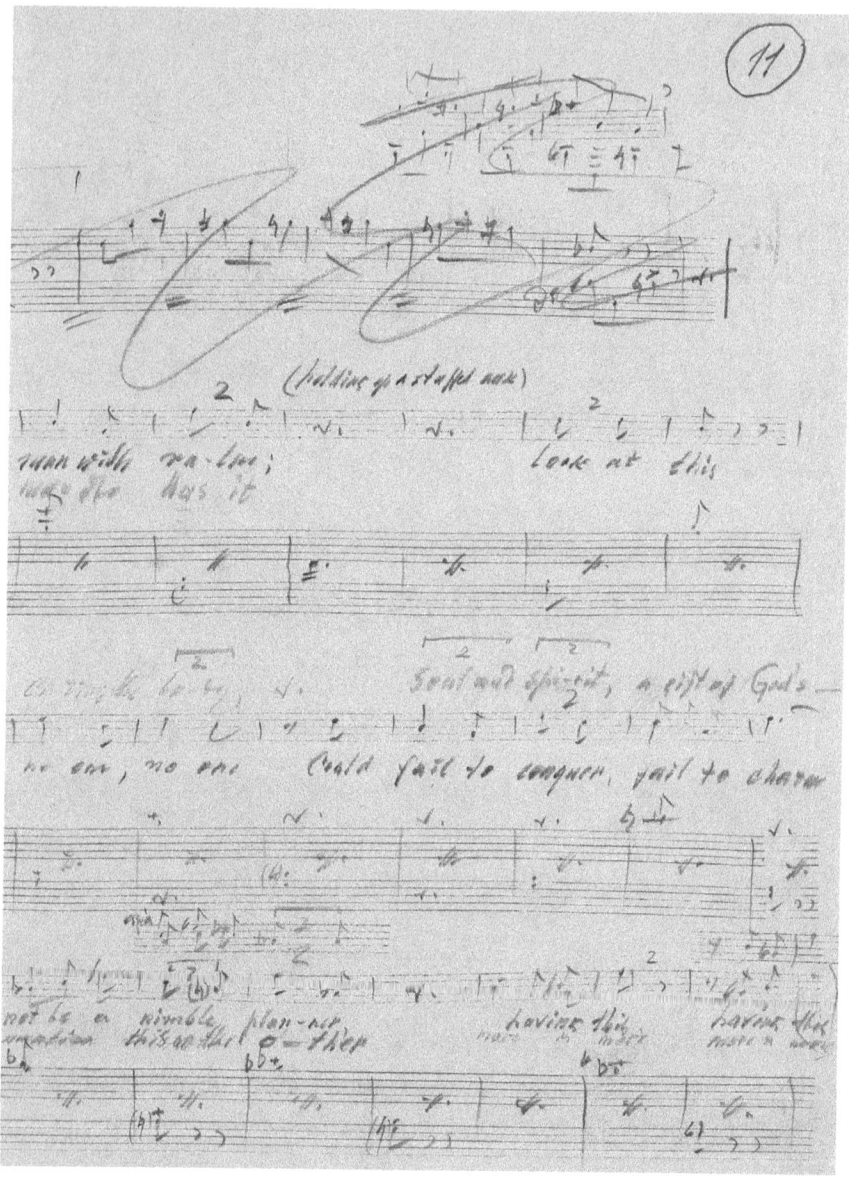

Fig. 5.1. *(continued)*

"spirit," so the rest is inappropriate. Example 5.5 juxtaposes the sketch and the final version, showing how Stravinsky eliminates the two breaks in his final setting and imposes a measure of rest before "a gift of God's," which he repeats for emphasis. In both sketch and final setting, though, he avoids in the repeated statement the accent on the article "a" so that "gift" receives proper emphasis.

Example 5.4. "The man who has it" from Sellem's aria.

Example 5.6 compares the sketch and final setting of the last tercet. Here Stravinsky eliminates the repetition of "more and more" so he can set off "so help me." Far from bluntly forcing the second verse onto the music of the first, the composer in every line works to accommodate the subtle grammatical and poetic differences. The result is both crystal clear and ideally paced for Sellem's histrionic delivery.

Subverted Declamation—"Lanterloo" Chorus (1.2)

Most formal numbers in a conventional opera may, to some degree, forgo textual clarity. This latitude affords a "music first" composer room to indulge, no finer example of which is the "Lanterloo" chorus from act 1, scene 2. Stravinsky himself wondered "whether any poet since the Elizabethans has made a composer such a beautiful gift of words for music as the 'Lanterloo' dance in our opera."[24]

> The sun is bright, the grass is green;
>   Lanterloo, lanterloo.
> The King is courting his young Queen.
>   Lanterloo, my lady.
> They go a-walking. What do they see?
>   An almanack in a walnut tree.
> They go a-riding. Whom do they meet?
>   Three scarecrow and a pair of feet. (1.2)

Auden here parodies a nursery rhyme. The composer responded by displacing accented words and syllables, just as he did in his Russian-period settings, with one major difference. In *Les Noces*, Stravinsky typically adjusts the meter so that metric stresses coincide with parallel musical lines and text; that is, he makes the radical choice to rebar the measures.[25] By contrast, he conserves a 6/8 meter throughout "Lanterloo." In example 5.7 I highlight his displaced stresses by superimposing the implied meter changes. As my "radical" rebarring shows, Stravinsky shifts the accented downbeat from the first dotted-quarter to the second by interposing an extra beat of running sixteenths in m. 3, thus creating the momentary sense of 9/8. He repeats the same five-beat phrase so as to shift the downbeat back to beat 1 at R164, coinciding with the chorus's entrance.

Stravinsky also shifts the chorus's downbeats, but not always in the same way as those for the orchestra, thereby creating a counterpoint of sorts between the perceived meters of each. For instance, the chorus enters at R166 on the downbeat (shown in example 5.7) rather than the upbeat as before. Because the melodic pattern is the same, the shift may be heard in two ways: conservatively

Example 5.5. Draft and final version of the second tercet, verse 2, of Sellem's aria.

Example 5.6. Draft and final version of the final tercet, verse 2, of Sellem's aria.

Example 5.7. Introduction and first verse of "Lanterloo" Chorus (1.2).

as a displaced metric stress from "King" to "The," or radically as a delay of the downbeat by an eighth note, thus creating a 5/8 measure in metrical counterpoint with the 6/8 accompaniment. This play with meter becomes even more obvious in the choral refrain that immediately follows, where the final stressed syllable—the first of "<u>La</u>-dy"—feels like a cadential downbeat but actually occurs on the second eighth.

As with example 5.1a, in suggesting alternate metrical interpretations I don't mean to question Stravinsky's choices. Sensitive performers should be aware of and may even preserve the tension between radical and conservative hearings.[26] Exactly what difference metric notation makes remains an open question—one that Craft put to Stravinsky in their published conversations. Asked whether accents could achieve the same effect as changing the meter, the composer responded, "Up to a point, yes, but that point is the degree of real regularity in the music. The bar line is much much more than a mere accent and I don't believe that it can be simulated by an accent, at least not in my music."[27] Consider a conspicuous pattern like the double bass's march at the beginning of *Histoire du Soldat* or the repeated opening phrases of "Lanterloo." Notated against the prevailing meter, these regular rhythms almost demand to be heard in a different metrical context. In fact, Stravinsky's initial sketches for "Lanterloo" confirm that he conceived several melodic ideas in meters other than the 6/8 he eventually settled on—meters that continue to sound in the chorus's shifting accents.

Early sketches for the orchestral ritornello and miscellaneous choral fragments are reproduced in figure 5.2 and transcribed in example 5.8. Fragment B confirms that Stravinsky indeed first notated the orchestral ritornello in 9/8. Likewise, his initial setting of "Lanterloo," sketched in fragment A, clarifies the underlying metric play. He originally conceived the refrain in 2/4, where the stressed first syllables of "<u>Lan</u>-ter-loo" and "<u>La</u>-dy" fall on downbeats. In the final setting, he essentially superimposes this 2/4 meter over the orchestra's 6/8. Had he done so exactly, the downbeats would have lined up again after two measures, so he perhaps added an extra eighth to the second "Lanterloo" (R166+4) to delay the arrival of "Lady" in the next bar.

The 2/4 origin of the "Lanterloo" refrain supports the interpretation of the chorus in metrical counterpoint with the orchestra's 6/8 dance. The two-versus-three conflict is most explicit at R172+3, shown in example 5.9, where the singers' octave leaps emphasize the 2/4 pattern. Stravinsky again alters his original idea in the final statement at R173, where he delays the chorus's downbeat by one eighth, thus setting up the final two "Lanterloos" for downbeats. Notice that the final metric stress on "La-<u>dy</u>" functions as a downbeat for neither the chorus nor the orchestra. Their implied meters become retroactively realigned on the subsequent "downbeat" in the middle of R173+3.

A different kind of metrical counterpoint plays out in the internal couplets. These lines pair questions with nonsensical answers: "They go a-walking. What do they see? An almanack in a walnut tree." Stravinsky sets each question in a pattern of four quarters repeated twice over three 6/8 measures, shown at the

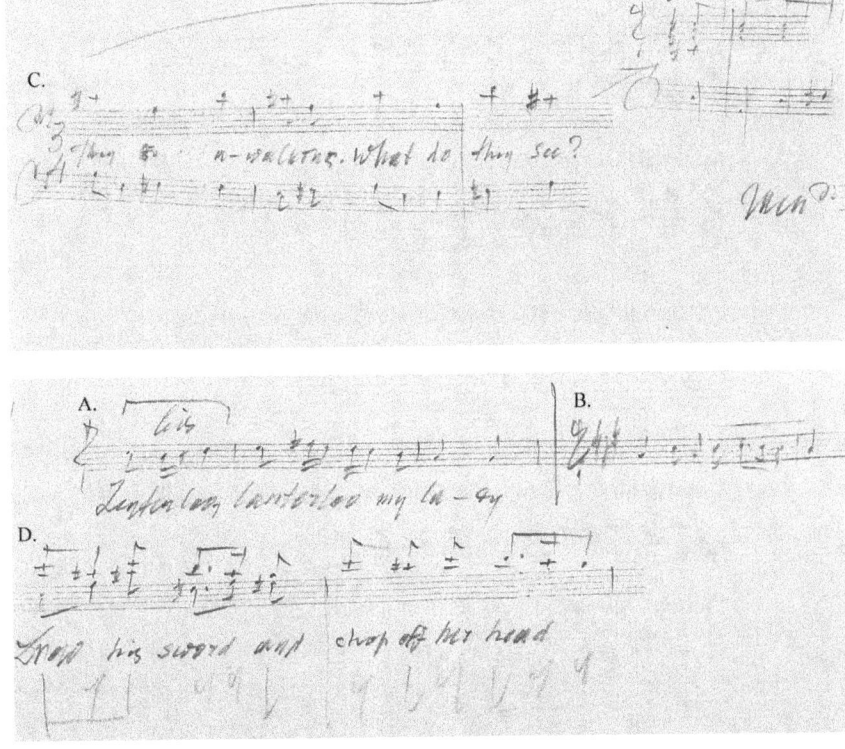

Fig. 5.2. Facsimile of the first sketches (labeled A–D) for "Lanterloo" chorus. (Igor Stravinsky Collection, Paul Sacher Foundation)

beginning of example 5.9. But this four-beat pattern does not feel like a simple 4/4. The number of syllables in the first poetic foot—"They go a-"—implies a 3/4 pattern and the second foot—"walking"—is squeezed into a single beat. The resulting pattern of alternating 3/4 and 1/4 measures creates an imbalance between the poetic feet, in keeping with the overall nonsense. This playful asymmetry pervades the entire couplet when each "answer" resumes the quick 6/8; Stravinsky gives each jerking question a smooth-flowing answer. And once again, he anticipated this metric play in his initial sketches (fig. 5.2): the "question" is notated in 3/4 (fragment C)—even here he forces the four-beat pattern into a 3/4 measure— and the "answer" is in 6/8 (fragment D).

The four fragments reproduced in figure 5.2 provide a key for deciphering the ever-shifting accents in the "Lanterloo" chorus. Here, concisely displayed, are the prototypes of the underlying meters at play throughout the number: the orchestral ritornello in 9/8, "Lanterloo" in 2/4, "They go a-walking…" in 3/4, and "Draw his sword…" in 6/8. Stravinsky does not simply adapt the different rhythms to conform to a common 6/8. Rather, the conserved 6/8 meter disguises possibly

a. Sketch for choral refrain

Lan - ter - loo,   Lan - ter - loo__ my   La - dy

b. Sketch for orchestral refrain

c. Sketch for line 5 (the first "Question" of the internal couplets)

They go   a   walk ing What do   they see?

d. Sketch for line 13 (the final "Answer" of the internal couplets)

Draw_ his sword__ and chop off her head____

Example 5.8. Transcription of figure 5.2.

his richest use of polymeters since *Histoire du Soldat*. The perverse accentuations perfectly match the childish hedonism of the Brothel.

Heightened Declamation—Anne's Aria (1.3)

Such empty revelry is the emotional opposite of the following act 1, scene 3, in which Anne ponders her absent beloved and prepares to depart for London to find him. To be sure, Stravinsky distorts the text in Anne's aria as well but differently than in the "Lanterloo" chorus and, I argue, to the opposite effect. Rather than subverting the natural stress of nonsensical verses, he heightens the meaning of Anne's heartfelt words through expressive text painting, like a classical composer.

That said, Anne's aria presents a particularly awkward fit between text and music, a feature I attribute less to Stravinsky's distortions than to Kallman's abstruse lyrics (see verse 1 on p. 68). The sentences are long and the connections obscure. His undeniably beautiful words may make for moving poetry but not for a neoclassical libretto. That the aria nonetheless succeeds as a touching expression of Anne's faith in love is testimony to the composer's skill and sensitivity.

Stravinsky notated what was probably his first musical idea for the aria at the top of a large sketch page filled with various fragments of the preceding recitative,

Example 5.9. Metrical counterpoint in "Lanterloo" chorus.

Fig. 5.3. Facsimile of first sketch for melody from Anne's aria (1.3). (Paul Sacher Foundation)

Fig. 5.4. Facsimile of first sketch setting of final two couplets of Anne's aria. (Paul Sacher Foundation)

shown in figure 5.3. This textless melody, a descent from F♯–B embellished with ascending thirds and falling seconds, is the basis for the setting of the last line of verse 1 ("Although I weep, it knows of loneliness") and two couplets in verse 2 ("And warmly be the same . . ." and "It cannot be thou art . . .") (see example 4.9 for an analysis of its tonal structure). As he did with the verses of Sellem's aria, Stravinsky initially imposed the two parallel couplets of verse 2 over the same notation, shown in figure 5.4. But even in this simple, mostly syllabic setting, Stravinsky has altered his original by extending the E through repetition and lengthening. Example 5.10 follows the evolution of the textless melody into the first of its final settings.

Stravinsky's first attempt at "Although I weep," shown in figure 5.5, is also largely syllabic with a brief melisma on "weep." Crossing out that first underlay, he made room for another melisma on the unstressed "Al-" by delaying "-though I" in a revision Taruskin calls deliberately "inept."[28] However, such a distortion—especially on an open vowel—is typical of expressive vocal settings. Craft, in a more generous early commentary, explains: "The claims of English stress and accent did not trouble him very deeply. He was far more concerned with singability, with vowel sounds in vocal ranges, with the effect of words on vocal quality and the other way round."[29] Concern with singability is very different from the metric play and shifted accents of the "Lanterloo" chorus. Anne's melismas

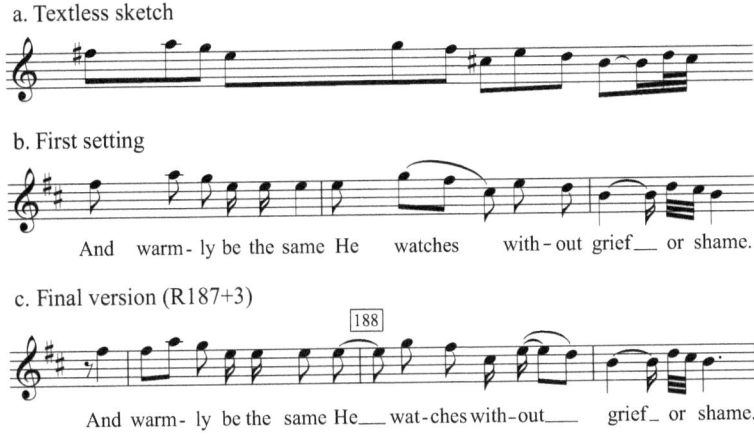

Example 5.10. Successive stages of "And warmly be the same" from Anne's aria.

Fig. 5.5. Facsimile of first sketch setting of final line of verse 1 of Anne's aria. (Igor Stravinsky Collection, Paul Sacher Foundation)

reflect a tradition of text painting going back to the Renaissance, not the arbitrary play of a modernist.

Stravinsky's final setting carries the image of weeping to even greater expressive heights. Tracing the various stages, example 5.11 demonstrates the complexity of the final version by showing the extended text repetitions and melismatic interpolations on successive staves, thereby exposing both melodic and rhythmic development as well as the various settings of each word.

The musical and emotional culmination of Anne's aria comes in the final couplet of the second verse. Though highly embellished, this line can still be traced to the original melody (fig. 5.3). Figure 5.4 shows how Stravinsky first simply imposed the text over "And warmly be the same." In example 5.12, I juxtapose this first attempt (b) with the short score (c) and final version (d). The short score already introduces oscillating thirds to the words "cannot be." In the final version Stravinsky extends the phrase, first repeating the embellishments and then delaying the cadence by repeating "a colder moon."

a. First sketch

b. Revision of first sketch

c. Final version (R185+1)

Example 5.11. Successive stages of setting for "Although I weep" from Anne's aria (various settings of each word aligned for comparison).

Example 5.13 shows how in the short score, the oscillating thirds project a 3/4 (or hemiola) against the 6/8. In the final version Stravinsky displaces the motive so that the first three thirty-second note groups each begin on a different triplet subdivision. By placing the final two on the same triplet (the second), he stabilizes the metrical sense just before the final sustained high B.

These extended embellishments make some words difficult to comprehend, but the emotional meaning could not be clearer. They express Anne's desperate need to believe she is still loved, even as her unaccompanied and ultimately unembellished final cadence portrays a distant, indifferent moon. This bel canto style bears little resemblance to the nonsensical "Lanterloo" settings. In those subversive settings, syllables detached from their conventional meaning lose their expressive qualities. Anne's vocal line, by contrast, heightens the poetic feeling even as it violates conventional prosody, like a *cantabile* aria by Mozart or Donizetti.

Example 5.12. Successive stages of setting for "It cannot be thou art" from Anne's aria.

Example 5.13. Comparison of motivic groupings for "It cannot be thou art": (a) short score; (b) final version (R188+2).

Similarly embellished settings permeate Anne's music, as well as Tom's cavatina in act 1, scene 2, and aria in act 2, scene 1; the lovers' duet in act 2, scene 2; and their farewell in act 3, scene 3. What does it mean that Anne and Tom engage the listener's emotions in these moments? How and why they stand out from the surrounding playfulness is the subject of the next chapter.

Notes

1. Letter of December 10, 1947, in Robert Craft, ed., *Stravinsky: Selected Correspondence*, vol. 1 (New York: Alfred A. Knopf, 1982), 335.
2. Ibid., 339–40.
3. Comparisons to Boswell's relationship with Samuel Johnson or that of Eckermann to Goethe fail to capture the young American's evolving role over their twenty-three years together. Craft corrects a common observation, "The Stravinskys and I were more like companions than parents and son" (*Glimpses*, 46). But the connection went deeper. Stephen Spender observed that the three were "all in love with each other, like characters in a Henry James novel," as quoted in Stephen Walsh, *Stravinsky—The Second Exile: France and America, 1934–1971* (New York: Alfred A. Knopf, 2006), 423.
4. Robert Craft, *Stravinsky: Glimpses of a Life* (New York: St. Martin's Press, 1992), 53.
5. Robert Craft, "A Personal Preface," *Score* 20 (1957): 7.
6. Robert Craft, "Words for Music Perhaps," review of *The Complete Works of W. H. Auden: Libretti and Other Dramatic Writings (1939–1973)*. *The New York Review of Books* 41, no. 18 (1994): 55.
7. Vera Stravinsky and Robert Craft, *Stravinsky in Pictures and Documents* (New York: Simon and Schuster, 1978), 361.
8. Robert Craft, "Reflections on 'The Rake's Progress,'" *Score and I.M.A. Magazine* 9 (1954): 27–28.
9. "Craftsman, Artist, Genius," quoted in V. Stravinsky and Craft, *Pictures and Documents*, 406.

10. Robert Craft, *Stravinsky: The Chronicle of a Friendship: 1948/1971* (Nashville: Vanderbilt University Press, 1994), 97. Craft had despaired about Stravinsky's settings as early as October 1949, when he confided to harpsichordist Sylvia Marlowe: "Saw new pages of 'Rake' and the English is hideously mis-set, impossibly awkward. What can I do with that man" as quoted in Richard Taruskin, *The Danger of Music and Other Anti-Utopian Essays* (Berkeley: University of California Press, 2008), 110. The skeptical Taruskin claimed it also "well known that Auden and Kallman were at first appalled at the way Stravinsky had mauled their libretto . . . and proposed numerous 'revisions' as a way of salvaging a proper scansion" in *Stravinsky and the Russian Traditions: A Biography of the Works through Mavra*, 2 vols. (Berkeley: University of California Press, 1996), 1198. However, the example he cites of "revision-as-salvage"—the act 1, scene 2, chorus, "Soon dawn will glitter," reproduced in Craft, *Correspondence*, vol. 1, 307—is, in fact, an additional verse that Stravinsky set to the same music.

11. Ernest Newman, untitled review, *Sunday Times*, August 30, 1953.

12. Virgil Thomson, *A Virgil Thomson Reader* (Boston: Houghton Mifflin, 1981), 513.

13. Walsh, *Second Exile*, 226.

14. Richard Taruskin, "Stravinsky's 'Rejoicing Discovery' and What It Meant: In Defense of His Notorious Text Setting," in *Stravinsky Retrospectives*, ed. Ethan Haimo and Paul Johnson (Lincoln: University of Nebraska, 1987), 194–96; van den Toorn makes the same observation in *Music of Igor Stravinsky* (248). Marina Lupishko reconsiders the folk settings on which Stravinsky supposedly based his practice in "'Rejoicing Discovery' Revisited." For a broader discussion of Stravinsky's neoclassical settings (including *Oedipus*, *Symphony of Psalms*, and *Perséphone*) and "classical" attitude in general, see Chandler Carter, "*The Rake's Progress* and Stravinsky's Return: The Composer's Evolving Approach to Setting Text," *Journal of the American Musicological Society* 63, no. 3 (2010): 555–72.

15. Igor Stravinsky and Robert Craft, *Expositions and Developments* (Garden City, NY: Doubleday, 1962), 134.

16. José Ortega y Gasset, *"The Dehumanization of Art" and Other Writings on Art and Culture* (Garden City, NY: Doubleday, 1956), 23–24.

17. Thomas Hulme, *The Collected Writings of T. E. Hulme*, ed. Karen Csengeri (Oxford: Clarendon Press, 1994), 61. Hulme's essay became widely known through the posthumously published collection *Speculations*. Stravinsky was unaware of his work until Craft sent him a copy in 1947 (Craft, *Correspondence*, vol. 1, 330–31).

18. Taruskin, *Russian Traditions*, 1230.

19. Hulme, *Collected Writings*, 69.

20. Igor Stravinsky, *Themes and Conclusions* (Berkeley: University of California Press, 1972), 57; see chapter 8, note 30 for more of this quotation.

21. Craft, *Correspondence*, vol. 1, 246. Contrast this statement with Stravinsky's very different ambitions for *Perséphone* (*Correspondence*, vol. 3, 189).

22. John Briggs, "Recording of 'Rake,'" *New York Times*, November 15, 1953.

23. Craft dubiously claims that, aside from *The Rake* and some of his Russian-language settings, "Stravinsky's practice of writing rhythmic values above the syllables and only later adding intervals or melodic ideas is not true of his vocal music generally" (V. Stravinsky and Craft, *Pictures and Documents*, 361). For evidence to the contrary, see Carr, *Multiple Masks*, figures 4.1, 4.3–4.5, 4.11 (163–93).

24. I. Stravinsky, *Themes and Conclusions*, 77.

25. See Carter, "*Rake's Progress* and Stravinsky's Return," example 1, 556. Van den Toorn introduces the terms "radical" and "conservative" to his metric analyses in *Stravinsky and "The Rite of Spring": The Beginnings of a Musical Language* (Berkeley: University of California

Press, 1987) 67; though he makes the same distinction, labeled Types I and II, throughout his earlier *Music of Igor Stravinsky* (227). See also "Stravinsky Re-Barred," *Music Analysis* 7, no. 2 (1988): 165–95, and Pieter C. Van den Toorn and John McGinness, *Stravinsky and the Russian Period: Sound and Legacy of a Musical Idiom* (New York: Cambridge University Press, 2012), which consolidate van den Toorn's work on displacement and expressive timing.

26. I describe this relationship somewhat differently from van den Toorn, who contends, "The two readings are not reconcilable. Although listeners may switch from one reading to the other, or sense one in relation to the other, they cannot attend to both simultaneously" in Pieter C. van den Toorn, "Stravinsky, *Les Noces*, and the Prohibition against Expressive Timing," *Journal of Musicology* 20, no. 2 (2003): 292.

27. Igor Stravinsky and Robert Craft, *Conversations with Stravinsky* (Garden City, NY: Doubleday, 1959), 24. Both van den Toorn ("Stravinsky Re-barred," 170) and Gretchen Horlacher in "Metric Irregularity in *Les noces*: The Problem of Periodicity," *Journal of Music Theory* 39 (1995): 285 consider Stravinsky's less than conclusive answer.

28. Taruskin, *Russian Traditions*, 1234.

29. Craft, "A Personal Preface," 8.

6

STRAVINSKY'S TRUTHS AND MOZART'S LIES—MUSIC, EMOTION, AND THEATRICAL DISTANCE

"Perhaps the oddest thing about this music," observed Phillip Hope-Wallace, "is that as it grows upon the ear it seems more and more to be loaded with that very emotionalism which it is supposed to renounce if not to deride.... We find the musical language affecting us in precisely the 'old' way."[1] Even so harsh a critic as Deryck Cooke admitted to being moved by Tom's death, though he found its expressiveness disturbing: "Even such a 'beautiful' and 'moving' number as 'In a foolish dream,' ... still relies too heavily on its original: the intense emotional effect is due to Bach's genius rather than Stravinsky's." He went on, "And when the pasticheur slips up, and lets the great model himself loom through the flimsy mask for a moment—as when two bars of Bach's own poignant melodic-harmonic-rhythmic style intrude into 'Love, too frequently betrayed'—the effect is devastating. The noble reality dwarfs the heartless, purely technical imitation surrounding it."[2]

That passage from Tom's Cavatina in act 1, scene 2, shown in example 6.1a, merits a brief look. Knowing Stravinsky studied examples of Purcell's vocal music, a passage like the following from *The Fairy Queen* (1692) in example 6.1b makes for a more apt comparison than Bach, at least for the handling of text (see example 6.8 for a tonal analysis). Both passages are laments for lost love and feature conventional sighing figures.

As long as Stravinsky limits himself to brittle harpsichord flourishes and wooden ballad tunes, Cooke could dismiss him as a "pasticheur." But when he heightens expression through melodic embellishments and moving harmonies, the line separating modeler and model—like that between signifier and signified—becomes blurred. This distinction is especially fuzzy in music, as Anthony Newcomb observes, because "a musical sign is not transparent—that is, the sign does not disappear in favor of its function as pointing to the signified."[3] In other words, even a stylized gesture—for example, a bel canto melisma or ornamented cadence—registers first as musical sound and only secondarily as rhetorical gesture. More directly than words or images, music engages the receptive listener's emotions, bypassing extra-musical associations. This phenomenon helps explain why lovers of conventional opera are not especially bothered by distorted settings or languages they do not comprehend. At such heightened moments, it matters not if we understand the words or pick up on the stylistic allusions, whether the music is "classical" Purcell or Mozart or "neoclassical" Stravinsky. *The Rake's Progress* ceases to be a modernist work modeled on old-fashioned Opera and becomes just an opera.

This chapter addresses not so much why conventional opera engages our emotions—that seems obvious—but how composers, especially of comic opera, manipulate our emotions for dramatic effect. Perhaps no one does so more expertly than Mozart in *Così fan tutte* (1790), the work on which Stravinsky admittedly modeled *The Rake*. Yet, aside from obvious surface resemblances, Mozart's cynical farce seems less influential than the tragicomic *Don Giovanni*. Understanding what Stravinsky learned from *Così* may explain why this artist who once claimed to disdain expressive music—and opera!—became so drawn to it.[4] Delving into the intricate relationship between emotion and theatrical distance also sheds light on his aesthetic evolution introduced in the previous chapter.

Theatrical Distance Defined

Distance here refers to the sense of separateness rooted in the psyche. Indispensable to any theatrical event, psychological distance enables the viewer to recognize *play* as an imagined reality. Lines connecting the audience and the "play" in figures 6.1–6.4 represent not just the physical distance of a staged drama but also the metaphorical distance the viewer imagines. In the Western tradition dating back to the Greeks, the stage functions as a "safe haven" onto which viewers can project their emotions. The play thus becomes a venue for vicarious emotional experience.

Emotion has a profound impact on our theatrical experience. For Sartre, "True emotion . . . is accompanied by belief" and thus mitigates distance; one loses one's self in the drama.[5] Roger Scruton conceives this imaginative experience in cooler terms—as a nonliteral "seeing as" rather than a literal "believing in."[6] Viewers can imagine the aesthetic object yet remain aware of its unreality. Sartre and Scruton differ only in emphasis. For both, the intensity of the aesthetic emotion and, thus, the degree of distance depend on the viewer's imaginative involvement.

Bertolt Brecht famously distrusted the "Aristotelian" conception of drama as vicarious experience. In that, he bears a strong affinity with Stravinsky. "One can only imagine if Stravinsky and Brecht had collaborated in the twenties," Boulez enthused. "My God, what would have resulted!"[7] He isn't the only observer to recognize that the two agreed on "the heightening of theatrical effect" (even if the composer would have disdained the dramatist's Marxism).[8] By making explicit the unreality of their stories and characters, both hold the audience at

Example 6.1. Comparison of text setting and melodic figuration.

an emotional arm's length. Brecht's actors break the "fourth wall." They carry placards with moralizing slogans and adopt stylized gestures and exaggerated attitudes—what the dramatist calls *gestus*.[9] Such alienating effects encourage the viewer to experience the drama at a higher dramaturgical level—"higher" because it is conscious and intellectual rather than unconscious and primarily emotional.

Stravinsky, though, had mastered musical alienation in *Petrushka* and *Renard* well over a decade before Brecht's collaborations with Kurt Weill. Although too early to have been derived from Pirandello, as Stravinsky claimed, even the narrator's "Pirandellian" intercession in *Histoire du Soldat* was common in early twentieth-century theater as was the positioning of musicians, dancers, and actors on stage in full view.[10] Vsevolod Meyerhold and Alexandre Benois, both members of Diaghilev's "World of Art" circle, created a sort of anti-*Gesamtkunstwerk* by separating singing and movement rather than unifying them as Wagner had aspired. Benois, who closely collaborated with Stravinsky on *Petrushka*, staged the 1914 premiere of *Le Rossignol* as a "ballet-opera"; that is, dancers mimed the action while singers performed from the orchestra. In the words of an early critic, this separation of music and action replaces "the false illusionism of the old ballet and the old opera."[11] Stravinsky would continue to disassociate music and action in his staged works until *The Rake's Progress*.

Ortega y Gasset reminds us this rejection of theatrical illusion was part of a more general reaction to realism. Modernists adopted a more objective, consciously "artistic"—in a word, distant—stance, what Ortega calls the "dehumanization of art." His description encapsulates a spirit that permeates the modernist age: "Seeing requires distance. Each art operates a magic lantern that removes and transfigures its objects. On its screen they stand aloof, inmates of an inaccessible world, in an absolute distance."[12] For Ortega, aesthetic distance is not simply an archaic technique borrowed from folk or comic traditions, rather it is an essential component of all true art.

Distance in Music

Andre Bouchourechliev describes *Histoire du Soldat* as "simple, even commonplace, but 'structured to the second degree,' having undergone . . . distortions to which it owes its uniquely fresh quality."[13] He could as easily be describing the prelude and introduction to *The Rake*, excerpted in example 6.2, which similarly refract the opening fanfare and flowing melodies of Monteverdi's Prologue to *L'Orfeo* (1608). There, La Musica famously proclaims: "I am Music, who in sweet accents, know how to calm every troubled soul."[14] Stravinsky even borrows her "*dolce accenti*" to mark his descending wind melodies (example 6.2d). These allusions in turn mark *The Rake*, like *Histoire*, as "an archetypal fable beyond all doubt, but . . . also an archetype of music itself. All these constructions, these melodies, these rhythms and even the apparently most trivial—though in fact

Example 6.2. Comparison with opening of Monteverdi's *L'Orfeo*.

the most incredibly refined—phrase . . . represent music, are the original outline, the sign manual, the very ideogram of music."[15] Falling upon late modern ears like faint echoes, these "sweet accents" connect the opera to its origins in European sung drama, yet they also distance the work from its modernist surroundings. From the moment it begins, *The Rake's Progress* is already steps removed from its listeners, which is to say, it is an "Opera."

Comic Theater and Distance

Hardly unique to modernist theater, exaggerated gestures and cultivated falsity are fundamental to comic theater, especially opera buffa. "It is artificial comedy of the best," writes Edward Dent of *Così fan tutte*. "Don Alfonso is a real

che poi sì ce - le-bre   là in Fran   -   cia fù.

trans.: ... *who was then celebrated in France.*

Example 6.3. Mozart, *Così fan tutte*, act 1 finale (Despina as Doctor).

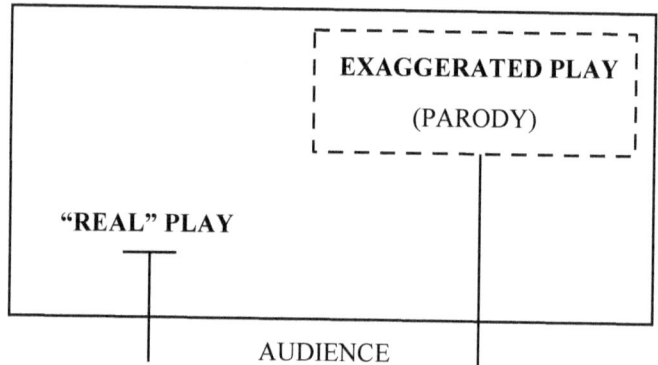

Fig. 6.1. Effect of parody to increase distance.

person . . . ; Despina too has a certain reality . . . But the four lovers are utterly unreal; they are more like marionettes than human beings. . . . *Così fan tutte* is the apotheosis of insincerity."[16] Mozart and every other composer of comic drama create this distinction by manipulating theatrical distance. His unreal characters, often ridiculously disguised, sing and act in wooden or overblown gestures that betray their professed passions. Example 6.3 shows one such melody, sung by the chambermaid Despina (impersonating a doctor) as she wields a giant magnet to extract "poison" supposedly swallowed by the pretend suitors, Ferrando and Guglielmo. Her aggrandizing fermatas and trills betray the farce.

From a semiotic point of view, one imagines Despina's exaggerated music and character as set apart from the surrounding action. According to Robert Hatten, music signals such shifts in discourse "by means of extreme contrasts of style or stylistic register."[17] The cultured listener recognizes, consciously or not, the convention and its correlation—that is, the context, the genre, or the emotion with which the convention is commonly associated. Figure 6.1 represents such exaggerated musical "objects" as set off from "normal" (contextually speaking) music. By extending distance, these distorted gestures—both musical and physical—create a play-within-the-play.

The score of *The Rake* brims with such stylized music. The ludicrous "bread machine" in act 2, scene 3 (R189–92), is the most obvious example; Stravinsky's "deliberately indifferent" hurdy-gurdy music recalls the organ-grinder from

Petrushka. Earlier in the same scene Baba's cloying "love song" is immediately betrayed by her stormy tirade. Even Tom's half of the opening duet is put on, though what makes him less sincere than Anne has more to do with the characters' subsequent development than any musical differences. Speaking more broadly, almost everything the chorus sings projects some form of hyper-reality. We know from the previous chapter how Stravinsky's distorted settings capture the perversity of Auden's brothel verses. The Auction chorus recalls the campiness of Gilbert and Sullivan operetta rather than Mozartian buffa. And the final "mourning" chorus achieves something like the choric parabasis Auden originally proposed in his first letter to Stravinsky.[18] (It would take the masterful direction of Ingmar Bergman, described at length in chapter 10, to realize the chorus's independent role within the opera.)

Expressive Music and Distance—Tom's Catechism (1.2)

Perhaps the most important lesson Stravinsky absorbed from Mozart's morally dubious comedy was not to delineate but to confuse the "real" and the "imaginary." In *Così*, Andrew Steptoe observes, "the mixture of real and feigned emotion is completed at a musical as well as dramatic level; truth and deception are confounded and seemingly inseparable."[19] Distinguishing "real" from "feigned" emotion raises again the question of musical expression, about which Stravinsky declared: "If, as is nearly always the case, music appears to express something, this is only an illusion and not a reality. It is simply an additional attribute which, by tacit and inveterate agreement, we have lent it, thrust upon it, as a label, a convention."[20]

The composer's dismissal of musical expression resembles Hatten's conception of the musical sign. Stravinsky rejects such interpretation as merely subjective, but as the philosopher Charles Pierce contended, the interpretation of all signs is subjective. Although unique to the interpreter, the idea prompted by a signifier/signified relation—what Pierce calls the *interpretant*—nonetheless does not float freely. Music theorist Naomi Cumming applies this insight to music: "[Musical] signs are not, then, private mental items; neither, on the other hand, can they be isolated from the 'material' of score or style. The interpretant links mind and material to form the sign. It is defined as a mental event, but it is intrinsic to the semiotic realization of musical structure, not an imposition of the listener's individuated subjectivity."[21] The subjective nature of the interpretant likewise applies to how the viewer imagines a theatrical play. And just as the staged act prompts us to project our own emotions, so does music. As Sartre asserts, whether inspired by a play, an opera, or a musical performance, such emotional projection promotes empathy and thereby lessens distance.

Highlighting the fundamental connection between aesthetic emotions in the theater and at a concert, Cumming describes our experience of expressive music as "hearing as." Drawing together theories of musical expression involving vocality, gesture, and agency, she writes: "The violin is heard as a voice; the [musical] figure as a gesture, a tonal resolution as the fulfillment of a causal agency. Together these are heard as the utterance of a subject." Just as Scruton's "seeing as" transforms staged actions into a fictional "play," Cumming asserts that "the act of 'hearing as' turns a property of sound and score into a vehicle of signification."[22] Once music is "heard as" an individuated voice, the listener identifies with the aesthetic subject—the opposite of Brechtian (and Stravinskian) estrangement.

Stravinsky regarded sincerity as "a sine qua non that at the same time guarantees nothing," though, perhaps thinking of *Così*, he admitted "some insincere art (sincerely insincere) is quite good."[23] Yet to be immersed in music is to hear it as sincere. Like Mozart throughout *Così*, Stravinsky confuses "feigned" and "real" emotions during Tom's catechism in the Brothel scene. For this first step of his Progress, Nick has prepared his master/student for initiation into the "newly found state of manhood" (1.2). Another composer and librettist might have written a lusty, Venusberg-like episode; Auden and Stravinsky, by contrast, indulge their penchant for game-playing and ritual. Nick asks a series of questions in static but smoothly turning lines, as shown in example 6.4.

Tom first answers in rigid monotones, shown in example 6.5a, not those of secco recitative that invite rhythmic flexibility but those of accompanied recitative that require stricter adherence to the conductor's beat. Asked to define the "Beautiful," he loosens up a bit; supported by Mozartian *accompagnato* with a twist of Stravinskian displacement, he takes on Nick's gentle turns and reaches farther afield melodically (example 6.5b). The young initiate discourses on "pleasure" with equal confidence, though still within narrow musical confines. But Nick's final question, "Love is . . ." throws him off his game. The tonality lurches into E♭ minor, the strings skitter in disarray, and Tom recoils (example 6.5c).

Tom's unexplored and uncontrolled feelings have effectively burst forth to disrupt the mock ritual: "No, no more . . . Let me go." The dotted arrows in figure 6.2 map his progression from rigid and aloof to agitated but emotionally engaged. In breaking character, Tom takes a shaky first step toward greater consciousness (see table 3.4d).

Expert but hardly innovative, Stravinsky's sudden shifts of texture and mood follow the classic technique Gluck pioneered in *Orfeo ed Euridice* (1763) that marks the true beginning of modern operatic drama. Emotional breakthroughs like that of Tom usually find voice over flexible accompanied recitative. Mozart, though, uncovers unexpected emotional depth within a formal number, the act 1 quintet, "Di scrivermi ogni giorno," from *Così*. The paired lovers bid their half-comic, half-touching farewell as the amused Don Alfonso comments from the side. The men's departure is of course faked, as is their grief; oblivious to the ruse, the overly dramatic women profess sorrow more profuse than profound. In comically broken syllables over a static I-V^7 in F major (repeated six times), shown in example 6.6a, the sisters insist their lovers write every day—twice a day for Dorabella! Yet, as their voices bloom into sustained lyricism and chromatic

So tell my La-dy Bi-shop of the game What I did vow and pro-mise in thy name.

What is thy du-ty to thy-self?

Example 6.4. Nick's catechism questions (1.2).

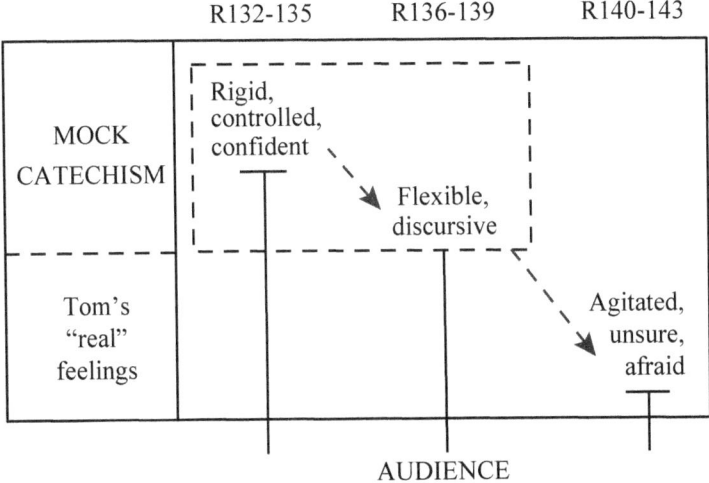

Fig. 6.2. Diminishing theatrical distance in Tom's break from the mock "ritual."

harmonies begin to move (example 6.6b), the lovers' feigned emotions seem to mix with true feeling, and with their harmony and voices so are we as listeners moved. In a span of a few measures, the music penetrates their brittle facade to discover true affection.

Such a metamorphosis would be impossible in elaborate baroque style. Classical clarity allows us to empathize momentarily with Mozart's lovers in their moment of "parting" before the laughing Don Alfonso instantly reminds us it is just a game. This flexible push and pull virtually defines buffa and, more broadly, classical style. Mozart's quintet, though, presents a special case. As a theatrical medium, formal musical numbers impose greater distance from the listener's natural discourse than spoken dialogue, secco, or even accompanied recitative; however, they can compensate by inspiring emotional attachment. A given classical number usually presents, if not a single emotion, at least a stable degree of attachment to a single character or group of characters.

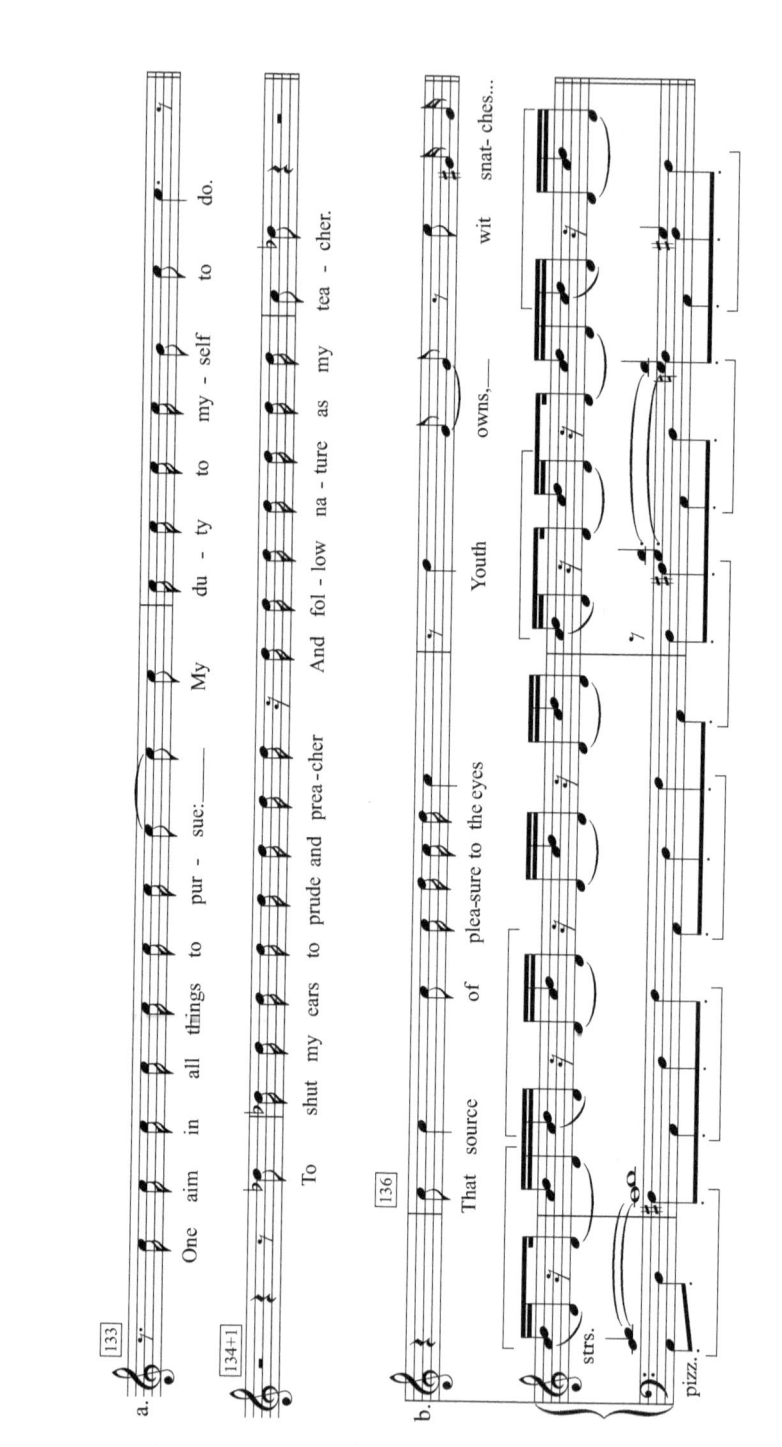

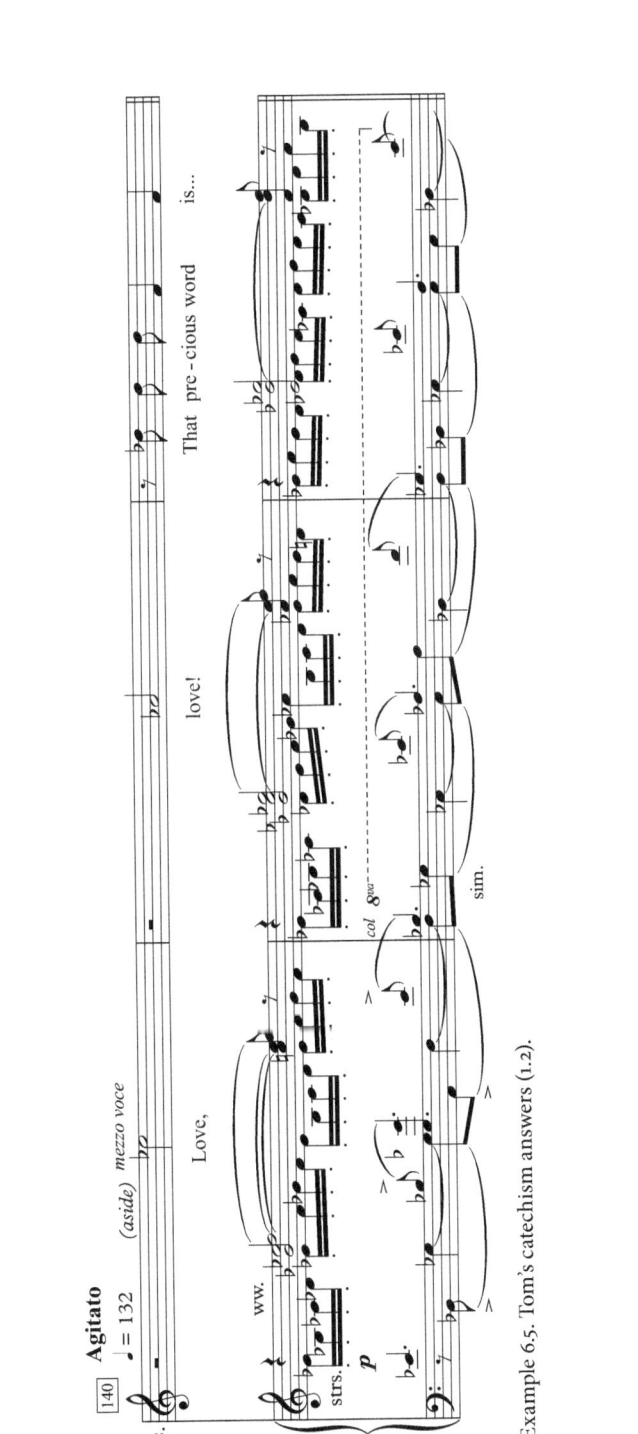

Example 6.5. Tom's catechism answers (1.2).

a. mm. 1–2

translation: Fiordiligi: *Write to me each (day.)*
Dorabella: *Two (more times write to me.)*

b. mm. 17–22

trans: *I divide my heart, my beautiful idol.*
Don Alfonso: *I'll burst if I don't (laugh).*

Example 6.6. Mozart, *Così fan tutte*, act 1 quintet "Di scrivermi."

However, within the quintet, subtle changes in articulation and harmony effectively draw in the audience, as the dotted arrows in figure 6.3 show. The direction of attraction arguably differs from Tom's emotional breakdown (fig. 6.2), where fragmented textures and dramatic shifts in vocal style essentially break through the boundary separating the stiffly formal catechism from the character's "real" feelings. By contrast, nothing overtly dramatic happens

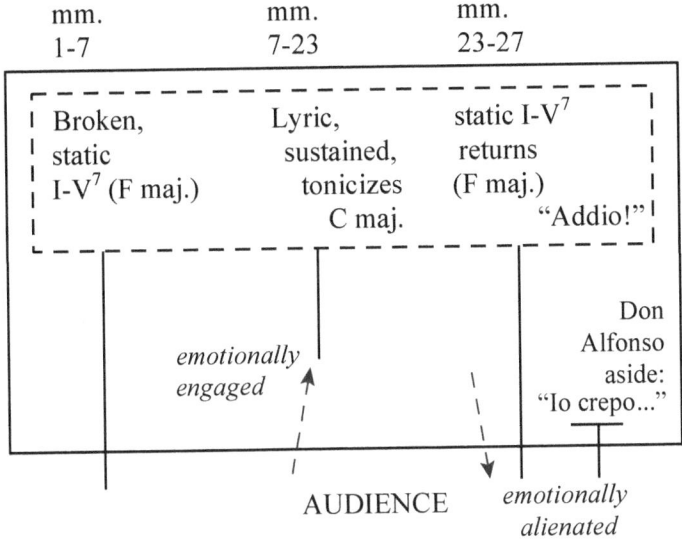

Fig. 6.3. Three theatrical levels in quintet, "Di scrivermi."

either onstage or even in the music of the quintet. There, a subtle but palpable new depth of character is realized primarily through the listener's imaginative engagement.

Note, though, the knowing Alfonso's asides; his clipped rhythms and verbal snickering signal his grasp of reality even as the lovers indulge in their sorrowful "play-within-the-play." Stravinsky apparently noticed too, for he also lets slip from his shallow hero a hint of emotional depth as the controlling Shadow looks on. He would also steal Mozart's static accompaniment figure, not to mention the opening motive from Ferrando's aria "Un' aura amorosa." What he learned from the master, though, extends far beyond those surface gestures.

Turning Back Time—Tom's Cavatina (1.2)

The sinister Nick represents a far more controlling presence than Alfonso because he has the power to turn back time, not to mention the power to claim souls. Offering Tom what is essentially a do-over, he foreshadows their decisive card game in the graveyard. (The November scenario makes no mention of a breakdown. There the villain turns the clock back because the reluctant hero simply claims "it is late," not the pregnant "it is *too* late.") Stravinsky marks the twelve "cuckoos" of the retrogressive clock with twelve pitches of a descending B♭ V^7 plus C and low D♭ shown in example 6.7. The extra pitches add to the foreshadowing by generating the 014, 015, and 016 trichords familiar to us from the

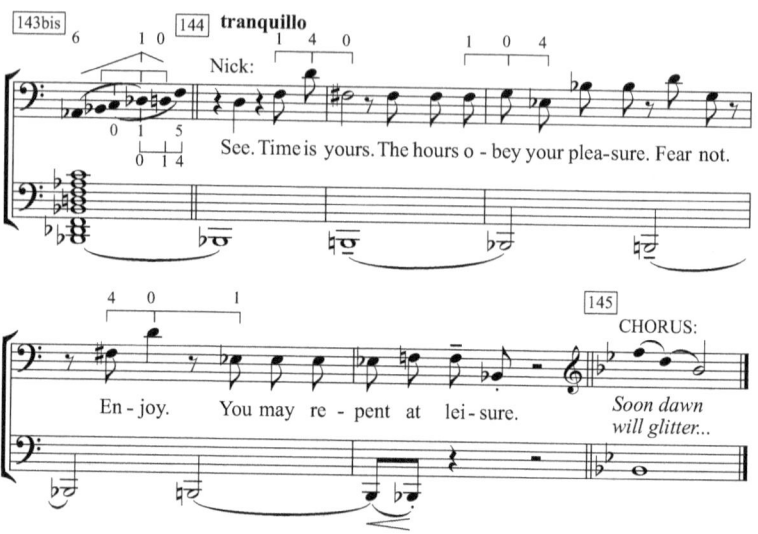

Example 6.7. Nick turns back the clock (1.2).

Graveyard prelude (cf. example 4.2). In his "consoling" words, Nick vacillates between B♭ major and G/B, the overlapping of which yields melodic 014's not unlike the octatonic span that precedes the Duettino in act 3, scene 3 (cf. example 4.10c). In that scene, B♭ is associated with "Adonis's" mad illusion. However, prior to his insanity, the key of B♭ signals Tom's desires: prurient (the brothel), melancholy ("Vary the song" in act 2, scene 1), and noble (his prayer in act 2, scene 3). Nick stakes a claim to B♭ as well: here resetting the clock; his aria in act 2, scene 1; and his descent into Hell in act 3, scene 2. These associations are not necessarily contradictory, though, for the Mephistophelean Shadow personifies his master's desires, as Auden explains: "The story of Faust is precisely the story of a man who refuses to be anyone and only wishes to become someone else. Once he has summoned Mephisto, the manifestation of possibility without actuality, there is nothing left for Faust to represent but the passive consciousness of possibilities."[24]

Set back one hour, the chorus rewinds to its opening "marche militaire" (as the original scenario calls it), this time in Nick's B♭ instead of C major. The scenario also calls for a "Serenade of the conventional gallant" to follow the "Catechism of Pleasure." In the libretto, Nick introduces Tom's confirmation piece as a "song in earnest," whereupon Auden has him return to the theme that previously rattled him: love. Patricia Blake, who at age twenty-three witnessed Stravinsky and Craft muscle through the first reading with Auden, Balanchine, and others "screaming parts," would underline the importance of this episode almost fifty years later. Responding to Taruskin's curt dismissal of the "dowdy brothel scene," she wrote to the *New York Times*:

On the contrary, it is the real site of love in this drama . . . It is a richly exuberant, bawdy scene, a choral celebration of Venus and Mars by the whores and roaring boys, while the rake-in-progress is readied for his initiation. Suddenly, at the sound of the word "love," Tom exclaims in a heartstopping aside, "Love, love! That precious word is like a fiery coal / It burns my lips, strikes terror to my soul." There follows Tom's aria, a cavatina so beautiful and so moving as to rival the greatest tenor love music in all opera. Whoever ventures to sing it, its musical and verbal meaning is wholly intelligible, capturing as it does the deepest sense of this great work of art. . . . Like others in the audience, I weep every time I hear it.[25]

What so moves Blake, Deryck Cooke, and others is not that the Cavatina borrows an opening arpeggio from Ferrando's aria.[26] Its Purcellian text setting (example 6.1) points to a much deeper connection with the "melodic-harmonic-rhythmic style" of the high baroque, as Cooke rightly observes (note 2 above). Paradoxically, Stravinsky's conservatism here confuses real and feigned emotion. Unlike his appropriations of Monteverdi (example 6.2), which he distorts just enough to remind us who composed them, the Cavatina hews closely to tonal convention and refrains from rhythmic displacement altogether. The reductive graph in example 6.8 shows how this noble-sounding air modulates, tonally pregnant harmonies (Neapolitan chords and a German augmented sixth) draw us in, and sequential progressions pull us along.

Stravinsky does not entirely hide behind a baroque facade; in measures 4–6 he constructs a virtual nest of 014's and 016's by inserting C♯s. Spelled as leading-tone B♯, this pitch forms a VII°7 over the outlined tonic in the bass. The clarinet's embellishing F♯♯'s at R152 (and throughout the aria) anticipate the "tonic+♯4" 0147 that introduces Anne's B-minor aria in the following scene (cf. example 4.9). More unsettling is the virtual collapse of the otherwise stable tonal structure at the end of the first verse (". . . thy wounded shade"), where a striking Neapolitan harmony (♭II⁴/³ at R155) dissolves into a chromatic morass. A similar collapse undermines "darkest hour that I . . ." (example 6.1a, mm. 5–6). Meandering sixteenths and a lone <–1,+2> in the bass threaten to derail the final cadence before the sighing gesture ("Dying, dying") returns, transposed to E minor, to anchor the tonality. In exactly what key the aria will conclude, though, remains unclear. The tonal center shifts at R157 but refuses to settle until Tom's E-minor sighs. The Neapolitan chord at R159 seems poised to cadence there before Stravinsky finally forces it back to C♯ minor.

Griffiths notes how tonally removed the Cavatina is from Tom's G-major music in act 1, scene 1, just as his previous outburst in E♭ minor (example 6.5c) marks his alienation from Anne's opening A major.[27] This tonal distance is especially palpable in the context of the Brothel, where much of the catechism and Mother Goose's later interruption (R162) also veer toward G major. The dramatic significance seems clear: Tom realizes his betrayal of Anne (E♭ minor against A major) and tries to pull back from his progress (C♯ minor against G major). His hesitation may also explain Stravinsky's otherwise surprising choice of the tonally proximate A major for the concluding "Lanterloo."

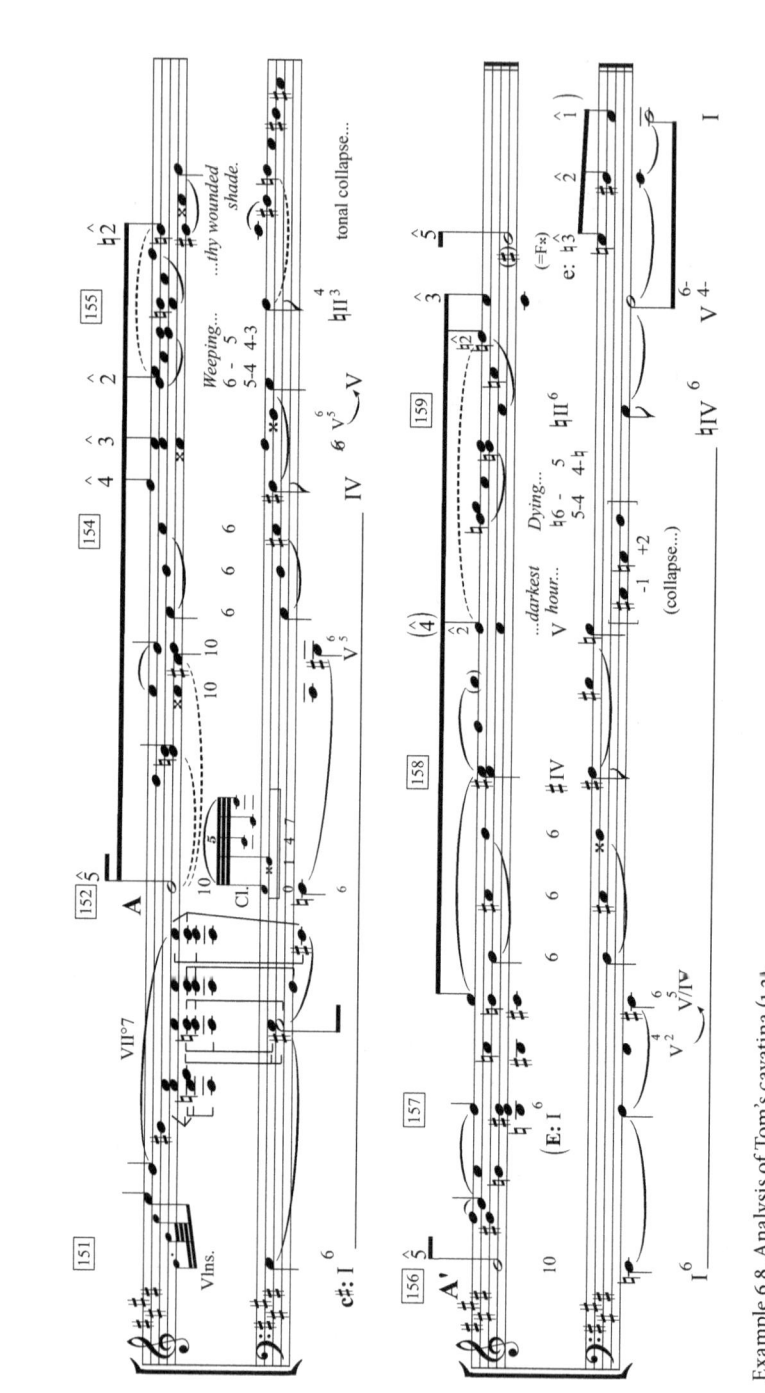

Example 6.8. Analysis of Tom's cavatina (1.2).

Example 6.9. Stages of final cadence, cavatina: R159.

Straus has discovered in the preliminary sketch an even stronger connection between the Garden and Tom's lament. There, rather than abandoning his cadential descent, Stravinsky has Tom lead strongly from B♯–C♯, thus recalling Anne's signature motive. Viewed in this light, the C♮/B♯'s in the opening phrases, which never resolve to the promised C♯, represent thwarted attempts to invoke her memory.[28] Even more broadly, the modulation to E minor, culminating on the Neapolitan six at R159, recontextualizes that same C♮. While Stravinsky reconsidered the direct resolution, his willful return to C♯ minor implies it. As Straus notes, B♯–C♯ exerts a background presence.

Another detail in the final cadence elegantly brings together the Cavatina's surface and background harmonic structure. The inner-voice F♯♯–G♯ at R159+1 recalls the clarinet's obbligato motive, but also 3̂ in E minor. Two further sketches—below and on the reserve side of Straus's example—shown in example 6.9, clarify the connection. Stravinsky first writes G♮–F♯–E (3̂-2̂-1̂ in E minor) in an alto voice, even as he arpeggiates tonic C♯-minor in the bass (example 6.9a). In introducing more details (example 6.9b), he adjusts the vocal line, augments the rhythm, respells G♮, and adds instrumentation to clarify his intended voice

a. mm. 1-2

b. E-major progression over c♯–minor ostinato

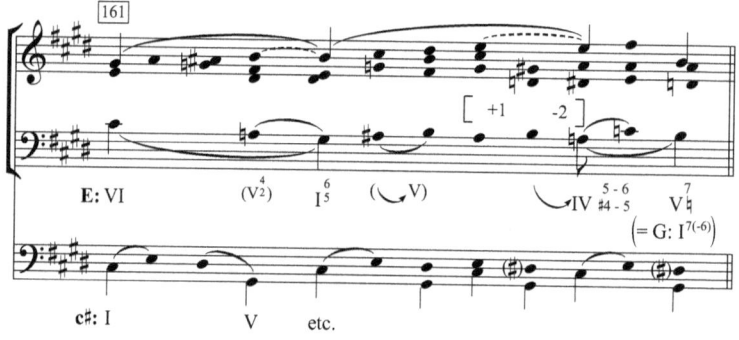

Example 6.10. Analysis of whore's chorus (1.2).

leading F𝄪–G♯ and F♯–E, which both echoes the original motive and obscures its E-minor origins.

Auden's text for the women's chorus, "How sad a song," prescribes the "expressive" cavatina that precedes it. The whores, though, are more attracted to his affect than empathetic: "But sadness charms. How handsomely he cries." Stravinsky certainly recognized the artifice when he chose to lift and repeat ten times—Mozart's static bass line from "Di scrivermi" (example 6.6a). Even with its broken melody, shown in example 6.10a, the minor mode and inner voice suspensions still resonate with Tom's sadness. But Stravinsky betrays their lustful compassion with posttonal dissonance (similar to the numbers analyzed in chapter 4). In keeping with the Cavatina's modulation and starting at R161, he overlays the C♯-minor ostinato with a chromatic (though mostly conventional) progression in E major, summarized in example 6.10b. By themselves, the upper voices seem to modulate seamlessly toward G major, the key of Mother Goose's interruption. Over the static bass, though, the progression becomes an increasingly crowded, dissonant tangle.

Set pieces like Tom's Cavatina, by definition, stand out from the surrounding music, as my summary of the Brothel scene in figure 6.4 shows. The three choral numbers establish a "middle ground" against which the formal catechism

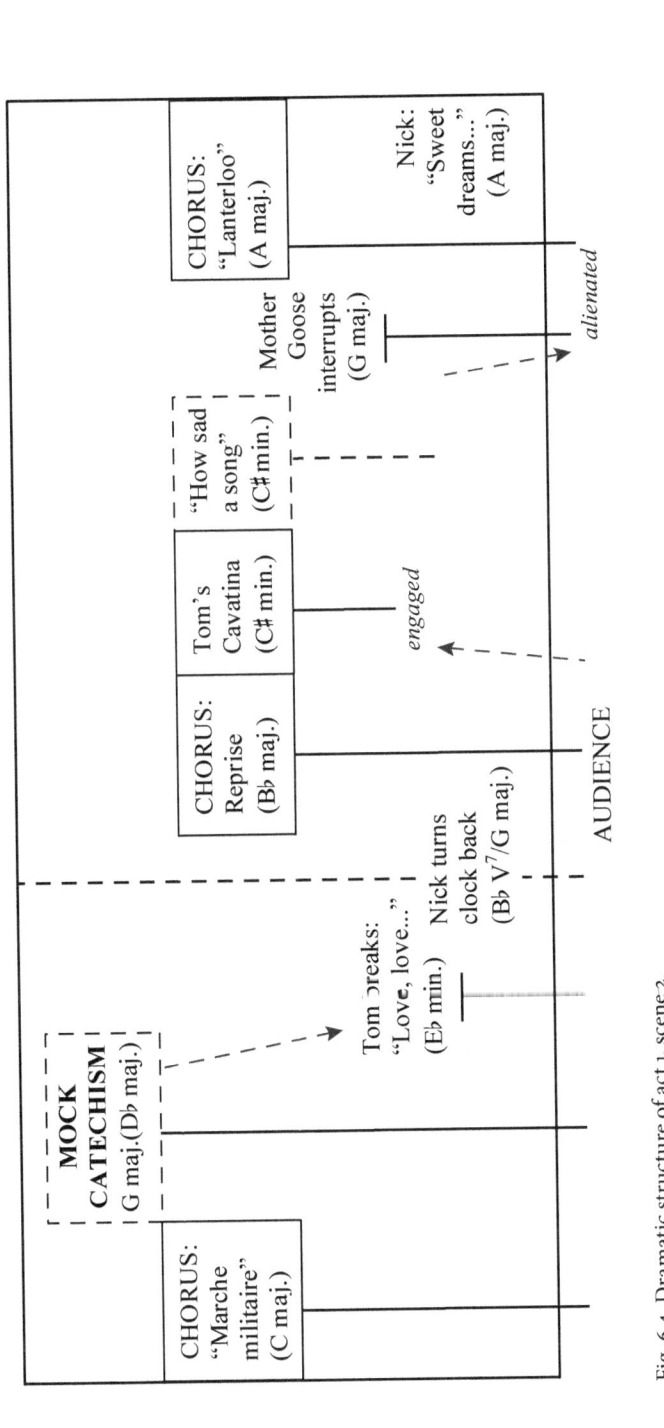

Fig. 6.4. Dramatic structure of act 1, scene 2.

and Tom's breakdown stand as more and less distant, respectively. Nick's position in the play between real and unreal seems ambiguous. Like Don Alfonso he stands aside, controlling the action. We see through his oily manipulation as easily as Despina's silly disguise, but that makes him as a character (like Despina) all the more real. As Auden claims, Nick is an actor, a sort of demon "stage manager" from Thornton Wilder's *Our Town*. I therefore place him, like Alfonso, at the metaphorical edge of the proscenium. As a formal number, the Cavatina sits back from Tom's "heart-stopping aside" at R140 (example 6.5c), yet its expressive music draws in the listener; Patricia Blake claims to weep "every time she hears it." Bitonal dissonance exposes the whore's sentimentality before Mother Goose interrupts to dispel altogether any remaining emotional attachment. As I suggest in chapter 4, posttonal elements in the opera generally function to dispel illusion, thus mitigating distance. But dissonance can also alienate. If such phenomena could be measured, the absolute distance would remain fairly consistent. Depending as it does on each listener's subjective engagement, I can only generalize about its effect.

From the mock formal catechism to Tom's touching Cavatina, the whores' empathetic response, Mother Goose's grotesque interruption, and the perverse "Lanterloo," Stravinsky structures the Brothel scene like an elaborate game. Just as Don Alfonzo manipulates the pairs of lovers in *Così*, crafty Nick controls his master like a puppeteer. With his usual assurance he pronounces a final "blessing":

> Sweet dreams, my master. Dreams may lie,
> But Dream. For when you wake, you die.(1.2)

However, the key of his soothing melody—A major—points back to Tom's pastoral home, not the impulsive Progress that lies ahead. In tonally linking the close of the Brothel scene with Anne's recitative that opens the next scene, Stravinsky may be telling us something. Perhaps Tom has not progressed as far as Nick imagines. I return to the composer's choice of keys and how he uses them to structure scenes and the opera as a whole in the next chapter.

To the extent expressive music engages the listener's emotions, theatrical distance is diminished. Yet might the expressiveness of Anne's B-minor aria and Tom's Cavatina function as just another conventional type—namely, the *sehnsucht* and *ausdrucksvoll* that Stravinsky usually eschews? Perhaps, but such posed expressivity is by its nature elusive. Unlike the feigned passions in *Così fan tutte* or the cultivated triviality of *Histoire du Soldat*, this type of expression disguises itself. Even stylized music, when allowed to work its spell, encourages the listener to suspend disbelief. Stoking our passions, expressive music evokes, as Sartre put it, "the return of consciousness to the magical attitude." Ortega asserts that we become fully conscious again through another magic, the "lantern" through which each art "removes and transfigures its objects" (see note 12). The contrast between these two images is revealing. Ortega's lantern separates us from the aesthetic object; Sartre's magic draws us into a shadowy, primal consciousness upon which categories of the world act immediately, *"without distance."*[29]

Stravinsky, as we know, usually prefers to shine Ortega's lantern. He imitates, but not too closely, for "real" music—that which is indistinguishable from its model—even if archaic, draws us into Sartre's magical world. That may explain why he long avoided conventional opera, a genre created to make us believe in unnatural characters and relationships. It comes as no surprise then that at certain moments *The Rake* lures us into the emotional world of its moral fable. Wooden, "pretend" stereotypes in one scene emerge as thinking, feeling, "real" beings in the next. The result can be inspiring, as when Anne finds the courage to pursue her errant beloved; or disarming, as when Baba shows empathy during the Auction scene; or even "devastating," as Cooke reacted to Tom's Cavatina and death scene.

And yet, the composer is not entirely in control of the matter. Musical—indeed, all—expression requires a receptive listener. Cooke and Blake experience Tom's Cavatina as "expressive" because they imagine it so. Lovers of opera and music in general (as well as theater and art) are conditioned, unconsciously, to project emotion onto the aesthetic object. Composers who wish us to respond otherwise must disengage. Mozart must overstate a musical type; Stravinsky must evoke and then arbitrarily violate established conventions, even his own. Immersing himself in Mozart's "lies" perhaps inspired him to discover deeper "truths" within his own characters.

Notes

1. Phillip Hope-Wallace, "'Rake's Progress' at Glyndebourne," *Manchester Guardian*, July 18, 1954.
2. Deryck Cooke, "'The Rake' and the 18th Century," *Musical Times* 103 (1962): 22.
3. Anthony Newcomb, "Sound and Feeling," *Critical Inquiry* 10, no. 4 (1984): 623.
4. In 1913 Stravinsky piously announced: "I dislike opera. Music can be married to gesture or to word—not to both without bigamy. That is why the artistic basis of opera is wrong and why Wagner sounds at his best in the concert-room," as quoted in Richard Taruskin, *The Danger of Music and Other Anti-Utopian Essays* (Berkeley: University of California Press, 2008), 110.
5. Jean-Paul Sartre, *The Emotions*, trans. Bernard Frechtman (New York: Philosophical Library, 1948), 73.
6. Roger Scruton, *Art and Imagination: A Study in the Philosophy of Mind* (London: Methuen, 1974), 107.
7. Pierre Boulez, "Blow up the Opera Houses!" Interview in *Der Spiegel*, September 25, 1967.
8. Mikhail Drushkin, *Igor Stravinsky: His Personality, Works and Views*, trans. Martin Cooper (New York: Cambridge University Press, 1983), 55; see also Jürgen Engelhardt, *Gestus und Verfremdung: Studien zum Musiktheater bei Stravinsky und Brecht/Weill* (Munich: Katzbichler, 1984). Stravinsky claimed to admire *Die Dreigroschenoper* (1928), though no evidence suggests any influence (*Expositions*, 93). He and Brecht, though, share a common lineage. Frederic Jameson traces Brechtian *Verfremdung* or "estrangement" to "the 'ostranenia'

or 'making-strange' of the Russian Formalists." In *Brecht and Method* (New York: Verso, 1998) 39, 86n, Rudolf Stephan also connects to Stravinsky ("Zur Deutung von Strawinskys Neoklassizismus").

9. Bertolt Brecht, *Brecht on Theater: The Development of an Aesthetic*, ed. and trans. John Willett (New York: Hill and Wang, 1964), 42.

10. Igor Stravinsky and Robert Craft, *Expositions and Developments* (Garden City, NY: Doubleday, 1962), 102. Simon Karlinsky attributes the novel staging of *Renard* and *Histoire* to Russian folk theater in "Stravinsky and Russian Preliterate Theater," in Jann Pasler, ed., *Confronting Stravinsky: Man, Musician and Modernist* (Berkeley: University of California Press, 1986), 12–13. The stylized gestures of Russian folk and Oriental theater permeated Diaghilev's "World of Art" circle and the Ballets Russes; see Glenn Watkins, *Pyramids at the Louvre: Music, Culture and Collage from Stravinsky to the Postmodernists* (Cambridge, MA: Harvard University Press, 1994), esp. 32–49, 280–95.

11. Quoted in Richard Taruskin, *Stravinsky and the Russian Traditions: A Biography of the Works through Mavra* (Berkeley: University of California Press, 1996), 1071.

12. José Ortega y Gasset, *"The Dehumanization of Art" and Other Writings on Art and Culture* (Garden City, NY: Doubleday, 1956), 26. André Gide anticipates Stravinsky, Brecht, and the Russian formalists in his 1904 essay, "The Evolution of the Theater," in which he advocates a return to the ancient conventions of liturgy and masked drama: "The artist chooses figures distant from us for the reason that time, or any kind of distance, allows an image to reach us only after it has been stripped of everything episodic, bizarre, and transitory, leaving only its portion of profound truth for art to work on. And the sense of strangeness that the artist seeks to produce by putting his characters at a distance from us indicates just this desire: to give us his work of art as a work of art, his drama as drama simply, and not to run after an illusion of reality . . . " quoted in Maureen Carr, *Multiple Masks: Neoclassicism in Stravinsky's Works on Greek Subjects* (Lincoln: University of Nebraska Press, 2002), 8.

13. Andre Bouchourechliev, *Stravinsky*, trans. Martin Cooper (New York: Holmes and Meier, 1987), 130.

14. Alessandro Striggio, *L'Orfeo*, trans. Nigel Rogers (London: EMI Records Ltd, 1993), 44.

15. Bouchourechliev, *Stravinsky*, 130.

16. Edward Dent, *Mozart's Operas: A Critical Study* (New York: Oxford University Press, 1947), 192.

17. Robert Hatten, *Musical Meaning in Beethoven: Markedness, Correlation, and Interpretation* (Bloomington: Indiana University Press, 1994), 174.

18. Robert Craft, ed., *Stravinsky: Selected Correspondence*, vol. 1 (New York: Alfred A. Knopf, 1982), 300.

19. Andrew Steptoe, *The Mozart-Da Ponte Operas: The Cultural and Musical Background to Le Nozze di Figaro, Don Giovanni, and Così fan tutte* (New York: Oxford University Press, 1988), 230. Yet Steptoe also notes, "'Flat' keys are used to depict false or shallow feelings, while authentic emotion is presented in dominant 'sharp' keys," a practice that may have inspired Stravinsky to associate keys with specific dramatic ideas (232).

20. Igor Stravinsky, *An Autobiography* (New York: Norton, 1962), 53–54; see chapter 2, note 16, for beginning of quotation and possible influences.

21. Naomi Cumming, "The Subjectivities of 'Erbarme Dich,'" *Music Analysis* 16 (1997): 16.

22. Ibid., 15, 17; see also note 6 above. Because individuals necessarily respond differently even to expressive music, it is impossible to measure psychological distance precisely. For this discussion we only need to recognize the general effects of musical and theatrical conventions.

23. Igor Stravinsky and Robert Craft, *Conservations with Stravinsky* (Garden City, NY: Doubleday, 1959), 120.

24. W. H. Auden, *The Dyer's Hand* (New York: Vintage International, 1989), 115.

25. Quoted in Taruskin, *Danger of Music*, 116.

26. Reproduced in Watkins, *Pyramids at the Louvre*, 356.

27. Igor Stravinsky, *The Rake's Progress*, libretto by W. H. Auden and Chester Kallman (New York: Boosey & Hawkes, 1951), 35.

28. Joseph N. Straus, "The Progress of a Motive in Stravinsky's *The Rake's Progress*," *Journal of Musicology* 9, no. 2 (1991): 175–77; Straus reproduces the original sketch in his example 10.

29. Sartre, *The Emotions*, 90.

7

THE STRUCTURE OF SCENES

As baffling as it is indisputable, Stravinsky carefully notated a key signature of three sharps, shown in figure 7.1, before sketching the first musical idea for his new opera (transcribed in example 4.8a). It would be weeks before Auden would send the first installment of his libretto, so the eager composer jumped ahead to the only instrumental number their scenario called for: the "Orchestral Prelude" to what was then act 3, scene 1 (Auden would later reposition the Auction scene to open act 3). Natural signs clutter the first five measures to cancel out the default sharps. The signature disappears altogether by the middle of the page.

Almost six months later, on May 8, 1948, Stravinsky would renotate the key signature for A major, the home key of his long-planned opera, and this time really mean it (though Anne's first pitch, C♮, still requires an accidental). The opening, closing, and every number in between either situated in or referencing the Garden are firmly rooted in A. But what was Stravinsky thinking when he first sketched the Graveyard prelude? Judging from the gravelly opening cello line, he notated three sharps to remind him of which pitches to avoid, not to use, wherein may lie the answer.

The inescapable conclusion is that, before he sketched a note, Stravinsky planned to structure his three-act opera within an A-major tonal frame. In jumping ahead, he knew the graveyard would be the most alien environment (aside from the prelude to act 1, which he composed last, he would not compose another number out of order).[1] As it circuitously labors toward the cadence on F major, the prelude progresses away from the tonal home implied by the key signature. Indeed, "dramatically and emotionally the Graveyard is as far as possible from the Garden," Straus observes. "The distance between them is the full extent of Tom's 'progress.'"

Straus sees C–C♯ as a structuring motive that, "held invariant between the two scenes, gives us a fixed musical point from which to measure that distance musically."[2] One can imagine Stravinsky focusing on the viola's repeated D♭–C's as a potential link when, six months hence, he took up Anne's opening line. The cello's "phrygian" B♭–A would be too alien to her pastoral verse. But C–C♯ offered just enough ambiguity—that is, more a classic ♯$\hat{2}$-$\hat{3}$ than modal mixture—without

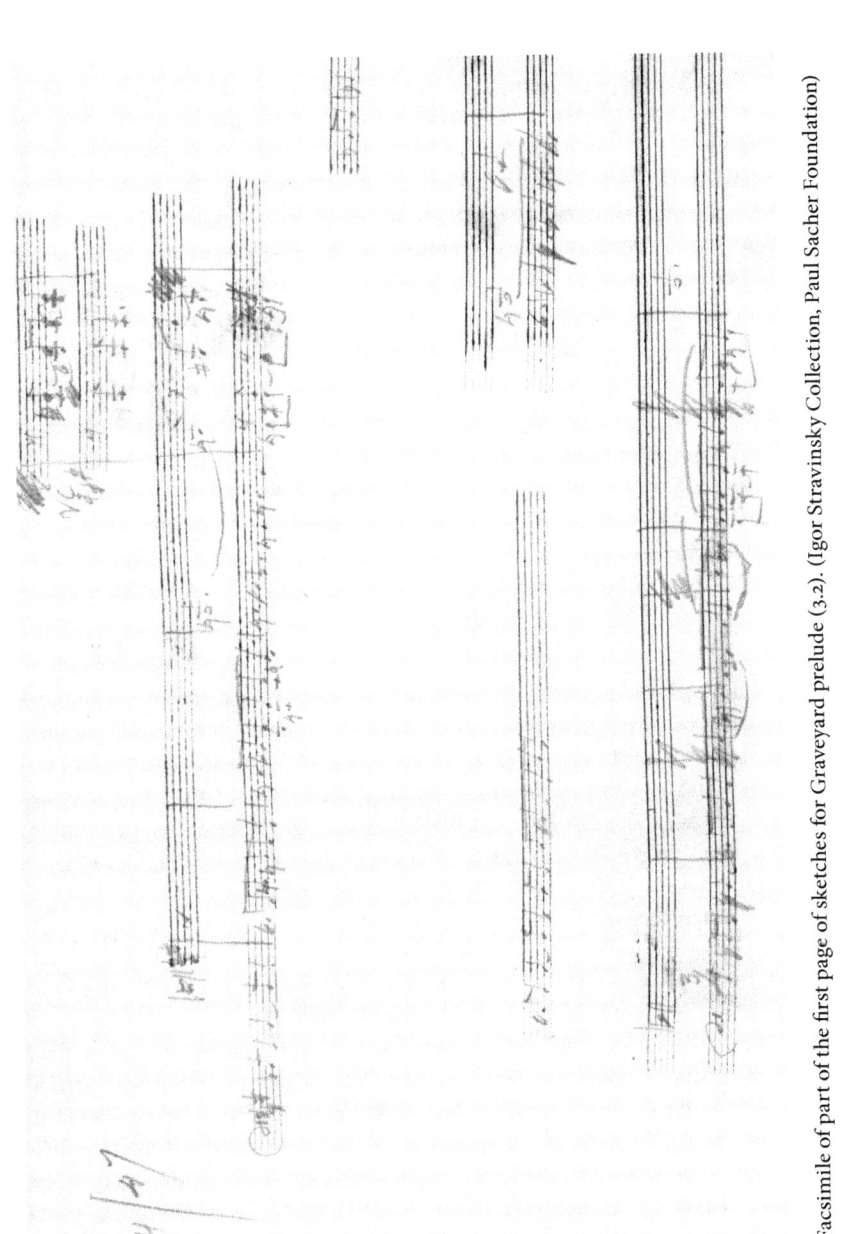

Fig. 7.1. Facsimile of part of the first page of sketches for Graveyard prelude (3.2). (Igor Stravinsky Collection, Paul Sacher Foundation)

seriously undermining the key. Whatever his reasoning, Stravinsky never waffled on his choice of pitches, even as he experimented with various metrical placements and accompaniment figures (cf. preliminary sketches in example 5.1b–e). Balanced on this simple fulcrum, the tonal distance spanning the Graveyard prelude and Trulove's Garden would serve to orient Stravinsky's structure for the entire opera.

Untied to a characteristic rhythm or tonal context, C–C♯ serves a more abstract unifying role than a thematic reminiscence or Wagnerian leitmotif. The few instances where Stravinsky does reuse a melody or idea are dramatically significant but isolated:

1. Tom assumes Anne's prayer from act 1, scene 3 (R192) when he prays for forgiveness in act 2, scene 3 (R204);
2. Anne's resounding "A love sworn before thee" from act 2, scene 2 (R93) saves Tom in the card-guessing game (3.2, R197); chords from her Cabaletta (1.3) herald his winning answer (R198);
3. Tom and Nick's Ballad tune that first interrupts the Auction (3.1, R134, R146) recurs transformed in the Graveyard, first by Nick (3.2, R165, R170) and then by Tom (R207);
4. The trilling motive that accompanies Tom's entrance into the Graveyard (R161) marks his transformation at the end of that scene (R206) and in his and Anne's Bedlam Duet (3.3, R249).

As I and others have described, rather than a network of motives or a conspicuous theme, Stravinsky uses tonal keys to connect dramatic motivations between scenes and structure the succession of numbers within them (see table 7.1). The composer right away establishes the succession from A major to G as significant in act 1, scene 1: Tom transposes Anne's opening verse down a step at R7; Nick explains Tom's inheritance in G major at R51; the lovers bid each other farewell in a G-major duettino (R81–88). In case we missed the point, the scene concludes when the isolated bass drops from A to G and Nick pronounces to the audience: "The PROGRESS OF A RAKE begins." An exclamatory G-major chord catapults the opera into the C-major march that opens scene 2. The message is clear: G major is the tonal engine driving Tom's Progress.

Although these passages seem dramatically convincing, one cannot always ascribe meaning to Stravinsky's choice of key. The E-major prelude functions as a supporting V to the initial A-major duet; if the latter identifies Trulove's Garden and all that it implies—for example, pastoral bliss, Anne, and so on—the former seems only structural. Likewise, a key with unambiguous meaning in one scene may not necessarily retain that meaning elsewhere. Is the A-major "Lanterloo" meant to recall the Garden or to prepare a smooth transition to Anne's recitative? (Yet, as discussed in the previous chapter, the fact that Stravinsky chose not to emphasize a tonal/dramatic disjunction may be equally significant.)

Even as extra-musical factors prescribe certain keys for certain dramatic situations, Stravinsky still adheres to a strict musical development. From section

Table 7.1. Dramatic Association of Keys.

Key	Dramatic Idea	Major	Minor
A	Garden, home, return (Anne)	1.1, 3.3, epilogue	1.3, 3.3 (R273)
G	Progress	1.1, 1.2, 1.3, 2.1, 2.3, 3.2, 3.3	3.1, 3.2, 3.3
B♭	Tom's desires (Nick); madness	1.1 (R58), 1.2, 2.1, 2.3, 3.1, 3.2, 3.3	3.2 (R201)
C	Love	1.3, 3.1, 3.2	3.2, 3.1
B	Anne's doubt; Tom's demise	3.2 (R185)	1.3, 2.2, 3.2 (R174)
D	Baba	2.2	2.3, 3.1

to section and number to number, the succession of tonal centers, along with thematic development, tempo, meter, and instrumentation, anchors his larger organization. How and why he proceeds from one tonal area to the next varies as widely as his foreground play with tonality. In this chapter I examine two possibilities: a linear span and a motivic span.

Linear Span—Act I, Scene 3: Anne's Recitative, Aria, and Cabaletta

The shortest and most easily decipherable scene follows a simple succession from A minor to B minor to C major. Anne's Recitative, Aria, and Cabaletta dramatize her decision to venture to London where she hopes to reunite with Tom. Besides some notable harmonic diversions (R184–85, R200–1, and R205–6), Stravinsky generally adheres to these tonal centers, projecting fully formed structural descents: F♯–B in the Aria and G–C in the Cabaletta, the middle and background of which are shown in example 7.1a and 7.1b.

The scene opens in the safe confines of Trulove's garden as the spurned Anne prepares to leave. The A-minor introduction (R177–80), scored for double reeds, recalls the introduction to scene 1. Having received "no word from Tom," Anne questions whether love can survive away from her pastoral home. Casting aside her doubt, she resolutely climbs from e^2 to $f\sharp^2$ to g^2 (R182), declaring: "Love hears, Love knows, Love answers him across the silent miles, and goes." The supporting progression, a^7–b^7–C^7, anticipates the background structure of the entire scene before concluding on V^6 of B minor.

In the melancholy Aria (R183–90), Anne desperately hopes Tom will still respond to her affection: "It cannot be thou art a colder moon upon a colder heart." Her beckoning father prompts a new pang of doubt. In an accompanied recitative (R190), she reconsiders deserting him "for a love who has deserted me." The bass retreats auspiciously from B to A; the plaintive winds take over and the bassoon continues down to F. Again resolute, Anne returns to her original plan

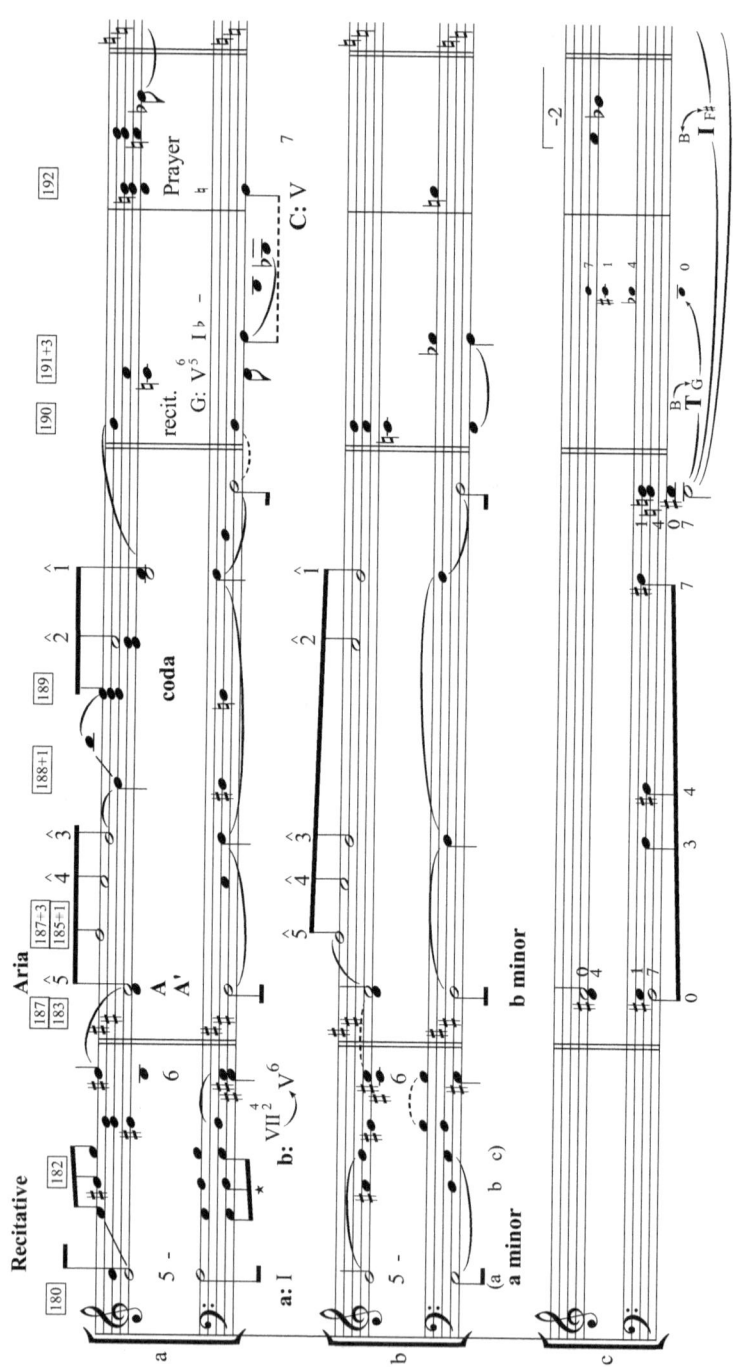

Example 7.1. Middle ground (a), background (b), and posttonal (c) structure of Anne's aria and cabaletta (1.3).

and the cello F♯ guides the harmony gently to G major, the key of her departing prayer (R192–93). Her faith in the power of Love fully restored, Anne bursts into an exuberant C-major Cabaletta: "I go to him. Love cannot falter, Cannot desert;... If love be love, It will not alter." From this point on, the tonal center of C firmly identifies the power of Love.

Anne's scene closely follows the multipart structure (also known as *solita forma*) of the nineteenth-century *scena ed aria*: introductory accompanied recitative, slow *cantabile*, intervening recitative or *tempo di mezzo*, and allegro *cabaletta*. The progression from slow to fast and lyric to florid underscores a dramatic change (usually from reflective to active), often instigated by a brief interjection from another character or even chorus. A hallmark of Donizetti, Bellini, and early Verdi, this musical structure typically dramatizes a pivotal change in character, as is the case with Anne.

(A brief comparison with Tom's equally expansive aria the opening of act 2, "Vary the Song," reiterates the essential stasis of his character. From his accompanied recitative [R10] and accelerating allegros [R12 and R19] erupt previously unexpressed layers of feeling, but his reprise of the plaintive aria at R23 serves to repress it all. While Tom here uncovers even greater personal depth than in his earlier Cavatina, he remains as yet unenlightened and unchanged.)

Critics never fail to cite Stravinsky and Auden's wholesale embrace of bel canto conventions in Anne's scene. However, its dramatic arc and even certain musical ideas also point to the Countess's act 3 aria from *Le Nozze di Figaro*, itself a precedent for bel canto composers. Depressed by her husband's lack of interest and infidelity, the Countess decides to take action. In her opening recitative, she pities herself for having to resort to trickery. In the nostalgic andantino she asks, "Where are those sweet moments?" when he still loved her. Finally, in a thrilling allegro she determines to win him back through her own constancy. Example 7.2 shows that besides the dramatic and formal parallels, the two C-major arias also share an opening allegro motive (a and b) and strikingly similar instances of modal mixture (c–f).

Mixture also figures prominently in Anne's slow aria, where the oscillating bass D and D♯ (R188–89) raise modal conflict to the structural middle ground (represented as a linear 0347 in example 7.1c). The cadence preceding her G-major prayer likewise projects a middle-ground modal shift. (Stravinsky also briefly inflects G minor to major in the medial dominant leading from the Cabaletta's B section at R206+4.) A similar inflection from C minor to major literally replaces the traditional cadence in the dramatic transition from the Prayer to the Cabaletta (R193). The sections nominally progress from G major to C major, but instead of resolving the B to C and F to E, Stravinsky anticipates the tonic minor and foregrounds the subsequent resolution from E♭ to E♮. Here and elsewhere, mixture entails a <–2,+1> between the soprano's F–E♭ and the trumpet's subsequent E♮ (example 7.1c). In fact, almost every instance of mixture in the Cabaletta—namely, at R195+1, R198+1, R201, R204+2, R208+2, and R209+1—either implies the motive at the middle ground (e.g., <–2,+1> in example 7.2d) or on the surface

a. *Le Nozze di Figaro,* act 3, "Dove Sono," allegro, mm. 12-15.

b. Cabaletta (1.3)

c. "Dove Sono," allegro, mm. 3-7.

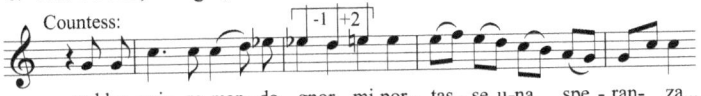

nel lan guir - re man - do gnor, mi por - tas - se u - na spe - ran - za...

trans: ... *in langueur always loving bring me hope...*

d. Cabaletta (1.3)

e. "Dove Sono," allegro, mm. 22-25.

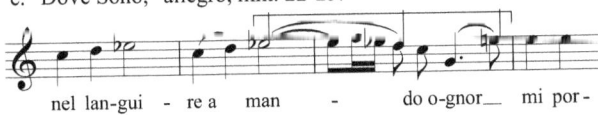

nel lan-gui - re a man - do o-gnor__ mi por -

f. Cabaletta (1.3)

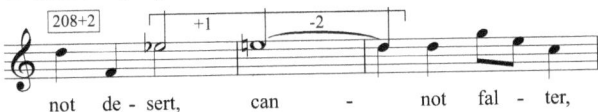

not de - sert, can - not fal - ter,

Example 7.2. Comparison of Anne's cabaletta with the Countess's allegro.

(example 7.2f), as it likewise does for "Dove Sono" (example 7.2c and 7.2e). The motive even spans the ten measures from R201 to R203+1 in the soprano's highest register: A♭–A–G.

Example 7.1c also shows how posttonal harmonies connect different parts of the scene. My previous analysis of the slow Aria (example 4.9) traces the transformation of the B minor+♯4 0147. Though never again a stable tonic, 0147 punctuates several subsequent transitions. In the central recitative, an ambiguous progression in G minor (R191+3) contains a link (D–C♯–B♭–G) highlighting the transposition from the original B minor+♯4. The chromatic 0147 also marks several fleeting diversions in the Cabaletta. The B–C–E♭–F♯ at R197+2 and R200+2 combines the boundary B/F♯ of B minor with the Cabaletta's minor-mode C/E♭. The same chord with B instead of C in the bass and an added A functions as a pivot in the abrupt transition at R204+2. One last diversion at R209+1 (D–E♭–F♯–A) both preserves the previous E♭/F♯ and recalls the D/F♯ from the original. Not coincidentally, these chords all mark incursions into the minor; both modal mixture and posttonal dissonance remind us of Anne's earlier doubt, just as the subsequent returns to C major reaffirm her newfound faith.

Over the course of act 1, scene 3, posttonal transformations and modal ambiguity encroach upon a conventional tonal background to highlight Anne's emotional transformation from passive victim to active agent. In that, she joins Mozart's Countess in the great musical and dramatic tradition of operatic heroines. Stravinsky's original ending (see prelude, example 0.1a) may have disappointed Auden, but even without her glorious final high C, Anne's aria "demolishes the theory that we are the irresponsible puppets of fate or chance."[3]

Motivic Span—Act II, Scene 2

Scenes involving several characters and situations tend to be longer, more varied in their succession of numbers, and more complex than Anne's aria. Though the librettists avoided the classic midpoint finale (a problem I address in chapter 10), some scenes in acts 2 and 3 are structured like extended finales. Stravinsky explains: "In the earlier scenes the mold is to some extent pre-Gluck in that it tends to crowd the story into secco recitatives, reserving the arias for the reflective poetry, but then, as the opera warms up, the story is told, enacted, contained almost entirely in song."[4]

The first such extended scene is act 2, scene 2. Anne arrives in London to discover Tom has married Baba the Turk. Stravinsky presents the events of this complex scene in a series of mostly discrete numbers organized into three basic harmonic regions, summarized in example 7.3: from the melancholy introduction to Anne's apprehensive Arioso (C minor/E♭ major); a festive interlude and Anne and Tom's turbulent Duet (F major/minor); Baba's comical entrance, a moving Trio, and the majestic Finale with chorus (D major).

As the summary graph shows, unlike act 1, scene 3, foreign keys intrude into each region: B minor in the arioso, D major and G major in the servants' procession, E♭ minor in the trio, and a bass F♮ in the chaconne. These passages represent more than the surface diversions of Anne's previous scene. They embed into the harmonic background familiar foreground motives, like 014 and (+1,−2), to create distinctive chords and abrupt juxtapositions that support the complex drama unfolding on stage. From Anne's chilly arrival to her bitter exit amid the gawking crowd, she and her fellow characters progress through a series of doubts, deceptions, charades, confrontations, and revelations, all of which Stravinsky tells, enacts, and contains "almost entirely in song."

Stravinsky alludes to Gluck's reformed opera seria, even though most of *The Rake* follows the mold of Mozartian buffa. A typical buffa finale constantly introduces new dramatic situations and combinations of characters, usually culminating in an accelerating swirl of tempos and plot twists. The London scene follows this pattern, though its grand chaconne concludes more like the stately act 3 of *Figaro* (a much happier wedding celebration) than the chaotic midpoint finales of *Figaro*, *Così*, and *Don Giovanni*. Stravinsky, of course, also deviates tonally from these integrated models; though, as is usually the case in *The Rake*, tonal/dramatic connections justify the larger disjunction. The C-minor introduction anticipates parts of Anne's Arioso (R93) and her Duet with Tom (R117), but Baba's entrance in D major at R127 utterly disrupts the scene's tonal unity. The dramatic justification is clear: Anne's faith in love—and the waning power of C—is dashed when Tom's new wife arrives. Baba's D major dominates the rest of the scene.

Introduction and Arioso (R79–97)

A succession of three startling chords, shown in example 7.4a, introduces the bleak world of London. Meandering string thirds, reminiscent of the tranquil "Soave sia il vento" from *Così* (example 7.4d), accompany a melancholy trumpet solo that Stravinsky admitted he derived from the beginning of act 2 of Donizetti's *Don Pasquale* (example 7.4c). He stole the opening chords, too (example 7.4b).

As we know, *The Rake* is full of such "borrowings." The unique variety of them at the start of act 2, scene 2, though, perhaps best demonstrates Watkins's point that Stravinsky's personal "style was . . . coined not so much through the appropriation of ingredients from a particular historical or cultural model as through their fracture and purposeful reassemblage: criticism of received materials becomes the modus operandi for the creative act."[5] The composer, in reference to *Oedipus*, likens his approach to a "*Merzbild*, put together from whatever came to hand . . . the Alberti-bass horn solo . . . the *Folies Bergères* tune . . . and the Wagnerian 7th-chords. . . . I have made these bits and snatches my own, I think, and of them a unity."[6] And by all evidence, he achieved a more integrated "unity" from such disconnected ideas in *The Rake* than in any of his other works.

The three opening chords also introduce the only chromaticism of the first twenty-six measures, though only the third (B♭–D–F♯–G–C) would sound out of place in *Don Pasquale*. As set-class 01468, it contains each of the three trichords 014, 015, and 016 featured in the Graveyard prelude. Knowing where the scene

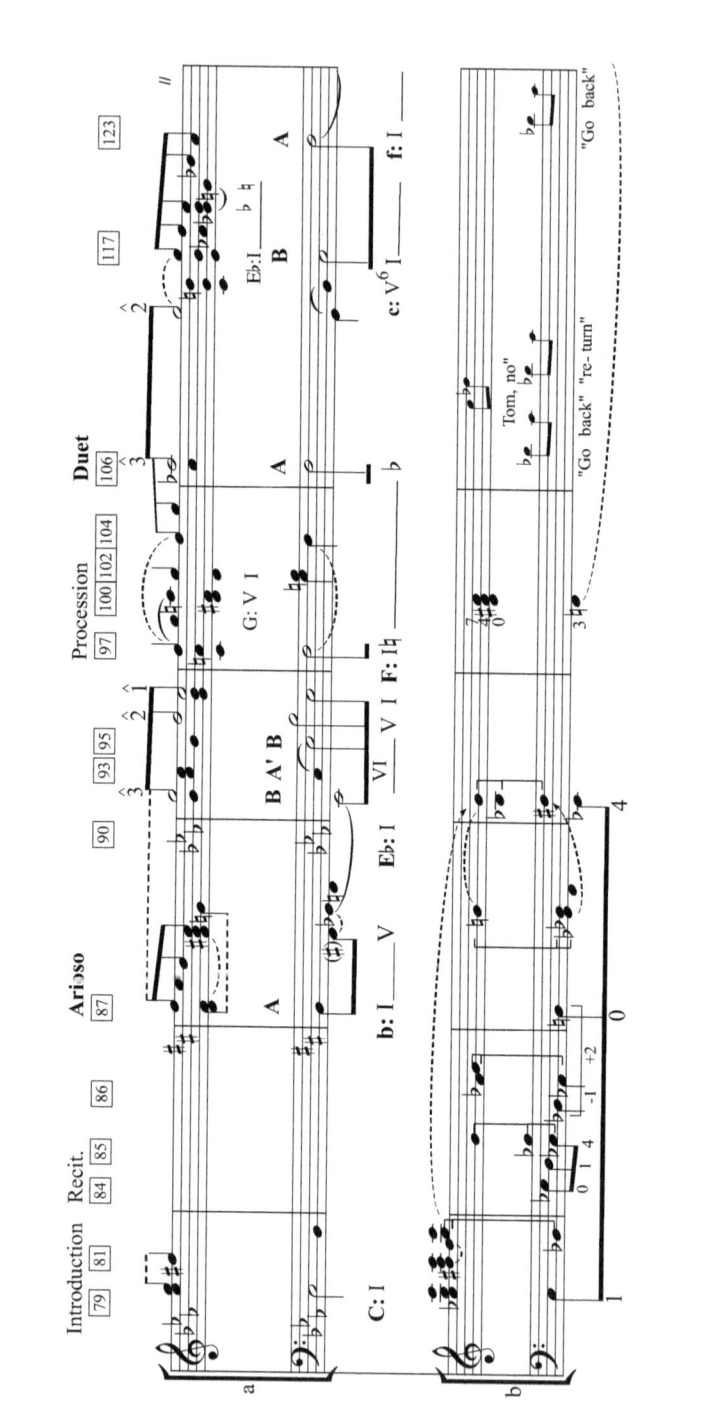

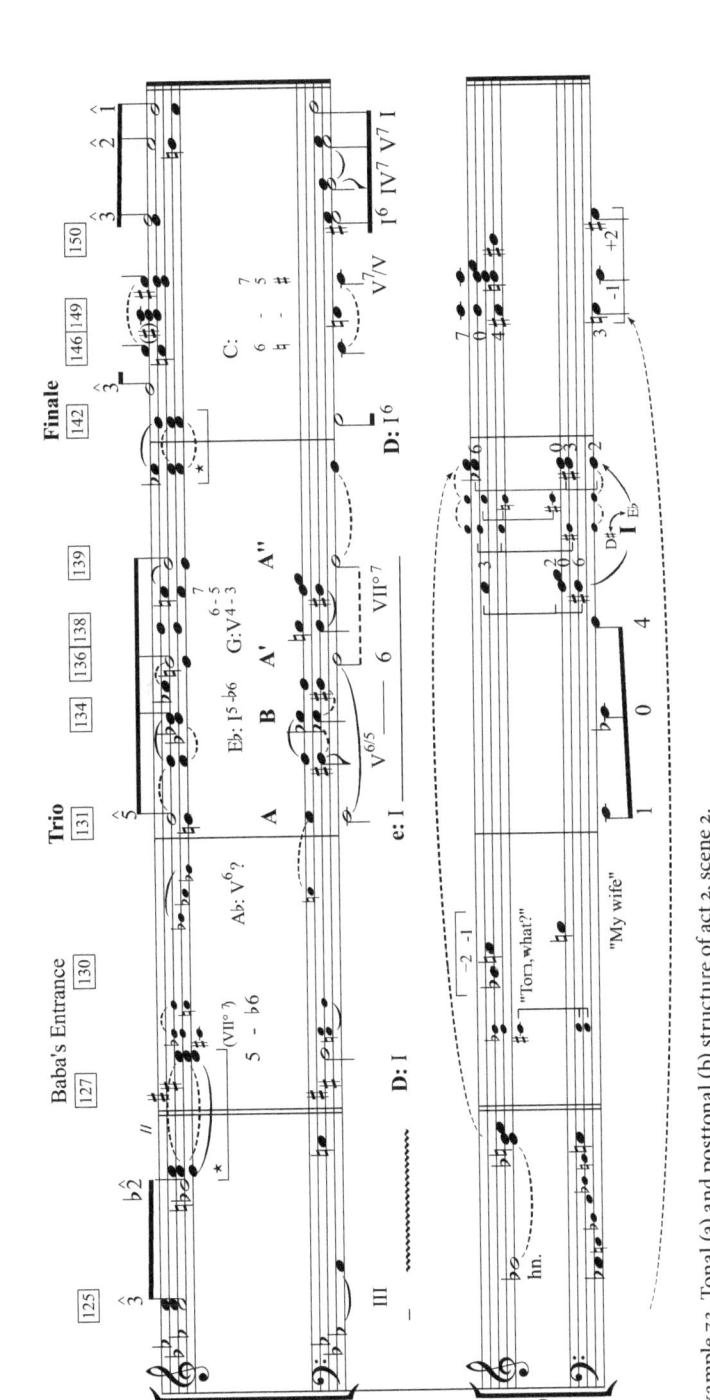

Example 7.3. Tonal (a) and posttonal (b) structure of act 2, scene 2.

a. *The Rake's Progress*, act 2, scene 2.

b. Donizetti, *Don Pasquale*, act 2, mm. 1-3.

c. Donizetti, *Don Pasquale*, act 2, mm. 6-10.

d. Mozart, *Così fan tutte*, act 1 trio "Soave sia il vento."

Example 7.4. Comparison of opening of act 2, scene 2, with passages from Donizetti and Mozart.

is headed, one may interpret the D/F♯ as foreshadowing Tom's imminent marriage (otherwise the chord is voiced the same as Donizetti's opening $V^{4/2}$), but this disturbing harmony portends unsettling harmonic changes well before Baba arrives.

Anne meekly interrupts the somber prelude (R84) in a recitative that transitions to the alien B minor of her Arioso (Stravinsky originally sketched this opening section in C minor, discussed below). The music progresses to nearby F♯ minor (R89+1), at which point Anne decisively turns on the pivot tone g^1 to distant E♭ major (R90). Her tonally unstable tune gravitates back to C minor, where Stravinsky recapitulates the material previously heard in B. This peculiar tonal path from B to E♭ to C, besides projecting a background 014 (shown in example 7.3b), also carries profound dramatic implications. Anne admonishes herself—"O heart, be stronger"—in B minor, the key of her desperate Aria from act 1, scene 3. Her lively E♭-major song ("No step in fear shall wander") musters courage for her forceful affirmation in C minor: "A love that is sworn before Thee can plunder Hell of its prey." Remember this line, for its return at the moment of Tom's deepest despair in act 3, scene 2, will be the turning point of the opera.

Stravinsky's setting, shown in example 7.5, strikes a perfect balance between smooth and angular melody and between placed and displaced accents. The keywords "love" and "sworn" get it all: flowing melismas and angular leaps; stressed beats and off-beats. However, the high point of the Arioso—and, in its return in act 3, of the entire opera—is "plunder hell of its prey." The compound melody reaches both upward (climbing stepwise E♭–F–G) and chromatically downward (E–E♭–D) to "hell," no less. The final "its prey," a seemingly straightforward cadence, merits a rhythmic analysis on its own. This simple descending third recurs throughout the short aria in varied metric placements, both within phrases and as a cadential gesture (see also example 7.6 below). However, only in setting "<u>its</u> prey" does Stravinsky go out of his way to stress the wrong syllable.

Stravinsky's placement of bar lines also seems fussy if not bizarre. He indicates an *allargando* for the final "plunder hell," but the dotted bar line marked in the piano (though not in the orchestral) score indicates he probably wanted it to begin only after the bassoon's rising sixteenths. But again, why not just place the bar line there to start with, and why not return *a tempo* on a downbeat? Mozart or Donizetti would have. Stravinsky goes out of his way to avoid the "natural" solution. For Anne to hold "of" until the end of a bar is too easy. The singer (and conductor and orchestra) would simply stop counting until she was ready to go on. "Its prey" must come in the middle of the bar so that the phrase remains rhythmically taut. These peculiarly placed accents and tempo changes are Stravinsky's unique way of painting Anne's resolve. She will not take the passive course. Still, her bold words cannot yet sway events, and she ends timidly with a brief return to her E♭-major ditty (R95–96).

While abrupt, Anne's tonal shifts are not disjunct, as Stravinsky constructs his surface harmonies to integrate the background 014. The transitional recitative at R84–87 is a case in point. After the diatonic trumpet solo, Stravinsky hints at

Example 7.5. Setting of "A love that is sworn before Thee" (2.2).

Example 7.6. Draft of act 2, scene 2: R89–90 showing B minor glued over C minor, with adjusted chords (analytical notations added).

the distant B minor to come in a succession of 014-related chords—articulated, not coincidentally, like the "aftershocks" of the fortissimo jolts that open the scene—shown in example 7.4a. The bass line itself, E♭–D–C♭, both emphasizes the tonal goal (B minor) and 014. Notice that the bass voice leading into the Arioso—B♭–A–B—also follows the familiar <−1,+2>.

Stravinsky's first thought, though, was to integrate the entire Arioso within the C-minor/E♭-major frame. He literally glued the B-minor transposition of the lines "O heart, be stronger" (R87–89+1) over his first attempt in C minor. No evidence indicates that he revised the preceding recitative to accommodate the new key (being on a separate sheet, he could have composed it after completing the Arioso), but he definitely adjusted the transition into E♭ major. Example 7.6 shows his original and alternate version (marked "better") of the three transitional chords before R90. The copious accidentals of the "ossia" account for the new key signature.

So what did he change? Because the first chord, G♭/B♭/G, is an 014, it shares pitches with both previous tonics, F♯ and G, and thus transitions smoothly from either one. In his first version, the bass descends chromatically (G–G♭–F–E–E♭) while the upper voices change only slightly. In the second and final version the bass progresses more directly (G♭–F–E♭) but now guides the changing harmonies, pregnant with 014's and 016's, through inversion. Even in the E♭ major that follows, the clarinet retains F♯–G, the familiar ♯$\hat{2}$-$\hat{3}$ that haunts Anne's music from the beginning of the opera. Whether as a vestige of B minor, the key of her self-doubt, or a portent of her rival to come, F♯ lingers to the very last measure of the arioso. Perhaps most striking, the F♯/G/B♭ connects back to the last fortissimo chord of the introduction (R80+3). Stravinsky typically uses posttonal cells like 014 to mediate between distant keys, but rarely does he so strongly integrate them into the background harmonic structure as in the Introduction and Arioso of act 2, scene 2.

Procession and Duet (R97–127)

The mood changes quickly with the festive F-major procession of Baba's servants (R97). Stravinsky here generally avoids 014, with its minor mode implications, in favor of the diatonic 027.[7] Casting a shadow over the proceedings is the sudden D major over F♮ at R100 (see example 7.3). The resultant 0347 (D/F/F♯/A) reflects less a modal conflict (D major/minor) than bitonal tension between G major in the upper voices and the persistent F major in the bass; Anne senses an underlying dark presence. (Oddly, this diversion to G major anticipates the structural conflict of the bitonal Duettino in act 3, scene 3, as analyzed in example 4.10. There G major signals Anne's departure from Tom; here G major portends Tom's betrayal of Anne.) At R102, subdued divided strings continue the elegant procession as both the upper voices and bass resolve to G major. Yet Anne becomes so spooked she ceases even to sing, observing in spoken voice: "I tremble with no reason." The bass descent after R103 steers the passage back to F major (R104).

Stravinsky shifts to F minor the moment Tom arrives (R106). Each time he demands that Anne "Go back" (R110 and R124+2), he sings D♭-C. She responds, "Tom, no!" on an ascending C-D♭, the same pitches (spelled C-C♯) she sang in her idyllic opening (see example 5.1a). The contrast between C-C♯ (♯$\hat{2}$-$\hat{3}$) in A major and C-D♭ ($\hat{5}$-♭$\hat{6}$) in F minor thus encapsulates the state of their—and the opera's—central conflict: her ascending motive calls for his return; his descending versions mark his refusal.

Saturated with chromatic inflections and posttonal dissonance, this turbulent duet eventually winds its way to a G minor^6 chord (with added C), ostensibly V^6 of the following B section (R117). Here, in a much slower tempo, Tom tries to reason with Anne. He sings essentially in E♭ major, ignoring the steady C-minor bass, and even briefly tonicizes A♭ (R118). But he cannot keep up the pretense of major, as G♭'s creep in at R118+2 and R120+1, like the clarinet's nagging

F♯'s throughout Anne's E♭-major Arioso (R90–96). His repressed anxiety erupts again with the agitated return to F minor at R123.

Anne futilely responds to Tom's outburst in the relative major, A♭ (R125), while the bass ascends chromatically. Full of 014's, the progression effectively obliterates any strong tonal sense. The troubled pair gravitate to E♭/G♭ before stopping abruptly, leaving a single horn E♭ hanging in the tense air. The opera's most impassioned and anxious moment is interrupted by its most banal. Piping along in a static D major (R127), two bassoons, marked *tranquillo*, accompany the arrival of exotic Baba the Turk in her sedan-chair. The disjunction is no mere comic relief; Baba and her materialistic caravan have supplanted poor Anne, at least for the time being. Stravinsky already planted the seed in the servants' procession (R100). More specifically, F♯/G♭ has infiltrated both earlier sections in E♭ major: Anne's song (R90–97) and the duet (R117–23). The culminating sonority at R126 recalls Tom's earlier hint of E♭ minor (R120). The only change required for Baba's arrival is the resolution to D.

Trio (R127–42)

Waiting in her sedan, Baba quickly lapses from her sedate D major into impatient chromaticism. Noticing Anne, she shifts first to VII^{o7}, then B♭^{6}. Anne too notices; rising from B♭ to C, she asks, "Tom, what?" Punctuated by the returning solo horn, he intones his regretful response, "My wife, Anne" on B♮, thus completing <+2,–1> (example 7.3b). Tom has revealed the painful truth. This most awkward moment most clearly demonstrates the dramatic function of (+1,–2). Its chromatic intensity undermines not only the prevailing tonal sense but the prevailing sheen of pretense and deception as well.

Shocked and heartbroken, Anne takes up Tom's B and descends chromatically (with the solo horn) in her uncharacteristically ironic response: "I see, then, it is I who was unworthy." Anne's line here recalls her hesitation at R85+2 when she first arrived in London ("The hand draws back"); her G♭-F♭-E♭ sets up the E minor to come (R131). But the horn's G implies V^6 of A♭. Like the earlier motion to D major (R127), the arrival of E minor at R131 depends not on a directed progression but on the resolution of a solitary E♭ to E♮. Consequently, both successions seem alienating, even arbitrary, like Tom's marriage.

The following Trio is essentially a mournful duet between the two lovers, repeatedly interrupted by the peeved Baba. Like numerous similar combinations, especially in Mozart's ensembles, this number contrasts two vastly different emotional states by interposing Baba's recitative-like patter around Anne and Tom's lyrical lines. One of the most moving settings in the opera, the text required some adjustment before Stravinsky could strike the right balance. Auden originally composed a much longer prosaic passage for Baba:

> *I believe* I explained that I was waiting. . . . *Who* can this person be? . . . It could hardly be thought that wedded bliss entailed *such* manner of attention. . . . I confess

that I do *not* understand.... When am I to be helped from this infernal box?... Should I expire, the world will know whom to blame.... Tell her to go, you have your duties as a spouse, you know, and I cannot but feel this is the least of them.... Allah!... I'm suffocating.... Hussy, begone, or I shall summon spirits and have you well haunted for your presumption.... A plague upon matrimony.... My love, if you do not wish Baba to be piqued, do see that she is not condemned to remain immured in this conveyance forever.[8]

This then prompted Stravinsky's only request for a major revision:

I have just driven my music to the TRIO.... and my composition is stalled because any music I might compose for Anne and Rake will be drowned under Baba's comic interference and the audience's laughs (I am positive about this).

My first move has been to reunite Anne's and Tom's verses by staggering their lines until the very end when I let them sing twice together.... As my efforts to hold the audience's attention focused on a single action are vain, as long as Baba keeps interfering by inserting her parlando monologue while Anne and Rake sing, I cannot figure any other way out but for you *to compose verses for Baba's grumbling*. The verses that I want you to compose should match those of Anne and Rake, and might stagger with them most of the time, except when you would find it possible to melt them with the words of Anne or Rake, without, of course, drowning any of them.

Be an angel and send me this overhauled TRIO as soon as possible. It will then be a genuine trio and not a duo with a third person's intervention.

My suggestion would be to reduce Baba's words to not more, and even rather less, than either Anne's or Rake's.[9]

Recognizing that a "genuine trio" might muddle the emotional differences between the characters, Auden responded: "In order to distinguish Baba in character and emotion from the two lovers, it seems to me that her rhythm should be more irregular and her tempo of utterance faster. In writing her part, therefore, I have given any line of Baba's twice the number of accents as compared with the equivalent line of Anne or Tom's. If you find I have given her too many lines, cuts are easy to make."[10] Auden then wrote out shorter versions of the first two verses and suggested any of the short phrases of the third could be "used or not ad lib." Figure 7.2 shows the complete revised text with his suggested deletions in brackets, plus the accent marks and stage direction he handwrote on the typescript. Stravinsky's response speaks for itself:

Pardon me for being so late in thanking you for your brilliant versified version of Baba's interfering recitative. I am delighted, and I have already composed the trio.

In Baba's first two interferences I dropped only the alternate words as per your advice; I kept the whole of her babbling in the third one.

And you sent it to me so quick! Thanks so much.

I am composing now the end of that scene which is a chaconne; even when the crowd greets Baba, the chaconne continues, thus ending the whole scene.[11]

```
                        ┌─────────────┐
    —   v  v    v  —    │she sees Anne│     —
                        └──────┬──────┘
                               ∨
Why this delay? Away, [or the crowd will...] O!

[And why, if I may be allowed to inquire, does my husband desire
                               —  v v  —
To converse with this person?] Who is it, pray,
v   v  —  v v  —  v v   v    —    v   —
He prefers to his Baba on their wedding day?
```

A family friend? An ancient flame?

[A bride has surely the prior claim

On the bridal night!] I'm quite perplexed

And more, I confess, than a trifle vexed!
                           [*little*]

Enough is enough! Baba is not used

To be so abused. She is not amused.

Come here my love. I hate waiting.

I'm suffocating. Heavens above!

Will you permit me to sit in this conveyance

Forever and ever?

Fig. 7.2. Auden's revision of Baba's text for trio (2.2).

    Auden's revision and Stravinsky's execution demonstrate a highly sophisticated handling of theatrical distance. Each of the three characters expresses sincere feelings, just at different levels of emotional depth. By giving Baba "twice the number of accents" per line, Auden creates a more naturalistic style to vent her superficial annoyance. Like the lovers in the *Così* quintet, Anne and Tom's lyrical singing is more distant, yet emotionally more engaging (cf. fig. 6.3); they express a deeper suffering. That listeners can attend both levels of discourse simultaneously is the unique magic—indeed, the miracle—of sung drama. Stravinsky and Auden here strike a nearly perfect musical and dramatic balance worthy of comparison with the great ensembles of Mozart and Da Ponte.

The Trio is organized in four clearly defined sections: A) R131–34 in E minor; B) R134–36 in E♭ minor; A') R136–39 in E minor; and A") R139–42 in E minor. As one would expect, the bass line gravitates to the leading-tone D♯ before each returns to E (the piano/vocal score mistakenly omits the ♯ on the last eighth note before R136). But when the second verse slips into E♭ minor (R134), the lower strings simply preserve the D♯/F♯ (as E♭/G♭) and the A and B "resolve" to B♭, similar to the earlier movements to D major (R127) and E minor (R131).

The return to E minor at R136 presents another noteworthy departure from tonal practice. Instead of leading to E, the bass D♯ falls to G. Stravinsky often emphasizes the chordal third in the bass to suggest an alternate tonal center, which he nearly realizes in Anne and Tom's G-major cadenza at R138. A dismissive Deryck Cooke spots the "cadential cliché of the [Classical] period, which always ends with the three notes [B-A-G], ... But Stravinsky omits the obligatory ending, and reaches no cadence at all."[12] Exactly. In fact, the composer roughly sketched the trivial "obligatory" ending, shown in example 7.7b, probably only to remind himself what to avoid. The 0347 in example 7.7a and (+1,−2)'s in example 7.7c indicate the ideas he would eventually develop. Just as the lovers' hope for a life together languishes, his final version chokes off any tonal motion in vines of chromatic (+1,−2)'s and 014's.

As an anchoring bass, G again supplants E in the final section. Indeed, only the bass differentiates the final sonority of the Trio (G/F♯/A/E♭) and the fleeting final chord before Baba's first entrance (E/E♭/G♭/A), highlighted in example 7.3b. The harmonic connection, though, also reveals a contrast: leading up to that dramatic moment a chromatically rising bass buffets the horn's sustained E♭; at the end, sustained high and low G's envelop the floating inner voices (a series of 014's—F♯/F/D, C/C♯/E, G/F♯/E♭—in the final measure alone).

This final chord also preserves that key-defining tritone (A/D♯) of E minor but is stripped of its tonal implications. The dyad punctuates all four sections of the trio, but only two follow its tonal lead (before R136 and R139), and even there the bass D♯ falls to G. In fact, the Trio's large-scale bass, E–E♭–G, follows the same "voice leading," <−1,+4>, as the earlier succession of keys in the introduction and Arioso: C–B–E♭. By juxtaposing tonally alien keys, these background 014's form an abstract connection between the beginning and end of the scene. The E♭-minor section of the Trio is linked to the E♭-major conclusion of the Arioso; similarly, the Arioso's opening B-minor relates to the E-minor trio. The Arioso and Trio also balance each other dramatically—the first nurturing Anne's hope, the second burying it. Anne's nagging doubt has unfortunately proven true.

Finale (R142–52)

Just as it transitioned into Baba's first appearance, the final chord of the Trio progresses to the D-major Finale. As he described to Auden, Stravinsky composed a

Example 7.7. Sketches (a–c) and final version of cadenza (2.2) (analytical notations added).

pompous chaconne to accompany her to center stage. He organizes the baroque structure in ten four-measure phrases: the first four (R142–45) and last two (R150–51) are self-contained progressions in D major; two C-major phrases accompany the entering chorus (R146–47); the segment at R148 modulates back; and a fortissimo D major with F♮ in the bass—the same 0347 that underscores the servants' procession at R100—extends the climactic moment when Baba reveals her beard (R149). Just as the earlier superposition hints at the caravan's sinister meaning, the F♮s and C♮s throughout the chaconne belie Baba's celebratory recession. And once again, this bitonal conflict creates a final, loud, and extended <−1,+2> in the bass: F–E–F♯ (R150).

Stravinsky uses the same posttonal harmonies, motives, and general techniques in act 2, scene 2, as he does in the isolated numbers analyzed in chapter 4. Analyzing an entire scene, though, reveals not just its structural logic but also the dramatic implications of its musical relationships. The opening C minor and closing D major create tensions at every structural level that are integrally tied to the dramatic process; the harmonic jolts of the introduction (R79–80) anticipate the ultimate resolution of G to F♯ for the D-major chaconne (R142); the 014's that populate the musical surface penetrate the background structure of the Arioso and Trio; the superposition of D major over F♮ links the servants' procession with Baba's recession.

As in the classic midpoint finale, everyone's fate hangs in the balance at the conclusion of the London scene, not that Stravinsky and Auden ever intended for it to conclude an act. The loud F♯s undermining Baba's garish D major point to a less than happy union for these newlyweds; meanwhile, determined Anne will not yet give up her beloved. Most importantly, even as Nick leads him from one disastrous mistake to the next, Tom, despite himself, continues to grope his way toward enlightenment. The culmination of this rake's progress, both musical and dramatic, is the subject of chapter 8.

Notes

1. Craft annotates a chronology with some errors (see chapter 1, note 12) of the opera's creation in Vera Stravinsky and Robert Craft, *Stravinsky in Pictures and Documents* (New York: Simon and Schuster, 1978), 396–415.

2. Joseph N. Straus, "The Progress of a Motive in Stravinsky's *The Rake's Progress*," *Journal of Musicology* 9, no. 2 (1991): 174.

3. See prelude, note 11 for context.

4. Igor Stravinsky, "The Composer's View," in Paul Griffiths, *Igor Stravinsky: The Rake's Progress* (New York: Cambridge University Press, 1982), 2.

5. Glenn Watkins, *Pyramids at the Louvre: Music, Culture and Collage from Stravinsky to the Postmodernists* (Cambridge, MA: Harvard University Press, 1994), 2–3.

6. Igor Stravinsky and Robert Craft, *Dialogues and a Diary* (Garden City, NY: Doubleday, 1963), 11.

7. A Stravinsky favorite, 027 probably occurs at least as much as 014 in the opera; see example 11.1, example 1, and Joseph N. Straus, *Introduction to Post-Tonal Theory*, 4th ed. (New York: Norton, 2016), 15.

8. Robert Craft, ed., *Stravinsky: Selected Correspondence*, vol. 3 (New York: Alfred A. Knopf, 1985), 509.
9. Letter of October 18, 1949, Craft, *Correspondence*, vol. 1, 309–10.
10. Letter of October 24, 1949, ibid., 310.
11. Letter of November 15, 1949, ibid., 311.
12. Deryck Cooke, "'The Rake' and the 18th Century," *Musical Times* 103 (1962): 22.

8

RUIN, DISASTER, SAVING GRACE

For all its admitted flaws, those who love *The Rake's Progress* find redemption in the final act, "one of the most perfect and most moving in all opera."[1] By the time Stravinsky and his librettists reached act 3, they seemed to have mastered the neglected craft of Opera. Absent are the stiffness of the opening scene and the awkward pacing and redundancy at the end of act 2. The final three scenes are also interconnected in ways the previous acts are not. The ballad tune Nick and Tom sing from offstage during the Auction scene resounds uncannily in the graveyard. Stravinsky even uses that trivial melody to define tempo relationships throughout the Graveyard scene. He also develops the metrically unsettled motive accompanying Tom's entrance into an altered sense of time in Bedlam. There he builds on established tonal associations to construct a harmonically distinct world for the imagined "Venus" and "Adonis." These musical features in turn support an increasingly sophisticated handling of theatrical effects, culminating in Tom's touchingly credible death.

The Auction: Act 2, Scene 4?

In their original outline Stravinsky and Auden imagined a two-scene final act, positioning the auction at the end of act 2. Upon sending the first installment of libretto, the poet curtly explained: "It seemed best to transfer the Auction Scene to Act III, as that is where the time interval occurs."[2] When prolonged set changes at the premiere prompted calls to reposition the scene for the 1953 Metropolitan production, Kallman responded with a lengthy argument that reveals more of his (and presumably Auden's) thinking about dramaturgical structure than any other source:

> I have grave doubts about the new alignment of the scenes. Leitner, as you know, suggested it at La Scala. . . . What I feel is that the *unity* of the Rake, depending as it does a great deal on the balance between its parts, is certain to suffer slightly by shifting the Auction to the end of the Second Act. Musically, dramatically and scenically the Second Act seems to me so absolutely to run in the classic a-b-a form, with its highest point of intensity in the trio of the second scene, that the Auction could not but seem to be tacked on to it, if placed immediately after. And the brilliance of Sellem's scene, wonderfully effective as the opening of an act,

would, since it does not really advance the action, be in the nature of a parenthesis if placed as the opening of a fourth scene. . . . Also, to follow the brio of the Rakewell-Shadow duet with the brio of the Auction scene prelude, must inevitably diminish the effect of the second. And the link between the Auction scene and the Cemetery scene, the offstage ballad-tune, will be lost in the intermission that should, in my opinion, serve rather as marking the months of Baba's sleep. To discover her still seated in her place in a new act is surely more effective than discovering her a moment later. . . . Further, I think the back-stage chorus (Ruin, disaster, shame) a shade too striking a device to place between two scenes; it is so much a call to attention for the opening of an act, a post-intermission device. Moreover, the original act endings were in the nature of two precipices: Anne on the edge of going [to] London and finding Tom, Tom on the edge of his financial ruin. Shifting the auction scene would mean that the suspended action at the end of the second act was the same as that of the first: Anne seeking her tenor again—"I go, I go to him." Also, I understand that, in order to get the stage prepared in time for the cobwebs and dust of the auction scene, it will be necessary to play the end of the Rakewell-Shadow duet in front of the drop; which means that the lines: "I have no wife . . . etc" are sung *without* Baba's visual presence to give them point. . . .

Probably my objections might be answered by the fact that the auction scene has a more effective curtain than the other; but really, does that balance all the disadvantages? And is that the kind of effectiveness we want for the Rake? . . . I feel, more strongly than any of my other objections, that it is necessary for us, at certain points, to *flout* the theater a bit. To say, in effect: "Yes, we have our big curtains, our finales with grand gestures; that's easy. We can afford to throw them away, because the effects we want are, in the end, better, truer and, as a matter of fact, bigger."[3]

Stravinsky responded: "Your whole reasoning makes sense, indeed, but I do not quite agree with your estimate of advantages compared to disadvantages in either one solution. . . . It is quite impossible to review all angles of the problem in writing and I have but to leave it up to you and Wystan to decide what to do. . . . I insist and warn you that *I will not accept* any stops between scenes as it was in Venice."[4]

Two glaring, and related, misjudgments undermine Kallman's argument. First, the "classic a-b-a form" he ascribes to the second act applies—at least in conventional Italian opera—to single numbers or sections, not to full acts. Wagner embraced such a rounded act structure (e.g., act II of *Tristan und Isolde*), but his was certainly not the model Stravinsky and Auden had in mind. The dramatic high point of an act in a Mozartian—or any Italian—opera tends to culminate near the end.

Furthermore, Kallman contradicts himself when he asserts the necessity "to *flout* the theater a bit." He first justifies the three-times-three scene arrangement for its dramatic/theatrical effectiveness: "I think the back-stage chorus (Ruin, disaster, shame) . . . a call to attention for the opening of an act"; "the original act endings were in the nature of two precipices." To then argue that they wish to "flout" the theater by placing rousing finales like Baba's beard revelation and the Auction in the middle of acts seems arbitrary.

Kallman is groping for the fine line between parodying operatic conventions and embracing them. The entire exchange suggests the three creators did not plan the emotional intensity they ended up with. In his first letter to Auden, Stravinsky imagined a "choreographic divertissement" at the end of act 1 and suggested the "hero's end in the asylum scratching a fiddle would make a meritorious conclusion to his stormy life."[5] One glimpses the poignancy of Tom's death in "pleurez, pleurez pour Adonis" from the original scenario; otherwise, that bare-boned outline is mostly a map of operatic clichés. Seduced by the high operatic style, though, the librettists and composer fleshed out the skeletal plot with an emotional eloquence scarcely hinted at previously. Perhaps they always intended it so, but one senses from Kallman's hit-and-miss arguments that the collaborators at times misgauged the effect of their work.

Keeping a Distance

Before the curtain even rises, Kallman plays with distancing effects by specifying "a great choral cry of 'Ruin, Disaster, Shame,' is heard from behind it." Offstage voices, shown in the dotted blocks in figure 8.1, play a recurring role throughout the scene. Either clichéd (the ominous chords for "Ruin . . .") or trivial (the Ballad tune), these episodes belong most clearly to the puppet-show Progress Nick has been staging all along. Once the curtain rises, the campy chorus of "Respectable Citizens" establishes an archly comical distance even as unseen "voices" continue to loom behind the scenes (R11).

Just as he used the three jolting chords to introduce act 2, scene 2 (example 7.4), Stravinsky latches onto Kallman's ominous refrain to establish the harmonic trajectory of the Auction scene, sketched out in the three block chords shown in example 8.1a. Diminished seventh chords establish the mock ominous tone. Stravinsky initially gave each word its own chord; in the completed scene the chords demarcate the larger sections. The first (example 8.1b), built on G♯, closes off the busy E-major opening. The second, built on C♯ over a bass B♮ (example 8.1c), transitions to G minor. The final statement (example 8.1d) veers from his preliminary A minor to B♭ minor. Here the blurred connection between the key of Tom's Progress and the key of his Desires becomes explicit; the diminished seventh (C♯–E–G–B♭) encompasses both. This harmonic and theatrical diversion conveys a dramatic message: the crowd buzzes with excitement in the opening E major but turns to the audience at R13 to denounce the name of "Rakewell" in the keys of his ruin: G and B♭. This tonal disjunction will prove significant over the course of the scene.

Unconnected to the unfolding drama, the auctioneer Sellem ranges over the tonal map (see example 8.3). Only when he turns to the "unknown object" at R86 does he settle into a stable E♭ major, which in turn gets lost in the final and most excited flurry of bids (R91). As figure 8.1 shows, he and the Auction crowd establish the scene's default distance. Once that alluring object is uncovered, Sellem, despite his protests, must yield his spot in the limelight.

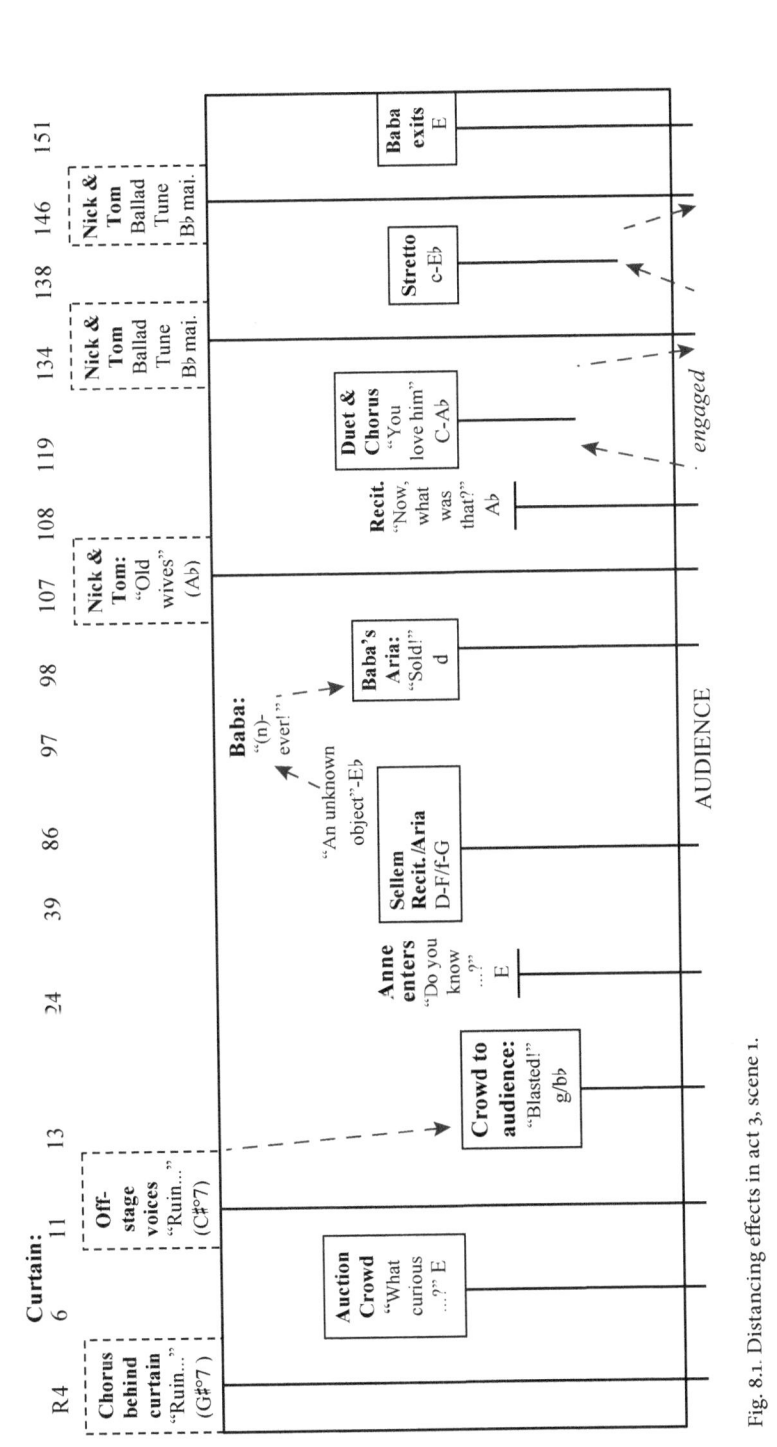

Fig. 8.1. Distancing effects in act 3, scene 1.

Example 8.1 Initial sketch (a) and three final settings (b–d) for "Ruin. Disaster. Shame." (3.1).

Baba's Return

"The day Baba the Turk was born and named," recalled Kallman, "we both laughed until we could no longer stand up straight."[6] Not everyone shared their amusement. Stravinsky's attorney Aaron Sapiro advised, "I do not think it is necessary to provide Baba with a beard—and I think this is not merely unwholesome but likewise pushes the opera into slapstick farce."[7] According to

Craft, he even privately urged Stravinsky to reject the libretto "on the grounds that it would make him an accessory to the 'homosexual joke of Baba the Turk.'"[8] Lincoln Kirstein claims the librettists modeled their bearded lady on the French artist Christian Bérard (coincidentally, the lover of *Mavra* librettist, Boris Kochno). Taruskin even asserts: Baba, "a madcap gay inversion of the conventional 'trouser role,' was Auden's and Kallman's catty little joke at the expense of the elderly, conventionally homophobic and decidedly unhip composer."[9]

First, the notion that someone mentored by Serge Diaghilev could be hoodwinked by an inside gay joke strains credulity. Stravinsky understood full well the character's gender-bending nature and the operatic tradition to which she belonged. Second, though Kallman would later insist "Baba is, and must be played by, a dyke"—a comment prompted by Blanche Thebom's voluptuous interpretation at the Met—his point was precisely not that Tom's marriage vents a repressed homosexual desire (in which case her character should attract him) but that he must find Baba repulsive.[10] Her character is certainly campy, but she is no more obviously gay than the drag Bugs Bunny and Elmer Fudd in those supreme tributes to operatic camp, "The Rabbit of Seville" (1950) and "What's Opera Doc?" (1957).

The fretful lawyer was not entirely wrong, though, to perceive a connection to gay culture. Yet what he imagined a "homosexual joke" is, in truth, part of a centuries-old tradition of comic transvestitism extending well beyond the claque of contemporary opera queens. "After all," Stravinsky himself pointed out in approving Sarah Caldwell's choice to cast Baba as a countertenor, "the opera takes place in the age of Farinelli, when operatic sex-swapping was conventional."[11] That tradition, in its flexible attitude toward gender and sexual identity, overlaps with central concerns of postmodernism. Thus, in her 1967 "mod" interpretation Caldwell amplified the androgyny that so offended Sapiro by accompanying Baba's arrival "with an entourage of transvestite groupies in leather riding motorbikes."[12]

Baba is much more than an androgynous freak; she is an Artist. "The beard," Auden explained in a BBC radio broadcast, "represents her genius, something which makes her what she is and at the same time cuts her off from other people, so that her mistake in accepting this proposal is that she tries to fit into an ordinary family life, to be an ordinary person, and of course, the whole thing breaks down."[13] Edward Mendelson interprets her as an "imaginary portrait" of the closeted Henry James, writing, "Baba is too wounded and exceptional for marriage.... But when she accepts celibacy, she makes herself the defender and patroness of those who love."[14]

The revelation of Baba's depth during the Auction scene is perhaps the librettists' most surprising twist, even more so than Tom's Kierkegaardian redemption. (The scenario merely calls for the revivified Ugly Duchess to recognize the Girl and break "into a tirade, blaming her for everything."[15]) Nothing in act 2 anticipates this transformation. The opera's most cardboard character lurches

a. Reprise of Baba's aria (3.1): R97.

(n) - e _____ ver!

b. Offenbach, *Les Contes d'Hoffman*, act 1, "Les oiseaux dans la charmille."

(gen) -til _____ le, La...

Example 8.2. Comparison of Baba's and Olympia's melismas.

from complaining bride to chatterbox, cloying wife, then hysterical harpy before devolving into an inanimate wind-up toy, at which point Tom shuts her up altogether. This last action indeed "pushes the opera into slapstick farce," precisely as the librettists intended. Her increasingly unhinged coloratura resembles the ever-widening leaps of the mechanical doll Olympia from Offenbach's *Les Contes d'Hoffman* (1881), shown in example 8.2. Baba, of course, possesses none of Olympia's playful charm—she's coming apart rather than winding up—but her exaggerated skips project a similarly stiff artifice.

Mechanical Baba stands at a distance even from the comical chorus and auctioneer and draws them further away before shattering the conceit like the objects she fitfully throws. Reawakened, she takes the stage as perhaps no mortal operatic character ever invented (Caldwell even experimented with interspersing the chorus throughout the theater and projecting Baba's enlarged image onto the curtain).[16]

Baba's tirade is broken in turn by the literally distant voices of Tom and Nick. At first chanting "Old Wives for sale . . . ," the carousing duo twice more interrupts by singing the nonsensical Ballad tune. (Bergman positioned the pair at different places in the audience, reinforcing the sense of them being "at large.") The interruption prompts Baba to bond with Anne, creating the one moment of true intimacy—that is, between two level-headed, caring individuals—in the opera. Like a Greek chorus, the sympathetic crowd mediates and amplifies our reaction: "He loves her still. The tale is sad."

The situation is tailor-made for opera, but the librettists were not confident the composer fully understood their intent. After hearing the first-act read through, they worried that, "in the interest of verbal distinctness, Stravinsky had tended to alternate the voices in duets and trios, rather than to blend them."[17] To address the problem, Kallman diagrammed Anne and Baba's culminating duet with chorus, shown in figure 8.2, specifying not only what lines were to be sung together but also how to pace their entrances. No simple duet (as designated in the libretto and score), the ensemble is a complex series of lyric solos, layered vocal settings, and sung dialogue. The model is not Mozartian buffa but Verdian

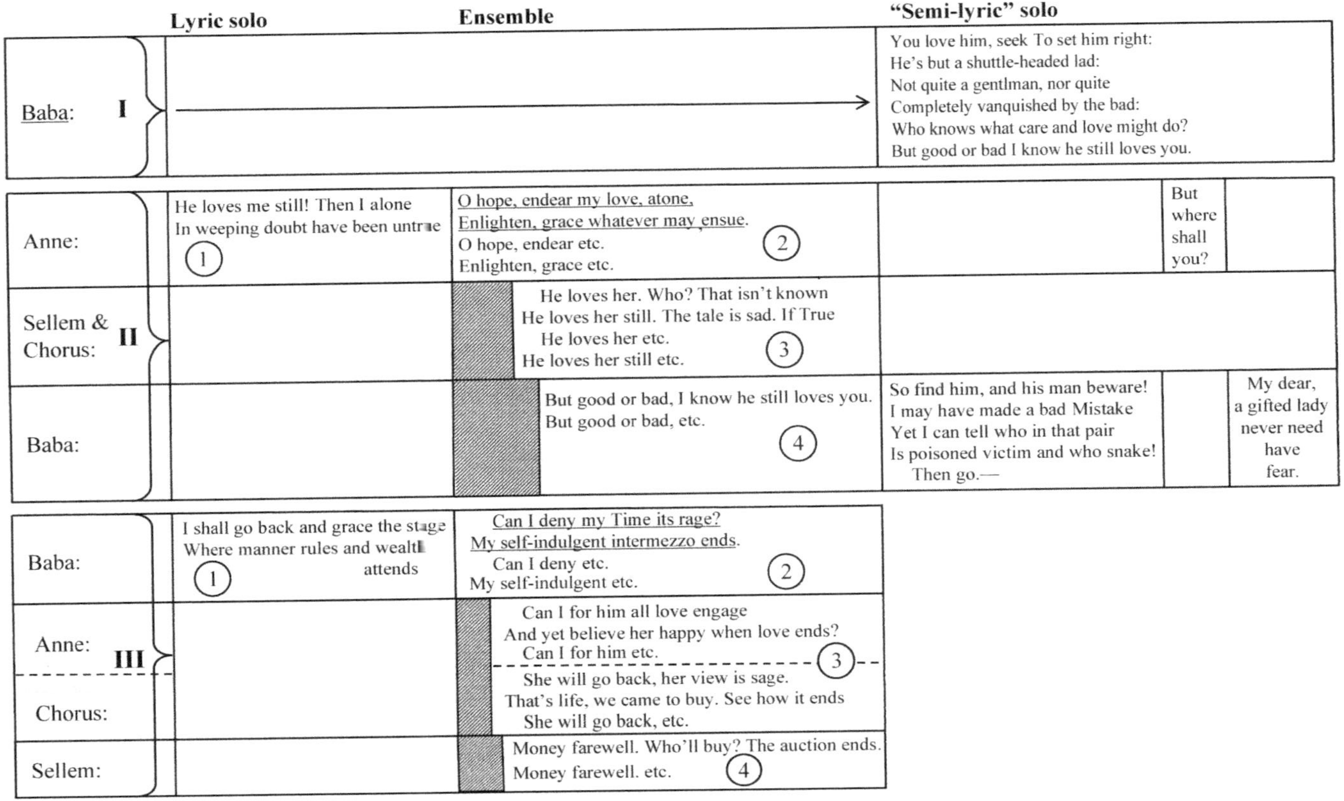

	Lyric solo	Ensemble	"Semi-lyric" solo
Baba: **I**			You love him, seek To set him right: He's but a shuttle-headed lad: Not quite a gentleman, nor quite Completely vanquished by the bad: Who knows what care and love might do? But good or bad I know he still loves you.
Anne:	He loves me still! Then I alone In weeping doubt have been untrue ①	O hope, endear my love, atone, Enlighten, grace whatever may ensue. ② O hope, endear etc. Enlighten, grace etc.	But where shall you?
Sellem & Chorus: **II**		He loves her. Who? That isn't known He loves her still. The tale is sad. If True ③ He loves her etc. He loves her still etc.	
Baba:		But good or bad, I know he still loves you. ④ But good or bad, etc.	So find him, and his man beware! I may have made a bad Mistake Yet I can tell who in that pair Is poisoned victim and who snake! Then go.—
Baba:	I shall go back and grace the stage Where manner rules and wealth attends ①	Can I deny my Time its rage? My self-indulgent intermezzo ends. ② Can I deny etc. My self-indulgent etc.	
Anne: **III**		Can I for him all love engage And yet believe her happy when love ends? ③ Can I for him etc.	My dear, a gifted lady never need have fear.
Chorus:		She will go back, her view is sage. That's life, we came to buy. See how it ends She will go back, etc.	
Sellem:		Money farewell. Who'll buy? The auction ends. ④ Money farewell. etc.	

Fig. 8.2. Kallman's diagram for Anne and Baba's duet with ensemble (3.1): R114–33.

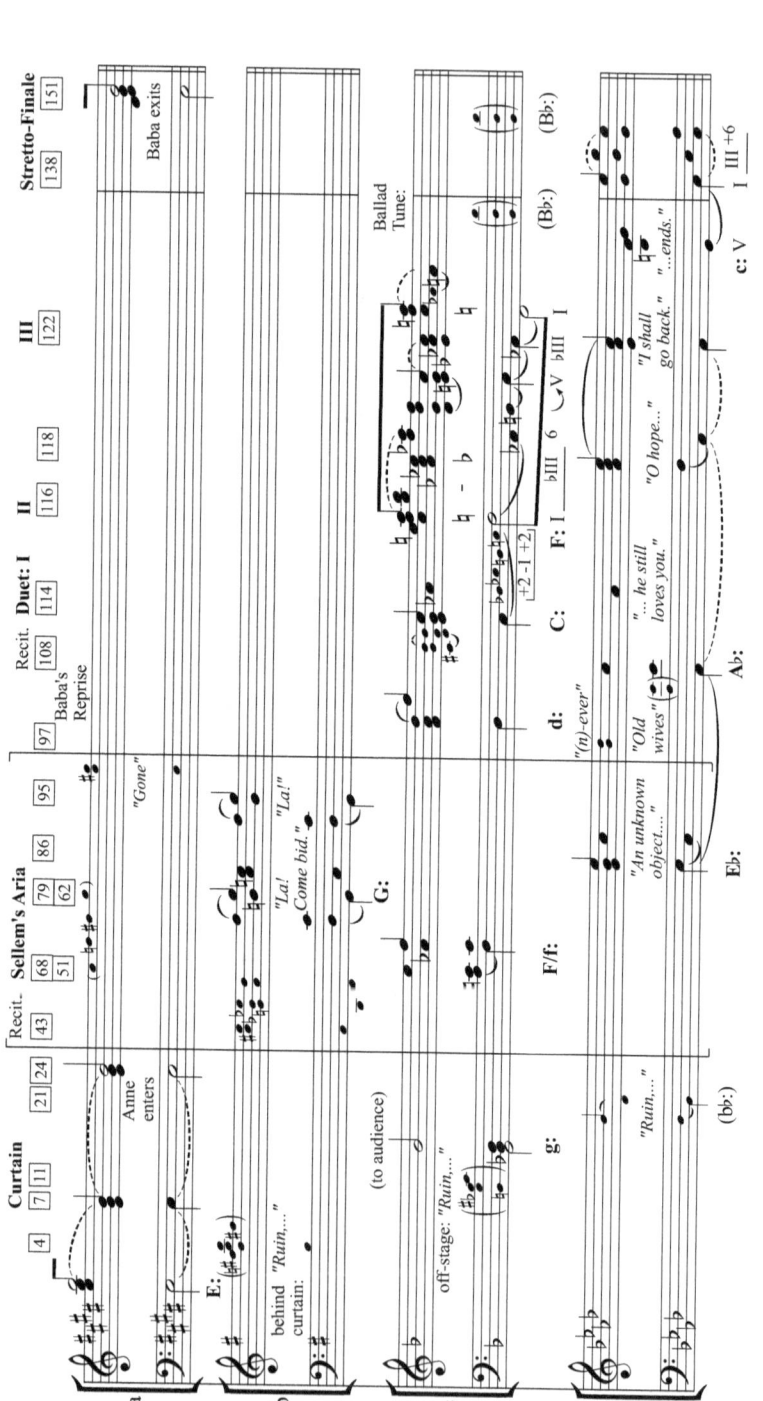

Example 8.3. Tonal structure of act 3, scene 1.

grand drama, where the chorus plays a role in its own right (cf. the act 2 finale of *La Traviata*). Kallman's diagram reads like a student's careful analysis—except in this case, Stravinsky was the attentive pupil.

The relationship in this scene between theatrical and tonal organization is less correlative than one might assume. The summary graph in example 8.3 shows how Stravinsky broadly distinguishes "sharp" (levels a and b) and "flat" keys (levels c and d) in the opening chorus. G minor and B♭ minor mark both Rakewell's infamy and the chorus's direct engagement with the audience (cf. fig. 8.1); later, Tom and Nick's droning interruption of Baba's D-minor aria (R107) sounds predictably jarring. However, much of the warm duet and chorus that follow gravitate toward their supposedly distant "flat" tonal world. Baba's C-major soliloquies, "You love him . . ." (R114) and "So find him . . ." (R122), stand as hymns to Anne's faith in Love, but they also frame the F-major Duet proper (R116 and 122 correspond to Kallman's sections II and III in fig. 8.2), which in turn slips seamlessly into the parallel F minor and its relative A♭ major.

The B♭-major Ballad tune presumably signals what remains of Tom's desires, which, judging from the silly rhymes, is not much, except that "he still loves you." How ironic that Baba intones these words on the same A♭ the scoundrel Nick previously mocked her. Commenting on her extended "I shall go back" (R122–27), Griffiths even claims Baba's "new tonic [A♭ major], diametrically opposed to her previous D, suggests that she has found a new, true home."[18] How does such a cartoonesque character transform so suddenly? As elsewhere, Stravinsky plumbs Baba's emotional depth by unmasking her tonal facade. Building on established associations, the line "The milkmaid haunts me," shown in example 8.4a, recalls her annoyed VII°7 from act 2, scene 2 (cf. example 7.3, R129); Anne's B♭–D♭ on "His wife!" echoes Tom's "My wife" from act 2, scene 3 (example 8.4b). Both references also share a common 014—D/D♭/B♭—which frames their exchange. The shift from C♯ (♯7̂ in d) to D♭ (♭3̂ in B♭) encapsulates Baba's transformation, which Stravinsky constructs like a puzzle made of 014-related trichords and tetrachords. The woodwinds at R110 invert the original D/C♯/B♭ around D, then transpose the whole progression to F. Baba's "All I possessed . . ." is similarly inverted around F/C♯ and then transposed down to D♭ for " . . . seems gone. Well, well." With that Baba puts C♯ and all her D-minor troubles behind her.

No longer self-obsessed, Baba now reveals the one truth Anne needs to reverse Tom's progress. In a circuitous transition from diatonic C-major into the F-major duet, Stravinsky both underlines and validates her words with interlocking (+1,–2)'s (example 8.4c).

Following Baba's lead, Anne transfigures Tom's destructive Desire into Hope in her memorable shift to F minor/A♭ major ("O hope endear my love," R118). Will this A♭–/E♭–/B♭–/F-major world prove illusory? "That isn't known," as the nosy chorus responds, but we do know "He loves her still." The tonal connection between Anne and Tom, even at the point of their greatest separation, anticipates the crucial moment in the graveyard when Tom will hear and be saved by the graceful voice of his distant beloved.

Example 8.4. Posttonal chords and voice leading in recitative and duet (3.1).

The Graveyard: Empty and Full Vessels

Despite their tonal affinity, Anne and Baba's sublime Duet stands in starkest contrast to Tom and Nick's ridiculous Ballad tune. Auden's devil-may-care text (see verse 1 on p. 67) recalls the formal verses, composed "without regard to content," with which he had entertained Stravinsky during their first visit.[19] The comparison suggests an absorption with form and process for their own sake, which likewise applies to Stravinsky's metrically regular and harmonically bland setting. Devoid of content, the words and music express essentially nothing—or at least the impression of nothing.

In short, the Ballad tune is as an empty vessel, ideal for reuse. So malleable is the melody, one hardly notices Nick singing it (now in G major) when he demands payment for his services in the graveyard. The ironic tension between its triviality and the deadly seriousness of his claim for Tom's soul makes an even more chilling impact. Stravinsky replaces the earlier amateurish progression, shown in example 8.5a, with static string configurations based less on what supports the melody than on convenient harmonics: violas oscillate an octave above the open G, D, and A strings and cellos arpeggiate the overtones of the open C and G (example 8.5b). He also undermines the metrical scansion. In the Auction scene, horn and clarinet sixteenths ground the meter with mundane regularity. That pattern is now expanded and in the consequent phrase displaced; there, harmonics and pizzicatos form 5/8 and 3/4 cross-rhythms against Nick's 3/8 tune. In a telling detail, the end of the jaunty 5/8 pattern coincides with the silent downbeat of Tom's awkward reentrance.

Stravinsky further transforms the sixteenth-note pattern when Nick reveals his true intentions at R170 (example 8.5c). Now the flute and clarinet pipe the Ballad tune and the singer arpeggiates, "'Tis not your money but your soul . . . ," retaining the strings' five-beat pattern and thereby displacing the repeated words. By aligning "soul" with the downbeat at R171, Stravinsky shifts back to the 3/8 tune to complete the phrase ("Which I this night require"). "Look in my eyes and recognize" and "Whom, Fool! you chose to hire" similarly alternate from sixteenth-note patter to jig-like tune, making Nick seem not only gleeful, but eager.

Contrast the emotionally empty Ballad tune with Anne's "A love that is sworn before Thee" (or any of the heightened settings analyzed in chapter 5). Expressing the heart of the opera's message, her disembodied voice recapitulates this line, unaccompanied and tellingly altered from its original iteration (example 7.5), to rescue Tom from certain damnation. As example 8.6 shows, Stravinsky slows the tempo by half, eliminates all bar lines, omits the repetition of "a love" and "is sworn," and introduces a new setting of "can plunder hell." Though inferable from the earlier setting, the absence of explicit meter and the slower tempo allows the singer considerable rhythmic freedom. The agogic accents on "can" and "of" are misplaced by conservative standards but intensify the impact. The setting has lost its previous rhythmic tautness but has gained in emotional intensity and expressiveness.

Example 8.5. Comparison of Ballad tune settings: (a) act 3, scene 1; and (b, c) act 3, scene 2.

Example 8.6. Recapitulated setting of "A love That is sworn" (3.2).

Time and Distance

Like the thematic reminiscences of nineteenth-century opera, Anne's emotional message is preserved and even amplified in repetition because her music is inextricable from her words—that is, it expresses the text. The Ballad tune, by contrast, registers no substantive emotional impact—it expresses nothing—and therefore can be recreated according to a new dramatic context. That both passages are heard from offstage presents in sharp relief the effect of expressive music in a theatrically distant context, as a comparison of figures 8.1 and 8.3 demonstrates.

Though one would hardly notice, these offstage interruptions are also related by tempo: the Ballad-tune eighths and Anne's sixteenths share a metronomic value of 168. In fact, metronomic relationships determine the tempos in the Graveyard scene more strictly than any other scene in the opera and possibly more than any Stravinsky piece since the *Symphonies of Wind Instruments*.[20] As we know, he composed the prelude in December 1947, almost three years before he would complete the rest of the scene. As if to compensate for the gap, the composer calculated nearly every new tempo in relation to either the prelude (♩ = 69), marked by dashed lines in figure 8.3, or the Ballad tune (♩. = 56), marked by solid lines. The latter pulse forms a 2:3 ratio with the opening ♪ = 84, which in turn determines every subsequent tempo—whether hesitant (Tom at R161 and 168), lively (Nick's Ballad tune at R165 and 170), or fast (Tom's *agitato* at R176)—until R185, at which point Nick suddenly stops the chiming clock. Thereafter—except for Shadow's aside at R188 (where ♩ = 112 doubles the Ballad tempo)—up to the anomalous ♪ = 76 at R193 (explained below), they play their card-guessing game according to the pulse of the prelude.

To further signal the cessation of time, Stravinsky couples this metronomic shift with a dramatic change to solo cembalo, and not just for the initial secco

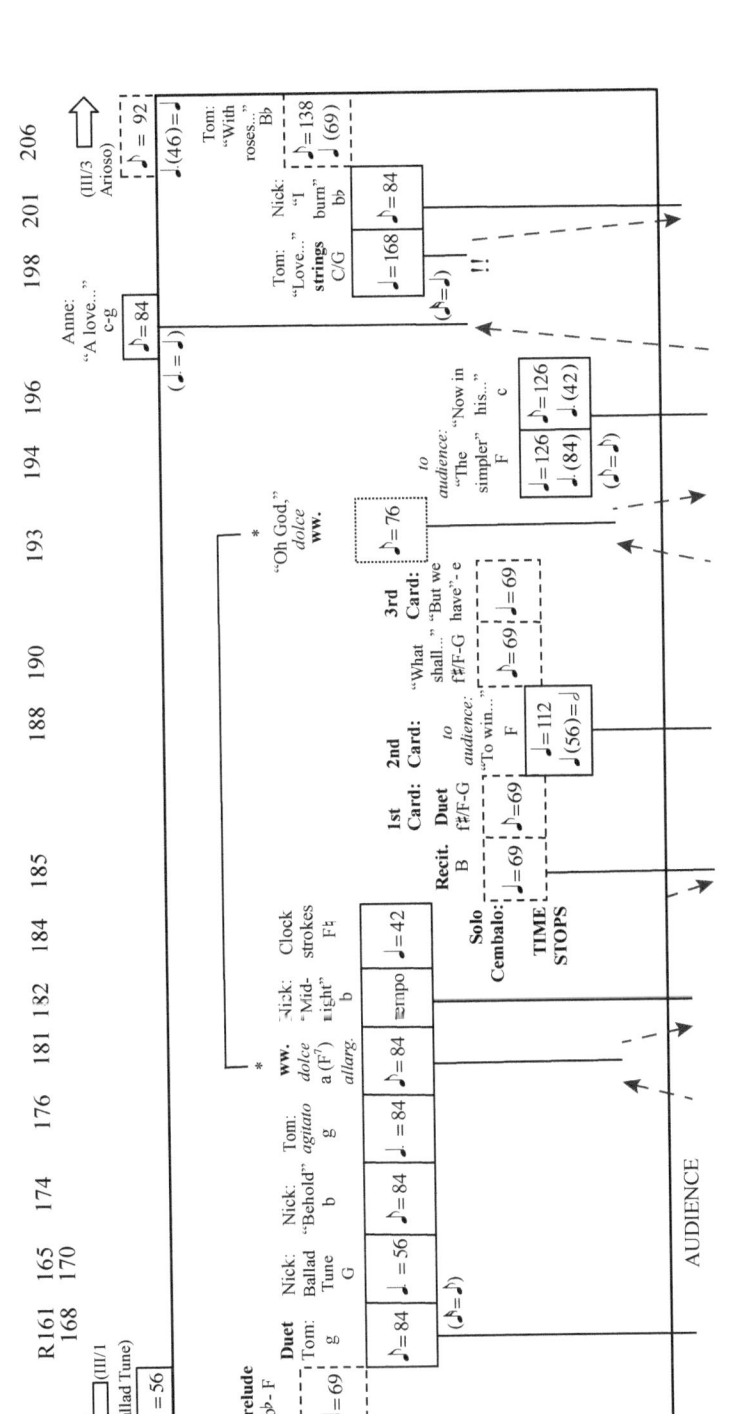

Fig. 8.3 Tempo relationships in act 3, scene 2.

recitative but also as a creeping accompaniment to the entire game. The new tempo and texture coincide with a fundamental harmonic shift as well, highlighted in example 8.7a. Tom and Nick's tense opening exchanges play out in the modal conflict between G minor and major, summarized in example 8.7b (R161–180). The exceptions are Nick's B-minor pronouncements at R174 and 182, in which he discloses Tom's fate: "Behold your waiting grave." The F♮ bell strokes at R184 recall the cadence to the dour prelude, as does Tom's D♭ for "Too late." That single pitch encapsulates almost every mistake he has come to regret—for instance, his rejection of Anne in London (example 7.3, R106); his marriage to Baba (example 8.4b)—and now as ♭3 in B♭, it confirms the tragic end of his Progress. But not quite yet; again inflecting minor to major, the former servant stops Time—"No, wait."—so he may relish his master's despair a few moments longer. As in the previous scene (cf. example 8.4a), the resulting B♭–D♭–D also forms a posttonal link, traced in example 8.7c.

Now in complete control, Nick reorients the scene toward B major, where he proposes the card-guessing game. Stravinsky initiates each shuffle of the deck with superimposed F♯-minor/F-major triads, conceived, as Straus demonstrates, expressly to support the C–C♯ motive.[21] Similar to other structural harmonies in the opera, this polychord 01478 features symmetrical 014's built around the common third, A. For the first two cards these tense tonalities slip into a comfortable G major (R187 and 191), where the "compassionate" Nick appropriates Tom's baroque turn to offer hints (see example 5.2b).

In between shuffles, Shadow addresses the audience in a simplistic F major (R188 and 194), made all the less engaging by the skeletal accompaniment (note in fig. 8.3 and example 8.7 how Stravinsky distinguishes Nick's asides to the audience by tempo and key). Emotionally dry, the intimate accompaniment nonetheless contracts theatrical distance. Stravinsky reverses the conventional relationship between recitative, which usually conveys a more naturalistic experience of time, and formal numbers, where time is suspended. Woodwinds intrude only at R193 to accompany Tom's "O God, what hopes have I," shown in example 8.8a, the very phrase for which the tempo is not derived from either metronome marking 84 or 69. A clue as to why Stravinsky here introduces other instruments and a single unrelated tempo lies in the equally brief woodwind interlude at R181 (example 8.8b). There the harmony (A minor), scoring (oboes and bassoons), and *dolce* marking distinctly recall the introductions to the two Garden scenes, act 1, scene 1 (example 6.2d) and act 1, scene 3 (example 8.8c). And while R193 bears little tonal relation to these earlier passages, its metronomic marking relates directly to the opening scene of the opera; Tom's vocal line is even marked *dolce*. (Stravinsky originally set the opening duet at ♩ = 84 before adopting the more sedate 76; see example 6.2d.) In instrumentation, expression, and either key or tempo, both wind interludes point back to the pastoral Garden.

Sounding at the moment of Tom's greatest despair, these *dolce accenti* perhaps reflect La Musica's claim "to calm every troubled soul." We too are momentarily soothed by the sustained winds, only to be jostled by the brittle harpsichord

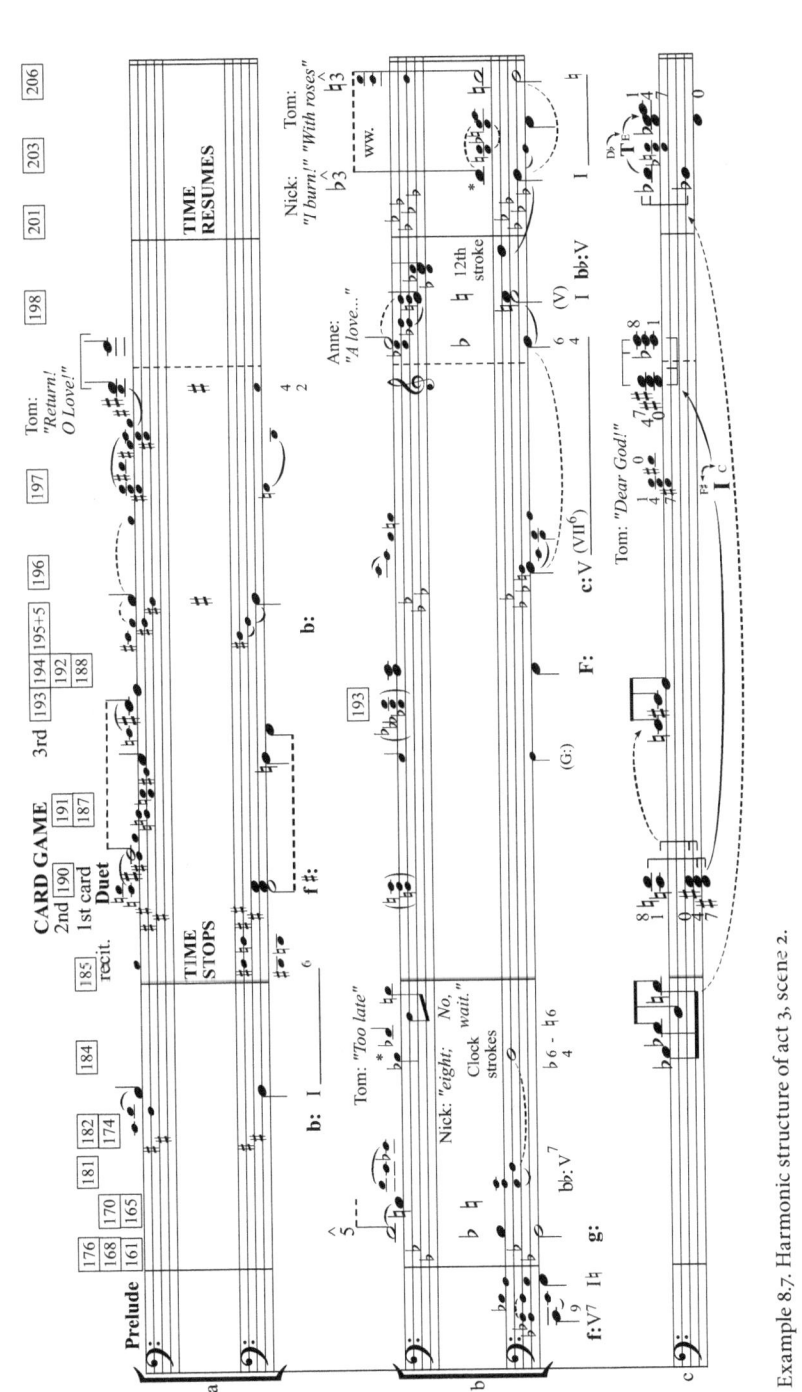

Example 8.7. Harmonic structure of act 3, scene 2.

Example 8.8. Woodwind interludes in act 3, scene 2 (a, b), and opening of act 1, scene 3 (c).

a. *The Nightingale*, Death's Music.

b. *The Rake's Progress*, "Now in his words..." (3.2).

Example 8.9. Comparison of Death's music from *The Nightingale* with the cembalo octaves in act 3, scene 2.

when Nick excitedly explains his final deceit, "The simpler the trick." To his master, though, Shadow will disclose no more hints: "Now in my words he'll find no aid." However, the key in which he sings these words suggests he may not be in control as he thinks. Stravinsky apparently reached back forty years into his subconscious for the accompanying cembalo octaves, shown in example 8.9b, which he admitted "have certainly come from the same well-springs as the octaves in Death's music in *The Nightingale*."[22]

Try as he may, the "knavish goat" cannot resist taunting the "spring's return" he hopes to harvest. From Nick's cryptic comments, "Love-lucky Tom" picks up just enough to awaken from his own unconscious the voice of Return and Love. Reaching his breaking point, the rake lurches back into Shadow's B major, thus replicating the succession of keys from Anne's Arioso in act 2, scene 2 (example 7.3, R87–90). Superimposing B minor into the Arioso forced Anne to progress from $f\sharp^1$-g^1, revealed in the altered short score in example 7.6. Now Tom sings the same F♯ to G to call forth her C-minor theme. Just as Anne overcomes her doubting B minor, Tom wrests himself from Nick's murderous B major. (This B major–C minor juxtaposition also inverts the earlier F♯ minor/F major 01478, shown in example 8.7c.) The frozen Shadow cannot hear Anne's distant response, but we can. Figure 8.3 suggests we remain drawn to her mysterious voice when the rising string tremolos, lifted from her Cabaletta, announce the outcome of the game even before Tom proclaims the final card. Stravinsky allows us one brief, unmitigated, undistanced triumph.

The Queen of Hearts again revealed, the clock finally sounds its twelfth stroke and Time resumes. It is now Shadow's turn to despair in the same tempo as Tom at the start of the scene, as he returns to his fiery home empty handed.

The rake's triumph is, of course, short-lived; Auden and Stravinsky could not allow the spirit of Goethe's romantic Faust to override completely Hogarth's "bourgeois cautionary tale." The stricken Hero greets the new day singing a familiar melody, the Ballad tune, in a familiar key, B♭. But now Tom is the one who inflects minor to major, not his defeated servant (cf. example 8.7, R184).[23] He also adopts the pulse, ♪ = 138, associated with the previous cessation of Time (see fig. 8.3).

Recall from our discussion in chapter 3 that in the original scenario it was the hero, not the villain, who declared, "J'arrête le temps." His madness was not a retribution for sins but a voluntary "leap into the absurd." Unafraid, the insane protagonist explicitly dramatized, as Auden later described in his essay on Kierkegaard, an "awareness of being *with* time, i.e., experiencing time as an eternal present to which past and future refer." The theatrical curse he and Kallman introduced into the libretto thus masks a spiritual transformation that Stravinsky, who also understood the Kierkegaardian "leap," would subtly dramatize in the music.[24]

Music without Time

A flute, oboe, and clarinet sweetly hail the arrival of dawn after the card-guessing game. Static harmonies, shown in example 8.10a, reduce the sense of tonal motion and irregularly placed trills seem to flutter aimlessly, obscuring the meter. Sitting atop his intended grave, the transformed Tom proclaims himself "Adonis" in the transformed key of B♭. No longer prodded by the worrisome clock of Progress, his 3/8 melody seems to float, ungrounded, on the airy accompaniment. By turning the most mundanely conventional music of the opera into an ethereal stasis, Stravinsky halts musical time.

The trill motive he uses to transform his rake into a babbling innocent is itself a recurring idea. We first hear it as Tom stumbles into the graveyard, feeling the true weight of his debt. Stravinsky repeats this idea three times: twice in G minor at the beginning of the scene (example 8.10b and 8.10c) and once in B♭ major to introduce the end (example 8.10a). Comparing the meter of each exposes the different effects of conservative and radical barrings and offers a clue as to why Stravinsky chooses one or the other.

The composer preserves 3/8 in the measures that introduce Tom's final ballad setting, displacing the stresses only slightly in the opening four-bar phrase. However, the second phrase disturbs the regular groupings. The sixteenth-note pickup from mm. 1 and 5 is contracted and displaced in m. 8, in effect shifting the sense of downbeat by a sixteenth. A subsequent 5/16 realigns the motive with the eighth-note pulse in the next measure, but the downbeat is still displaced, effectively suspending the sense of 3/8 before Tom even sings a note.

Stravinsky displaces the trill motive at the beginning of the scene as well, but without the leisurely repetitions the music conveys an unsettled urgency. More remarkably—at least for *The Rake*—he adjusts the meter to accommodate most of the displacements. The motivic parallels are easiest to gauge when comparing the instrumental introduction at R161 (example 8.10b) with the interlude at R163 (example 8.10c). The gestures of both phrases are a beat shorter than those of example 8.10a, but each is measured differently. The trills fall on downbeats at R163; the thumping bass presumably explains the motive's displacement at R161, though it is not aligned with any subsequent downbeats. The 2/8 measure at R161+3 is particularly perplexing. If Stravinsky is not conserving a regular meter, why not align the trill motive with the downbeat of a 2/8 in the next measure, as at R163+3?

Having conserved the meter and displaced the trill motive in example 8.10a and adjusted the meter to accommodate the irregular groupings in example 8.10c, Stravinsky appears to do neither in example 8.10b. His final draft of this latter passage, shown in example 8.11, explains his unusual choices and offers a glimpse into his thinking about meter. The pitches, rhythms, and scoring are almost exactly the same as the final version, but he had trouble deciding where to place the bar lines. Stravinsky's final drafts are usually neat and precise, with only details of articulation and slurring to be added to the final fair copy; for him to be rethinking his choice of meter at this late stage is highly unusual. Even without a time signature, it is fairly clear he originally notated it in 4/8: the only solid, neatly drawn—and therefore original—bar line is just before the bass C♯. Traces of another bar line are found four eighths later. The composer then began to experiment with different measures, erasing, penciling in, and scratching out lines, none of which seem to correspond to his ultimate choice. Unable to clarify his options amid this messiness, Stravinsky took out the trusty red and blue pencils he used to clarify voice leading, differentiate verse settings, bracket gestures for repetition, and designate scoring. Starting below and alternating between the bottom and top of the system, he bracketed groups of 4/8 in blue. Starting above and similarly alternating top and bottom, he bracketed groups of 3/8 in red. Dissatisfied with his options for conserving the meter throughout, he then along the bottom alternated between blue 3/8 measures and red 2/8 measures as his ultimate choice.

So Stravinsky actually conserves a five-beat pattern at R161, thus explaining why his irregular downbeats fail to align with the motivic parallels as they do at R163. The question remains as to how these three metrical choices affect the way one performs or perceives the music. To rephrase Craft's question: Is the same effect achieved with motivic parallels as with bar lines? Examples 8.10 and 8.11 help clarify Stravinsky's response: "not in my music."[25] When a salient motive is aligned with a metric stress, irregular or not, it is both played and heard with more attention and energy. The irregular meters Stravinsky favors in his Russian-period works account for much of their elemental dynamism. When he conserves the meter and lets the accents and motivic stresses fall where they may, as he does throughout most of *The Rake's Progress*, the energy is less intense, the accents less weighted, the effect more subtle. The sweetly fluttering woodwinds that introduce the childlike "Adonis" project a more subdued energy and very different sense of

a. End of act 3, scene 2, accompanying Tom as "Adonis."

Example 8.10. Comparison of meters for the trill motive.

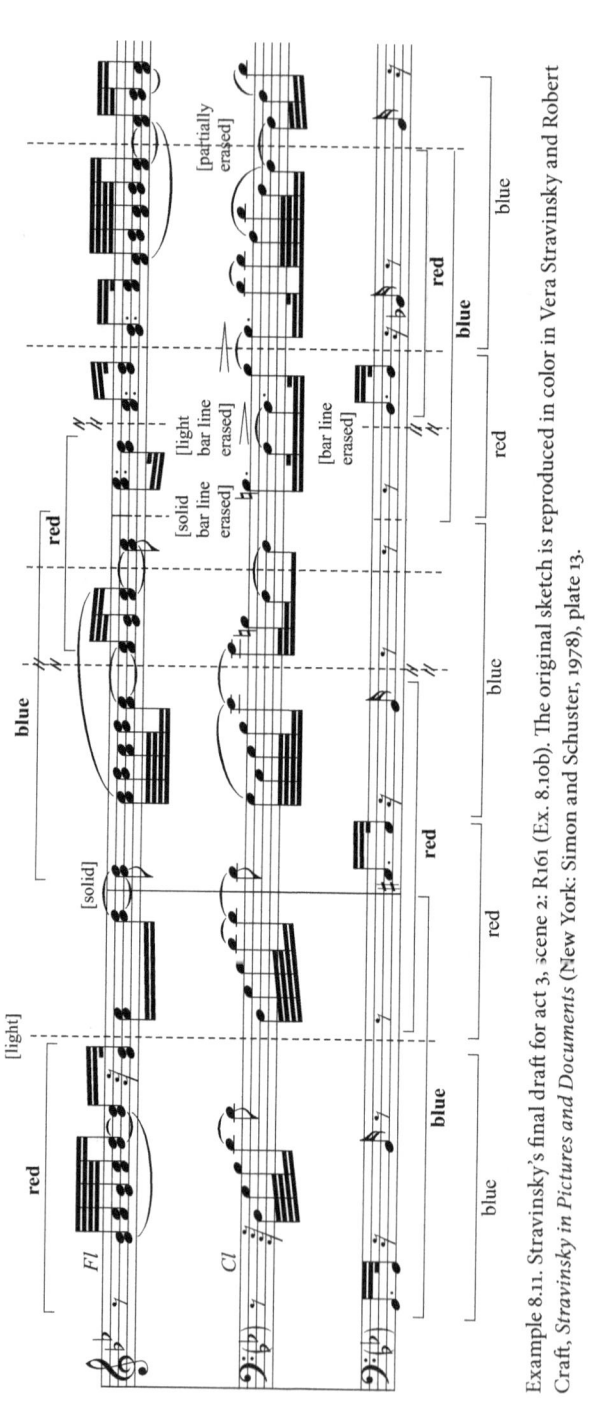

Example 8.11. Stravinsky's final draft for act 3, scene 2: R161 (Ex. 8.10b). The original sketch is reproduced in color in Vera Stravinsky and Robert Craft, *Stravinsky in Pictures and Documents* (New York: Simon and Schuster, 1978), plate 13.

time than the nervous, irregular phrases that interrupt the apprehensive Tom at the beginning of the scene. Stravinsky seems to have drafted his introduction assuming a conservative meter, as throughout most of the opera. But displaced motives over a regular meter could not supply the nervous energy he needed for Tom's entrance into the graveyard. And aligning the irregular groupings with irregular measures perhaps seemed too surefooted for the hapless rake. In the end, the composer opted for both misaligned stresses and irregular downbeats to usher this stumbling, frightened hero to his waiting grave.

Bedlam and Timeless Music

In the final scene, gone are the jaunty, driving tempos of Tom's opening aria and his rousing act 2 duets with Nick. The excited "Adonis" briefly sings allegro when he first encounters "Venus" ("I have waited for thee so long," R239). Otherwise, his tempos remain sedate and, nearing his end, he slips increasingly into accompanied recitative, with no strong metrical sense. Only in the lovers' final duet, "Rejoice, beloved," shown in example 8.12b, does Auden's original vision of timelessness find full expression. Here, for a brief moment, "Adonis" and "Venus" reunite in a changeless Elysium where neither space nor time can alter their love. To tie this utopian vision to Tom's insanity, Stravinsky recalls the fluttering motive from the end of act 3, scene 2, capturing their ecstatic but ultimately unreal emotion in music that is as embellished, but also as relentlessly displaced, as any number in the opera.

The singers join the accompanying woodwinds in concerted sixty-fourth notes to begin (because they share the same text and rhythms, I only show Anne's part). The upper strings waft in and out intermittently and pedal B♭'s occasionally weigh in; otherwise the trill motive and syllabic stresses provide the only metrical sense. Other than the opening <u>Re</u>-joice, Stravinsky aligns the vocal trills with stressed syllables, so words sound clearly and naturally enough. But without a score, the metric placement is indiscernible. Imagining how this music might fit within a regular meter, I have juxtaposed a hypothetical "normalized" version (example 8.12a) above Stravinsky's to show how he truncates, expands, or altogether changes the rhythmic groupings.[26]

By starting on a downbeat and adding extra beats in mm. 2–4, the melody fits comfortably in 3/8 for the first phrase; imagining 2/8 for "Space cannot alter nor time our love abate" is equally easy. This change of metric groupings would not be disturbing, except that Stravinsky begins the new phrase on the fourth sixteenth of m. 4, thus displacing the sense of downbeat to a subdivision of the beat. The shift can be heard in relation to the winds' interjections, which remain on the beat but now sound like an anacrusis to the stressed "Space." My attempt to normalize the meter is convoluted further in the third phrase ("Here has no words..."), which now seems to shift momentarily to a compound 6/16. The sense of 2/8 returns for good, except for a single grouping of 3/8 at R251, with "Absence or Estrangement."

Example 8.12. Comparison of a metrically regular recomposition (a) with the original "Elysium" duet (3.3) (b).

Other metrically regular versions of this music are plausible but would have to be similarly adjusted. Not only will a single meter not accommodate Stravinsky's groupings, but also one is hard pressed even to imagine a metrically regular prototype. Yet, neither does this music seem ametrical, which would contradict its classical allusions. The motivic parallels, especially when aligned with syllabic stresses, are too strong to ignore. The apparent 3/8, 6/16, or 2/8 meters seem to float like clouds, their momentary stability only an illusion in a world in which time is subject to no uniform gravitational pull. Like the love between "Adonis and Venus," neither space nor time (nor meter) seems to contain this music.

Example 8.12. (*Continued*)

Stravinsky also suspends the sense of harmonic movement. Anne's embellished melody descends conventionally until m. 10, at which point she simply skips to B♭. Taking up her suspended E♭, the strings' tranquil arpeggios hover over tonic B♭/D. Repeated only twice, they seem to continue forever, like the fluttering winds that first signal Tom's madness at the end of act 3, scene 2. In this exquisite moment, Stravinsky and Auden dramatize one of the most elusive but central tenets of Kierkegaard's existential philosophy: the leap from time-bound despair into the timeless absurd.

Illusion and Freedom

Tom's inflected D♭–D yet again haunts the cadence and following recitative, "I am exceeding weary" (example 8.14 below). Given its increasing musical/dramatic prominence, D♭–D can be heard as extending the central C–C♯ motive, making D♭/C♯ a sort of large-scale pivot tone for the entire opera. The resolutions to D♮ at the end of the Graveyard scene and Bedlam Duet seem to answer Tom's B♭-major prayer, "O may I not . . . deserve dear Anne at last?" (2.3, R204). This purified B♭ represents the new "Adonis," purged of idle desires (and Nick) but now obsessed with "Venus." Yet this mythic vision is as much a delusion as the "happy" marriage to Baba and "world-saving" bread machine. Described in Jungian terms, Tom is fixated on his projected anima raised to the height of spiritual devotion, which stymies his process of self-realization. Impatient, blind Progress has become static Regression. If the original scenario represented the hero's madness as a transcendent leap, the librettists ultimately chose for him a fate closer to Hogarth's pathetic final image: a nobler but still failed quest to balance shadow and anima. Their rake attains not a heightened awareness but a heightened state of denial.

Stravinsky now uses the fulcrum C♯/D♭ to distinguish Tom's mythical "illusion" from his "reality," summarized in example 8.13a and 8.13b. Building on the tonal polarity he constructed in the Auction scene (cf. example 8.3), Stravinsky projects Tom's illusion through (1) largely diatonic harmonies in (2) "flat" keys—E♭, B♭, A♭, and D♭ major; F and C minor—and (3) an obscured or loose sense of meter. Conversely, he delineates "reality" through (1) chromatic harmonies in (2) "natural" (i.e., white-note) keys—G major and A minor—and (3) strict four-measure phrases.

The pivotal nature of D♭/C♯ is never more explicit than the moment Anne sweetly addresses Tom as "Adonis" (R238+2). Her familiar B♭–D♭ prompts the winds' emblematic transition—A^6 to $E♭^7$—from Tom's A-major Arioso, "Prepare yourselves" (R213–23), to his E♭-major Arioso, "I have waited" (R239). Thereafter, the Duet and Lullaby are acted out as if "Adonis" and "Venus" are forever reunited. Stravinsky preserves a subtle tension between this illusion and reality in Tom's "In a foolish dream" (R243), where, over a steady B♭ pedal, the penitent lover confesses in G minor his vain hunt for "shadows." In yet another ironic transformation, the key of Nick's curse, B♭ minor, is echoed in Anne's blessing,

"What should I forgive?" (R246), and again subsumed by the glittering B♭-major of the Duet (cf. end of act 3, scene 2, example 8.7).

The D♭–D motive takes on a markedly different tone in the voice of the exhausted Tom. No longer a sign of hoped for transcendence, it now portends his impending death. Linear 014's mediate his brief shift to A minor, shown in example 8.14, and reintroduce D♭, now $\hat{4}$ of Anne's idyllic Lullaby. Similar 014 spans in the bass harmonize chromatically rising strings (cf. Baba's transformative recitative in example 8.4a) in sharp contrast to the diatonic A♭ major that follows. As elsewhere in the opera, posttonal dissonance reflects the true state of affairs.

Stravinsky creates an even more pronounced tonal opposition in the stoic Duettino (see example 4.10). In stark contrast to the static, ametrical flutterings of the "Elysium" Duet, its steady meter, strict four-bar phrases, and unambiguous resolution to G mark Anne's progress from that timeless illusion. Still, what are we to make of her departure? Whether they intended Tom's madness as a transcendent leap or a stagnant fixation, Stravinsky and Auden could have left their girl by his side, like Hogarth's ever-present Sarah Young. As Kerman asked, "What is the significance of having Anne save him in the graveyard, only to betray him now?"[27]

The moralistic Duettino—"Every wearied body must Late or soon return to dust"—is nearly the opposite of Anne's inspiring Cabaletta. Yet, in its own way, it presents her decision to leave as equally self-determining as her earlier choice to go to Tom. Stravinsky's dissonant, metrically restrained dirge perfectly embodies his demand for "something finite, definite" that can deliver us from the anguish of unrestricted freedom.[28] Anne's departure thus presents a different vision of the existential "l'acte gratuite," not Sartre's essentially arbitrary gesture but a morally reasoned act by a character uncompelled by passion.

"Holla!"

> The creator of the *Lamentation of Dr. Faustus* can abandon himself to subjectivity. Therefore, this, his strictest work, a work of utmost calculation, is simultaneously purely expressive. The return to Monteverdi and the style of his era is precisely what I called "the reconstruction of expression"—of expression in its first and primal manifestation, expression of lament. ... In the episode where Faust calls up Helen, ... there is a gentle reminiscence of the accents of Orphic lamentation, thus making Faust and Orpheus brothers in their invoking the world of shades. There are a hundred allusions to the sound and spirit of the madrigal.
>
> — *Doctor Faustus,* Chapter XLVI[29]

Sforzando pizzicatos at R266 startle Tom from his sleep. "It seemed ... Igor saved his finest inspirations for the last scene," wrote the composer's wife, "in 'Venus, mount thy throne,' in the duet, 'In a foolish dream,' and in 'Where

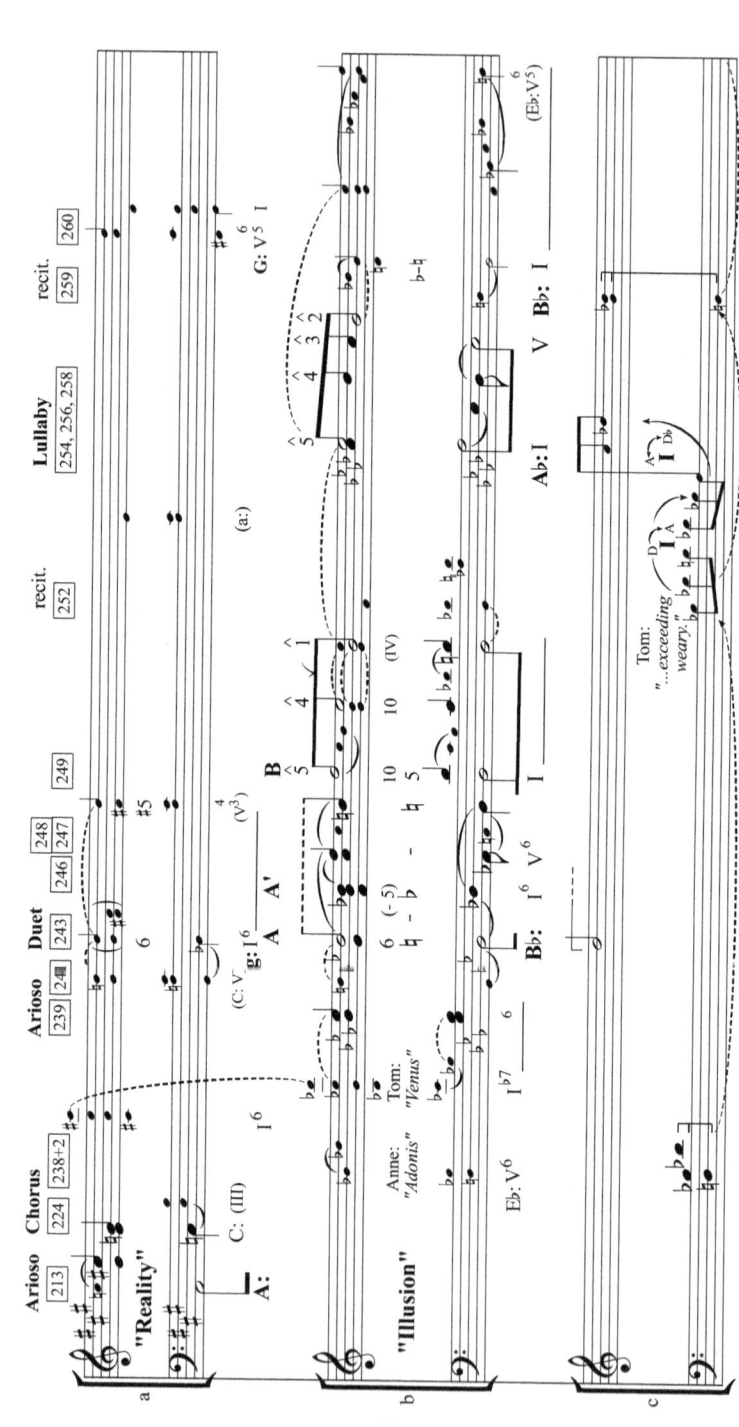

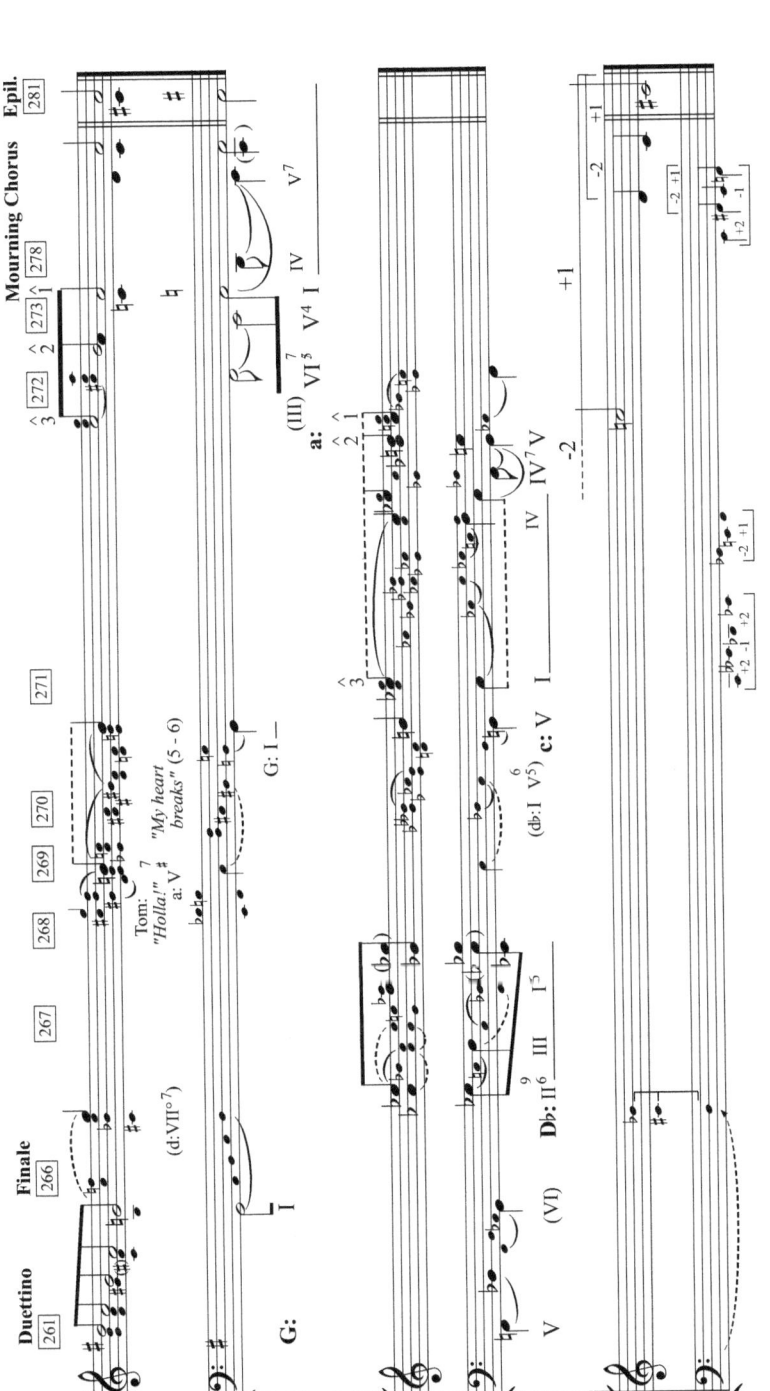

Example 8.13. Harmonic structure of act 3, scene 3.

Example 8.14. Transition from duet to lullaby (3.3).

art thou, Venus?' which to me is the most touching music he ever wrote."[30] A short F-centered progression leads to a terse D/C#/B♭: both VII°7 in D minor and the same 014 that has marked every important transition in the scene thus far (see example 8.13c). Without fanfare, a woodwind chord slips into D♭ major; the wind tremolos and singer's melismas recall the "Elysium" duet. Every musical device Stravinsky used to establish Anne and Trulove's sober reality—namely, bitonal dissonance, metrical regularity, four-square phrasing, syllabic setting—is now reversed. This florid setting also points to another, even more archaic operatic style devoted to ancient myth: seventeenth-century recitative. The deeper Tom's denial, the further back Stravinsky reaches for musical precedent.

Example 8.15 shows the singer moving easily from syllabic recitation into expressive melisma, like the flexible settings of Monteverdi and Purcell. Stravinsky anchors each accented syllable (in bold) to the quarter-note pulse but also subtly displaces and expands the melodic motive. The initial rising tetrachord ("ye nymphs") at R271+2 is shifted back a sixteenth in relation to beats 2 and 3

Example 8.15. Tom's "I feel the chill of death's approaching wing" (3.3).

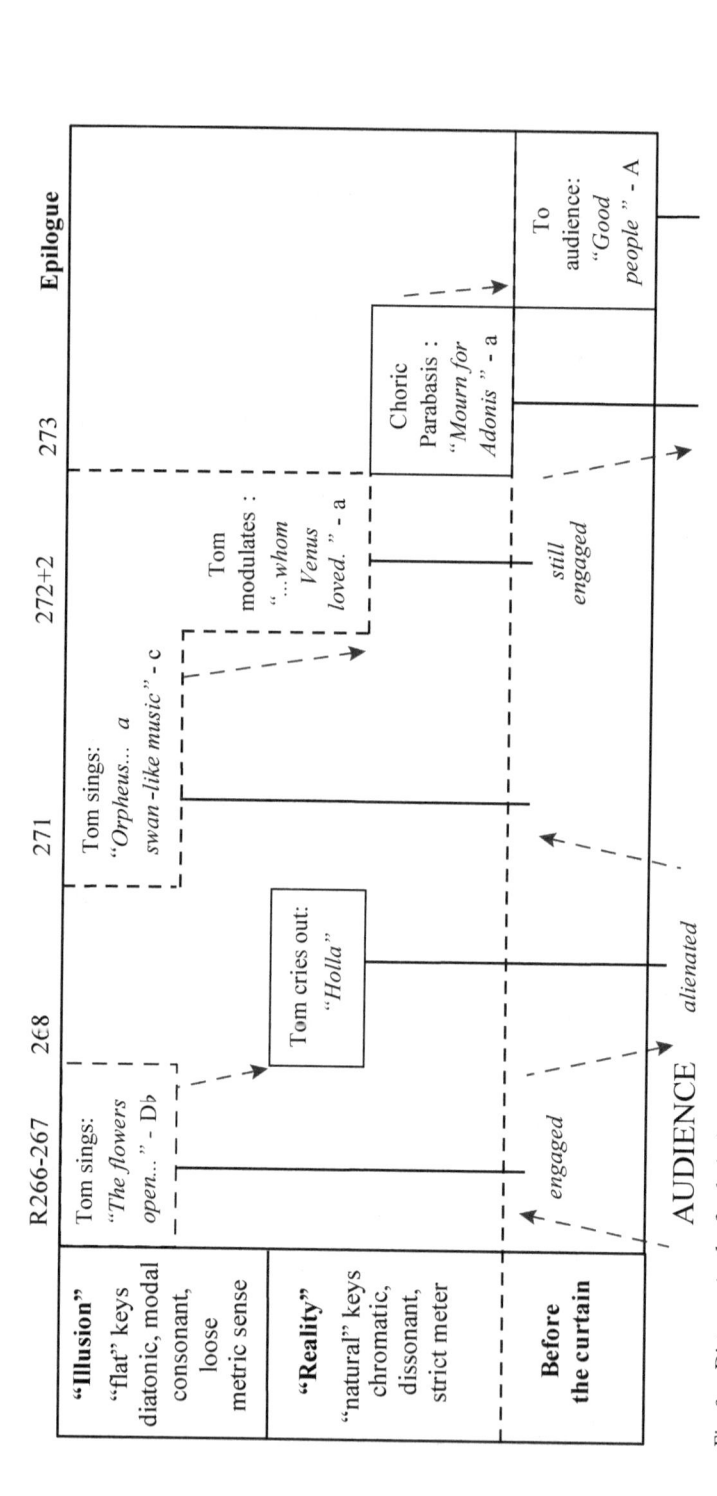

Fig. 8.4. Distance in the finale (3.3).

("and shep-herds" and "these Stygian") and spun out before returning to the goal tone C. He repeats the phrase up a step two measures later ("the beautiful...") and, with fewer syllables, the melody threatens to drift metrically; but the arrival of "young" on the following downbeat again stabilizes the meter.

Then, as smoothly as he lapsed into his springtime reverie, Tom abruptly cries out: "Holla!" (R268). Realizing "Venus" is gone, the frantic "Adonis" summons his fellow denizens of seventeenth-century Opera: Orpheus, Helen, Euridice, Persephone, Achilles. To gauge the emotional effect of this harsh disjunction, figure 8.4 compares three distinct moments in the Finale. The singer's expressive melismas around R267 draw us in; his spoken outburst shatters that lyrical world and disrupts our emotional engagement. Yet, less stylized than lyrical singing, these shouted lines also speak to us more directly. The difference between the two theatrical dimensions is not the absolute distance between audience and performer but who approaches whom. In either case, the abrupt disruption highlights the gap between Tom's "illusion" and his "reality."

In contrast to that harsh juxtaposition, Stravinsky transitions smoothly from "illusion" (C minor) to "reality" (A minor) at the moment of Tom's death (see example 8.13, R272). As the separate harmonic strata overlap and coalesce, so do the theatrical levels. His dying gesture—a leap to high A and slow cadential trill on B—prepares the subsequent resolution. Not only does Tom return to the key of reality, the un-Stravinskian process of modulation—as in the Cavatina in act 1, scene 2—lends special poignancy to his demise. Unlike his earlier outburst, this fluid transition does not disturb us. At the same time, in sadly accepting his fate "Adonis" moves closer to the reality of the story. Distance is diminished from both directions, creating perhaps the most expressive moment in all of Stravinsky's work.

With the strict meter and phrasing of the Mourning Chorus, Time and Reality resume. The Bedlamites' formal parabasis mediates the audience's reaction, and the return to A minor finally pulls the hoped-for D♮ of the Elysium Duet back down to C. Thus ends the Progress of a Rake—alone, unredeemed, and now dead.

Notes

1. David Schiff, "Redeeming the Rake," *Atlantic Monthly* (November 1997): 137.
2. Letter of January 26, 1948, W. H. Auden and Chester Kallman, *Libretti and Other Dramatic Writings: 1939–1973*, ed. Edward Mendelson (London: Faber and Faber, 1993), 590.
3. Letters of January 27, 1952, Paul Sacher Foundation.
4. Letter of January 31, 1952, Paul Sacher Foundation. Balanchine later assured him, "As for the continuation of the opera, I think it would be better divided as you yourself composed it.... It should not be a difficult problem because the stage is very large and there should be no delay between scenes. We can prepare very carefully in advance" (undated letter, Paul Sacher Foundation).

Presumably following Ebert's suggestion, Glyndebourne experimented with shifting the Auction scene to the end of act 2 for the British premiere in Edinburgh. When the company moved the production to their Sussex home the following year, they adopted a single act break after act 2, scene 2, which I discuss in chapter 10.

5. Robert Craft, ed., *Stravinsky: Selected Correspondence*, vol. 1 (New York: Alfred A. Knopf, 1982), 299; Auden and Kallman, *Libretti*, 578.

6. Quoted in Auden and Kallman, *Libretti*, 626.

7. Letter of August 29, 1948, Paul Sacher Foundation.

8. Vera Stravinsky and Robert Craft, *Stravinsky in Pictures and Documents* (New York: Simon and Schuster, 1978), 648.

9. Richard Taruskin, *The Danger of Music and Other Anti-Utopian Essays* (Berkeley: University of California Press, 2008), 110–11.

10. Robert Craft, *Stravinsky: The Chronicle of a Friendship: 1948/1971* (New York: Vintage Books, 1972); revised and expanded (Nashville: Vanderbilt University Press, 1994), 96.

11. Craft, *Chronicle* (1972), 350.

12. Daniel Kessler, *Sarah Caldwell: The First Woman of Opera* (Lanham, MD: Scarecrow Press, 2008), 74 (see detailed description in chap. 10).

13. Excerpted in Auden and Kallman, *Libretti*, 622.

14. Edward Mendelson, *Later Auden* (New York: Farrar, Straus and Giroux, 1999), 272.

15. Igor Stravinsky and Robert Craft, *Memories and Commentaries* (Garden City, NY: Doubleday, 1960), 162.

16. Michael Steinberg, "Mod 'Rake' Bold, Fantastic," *Boston Globe*, March 31, 1967, 18. Caldwell's touring production (which Stravinsky saw in Tempe, Arizona) replaced the "huge fuzzy image" with a small video monitor (Kessler, *Sarah Caldwell*, 74).

17. V. Stravinsky and Craft, *Pictures and Documents*, 402.

18. Paul Griffiths, *Igor Stravinsky: The Rake's Progress* (New York: Cambridge University Press, 1982), 42.

19. Craft, *Correspondence*, vol. 1, 301.

20. Edward Cone describes the metrical relationships in the *Symphonies* in "Stravinsky: The Progress of a Method," *Perspectives of New Music* 1, no. 1 (1962): 21.

21. Joseph Straus also discusses the structuring role of 014 in "The Progress of a Motive in Stravinsky's *The Rake's Progress*," *Journal of Musicology* 9, no. 2 (1991): 174–76.

22. Igor Stravinsky and Robert Craft, *Dialogues and a Diary* (Garden City, NY: Doubleday, 1963), 34.

23. Straus demonstrates how motion to G minor within Nick's aria (example 8.7) mediates the larger modal shift from B♭ minor to major in *Remaking the Past* (Cambridge, MA: Harvard University Press, 1992), 159–61. He also points out a striking harmonic connection between Nick's descent and the Commendatore's appearances in act 2 of *Don Giovanni* (156–59).

24. According to Souvtchinsky, Stravinsky composed in a Kierkegaardian state of "fear," "anguish," "emptiness," and "astonishment" as quoted in Tamara Levitz, *Modernist Mysteries: Perséphone* (New York: Oxford University Press, 2012), 160.

25. See chapter 5, note 27, for Stravinsky's complete answer.

26. Straus similarly recomposes "In a Foolish Dream" in "Three Stravinsky Analyses," *Music Theory Online* (2012): 18.4.6.

27. See chapter 3, note 38.

28. Igor Stravinsky, *Poetics of Music*, trans. Arthur Knodel and Ingolf Dahl (Cambridge, MA: Harvard University Press, 1970), 64. See chapter 11, note 53 for longer quotation.

29. Excerpt(s) from *Doctor Faustus: The Life of the German Composer Adrian Leverkuhn as Told by a Friend* by Thomas Mann, translated by John E. Woods, translation copyright © 1997 by Penguin Random House LLC. Used by permission of Alfred A. Knopf, an imprint of the Knopf Doubleday Publishing Group, a division of Penguin Random House LLC. All rights reserved. For the digital rights of Thomas Mann: All rights reserved S. Fischer Verlag GmbH, Frankfurt am Main.

30. Igor Stravinsky, *Themes and Conclusions* (Berkeley: University of California Press, 1972), 57.

PART 4

PERFORMANCE

9

VENICE

The ideal premiere would be La Fenice, don't you think?
—Auden to Stravinsky

THE COMPOSER OF *THE RAKE'S PROGRESS* NOW RESTS in Venice's island cemetery, San Michele, far from his native St. Petersburg and even farther from his home for the final decades of his life. There he lies beside his beloved Vera and steps from Serge Diaghilev, the man who gave the confident but untested composer his first great opportunity and in 1912 introduced him to "La Serenissima." The composer of *The Rite of Spring* or *Les Noces* is not buried there; Russia would have been his final resting place. Neither does the creator of the *Symphonies of Wind Instruments* or *Histoire du Soldat* lie there; a small French-Swiss town would host his remains. Nor is the composer of *Perséphone* or *Oedipus* there; a monument in Père Lachaise might have welcomed his admirers. Nor lies there the man who gave us the *Symphony in Three Movements* or the *Ebony Concerto*; he would have occupied a plot in the Hollywood hills or California desert. Not even the old man who imagined *Canticum Sacrum* or the *Requiem Canticles* is buried there; his ashes would have been scattered in the Venetian lagoon lest any admirers seek to venerate his earthly remains. No, the composer entombed in Europe's wilted bouquet of the eighteenth century is the one who lovingly embalmed the music of that era in the form that preserved most completely its artistic essence: as an Opera.[1]

The Venice to which tourists flock today is largely the same one Stravinsky fell in love with in the 1920s. It is also the city of Stravinsky's shadows, where Richard Wagner died and that Thomas Mann apotheosized. In truth, it is essentially the same Venice where the young Casanova fiddled and chased beautiful women and that Canaletto fixed permanently in our visual memory. However, even in the age of Casanova and Canaletto, Venice was a pressed flower, roughly preserved in the leaves of the antiquarian book of Old Europe. Though neither he nor Stravinsky had any inkling of the deal Nicolas Nabokov, at that very moment, was laying the ground for, Auden imagined it the ideal site for the debut of their opera.

Such a conclusion comes easily now, almost seventy years after that highly anticipated premiere, but at the time it was a controversial and improbable choice. Stravinsky's decision to place it during the Venice International Festival of Contemporary Music scandalized the major European companies that had been vying to present the most prestigious performance of a new opera since Puccini's *Turandot* in 1926. Especially chagrined were his publishers, Boosey & Hawkes, having assumed from their first discussions that Stravinsky's English-language opera would be performed first by the Royal Opera. From the beginning, however, Stravinsky rejected the idea of a premiere in large theaters like Covent Garden, the Metropolitan, or La Scala, each of which bid for the first performance.

The composer's first thought was to have the small but promising summer festival in Central City, Colorado, present a sort of out-of-town "preview." Having attended a "brilliant performance" there in 1948, Stravinsky was enchanted by the charming Victorian theater in this old silver boon town. He wrote to Craft the following December: "Played what is composed of *Rake* to Ralph Hawkes—he is enthusiastic about it. I told him I heard in July a very good performance of *Così fan tutte* in [Central] City, Colorado, and we conceived the project to give the world premiere-preview *there*."[2] Auden seemed guardedly enthusiastic when he informed Kallman in February: "There's a new plan about the *Rake*. To have premiere in Central City, Colorado in the summer of 1950.... Stravinsky has agreed that you and I shall direct the staging, for which we shall get paid."[3] (The poet's source could have been Craft or Nabokov, both of whom were in New York that winter. In any case, his source was wrong, as the composer never anticipated completing the opera by 1950 and did not consent for Auden and Kallman to direct).

Stravinsky's lawyer, Aaron Sapiro, confirmed that "[Hawkes] is not in favor of Denver [*sic*. Central City] for your opera; but he is eager to have it finished and enthusiastic about opening it in London [*sic*. Edinburgh] in 1951—and is anxious to have you make a preliminary tour in Britain in the summer of 1950, so as to re-acquaint England with you, as a person!"[4] The struggle between Stravinsky and his publisher boiled down to the trade-off between a lucrative composer's fee and a world-class premiere. The winner was never in doubt. Though Central City seemed provincial to Hawkes, he accepted Stravinsky's plan as an *avant* premiere and continued trying to schedule a still prestigious Royal Opera premiere at the Edinburgh Festival. In June he wrote:

> I have had an urgent cable from David Webster of Covent Garden, London, requesting information as to the availability of "The Rake's Progress" for world premiere at the Edinburgh Festival in 1950.
>
> I think this would be a magnificent opportunity for the theatre is small and the atmosphere correct having regard to your own views . . . not in Covent Garden Opera House, but in the King's Theatre, Edinburgh where [Carl] Ebert and the Glyndebourne people always give their Mozart performances.
>
> The main question is . . . is the work likely to be ready by August 1950?. . .
>
> I unreservedly recommend this production provided we get the right director, scenic designer, etc. The prestige of the Edinburgh Festival is enormous, but I

must tell you that it could involve your being there and there is no doubt that you would have many engagements at the Festival as well. In other words, the financial aspect of such a venture would be very favorable for you.[5]

En route from Australia via Honolulu (where he recuperated from a mid-flight heart attack), Hawkes stopped to visit Stravinsky in Hollywood on July 24, at which point he reiterated his desire to see the premiere at the Edinburgh Festival. In one of his last memoirs (2002), Craft ascribes to Stravinsky specific intentions about a premiere in Venice that the composer seems never to have expressed in writing:

> Stravinsky did not welcome [Hawkes's] opinion, having already decided that he wanted a small theater of the capacity of La Fenice in Venice. But he said nothing. . . . After Hawkes's departure that afternoon in 1949, Stravinsky began to address himself to the prospects of a Venetian premiere. He also invited me to attend it with him and his wife, and for the next year I lived happy and excited with this anticipation.
> But no response from the Italian cultural authorities was forthcoming. Lack of funds was a major obstacle, but apart from that, the Fenice orchestra and chorus were second-rate. The cast would have to be imported.[6]

In what way did Stravinsky "address himself" to such a prospect? Producer Mario Labroca, who would prove pivotal in facilitating that Venice performance, had conducted the premiere of the *Mass* at La Scala in October 1948 and may have already had his sights set on the opera. However, other than La Scala intendant Antonio Ghirighelli's obsequious offer in June 1950, which Stravinsky politely declined, no record of any exchange with an Italian cultural authority surfaces until Nabokov's letter of December 1950. The composer may have imagined aloud a Venetian premiere to friends and family, but I suspect Craft is conflating plans that took place a year and a half later in January 1951. (If Stravinsky had invited him to Venice for the premiere after Hawkes's visit, he would have had over two years to anticipate the exciting event, not one.)

Auditions

Presumably more reliable, in that he was an eyewitness, is Craft's recollection of the composer's concerted efforts to arrange a premiere in Los Angeles. German director Carl Ebert, who had cofounded the Glyndebourne Festival in 1934, was appointed director of the professional-quality student opera theater at the University of Southern California in 1948. Ebert encouraged Stravinsky to present his new work there with Otto Klemperer conducting. Craft recalled: "The dean of the music department, Raymond Kendall, insisted on seeing the score and asked his assistant, Ingolf Dahl, to borrow it from the composer. Reluctant to let it out of his hands, Stravinsky arranged for an audition. . . . Stravinsky taught the piece to Dahl, and asked him to play what he could of the vocal lines. . . . After a week or so of this coaching, a time was set and a few guests were invited . . . Afterward

Stravinsky told me that he had realized from the beginning that Kendall did not understand the music."[7]

Meanwhile, Hawkes continued to try to steer the reluctant composer toward a Scotland premiere:

> My dear Igor,
>
> David Webster from the Royal Opera is here in New York and he has already spoken to me about the RAKE'S PROGRESS for the Edinburgh Festival and Covent Garden in the summer and fall of 1950 [Hawkes meant to write 1951, but in fact, Webster had it slotted for 1950]. This would seem to me a very happy way of introducing this new opera. It will give you ample time to get it ready and it will give us ample time to prepare for other performances that will follow immediately. As I do not expect you to finish it before April or May 1950, and it is certainly going to take us nine to twelve months to get it all ready, the timing would seem to be good.
>
> I have told Mr. Webster that you would of course expect to be available in Edinburgh for its preparation but I am uncertain as to whether you would desire to conduct the first night.[8]

Of course, Stravinsky insisted on conducting the world premiere and, presuming a tour to follow, all subsequent first performances in the "continental music capitals." But the Royal Opera was not planning a tour and rejected Stravinsky's suggestion for an assistant conductor to handle rehearsals and subsequent performances. Most offensive was Webster's reluctance to let Stravinsky conduct at all. The composer responded by giving up on a Royal Opera premiere altogether:

> I realize now that our preceding conversations and correspondences on the subject of the *Rake's* Premiere under my direction, though extensive, have never meant to you anything but mere and vague talk.
>
> I have been interested both in creating myself the original tradition of my Opera and in cashing on my personal appearance to compensate for my loss of income during the time I work for nothing composing it, as this work is a non-commissioned one. I see that from now on I shall not expect any help from the sources we had considered.[9]

Though Hawkes was taken aback by Stravinsky's rejection, as it turned out David Webster had in mind only the 1950 season (he was apparently reserving 1951 for the premiere of Britten's *Billy Budd*). This was a year too soon no matter how much he was willing to pay, which, in any event, would never match what Stravinsky had in mind "owing to the extraordinary British tax situation."[10] Stravinsky imagined an American premiere would likely grant him artistic control and, more importantly, the hoped-for financial benefit, so he continued to entertain a variety of possibilities. Lincoln Kirstein, the commissioner of *Orpheus* and cofounder of the New York City Ballet, volunteered the idea for a production at New York's City Center or maybe even a lucrative run on Broadway such as Menotti had enjoyed with *The Medium* (1947) and *The Consul* (1950). To back the plan, he approached Huntington Hartford, heir to the A&P grocery fortune, who "insisted that Stravinsky play the score for him, which the composer refused to do for any non-musician. Eventually [Broadway producer] Billy Rose's opinion was sought . . . ; but like the others, he wanted to hear the piece, and therefore had to be smuggled, like Odysseus among Polyphemus' sheep, in a group of Stravinsky's musician friends for whom the composer had agreed to play the opera. After a very few minutes Mr. Rose's countenance implied that Tom Rakewell could expect a crueler fate in the commercial theater than in Bedlam."[11]

An embarrassed Kirstein later apologized, "You must have thought it very strange that I never wrote again after the fiasco of my attempts to get the [*Rake*] produced. I was terribly depressed by all the horror with Billy Rose."[12] However, he would not give up on the idea of a commercial run either in London or in New York. In early 1951, even as the Venice premiere was being negotiated, Kirstein introduced Stravinsky to Chandler Cowles (who had produced Menotti's operas on Broadway) and financial backer Anthony Brady Farrell to present the American premiere at the Mark Hellinger Theater as early as the fall of 1951.[13] That idea, too, came to nothing, though it reveals the extent of Stravinsky's eagerness and frustration in trying to reach a middlebrow audience, a factor that possibly contributed to his later ascetic turn.

Having apparently struck out with the auditors at USC and on Broadway, Stravinsky fell back on his original idea of a first performance in the Colorado Rockies. Meanwhile, Hawkes went ahead with plans to schedule the still highly sought-after European premiere at Covent Garden and the continental premiere at La Scala. However, the composer's attempt to negotiate terms with Central City shows that he needed tutoring in how to articulate in legal terms his goal of "cashing in on" his personal appearance. Bypassing his publisher, he directed artistic director Frank Ricketson to "start contacting [his lawyer] Mr. Arnold Weissberger . . . who will be in charge of carrying negotiations in order to assert my own author's rights including the World Premiere in the U.S.A. . . . Then you will be perfectly at ease to discuss the other matters with Boosey & Hawkes."[14]

Weissberger set the composer straight:

> I suspect that you do not fully understand the nature of this contract, if you believe that you have retained any rights as an author. What you have done here, in effect, is to turn over to the publishers your ownership of the work, and the publisher is under obligation to pay to you certain percentages of the different rights to be disposed of.
>
> . . . All the rights of every nature have been vested in Boosey & Hawkes, and your only right is to participate in the royalties. . . . You do not have the right to make a contract for the production of the opera. . . .
>
> An important result of this legal situation is that advance royalties paid by the Central City Opera Company would not go to you but to Boosey & Hawkes, and they would then give you your share. . . . What we must do, therefore, . . . is to demand not an advance royalty but a substantial fee payable to you, and to you alone, for your supervision of rehearsals, etc.[15]

Now better understanding his legal standing and confident that Weissberger fully appreciated his financial interests, Stravinsky confided his true intentions:

> As I have told you in New York I want to get some kind of "bulk" compensation for my three years of work as my opera has not been commissioned at the start....
>
> My single weapon in this move is to put pressure on the parties who want to secure for themselves the world premiere (and eventually, in case it proves necessary, I shall do the same with Boosey & Hawkes).
>
> The "pressure" I can use at will is not to deliver the completed opera under any kind of pretext. This, Boosey & Hawkes can do nothing against as no compulsory date has ever been set for such delivery in the contract with them.
>
> As you wrote in the last part of your letter what I want really now is a set fee (but I did not dare using [sic] the word so far) payable to me alone for any reason you may find suitable to the other party (supervision of rehearsals, creation of the tradition and, not the least, the choice for them either to get hold of my opera and its premiere at once, or to wait for years or forever).[16]

Stravinsky now realized his only trump card, to be played as needed, was to withhold completion of the opera.

In the midst of these increasingly complicated and entirely unresolved negotiations, Ralph Hawkes died of a heart attack on September 8, 1950. Betty Bean, director of the New York office, and Ernest Roth, managing director in London, now took over. To further unsettle matters, Ricketson waffled over committing his $5,000 offer, thus entailing a mad scramble for another, presumably American, venue for the world premiere. USC briefly seemed to be in the running again, but the money could not be raised in time for a 1951 date. The Juilliard School pops up repeatedly in correspondence, but nothing came of a proposed first performance there either. Nonetheless, Bean and Roth had good reason to presume that any new contender for the world premiere would have to be American. Only the previous May Stravinsky had reiterated to Hawkes, "Of course it is always to be kept in mind that the World Premiere in the U.S.A. will, under all circumstances, take place before Europe."[17]

Apparently confident of Stravinsky's desires and intentions, Roth proceeded with plans—though he could not issue contracts without the completed score—for the December premieres in London and Milan, both of which were contingent on a world premiere *outside* of Europe. As far as Boosey & Hawkes was concerned, were the American premiere not to take place before December 1951, the de facto world premiere would be at Covent Garden, which would offer Stravinsky only a modest conductor's fee (half of which would be taxed by the British government) and little artistic control. The composer attempted to disabuse Bean of that notion: "I am well able to visualize the end of the fully completed *Rake* this current season if I am given the means and the incentives for devoting all my energy and time to my opera without taking my usual series of seasonal commitments . . . which, on the other hand, I have all reason to accept as usual unless extraordinary circumstances worthy of my sacrifice [read: money] bring me to alter my course."[18]

Stravinsky probably had no serious intention of booking many concerts during the 1950–51 season (though he would conduct a crucial week's worth in Cuba in early March). The possibility of such engagements provided him a pretext to postpone completing the opera and thereby avoid an undesirable premiere.

With everything hanging in the balance, on January 24, 1951, Stravinsky cabled Ernst Roth at the London office the following message:

> HAVE GIVEN UP CENTRAL CITY PROJECT JULY STOP HAVE ACCEPTED CONDUCTING WORLD PREMIERE VENICE SEPTEMBER TWELVE STOP IN ORDER ENABLE YOU DELIVER MATERIAL VENICE IN TIME I WILL COMPLETE OPERA APRIL FIFTEEN STOP SCENES ONE AND TWO THIRD ACT ALREADY SENT NEW YORK STOP PLEASE CABLE CONFIRMATION BECAUSE SHOULD VENICE PROVE IMPOSSIBLE TO YOU I WOULD HAVE TO POSTPONE COMPLETION TILL NEXT YEAR. REGARDS STRAVINSKY[19]

Now he played his trump card. By reiterating his threat to postpone completion of the opera, Stravinsky essentially forced Roth to consent to his privately (and hastily) negotiated arrangement, about which the latter was completely uninformed until this moment. One can only imagine the publisher's reaction when he read it; his cabled response conveys well enough his alarm:

> STRONGLY ADVISE AGAINST IMPROVISED PREMIERE AT ANY FESTIVAL WHICH HAS NO OPPORTUNITY OF CAREFUL PREPARATION LETTER FOLLOWS REGARDS ROTH

To which Stravinsky responded:

> VENICE IS NO IMPROVISATION LABROCCA GAVE EVERY GUARANTEE OUTSTANDING PERFORMANCE ORIGINAL ENGLISH VERSION STOP WILL SUPERVISE MYSELF SINCE AUGUST STOP PLEASE CABLE URGENT CONFIRMATION DELIVERY MATERIAL IN TIME OTHERWISE ALL PLANS BE POSTPONED TILL 1952. REGARDS STRAVINSKY[20]

Roth had no choice but to deal with the fallout in London and Milan and then madly scramble to prepare for the September performance. More about that below but first: How did this Venice premiere suddenly come about seemingly out of nowhere?

"A Large Amount of Money in Dollars"

> What of the opera behind the opera? How much went
> on that was not visible on the opening night?
> —Jörg Immendorff[21]

In short, Nabokov placed it in his lap. In late 1950, with the premiere of—and remuneration for—Stravinsky's most ambitious work at a confused impasse, his dear friend demonstrated once and for all how he could most effectively help his esteemed compatriot. No longer the striving, young naïf whom Diaghilev had introduced to Paris over twenty years earlier or the frustrated lecturer and critic toiling in provincial America, the charming raconteur now showed himself to be not merely an adroit fixer but also an emerging world-class impresario. This unlikely and unforeseen transformation came about because Nabokov had thrust himself in the middle of the most divisive political and cultural conflict of the century: the Cold War.

While Stravinsky labored to complete the opera, Nabokov with Charles Thayer, brother-in-law of his State Department friend Charles Bohlen, helped establish the Russian broadcast service of the Voice of America. Frances Saunders even suspects he tried to join the newly founded Central Intelligence Agency (CIA).[22] In any case, in the spring of 1948 Nabokov definitely applied for a position on the State Department's Russian Policy Committee but failed to receive security clearance after the Federal Bureau of Investigation (FBI) "grilled him over his bohemian private life."[23] Chagrined and apologetic, his sponsor George Kennan nonetheless expressed confidence in Nabokov's value as an American asset: "I can only say that in my opinion the entire action of the Government in this matter . . . is unjust and quite inconsistent with any desire to utilize the services of sensitive, intelligent and valuable people."[24]

Meanwhile, oppressive control of Soviet culture had returned. In 1948, the director of cultural policy, Andrei Zhdanov, issued a resolution sharply reprimanding the most prominent composers, including Shostakovich and Prokofiev. With this internal shake-up also came a general denunciation of "decadent" modernists like Schoenberg, Stravinsky, and Hindemith. Indignant, Nabokov published articles calling out the renewed clampdown in prominent journals of the Non-Communist Left (NCL).[25]

Leery of America's extreme right wing, Nabokov became drawn to a group of activists known as the New York Intellectuals, which included Mary McCarthy, Arthur Schlesinger Jr., Sydney Hook, James Burnham, Clement Greenberg, and Irving Kristol, among others. Committed to artistic freedom but suspicious of capitalist mass culture, these writers and philosophers had embraced, in varying degrees, communist ideology during the early 1930s. Appalled by Stalin's purges and the 1939 pact with Hitler, they broke sharply with the Soviet cause. By the late forties, this small but highly influential group articulated the most intellectually credible defense, as opposed to Joseph McCarthy's right-wing demagoguery, against what they foresaw as potential Soviet domination of Europe. (Following Kristol's leadership, many from the NCL would continue to migrate rightward to form the neoconservative movement.) In 1948, the editor of *Politics*, Dwight MacDonald, formed with Mary McCarthy, Nicola Chiaromonte, and future Nobel laureate Albert Camus the "Europe-America Groups" (EAG) to sway the European Left to look to America rather than Russia. In April, Nabokov participated in an EAG-sponsored lecture and panel discussion, "The Soviet Attack on Culture." Stravinsky, who was in New York to conduct his first concert with

Craft, attended the lecture. The starstruck Craft describes accompanying "him, Nicolas and Patricia Nabokov to a debate at the Rand School (Mary McCarthy was brilliant)."[26]

The following year the Soviet Union, through a front group of the American Communist Party, sponsored the third in a series of four international "peace conferences" at the Waldorf-Astoria (the previous two were held in Berlin in 1947 and Wroclaw, Poland, in 1948; a fourth was scheduled for Paris in April 1949). Purportedly a forum for international writers and artists to advocate for a reduction in East/West tensions, the "Cultural and Scientific Conference for Peace" was really designed to mask the spread of Soviet hegemony in Eastern Europe and showcase artists who articulated the party line. Stravinsky shared with Craft the following invitation from the *New York Times* music critic (whom he held in contempt):

> Will you join with other outstanding American musicians in sending the following cable of greetings to Dmitri Shostakovich: "We are delighted to learn of your forthcoming visit to the United States and welcome you as one of the outstanding composers of the world. Music is an international language and your visit will serve to symbolize the bond which music can create among all peoples. We welcome your visit also in the hope that this kind of cultural interchange can aid understanding among our peoples and thereby make possible an enduring peace." Please wire me . . . Olin Downes
> The old fool! [Tom's reference to Father Trulove (1.1)]
> I answered him as follows:
> "Regret not to be able to join welcomers of Soviet artists coming this country. But all my ethic and esthetic convictions oppose such gesture. Igor Stravinsky."[27]

Downes published Stravinsky's curt response in turn prompting the Soviet paper *Red Star* to condemn "the composer as a 'traitor and enemy of our fatherland. . . .' This too appeared in the world press and, among other reactions, divided Americans into supporters of either Shostakovich or Stravinsky. On March 25, reporters converged on Stravinsky in his Beverly Hills home and asked if he would debate with Shostakovich on political or artistic issues. Stravinsky replied: 'How can you talk to them? They are not free. There is no discussion possible with people who are not free.'"[28]

According to Nabokov, at a dinner party he and Patricia hosted in their Upper East Side apartment, Mary McCarthy spearheaded the idea of forming a counter-group to infiltrate the conference.[29] In reality, the American Intellectuals for Freedom (AIF), as the group would be known, probably was instigated (and definitely funded) by the CIA through David Dubinsky, the head of the Ladies' Garment Workers Union. New York University philosophy professor Sidney Hook suddenly appeared to marshal the ad hoc counter committee from a suite of rooms in the hotel. Nabokov attended the session at which Shostakovich spoke (chaired by none other than Downes), fully prepared to expose the embarrassing constraints under which the star composer was forced to speak. Both of his later accounts profess a degree of sympathy for his fellow countryman's predicament:

> To me he seemed like a trapped man, whose only wish was to be left alone, to the peace of his own art and to the tragic destiny to which he, like most of his countrymen, has been forced to resign himself...
>
> After his speech I felt I had to ask him publicly a few questions. I had to do it, not in order to embarrass a wretched human being who has just given me the most flagrant example of what it is to be a composer in the Soviet Union, but because of the several thousand people that sat in the hall, because of those that perhaps still could not or did not wish to understand the sinister game that was being played before their eyes. I asked him simple factual questions concerning modern music, questions that should be of interest to all musicians. I asked him whether he, personally, the composer Shostakovich, not the delegate of Stalin's Government, subscribed to the wholesale condemnation of Western music as it has been expounded daily by the Soviet Press and as it appeared in the official pronouncements of the Soviet Government. I asked him whether he, personally, agreed with the condemnation of the music of Stravinsky, Schoenberg, and Hindemith. To these questions he acquiesced: "Yes," he said, "I completely subscribe to the views as expressed by ...etc...." When he finished answering my questions the dupes in the audience gave him a new and prolonged ovation.[30]

By contrast, his private letter to Stravinsky expresses only contempt:

> Dear Igor Fedorovich,
>
> The bolsheviks came in large numbers from all sides. Every Copland and Downes licked their seats and balls, gulped their shit, smacking with pleasure, and then grinned broadly: look how good we are, they tell us that we stink like carrion and we lovingly lick their asses for it. Some of my friends and I organized a very successful counter-meeting, where I read the paper which is enclosed on the back of this letter (and which was very enthusiastically received by press and audience). At one of the meetings, which was attended by the <u>scoundrel</u> Shostakovich (there is no other name for him), I asked him two questions <u>before</u> his speech: 1) why, if they are so interested in cultural exchange, do they not play there the new Western music; 2) whether or not he personally joins in flinging that mud at the masters of Western music in the USSR. In reply he delivered a mean, ugly-servile speech. And then answered me the following: "I fully join the criticism against the Western composers that were called masters; the important works of Western music have found their place in the Soviet repertoire." I loudly cut him short, having said in Russian: "You lie," and then the same in English, and after that I went out to the hissing and meowing of all pro-bolsheviks who clouded the room.
>
> What brutes, what shit they are.
>
> I heartily embrace you. Nika.[31]

Beside the complete absence of sympathy expressed in his published accounts is the subtle but telling discrepancy as to when Nabokov actually posed his questions. In the private letter he underlines both *scoundrel* and *before*, as if to correct preemptively his polite later versions. Shostakovich was far too popular for

Nabokov to voice his true feelings in public, which probably had little to do with Soviet oppression. Whether driven by refined taste, artistic outrage, or petty jealousy, he never respected even the early compositions of Shostakovich. For all the political importance of that notorious exchange—especially for Nabokov, who greatly impressed the CIA agents closely monitoring the conference—it is easy to overlook what the Soviet composer's stature meant to Nabokov and Stravinsky as musicians.[32] The following day he performed a two-piano version of the scherzo from his Fifth Symphony before a packed Madison Square Garden. Given his aversion to large opera houses, Stravinsky probably would not have wanted to perform in a 19,000-seat arena, but the spectacle of fawning attention paid to Shostakovich galled him.

Nabokov recounts the formation of the AIF counter-protest as remarkably efficient, even easy, especially when it came to finding money to cover hotel and publicity costs. Of course, by the time he published his second set of memoirs in 1975, it was public knowledge that the CIA had funded such ad hoc groups and, eventually, much more extensive cultural activities. Through its International Organizations Division (IOD), the spy agency would eventually establish permanent front organizations to publish journals and books and, following Nabokov's lead, even produce ambitious arts festivals, conferences, and exhibitions. Plans to develop such conduits for intellectual propaganda were just coalescing when, in 1949, a small group led by Melvin Lasky, an American journalist and editor of the US-funded magazine *Der Monat*, proposed an international conference in Berlin to counter the Soviet "peace" conferences. Out of the meeting would emerge a permanent "International Committee for Cultural Freedom," committed to the "cultural reconstruction" of Europe. According to Peter Coleman, the "costs would be met by the newly formed and generally unknown CIA."[33]

Most who attended the "Congress for Cultural Freedom" in June 1950 may not have heard of the CIA, but at least one member of the British delegation, Hugh Trevor-Roper, smelled an American rat: "When I arrived I found the whole thing was orchestrated on so grandiose a scale . . . that I realized that . . . financially it must have been funded by some powerful government organization. So I took it for granted that it was organized by the American government in one form or another."[34] Nabokov seems—or at least pretends—to have been less skeptical: "I do not remember when, where, and through whom I heard rumors about a grand, or even a grandiose, cultural conference planned for June 1950 in Berlin. I was told that the American government had agreed to offer financial help to the Mayor of Berlin from what used to be called 'counterpart' funds, to pay for that enterprise."[35]

If, as he claims, some vaguely defined authority invited him and Patricia to Berlin and paid for their lodging and travel, then that same authority the following September persuaded the newly formed executive committee to replace the abrasive and inflexible Lasky with the sociable Russian-born composer as the secretary-general of the new Congress for Cultural Freedom (CCF). Nicky's State

Department friends had finally found a way to utilize the services of this "sensitive, intelligent and valuable" person.

Counterpart Funds

On the one hand, Nabokov's accounts of the formation and funding of these various enterprises seem incredible. He, Patricia, and Mary McCarthy brainstorm over dinner about forming a counter-protest to the Waldorf conference; David Dubinsky gives him $1,500 to pay for it. He hears about a "freedom" conference in Berlin; the American Federation of Labor (AFL) offers to cover his travel and lodging. He asks AFL representative Irving Brown for another $2,000 a year in salary as secretary-general; political philosopher and activist James Burnham comes up with that amount, and more. He wants the Boston Symphony Orchestra to perform at his first CCF festival in Paris; arts patron Julius Fleischmann just happens to meet on a transatlantic voyage an unnamed "guy" who instantly raises $65,000. On the other hand, why question people who pay for activities you passionately believe in? Though it may seem tangential, the shady funding of such enterprises—and, more specifically, Nabokov's understanding of such funding—may explain how he found a solution to funding Stravinsky's exorbitant appearance fee for the premiere of *The Rake*.

Take, for example, the grandiose Berlin conference; Nabokov seemed satisfied that Germany's so-called "counterpart funds" paid for it. This money originated in local currency used to purchase American goods supplied by the Economic Recovery Program (ERP), the official title of the Marshall Plan (which Bohlen and Kennan were instrumental in drafting). The funds accumulated in special accounts administered by the Economic Cooperation Administration (ECA). An "Economic Cooperation Agreement" between the United States and each participating country set the conditions on spending, thus allowing the United States considerable influence over the participating country's economy. The agreement required no matching contributions as such, the source of the funds being the sale of imported American goods and services to local businesses. This innovative mechanism protected against inflation but also conveniently disguised the source of the money. "People couldn't say in the U.S. Congress, 'Oh, look what they're doing with taxpayers' money,'" former undercover agent Lawrence de Neufville explained, "because it wasn't our money, it was a by-product of the Marshall Plan."[36]

In fact, Americans determined much of the spending. The ECA required 60 percent of counterpart funds to be invested in industry, and a seemingly minor provision required each country to set aside 5 percent for American use. According to historian Armin Grünbacher, most of that money served "as a $200 million a year slush fund for the newly established CIA, which was able to pay for significant covert operations in particular in France and Italy."[37] It was this slush fund that paid for the 1950 Berlin Conference, including the transportation and housing of each invited participant. At the time, Nabokov was told his travel costs were covered by the American Federation of Labor through its European representative Irving Brown (another undercover agent). The spy agency had yet to establish credible and reliable channels for spending its supply of cash, so it used intermediaries like American labor unions to disguise the true source. Though he had access to cash, Brown wasn't yet sharing much of it with Nabokov, who had to fly to Europe via a student charter company called Youth Argosy (one of the CIA's intermediaries).[38] The composer describes the "thoroughly insecure" aircraft as "cheap, packed with guitared college youths and subdued professorial couples."[39]

Nabokov recounted his "awful journey" (with two-day layovers in Iceland and Nova Scotia) in the same long letter in which he informed Stravinsky of Mario Labroca's interest in premiering *The Rake*. Having not written since December 1949, he composed it over a period of days, filling in the details of his eventful year. Only recently appointed secretary-general, Nabokov was finishing out the school year at Peabody and his future salary and responsibilities remained unsettled. He would later recount in his memoirs: "Now I was to go to Paris to head something that did not exist and for which there were no modern precedents ... No one before had tried to mobilize intellectuals and artists on a worldwide scale in order to fight an ideological war against oppressors of the mind, or to defend what one called by the hackneyed term 'our cultural heritage.'"[40]

He privately confessed to Stravinsky an even less sanguine view of the fledgling organization:

> Congress for Cultural Freedom, in the work of which I am interested, is the only attempt at a lively opposition to the communal-Sartrian degradation. Several quite intelligent people take part in it (James Burnham, [Arthur] Koestler, [Ignazio] Silone, Raymond Aron, etc.) they try—alas, with some very little support from American Labor Unions—to organize a so-called *une seconde resistance anti-communiste*. ... I do not know what is going to come out of it, but I will send you the Manifesto of the Congress, and you will see that here there is at least ... *eine kleine popytka* [attempt] I look in the future without particular optimism. I am afraid that it won't be possible to make an army in Europe with the help of America, and that in a year people in America will deny Europe as a useless refuse pit. The Father of the People [Stalin] is of course waiting for it and then he will possess Europe by way of an inner seizure of power rather than by way of war, as they usually think here ... But the general situation is so disgusting that it is not pleasant to look into the future. In the end, the war is unavoidable and, alas, it will begin only when ... two thirds of the world are in the power of the Kremlin.[41]

Judging from his dour tone, it seems doubtful that Nabokov knew, at least in late 1950, that the CIA was the driving force behind the CCF. Why would he lie about labor union funding to Stravinsky, who at the moment was concerned only with obtaining a large fee for the premiere of his opera? Was it a coincidence that Nabokov had already proposed a solution to this problem in his sprawling, disjointed epistle? Or is the letter more connected than it appears?

To better understand Nabokov's thinking in negotiating the *Rake* premiere, we must first gauge his understanding of the sources for arts funding in Europe in 1950–51. His awareness of CIA backing (and his view of the CCF's prospects) may well have changed by the following May when he flew to Paris first class, a welcomed contrast to that torturous journey home the previous fall. He reports in *Bagázh* that during this flight

> was born the general outline of my first and far most exciting festival, *Masterpieces of the 20th Century*, held in Paris from April 1 to April 30 [sic], 1952.
>
> Curiously enough, not for a moment did the question of money cross my mind. It probably should have, because it was hard to imagine the American labor unions subsidizing a grandiosely expensive modern-arts festival and not in America, but in Paris, of all places.
>
> For no apparent reason, perhaps because of my innate optimistic insouciance [!], I assumed that money for my festival would come my way.[42]

This account must be taken with a grain of salt. First, Nabokov misreports the dates of the festival (it took place from April 30 to June 1). Second, he must have conceived it well before that flight to Paris; the CCF executive committee already had approved, in principle, the ambitious event on May 15.[43] Third, his claim, at that point, to be oblivious to matters of funding strains credulity. The previous January, after steering committee member James Burnham found money to augment his meager $6,000 salary as secretary-general, Nabokov matter-of-factly informed Brown, "Other arrangements to compensate me for my considerable loss of income will be made here, and will not appear on the books of the operation in Europe."[44]

Whatever the case, Nabokov feigned indignation after the whole scheme unraveled in 1966: "Not in my wildest dreams could I have expected that my 'dream festival' would be supported by America's spying establishment, nor did I know that the fare for my delightful first-class flight to Paris was being paid by the CIA via the labor union's European representative. . . . Was it really impossible to find open channels of subsidizing the CCF . . . ? Could it not have been done imaginatively, courageously, through the establishment of a worldwide fund made up of those famous 'counterpart funds' that in the late 1940s were spread all around the world? A kind of Marshall Plan in the domain of the intellect and the arts?"[45]

Nabokov again refers to those counterpart funds he was told paid for the 1950 Berlin conference. Of course, he's referring here not to the slush fund from which the CIA supported its covert operations—about that he claimed ignorance—but to the 95 percent aimed at reviving European industry and other parts of the devastated economy. Subtracting the lion's share earmarked for industrial investment and the Americans' 5 percent cut, there remained a sizable 35 percent that could pay for debt reduction, currency stabilization, and nonindustrial projects. The Germans used counterpart funds to make low-interest loans; the British paid down war debt. Other countries, like France and Italy, absorbed leftover counterpart funds for investment.[46] Though the Americans controlled more than they liked to admit, they didn't control all of the expenditures. In late 1950,

Nabokov may well have believed these funds had legitimately paid for that first Berlin Conference. They might as easily fund other ambitious events in a culture-starved Europe.

Nabokov's understanding—or lack thereof—of such byzantine funding details may shed light on his seemingly off-the-cuff but strangely fortuitous conversation with Mario Labroca, described in the middle of that December 23 letter to Stravinsky. He first recounts his busy—and for us revealing—travel schedule:

> I will start from the beginning and, so to speak, give you a brief picture of my movements for the last 6 months: I flew to Europe on June 1. Spent June: 12 days in Paris, 5—in Oxford, 3—in London, the remaining 10 days—mostly in Berlin at the anti-Soviet meeting of the so-called Congress for Cultural Freedom, to which I was sent or, rather, to which I arrived as one of the members of the American delegation (the congress was extremely interesting, and I have still been actively participating in its work, but I will tell you about it later in more details).
>
> In the end of June we settled in a *dacha* [near] Fontainebleau.... In the beginning of July we went to Aix-en-Provence, to a festival, where everything went well. ... Then I went to Switzerland and spent several days with my friend Isaiah Berlin. Then, in the end of my stay in Europe, in September, I went to my American acquaintances in Bonn for a week and, so to speak, inspected Germany up and down the Rhine. I came back on October 1 after an awful journey.... When I came back to America, a new rush-about began: the underwater life in Baltimore and half-above-water life in New York.... On November 23 I again flew out to Europe, this time for a meeting of the international committee of the same congress (to which I had been delegated in Berlin). I spent 3½ days in Paris, 4 in Brussels, where, so to speak, I "was in session." Flew for 2 days to Rome and came back here on December 2 or 3. Taking off from Rome at 3:35 on Sunday, next day, on Monday, I taught at 12 in Baltimore. So, *voici mes itineraries* for the last 6 months.

Then, as if beginning a new letter, reproduced in figure 9.1, he abruptly starts afresh:

> But first of all, how is your health? How is the music getting along? What are your plans for the first performance? Igor Fedorovich, dear, as I was in Rome I saw Labroca, the director of Radio and also more or less supervisor of the Florence and Venetian festivals. He was very interested in The Rake and asked me about its details. That happened only 2–3 weeks ago. He asked me to tell you that for the right of the first performance either in La Scala, or in Florence or Venice, he can get for you a large sum of money in dollars. I don't know why I told him that you, in my opinion, should be wanting $20,000. To this he said to me: "Tell Mr. Stravinsky that it is feasible and that furthermore we can produce the opera in English."
> The address of Labroca is the following:
> Mario Labroca, RAI via Botteghe
> Oscure *Roma*
> It would be marvelous if it comes out and Rake would be premiered in *schonem Venedig* in September of the coming year. If something will come of it I will demand a percentage from Boosey and Bean in the form of 2 tickets for the premiere.[47]

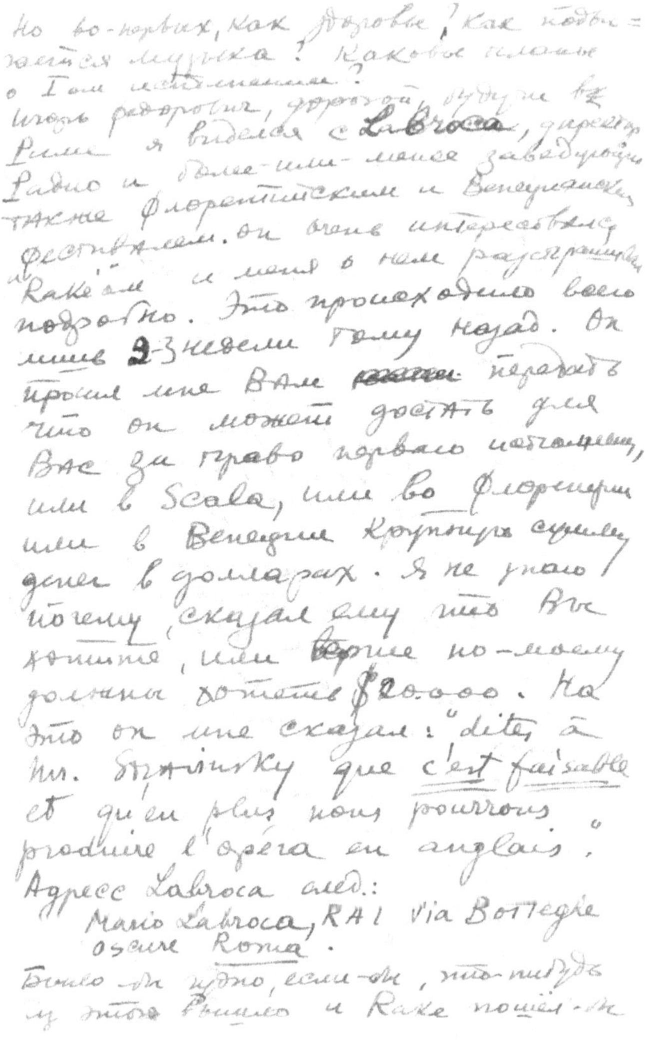
Но во-первых, как здоровье? Как подвигается музыка? Каковы планы о Там исполнении?
Теперь разговор, дорогой, будучи в Риме я виделся с Labroca, директор Радио и более-или-менее заведующий также Флорентийским и Венецианским фестивалем. Он очень интересовался "Rake'ом" и меня о нем расспрашивал подробно. Это происходило всего лишь 2-3 недели тому назад. Он просил мне Вам передать что он может достать для Вас за право первого исполнения, или в Scala, или во Флоренции или в Венеции крупную сумму денег в долларах. Я не знаю почему, сказал ему что Вы хотите, или вернее по-моему должны хотеть $20.000. На это он мне сказал: "dites à Mr. Strawinsky que c'est faisable et qu'en plus nous pourrons produire l'opéra en anglais".
Адрес Labroca след.:
Mario Labroca, RAI Via Botteghe oscure Roma.
Было-ли чудно, если-бы, что-нибудь у этого вышло и Rake пошел-бы

Fig. 9.1. Page from Nabokov's letter of December 23, 1950; see note 47, beginning "But first of all, how is your health?" (Igor Stravinsky Collection, Paul Sacher Foundation)

Just where did Labroca think he could find such "a large amount of money," when all of Europe, especially Italy, was so destitute? (By comparison, $20,000 in 1951 would be roughly equivalent to $191,500 in 2018. The average annual household income in the United States in 1950 was $4,237.[48] Biennale director Alessandro Piovesan even struggled to find the $15,000 for Stravinsky to compose and conduct *Canticum Sacrum* in 1956.) How could the Italian government afford to pay ten times the annual salary of the average worker to a foreign composer just to show up and conduct one performance? "We've got to remember," reminds Tom Braden, the head of the International Organizations Division that oversaw the CCF and other CIA fronts, "that when we're speaking of those years that Europe was broke... There wasn't any money. So they naturally looked to the United States for money."[49]

Did the CIA fund Stravinsky's exorbitant fee? Almost certainly not. The Farfield Foundation that would underwrite Nabokov's CCF festivals was not yet in place in late 1950, and even when it was, the secretary-general had a hard time persuading his executive committee to support his lavish spending; even as the featured star of the 1952 festival, Stravinsky received only $7,500 for conducting and travel expenses. In 1950, the only CIA conduits were American trade unions, through which Irving Brown was authorizing "counterpart" slush funds to break up Communist-run unions in France, not to entice a preeminent Russian American composer to headline an Italian contemporary music festival.

But there was that larger pool of counterpart funds. The Marshall Plan provided approximately $204 million in goods and services, or around 16 percent of Italian government income in 1950–51, the year of the ERP's highest impact on the Italian balance.[50] A sizable fraction of that amount was available to spend on various other projects, as long as the government and the ECA approved. So, did Nabokov fly to Italy for the express purpose of negotiating Stravinsky's appearance fee? Again, no. The itinerary he described to Stravinsky shows that, even before he was appointed secretary-general in November, Nabokov had touched base in every major Western European capital except Rome. Along with France, where the CCF home office was to be stationed, Italy was seen as especially vulnerable to the lure of Soviet-leaning Communists. For this reason, pro-CCF French editors Georges Altman and François Bondy traveled to Rome in late 1950 to help establish a CCF affiliate among Italians deeply suspicious of American backing. Bondy and Altman reported to Michael Josselson "'great possibilities' for the Congress in Italy, but these would mature only as the result of 'slow, indirect, diversified and extremely discreet action.'"[51]

Nabokov visited Rome in late 1950 for the same reason as Altman and Bondy: to promote the CCF. Of course, he met with Labroca, the country's most connected musical director, but it was Labroca, not Nabokov, who brought up the idea of premiering *The Rake's Progress*, just as the letter describes. As music director of Italian Radio, he understood his government was willing to support such a high-profile, morale-boosting cultural event as long as there was money to support it. Interrupted by the war, the contemporary music festival had started up again only in 1947 and became increasingly ambitious after Marshall Plan aid arrived in 1948 (the festival presented *Lulu* in 1949). The Italians could justify paying Stravinsky $20,000 because the money was underwritten by American aid. However, as long as it came from counterpart funds, the Americans could claim "it wasn't our money."

Thus did Nika Dimitrievich earn the enduring gratitude of his beloved Igor Fedorovich. Through the CCF, his network of personal contacts, and later directly through the American State Department and the city of West Berlin, he would go on to present Stravinsky and his works at international music festivals; he would arrange for important and lucrative commissions; he would even prompt a White House celebration for the composer's eightieth birthday. But nothing would match in sheer audacity the rabbit he pulled out of a hat in improvising the agreement to premiere *The Rake's Progress*.

"Je prefere La Fenice"

Nabokov had only set the table for the negotiation; it would be up to Stravinsky to settle the particulars. Labroca had conducted *Petrushka* and *Perséphone* in Florence in 1939 and more recently led the premiere of the *Mass*, so he and the composer were on familiar terms. In his letter of January 2, Stravinsky went straight to the point:

1) it must be done in English
2) I conduct the premiere
3) must be paid an absolute minimum $20,000 payable to my bank—all travel costs to my charge—could be performed at Venice, Florence or La Scala. I say to you right now that, of the 3 options, I prefer La Fenice.[52]

His conditions are telling:

"*1) It must be in English*": Auden's dismissively racist question to Stravinsky upon hearing the news—"Are they doing the *Rake* in English or Wop?"—seems to indicate even the librettist's indifference to the language of the premiere.[53] However, this first condition comes as no surprise, given that the composer's desire to create an important work in English was a primary driving force. Even in Nabokov's December 1950 letter, it is evident the composer's intent had been impressed upon Labroca ("Tell Mr. Stravinsky that . . . we can produce the opera in English").

"*2) I conduct the premiere*": Stravinsky's motivations for wanting to conduct are varied and complicated. He certainly thought himself up to the task, which may call into question his judgment, but not his sincerity. (After he came down with pneumonia during the voyage to Europe in August, Craft recalls that Vera, having attempted "to dissuade I.S. from conducting *The Rake* even if he *has* fully recovered, attributes some of his desire to conduct to vanity. I.S., in an access of pique, answers that he *is* a performer, and hence an actor, but not a vain one. . . . 'And besides, I *like* to perform.'"[54])

Stravinsky could be a competent conductor of prepared professionals under ideal conditions. However, even under the best of circumstances, conducting an opera is rarely ideal. La Scala's 1926 performance of *The Nightingale* was his only previous experience conducting opera, and Stravinsky had never overseen a premiere, which poses its own set of difficulties. Moreover, in rehearsal he could be oblivious to wrong pitches and often played over passages solely to satisfy his composer's curiosity. "During his *Rake* rehearsals and premiere he was capable of cueing singers too soon as well as too late," Craft later recalled. "At La Scala, rather than conduct himself he preferred to audit rehearsals of Ferdinand Leitner, his assistant conductor, and he did not undertake a run-through until the last day in Venice."[55] Writing to his American friend, Elizabeth Mayer, during the tense rehearsal period, Auden was less measured: "Stravvy insists on conducting and (1) He can't conduct. (2) He doesn't know the score. (3) He is deaf. Leitner . . . who prepared the pieces is excellent, but the singers are now in despair."[56]

Regardless of his adequacy, conducting fees now constituted an indispensable portion of Stravinsky's income. His insistence on leading the premiere served two purposes: for the record, it allowed him to exert nominal musical control; off the record, it justified his extravagant fee.

"*3) I must be paid $20,000*": Stravinsky's fee far exceeded anything he had ever commanded for conducting and "musical supervision," a fact for which many critics (including Craft) judge him harshly. To anyone familiar with the circumstances, the money represented a retroactive commission in all but name. Avoiding calling it that name, though, led to much confusion for his publisher and even Stravinsky himself. Having told Hawkes he wanted to conduct every major European city premiere, he decided he didn't want to commit himself; then, after Webster's rebuff, he gave up on Europe altogether and sought an American premiere, his services and fee ever in flux; then he negotiated on his own a European premiere anyway. Yet, for all of his posturing and vacillating, Stravinsky was sincere when he wrote to Bean in October 1950: "In the case of the *Rake*, my work comes to reach a scope with no precedent in all my experience."[57] As duplicitous as it seems, knowing the lucrative return future performances of his opera would earn for his publisher, he cannot be blamed entirely for selfishly guarding his own financial interests in the premiere.

Yet, for Auden, who was "delighted" by the choice of venue, Stravinsky's fee posed a different concern. Auden would later inquire meekly of the composer, "If it can possibly be arranged, Kallman and I would like to be present in an advisory capacity when rehearsals start." But he put it more directly, "strictly *entre nous*," to Craft: "It seems to us that, if there is, as I understand, a *large* sum of money being paid for the premiere rights, we are entitled to ten percent thereof. . . . Could you use your discretion and . . . mention the matter to *Il Maestro*?"[58] *Il Maestro* wouldn't budge: "Unfortunately, it is not my responsibility to provide for your active role with Kallman. I have not sold La Biennale anything but my conducting and musical supervision of the performance, and most of your problems are off bounds to me."[59]

Though his claim seems fair, Auden's reasoning is questionable. Stravinsky may have been disingenuous in claiming the fee solely for his conducting and musical preparation, but that was how he justified it all along, as his letters to Hawkes, Bean, and Roth indicate. Furthermore, he had never agreed to share a commission fee with Auden, as there was never an official commission. The 10 percent Auden thought he and Kallman should receive was wishful thinking. In 1948 Boosey & Hawkes agreed to pay him $3,000 as an advance against future royalties (he had asked for $5,000). Thereafter they were contractually entitled only to their librettists' share of the performance rights and royalties and a percentage of libretto sales.[60]

The matter was clearly a sore spot for Auden. He had already questioned Bean about "general arrangements" (meaning money) for him and Kallman in regard to the Central City offer and would continue to pester the publisher about their involvement in the Venice premiere. But Roth too washed his hands of the matter, about which Stravinsky coldly commented, "I believe Auden and Kallman are trying to find some way of getting something for 'unsolicited services.'. . . Unfortunately for them it seems to be nobody's business."[61]

The composer did eventually write to Ferdinando Ballo, the director of the Biennale Festival, on Auden's behalf: "My friendship and admiration for Auden, which is not a little, makes me strongly desire his presence on the occasion of this premiere, and naturally, if you were also able to invite his collaborator, I would rejoice greatly. However, I can only encourage you sentimentally in this way because the raising of funds is solely your jurisdiction."[62] Making arrangements for the librettists, however, was the least of Ballo's concerns, for at that moment he and Labroca were in the throes of an "incredible farrago" with La Scala over the Venice premiere.

"Of the three options, I prefer La Fenice": If only Ernst Roth had known that Stravinsky made Venice not a firm condition, but only his stated preference, perhaps he may have avoided getting caught up in a dispute lasting months that would postpone planning and severely compromise the first performance. Instead, Ballo leapt at the opportunity to secure the prestigious event for his festival, and the eager Stravinsky promptly accepted the terms and set his heart on Venice. Roth could say nothing to dissuade him, though he tried desperately. His letter details the publisher's short- and long-term thinking for the opera Boosey & Hawkes had so carefully cultivated:

> I only wish I had known that you were negotiating European performances yourself instead of being under the impression that it was *my* duty to get the best possible start for your work. Undoubtedly you are aware that the situation for us is extremely awkward.
>
> The following Festivals have been after me for the premiere of *Rake's Progress*—Salzburg, Maggio Musicale Florenze [sic], Venice and Edinburgh. Of all these, from the artistic point of view, Salzburg would have had the preference and from the financial point of view Edinburgh. . . . It is only Salzburg using the artists and the orchestra of the State Opera in Vienna which has an opportunity of proper and careful preparation and rehearsing. . . . All the other Festivals, namely Edinburgh, Venice and Florence, have no such artistic background. They collect the artists as they can find them. They have only two or three weeks at the most for any ensemble and stage rehearsals and all the singers have to learn their parts in various countries of the world with various coaches and as it usually happens, they

come to the place of actual performance rather unprepared, faced with the sudden demands of a conductor and producer, which almost invariably differ from what they have learned....

I, therefore, really cannot see the advantage artistically which Venice could offer over the Scala, which would equally invite you to conduct, would probably pay you more than Venice and would give you a performance which would be well studied, well rehearsed and played to an audience of at least equal distinction.

With these considerations in mind, I evaded all the Festivals and I think you were informed at the time that we had promised the European first performance to Covent Garden in December 1951, to be followed almost immediately by the Scala in Milan, with a first Continental performance, and this to be followed within short intervals by the Paris Opera, Zurich, probably Brussels and Stockholm. Particularly the commitments to Covent Garden and the Scala would put us into an extremely awkward position and the Scala especially would take great exception if the premiere went to Venice and there is no doubt that neither the Scala nor any other Italian Opera would perform the work for quite some time.

You are, of course, the master of the destinies of your work but I would really beg of you to consider all the arguments I have put forward, which in no way have any other purpose in mind but your work and the best possible start for it. After all, if you have the choice between Venice and the Scala, I do not think that there could really be much doubt... In Venice you would find yourself in a turmoil of disorganization which requires improvisation in the smallest matters. I have been there since the war repeatedly and have always been surprised that in the end the curtain could rise at all.

However, I want to stress once more that you are the master and if you decide definitively that the premiere should be in Venice, I certainly will comply with any request you may have in this respect. Please let me have your frank views about it.[63]

Of course, Stravinsky was informed about his publisher's agreements with Covent Garden and La Scala. That is precisely why he did not at least inform Roth about Ballo's offer, as he had been informing Bean of the details of his negotiations with potential American venues. Even as "master of the destinies" of his work, he didn't want to read Roth's arguments before signing the contract. It was easier to present his decision as a fait accompli.

And why not La Scala? The performance would have been much more easily and better prepared. Milan would have lavished money on Stravinsky and the production and avoided any further delay—for January was already late to start planning a December production—in contracting singers, directors, designers, and so on. Stravinsky knew all that. In June 1950 Ghirighelli had personally issued an invitation in language appropriate for a returning Lully: "Very illustrious Master, I want to express the strong desire of La Scala to present your new opera, if possible in the form of its creation.... We would be particularly happy if you would kindly agree to conduct."[64]

Ghirighelli seemed satisfied with Stravinsky's perfectly reasonable preference for an English-language premiere by an English-language company as long as La Scala could present the continental premiere. However, the composer had already expressed to Hawkes his "lack of enthusiasm to have my chamber *Rake* played in large theaters like the Met, Covent Garden, Grand Opéra Paris, and above all [!] La Scala."[65] Judging from the numerous and varied subsequent productions (discussed in detail in the following chapter), he was right. Stravinsky conceived his "chamber *Rake*" as an eighteenth-century-style opera, and it remains best experienced in eighteenth-century-sized theaters: hence, his serious pursuit of Central City. That would be Stravinsky's reasoning when, on January 18, before he had even informed Boosey & Hawkes, he wrote to Labroca and Ballo: "Central City wants an option for July 1951—without my conducting—considering it local American event. Hope you will not object as I have reasons not to antagonize them."[66]

Central City had already begun preparations for a July premiere. After consulting with his lawyer, Stravinsky offered to reduce his conducting fee from the Biennale to $15,000 in order to preserve his verbal agreement. Knowing how stressed the preparations for a September premiere were—he would not finish the opera until April—it seems incredible, not to say foolhardy, that Stravinsky was seriously considering a first performance in Central City in July 1951. In any event, Labroca and Ballo did object and the plan was dropped.

By far the most aggrieved party, though, was Ghirighelli, whom Boosey & Hawkes had assured would present the continental premiere. That La Scala now would not even present the Italian premiere nearly brought about a civil war, setting off threats of a lawsuit against Boosey & Hawkes and action by the Italian parliament to block payment of Stravinsky's fee. Finally in June, after much negotiation, machinations, and interventions facilitated by the long-suffering Roth, a compromise was worked out so that La Scala would provide the orchestra and chorus and oversee the production, thus claiming some face-saving credit for the premiere at Venice's La Fenice.[67]

In the end, *The Rake's Progress* resounded first where it was wanted most. Considered practically, the premiere should have taken place at the King's Theater in Edinburgh, in an English-speaking country by an English company; but the English were not flexible enough to accommodate Stravinsky's terms. Considered financially, the opera should have premiered somewhere in America, the richest country in the world; but in spite of Frank Ricketson's claim that the idea of a Central City premiere "has become almost a religion with our Executive Committee," the wealthy people in Denver (or in Los Angeles or New York) could not match the enthusiasm, much the less the money, the Italians were willing to put on the table.[68] Regardless of where that money actually originated, whether counterpart funds or the Italian government's culture budget, that Labroca didn't bat an eye before agreeing to pay Stravinsky $20,000 for the premiere, wherever, whenever, and in whatever language, as long as it was in Italy (one of the poorest countries in Europe), still speaks volumes about the relationship between Italians and opera.

The composer's confused pursuit of compensation uncovers forces that influenced, if not directly his work, then certainly the venue of its premiere. In this light is revealed another hidden motivation, unacknowledged and probably unknown to most of the parties involved in producing that memorable occasion. Whether or not the State Department knew exactly how Italy's counterpart funds were being spent, it makes sense that the world's most celebrated composer (and an American at that) would conduct the most anticipated premiere in a generation in a devastated part of Europe rather than a charming Colorado mining town or in Scotland, regardless of the language or setting. The Italian Ministry of Culture, which cared only that the premiere take place in the country where opera was born, certainly knew the source of the money. I suspect Nabokov had a notion as well.

The Performance

As with many ambitious works, the premiere was a shabby, if illustrious, mess. Stravinsky himself was mostly to blame. Had he informed his publisher of the offer from Labroca and Ballo before signing the agreement with the Biennale, the months-long delay in planning may have been avoided and stronger personnel secured. Had he flown to Cuba from Los Angeles in March instead of driving with Craft and Vera back and forth across the United States, he could have delivered the completed score at least two weeks sooner. Had he listened to his wife and let his assistant Leitner conduct, the lead tenor Robert Rounseville might have missed fewer cues.

But no. Only in late June would La Scala start planning for the off-site premiere. Producing a familiar standard in two and a half months would have been rushed. To try to launch a full-length new opera was courting disaster. The late start meant having to settle for second, third, and even fourth choices in important positions and roles. Stravinsky's tricky score posed few problems for La Scala's excellent orchestra, the same could not be said for its chorus, which had to pronounce Auden and Kallman's often complex English text. Gianni Ratto and Ebe Colciaghi would be the default choices to design the sets and costumes after the company failed to contract any of Stravinsky's preferences: his Hollywood friend Eugene Berman, French artist Balthasar Balthus, or English designer John Piper.

Only because the premiere offered such a golden opportunity were the producers able to contract world-class singers; still, only three of the seven roles would be sung by native English speakers. The one for which Stravinsky insisted on a native speaker was Tom. When the best tenors proved unavailable, the composer turned to his neighbor, the Baroness Catherine d'Erlanger, for a recommendation. She suggested, not inappropriately, Rounseville, a converted Hollywood operetta singer who had just starred in the film of Offenbach's *Tales of Hoffman*. Though stiff by today's standards, his lyric tenor suited Tom and his diction was good. However, he had little experience performing modernist music, which showed.[69] And to be fair, having been hired only in late July, he was not given adequate time to learn the opera's most difficult role.

In the end, La Scala engaged Auden as diction coach for the chorus (a task nearly as futile as getting Stravinsky to share his fee) and adviser to stage director Carl Ebert, a duty he ignored "since he disapproved of everything in the staging."[70] From the start Auden had opposed Ebert for his overly "refined and 'miniaturized'" direction and was even so bold as to suggest himself and Kallman: "at least we shouldn't sacrifice the music to the action, as most modern operatic directors do, in my opinion."[71] He minced no words to Elizabeth Mayer: "Worst of all, my dear, KARL EBURT [sic]. For vanity, insolence, and incompetence I have never met his equal. Just because Chester & I won't let him do his Max Reinhart [sic] tricks, he whether unconsciously or willfully rejects every suggestion we make."[72] The librettists further complained about Ratto's Italianate sets, the ill-prepared Rounseville, and privately about Stravinsky's conducting, though apparently not about the chorus butchering their text. Feelings of lingering resentment over Stravinsky's fee and dissatisfaction with being relegated to chorus coach probably contributed to the poet's embarrassingly emotional reaction to his shabby hotel room. Craft recounts:

> Wystan, finding his La Scala-financed accommodations at the Bauer to be bathless and viewless, flees to the I. S's over-upholstered and luxuriously uncomfortable Royal Suite and bursts into tears. V. calls the *"Direzione,"* explaining that Maestro Auden is not only the co-author of *"La carrier d'un Libertino"* but "a kind of Guglielmo Shakespeare, who, moreover, has been received at Buckingham Palace by the King." A better room is promptly found, of course, but Wystan's tears, exposing so much frustration and wounded pride, have watered us all a bit, not because he is beyond the most appropriate age for them, but because of his vastly superior mind.[73]

Auden's antipathy toward Ebert was especially intense, not simply because he wanted to stage the opera himself but also because the German director's approach to opera diametrically opposed his own. Ebert had been trained as an actor in the Stanislawsky method by Reinhardt in Berlin before gravitating in the late 1920s to the role of teacher and director. Frustrated with the stylized conventions that Auden and Kallman so loved, he introduced to the opera stage an unprecedented attention to dramatic detail so as to ensure "the essential unity between drama and music. That anybody coming from the 'straight' theatre could dare to disentangle the mysteries of a musical score and translate them into action seemed unheard-of."[74] However, for Auden and also Stravinsky, who since 1914 had embraced Meyerhold's strict separation of music and action, such a unity would seem, at best, illusory and, at worst, fraudulent. Craft reported his snide comments on the day of the premiere: "Auden, very out of patience with the stage director, proposes that we drink a bottle of champagne to his demise, and threatens to change the line 'A scene like this is better than a sale' to 'A scene like this is slower than a snail.'"[75]

In 1964, after the publication of *Dialogues and a Diary*, Stravinsky received a letter offering a very different, though perhaps equally biased, recollection of that tense rehearsal period:

> How well I remember those days in Milan and Venice. The harrowing first rehearsals; the stodgy La Scala chorus—prodded and protected by the venerable Maestro Veneziani, unforgettable in his squirming embarrassment at the scene which takes place in what he insisted be called by that lovely Italian euphemism, "casa di toleranza": Rounseville, in an agony of musical uncertainty, counting beats on his fingers right through dress rehearsal and premiere; Tourel—great singer and reluctant actress; the ever faithful Ferdinand Leitner and his invaluable labors in putting everyone through their musical paces; the stage and lighting crews with their creativity complex which, at the crucial moment, bade them disregard all instructions and follow the dictates of their own inspiration. Some of the events preceding the production, too—the choosing of director Carl Ebert, long before the completion of the opera; the decision to give the premiere to La Scala—despite the obvious disadvantages—for first performances at the prestigious Venice Festival. And, most of all, the frustration of W. H. Auden, and his insistence on retaining command—I remember thinking, if only Auden could now release his creation, could bring himself—as every creator must—to deliver its fate into the hands of the midwife and allow the child to be born. . . .
>
> All this came to mind when I read the paragraph [previously quoted]. . . . It was, to me, profoundly shocking and sad. Not a direct, honorable "I. S. was in total disagreement with the conception of director Carl Ebert because . . .", or "Ebert's production proved a great disappointment to I. S. by reason of . . .", but an ugly, petty, oblique reference, accompanied by a quote—albeit from a great poet—that is indeed obscene.
>
> Does one really toast the death of a man, justly famous in his field, because one disagrees with him? Does such an expression deserve public print, twelve years later, in the name of Igor Stravinsky?
>
> You see, Maestro, I was there too, in 1951, along with my father, Carl Ebert. And I write to you today less in filial piety (you will forgive me for saying that my father's reputation hardly needs defending) than in the desire to correct what I consider to be a distortion—by association, if you will—of the qualities of a man whom I deeply admire and respect, as an artist and as a human being. I do not believe that Stravinsky, whatever his flaws might be, is petty.
>
> Christiane Cooper

Stravinsky responded: "Although I share Robert Craft's reaction concerning the staging of Rake's Progress in Venice, personally I don't feel responsible for his sharp criticisms of it. If I were doing it I would find quite a different manner of expressing my disapproval of this particular staging. I wonder why did you write this letter to me and not to R. Craft who is the author of Diary, i.e. the second half of Dialogue and Diary."[76]

For the first and only time in writing, Stravinsky's letter clarifies his negative feelings about Ebert's staging, a vexing point given that, as Cooper notes, he had advocated Ebert for director as early as 1950, brushing aside Auden's expressed desire to stage the opera himself. Stravinsky also ascribes, cravenly, the criticism to Craft, whose diary coyly purports to describe only Auden's comments. Ebert's daughter sees through such passive aggressiveness directly to Stravinsky, whose attempt to wash his hands of Craft's gossip is perhaps more deplorable than Auden's open hostility. Understanding exactly what aspects of Ebert's staging Auden and Stravinsky objected to will be important, even key, to a successful production of *The Rake's Progress*. (Also dissatisfied with the premiere, Ebert would have a chance to redeem himself—and the opera—when he persuaded the Glyndebourne Festival to stage it in 1953, as discussed in chap. 10.)

Stravinsky was not reticent in expressing his frustration over the long delays between scenes caused by elaborate set changes, so typical of the large theaters he had railed against (and an issue directors and designers continue to struggle with).[77] The complicated change between the Auction and Graveyard scenes prompted Leitner, when he conducted the same production (in Italian) at La Scala in December, to propose making act 3, scene 1, part of a four-scene second act. Stravinsky and Auden even signed off on the change for the upcoming production by the Metropolitan Opera before Kallman raised objections.

Despite these shortcomings, the premiere was by most accounts a qualified success. The live broadcast recording by Radio Audizioni Italiane (RAI) verifies Craft's assessment: "At most changes of tempo the ensemble falls apart and there are a dozen near-disastrous entrances. But the opera survives, and we and most of the audience are deeply moved."[78] Other than the obvious scapegoat, Rounseville, the cast was fully up to the task. Though perhaps too lyrical for Baba, Jennie Tourel nonetheless proved herself worthy of creating the opera's most problematic character. Elizabeth Schwarzkopf's Anne and Hugues Cuenod's Sellem were, by all accounts, exemplary. The German soprano anchored musically every scene in which she sang and set the performance off on a solid, if stiff footing. The chorus-dominated Brothel scene was predictably incomprehensible. It would take Schwarzkopf's consummate artistry—and unforgettable high C (the idea for which Auden, it should be remembered, deserves credit) in scene 3 to set the performance aright.

The third act, with its numerous sudden changes in tempo and mood, fared the worst. La Scala's string section somehow managed to stay together, though at times apparently with little help from Stravinsky. Rounseville was lost through much of the Bedlam scene, but once again Schwarzkopf's rock-solid Anne, even truer to character than intended, rescued her aimless lover. The confused rake and messy chorus at least suited the madhouse setting.

None of these shortcomings seems to have fazed the composer. In the photograph we have already seen from the Taverna La Fenice (fig. 1.2) everyone is all smiles. More polished, nuanced performances and more thoughtful interpretations lay ahead, but the launching of *The Rake's Progress* had not failed and its creator had been well compensated. As for the opera, most critics wisely reserved judgment; "too soon to tell" was a recurring refrain. Roughly ten years would pass before the opera world would form a consensus about Stravinsky's *Rake*.

Fig. 9.2. Curtain call, Venice, September 11, 1951: (*from left*) Elizabeth Schwarzkopf (Anne), Nell Tangeman (Mother Goose), Igor Stravinsky, W. H. Auden, and Chester Kallman. (Igor Stravinsky Collection, Paul Sacher Foundation)

For all the hullabaloo, neither that first performance nor the city of Venice would play a significant part in determining the opera's ultimate fate.

Notes

1. Contrary to signs posted around Venice on the occasion of the funeral, Craft claims Stravinsky "never expressed any desire to be buried here; the responsibility of that decision is V's and mine. Moreover, St. Petersburg was the city he loved more than any other. But Venice reminded him of St. Petersburg, and he did love Venice. If he had died in California, the internment would have been there, but New York was only a way-station in his life, while burial in the USSR would have betrayed his good years in the U.S. France had become remote," as quoted in *Stravinsky: The Chronicle of a Friendship: 1948/1971* (Nashville: Vanderbilt University Press, 1994), 550.

2. Robert Craft, *Stravinsky: Glimpses of a Life* (New York: St. Martin's Press, 1992), 89.

3. Letter of February 24, 1949, Berg Collection.

4. Letter of March 20, 1949, Paul Sacher Foundation. Not only was Stravinsky unenthusiastic about a premiere in England, he could not have spared the time for an English tour in 1950 (see note 18 below).

5. Letter of June 23, 1949, Paul Sacher Foundation.

6. Robert Craft, *An Improbable Life* (Nashville: Vanderbilt University Press, 2002), 148.

7. Ibid.

8. Letter of October 7, 1949, Paul Sacher Foundation. Hawkes apparently charged Auden with the "ticklish diplomatic job to make the Maestro see that it is in his long term interests not to conduct the premiere at Edinburgh and then hand it over to a second-rate conductor[,] but to let Fritz Reiner do it from the start" (letter to Kallman of December 27, 1949, Berg Collection).

9. Letter of January 3, 1950, Paul Sacher Foundation.

10. Stravinsky continued: "(which means approximately 50% cut off) my English offer should have amounted to twice the Italian figures in order to let me break even" (letter to Roth of February 9, 1951, Paul Sacher Foundation). Of the impossibility of a premiere by the Royal Opera, Auden explained to Kallman. "England in '51 seems out as Bengy has the floor" (letter of September 20, 1950, Berg Collection). However, with plans for an American premiere in Central City seeming to move forward, Boosey & Hawkes informally agreed with Covent Garden and La Scala to present the European and Continental premieres in December 1951 (letter of May 18, 1950, Paul Sacher Foundation). The *Billy Budd* premiere seems not to have prevented the Royal Opera from also presenting Stravinsky's opera that fall. In the end, Britten's opera premiered during the time slotted for *The Rake*.

11. Vera Stravinsky and Robert Craft, *Stravinsky in Pictures and Documents* (New York: Simon and Schuster, 1978), 404. Stravinsky performed a four-hand arrangement of acts 1 and 2 with Marcelle de Manziarly in her Manhattan apartment on April 20, 1950. He later described Hartford as "Antimaecenas himself—a scion of grocery stores and sciolist of 'modern art'—who would have commissioned *The Rake's Progress* from me, had I agreed to his condition that he should sit in judgment while I played my music to him at the piano," as quoted in Igor Stravinsky and Robert Craft, *Memories and Commentaries* (Garden City, NY: Doubleday, 1960), 88.

12. Letter of August 23, 1950, in Robert Craft, ed., *Stravinsky: Selected Correspondence*, vol. 1 (New York: Alfred A. Knopf, 1982), 274.

13. Ibid., 280–82.
14. Letter of June 8, 1950, Paul Sacher Foundation.
15. Letter of June 26, 1950, Paul Sacher Foundation.
16. Letter of June 29, 1950, Paul Sacher Foundation.
17. Letter of May 20, 1950, Robert Craft, ed., *Stravinsky: Selected Correspondence*, vol. 3 (New York: Alfred A. Knopf, 1985), 331.
18. Letter of October 13, 1950, ibid., 335–36, Paul Sacher Foundation.
19. Cable of January 24, 1951, Paul Sacher Foundation.
20. Cables of January 25 and January 26, 1951, Paul Sacher Foundation.
21. "Jörg Immendorff to my Studio Ghosts in The Rake's Progress—Salzburg," Salzburg Festival, 1996.© The Estate of Jörg Immendorff, Courtesy Galerie Michael Werner Märkisch Wilmersdorf, Köln and New York.
22. Frances Stonor Saunders, *The Cultural Cold War* (New York: New Press, 2013), 36.
23. Peter Coleman, *The Liberal Conspiracy: The Congress for Cultural Freedom and the Struggle for the Mind of Postwar Europe* (New York: Free Press, 1989), 43–44. Based on an old French police file and rumors about intimate associates, the interviewer confronted Nabokov with "corroborated" evidence of his "homosexual tendencies" in Vincent Giroud, *Nicolas Nabokov: A Life in Freedom and Music* (New York: Oxford University Press, 2015), 205. Nabokov's laughing denials failed to convince him otherwise.
24. Quoted in Saunders, *Cultural Cold War*, 36.
25. Nicolas Nabokov, "The Music Purge," *Politics* 5, no. 2 (1948); Nicolas Nabokov, "Russian Music after the Purge," *Partisan Review* 16, no. 8 (1949).
26. Craft, *Correspondence*, vol. 1, 340; see also chapter 5, note 2.
27. Letter of March 16, 1949, in Craft, *Correspondence*, vol. 1, 358–59.
28. Craft, *Correspondence*, vol. 1, 358n. Artists and writers who professed support included Albert Einstein, Arthur Miller, Norman Mailer, Leonard Bernstein, Marc Blitzstein, Aaron Copland, Lucas Foss, and Eugene Ormandy.
29. Nicolas Nabokov, *Bagázh: Memoirs of a Russian Cosmopolitan* (New York: Atheneum, 1975), 232–33.
30. Nicolas Nabokov, *Old Friends and New Music* (Boston: Little, Brown, 1951), 204–5; cf. his briefer account in *Bagazh*, 237–38. Craft mistakenly conflates the panel at which Shostakovich spoke, held at the Waldorf on March 26, with his appearance the following day before an overflow crowd at Madison Square Garden (*Correspondence*, vol. 1, 358)
31. Undated letter, Paul Sacher Foundation (translated from Russian).
32. Josselson, who was monitoring the Waldorf conference for the CIA, lauded Nabokov: "This is a splendid affair you and your friends have organized" (Saunders, *Cultural Cold War*, 46).
33. Coleman, *The Liberal Conspiracy*, 15–16.
34. Quoted in Saunders, *Cultural Cold War*, 69.
35. Nabokov, *Bagázh*, 239.
36. Saunders, *Cultural Cold War*, 88.
37. Armin Grünbacher, "Cold-War Economics: The Use of Marshall Plan Counterpart Funds in Germany, 1948–1960," *Central European History* 45 (2012): 698–99.
38. Saunders, *Cultural Cold War*, 63.
39. Nabokov, *Bagázh*, 240.
40. Ibid., 242.
41. Letter of December 23, 1950, Paul Sacher Foundation (translated from Russian).
42. Nabokov, *Bagázh*, 243; see chapter 11 for a discussion of the CCF-sponsored festivals.
43. Giroud, *Nicolas Nabokov*, 251.

44. Quoted in Saunders, *Cultural Cold War*, 80. Starting in 1952, Nabokov's salary would be paid by the American Committee for Cultural Freedom (ACCF) through grants from the Farfield Foundation, the CIA front that supported all CCF's endeavors for its first several years. Nabokov privately acknowledged rumors of covert CIA funding (see Coleman, *The Liberal Conspiracy*, 49).

45. Nabokov, *Bagázh*, 243, 245–46.

46. Alan S. Milward, *The Reconstruction of Western Europe 1945–51* (Berkeley: University of California Press, 1984), 108; see also Grünbacher, "Cold-War Economics."

47. Letter of December 23, 1950, Paul Sacher Foundation (translated from Russian).

48. US Bureau of Labor Statistics. Incongruously, in this same letter Nabokov reflects on the dismal state of the continent (see chapter 3, note 9).

49. Braden quoted in Saunders, *Cultural Cold War*, 69.

50. Rigas Raftopoulos, "Italian Economic Reconstruction: A Reassessment," *Politische Italien-Forschung Occasional Papers* 3 (2009): 17; see also Martin A. Schain, ed., *The Marshall Plan: Fifty Years After* (New York: Palgrave Macmillan, 2001).

51. Saunders, *Cultural Cold War*, 86. Altman and Bondy's report is archived in the Irving Brown Papers, American Federation of Labor-Congress of Industrial Relations, George Meany Center, Washington, DC.

52. Paul Sacher Foundation (translated from French).

53. Craft, *Correspondence*, vol. 1, 315.

54. Craft, *Chronicle* (1972), 27–28.

55. Craft, *Chronicle* (1994), 69.

56. Letter of September 6, 1951, Berg Collection. Craft recounts the rehearsal period for *The Rake* premiere in *Chronicle* (1994), 54–60.

57. Craft, *Correspondence*, vol. 3, 335. Stravinsky betrayed a modicum of bad conscience by offering Boosey & Hawkes a reduced commission, calculated on the back of the envelope of Roth's letter of January 26, 1951, Paul Sacher Foundation: "Should have anything been contracted for my conducting and supervising the premiere through Boosey and Hawkes our basic arrangement would have provided for a commission to be paid to you. I think, under the present circumstances and owing to the exceptional and unforeseen outcome of the world premiere negotiations, I will prove to be playing fair by giving your firm a bonus of $800 (equivalent to half of what a regular commission might have been)" (letter of February 9, 1951, Paul Sacher Foundation). Roth declined the offer, his main concern being not lost income but the betrayed commitments resulting from Stravinsky's circumvention. See details below.

58. Letter of February 14, 1951, in Craft, *Correspondence*, vol. 1, 316; quoted in V. Stravinksy and Craft, *Pictures and Documents*, 407.

59. Letter of February 16, 1951, in Craft, *Correspondence*, vol. 1, 317.

60. Alan Ansen, *The Table Talk of W. H. Auden* (Princeton, NJ: Ontario Review, 1990), 95. Even this issue remained contentious. In June 1951, Stravinsky's lawyer, Aaron Sapiro, requested that the standard 60-40 percent split between composer and librettist be amended to 66 2/3-33 1/3 percent (the same as that with Gide for *Perséphone* and Jean Cocteau for *Oedipus Rex*). Auden's agent protested, asking for a 50-50 (!) split instead. The parties settled on the original 60-40 (Paul Sacher Foundation).

61. Letter of April 2, 1951, Paul Sacher Foundation.

62. Letter of April 13, 1951, Paul Sacher Foundation (translated from French).

63. Letter of January 26, 1951, Paul Sacher Foundation.

64. Letter of June 9, 1950, Paul Sacher Foundation (translated from French).

65. Letter of May 20, 1950, to Hawkes, in Craft, *Correspondence*, vol. 3, 331.

66. Paul Sacher Foundation.
67. Charles Joseph summarizes this complicated affair in *Stravinsky Inside Out* (New Haven, CT: Yale University Press, 2001), 199–200.
68. Letter of May 20, 1950, Paul Sacher Fountation.
69. Stephen Walsh, *The Second Exile: France and America, 1934–1971* (New York: Alfred A, Knopf, 2006), 265. Rounseville would go on to create other roles, including the title in Bernstein's *Candide*.
70. V. Stravinsky and Craft, *Pictures and Documents*, 413.
71. Letters of February 10, 1951 and July 25, 1951, in Craft, *Correspondence*, vol. 1, 316, 320.
72. Letter of September 6, 1951, Berg Collection.
73. Craft, *Chronicle* (1972), 28.
74. Hans Oppenheim, "Carl Ebert," *Glyndebourne Festival Program* (1953): 27.
75. Igor Stravinsky and Robert Craft, *Dialogues and a Diary* (Garden City, NY: Doubleday, 1963), 110. For reasons that will become obvious, Craft edited this passage in his subsequent published diaries to: "Auden, very out of patience, threatens to change the line . . ." (*Chronicle* [1972], 29). Such redactions and ample additions are typical of his successive editions.
76. Letters of January 27, 1964, and February 14, 1964, Paul Sacher Foundation.
77. See chapter 8, note 4 and note 63 above.
78. Craft, *Chronicle* (1994), 63. The RAI recording was issued by Fonit Cetra (DOC 29) 1982.

10

HOW *THE RAKE* BECAME A MASTERPIECE

The Rake's Progress made its way around the major and many minor European houses in quick succession: Hamburg, Stuttgart, Zurich, Basel, Milan, Rome, Düsseldorf, and Brussels before the end of 1951; Vienna, Geneva (with sets by Theodore Stravinsky), and Strasbourg, to name only a few, followed in 1952. Reviewers recognized the music and text as the product of a brilliantly imaginative composer and poet, but most of these early productions showed the work in a drab light. Skeptical critics and company directors were willing to grant the opera the benefit of the doubt, though; after all, good or bad, a Stravinsky premiere guaranteed an audience. Glyndebourne's founder John Christie, though tactless, was not alone in bluntly stating: "I don't like the music."[1]

Not all of the early critics were uncomprehending. In general, the German theaters and press best appreciated the subtle complexity of Stravinsky's seemingly old-fashioned music and the philosophical undertones of the libretto. Günther Rennert's staging of the German premier at the Hamburg Staatsoper was the first to penetrate the deeper issues at play. Having summarized the allegorical critique behind the Hogarthian mask, a reviewer concludes:

> The encounter with the eighteenth century already has been fruitful for the renewal of opera. But the path that Richard Strauss began in *Ariadne,* with all its consequences, Stravinsky has now followed to the end. From the spirit of Mozart, in the footsteps of the Italian operas up to middle Verdi, *bel canto* opera is here reborn in a prodigal wealth of melodies—not as a restoration or stylistic copy, but as a creative act of a great musician who in complete consciousness has collected and bound the still living forces of the European art of opera into a highly personal synthesis for the twentieth-century stage.
>
> This opera is so melodious, so "easy" is its musical language: never naturalistic background music, but strictly stylized, strangely "frozen," exquisitely orchestrated and the tonal foundations clearly indicated. But one should not underestimate this simplicity.... If you listen closer, the composer of *Histoire du Soldat* and *Mavra* is recognized again in this opera as the creator of *Apollon musagètes* and the *Mass*. Though transformed, mellow, [he is] nonetheless unchanged

in the profound novelty and boldness of his grammar, the ingenious structure of his rhythm, harmony and melody. Thus through a highly complex, multi-layered style—exactly equivalent to the underlying text—the music turns from the atmosphere of Hogarth to the landscape of Cubism and Picasso.[2]

Only in 1953, when the Metropolitan Opera in New York (February) and Glyndebourne Festival in Edinburgh (July) presented the American and British premieres, would *The Rake's Progress* be heard, as intended, by a native-English-speaking audience.[3] By then, the opera had been performed over two hundred times, with over fifteen productions in Germany alone. As for the Royal Opera, David Webster had been so incensed by Stravinsky's decision to sell the world premiere to the Biennale—"When . . . I told him that Venice had just secured for themselves my conducting and supervising of the premiere . . . he nearly fainted"[4]—that he promptly canceled any plans to produce the opera. London's major opera house would not present *The Rake's Progress* until 1979. (Central City, where the idea of premiering *The Rake* had become "almost a religion," has yet to stage the opera.)

The early productions at the Met and Glyndebourne, though almost two years in coming, would create the most important and lasting first impressions for *The Rake*. Not pressed by competition to be the first in their respective countries, both companies took time to plan carefully. Singers were well prepared; stage directors and set designers had time to develop their ideas; the mistakes and shortcomings of previous productions were worked out. The contrast between the two productions reveals much about how—and how not—to approach the opera.

The Metropolitan Opera (1953)

> No work of mine has been treated so unjustly as the RAKE and no work am I more eager to see performed in New York and outside of the two opera death houses.
>
> —Stravinsky to Lincoln Kirstein[5]

As expected, the Met contracted the finest singers money could buy. Eugene Conley and Mack Harrell sang Tom and Nick as well as any pair this writer has heard in a single cast.[6] The Texan Harrell combined operatic richness with the clarity and directness of a Broadway singer. Kallman complained about Blanche Thebom's Baba, which he thought inappropriately voluptuous. The only weak link was Hilde Gueden: her Anne was rhythmically sluggish and, surprisingly given her *fach*, strained in the highest register. Hugues Cuenod, who made such an impression as the first Sellem, was the only singer from the original Venice cast.[7]

To lead the production, the new artistic director Rudolf Bing assigned a pair of legends: musical director Fritz Reiner, one of the few major conductors to enjoy a mutually admiring relationship with Stravinsky, led the orchestra; and as stage director the composer handpicked his most trusted, sympathetic, and beloved collaborator, George Balanchine.

Downes provides a largely accurate, if disingenuous, summary:

> It may be said that the production was in every respect first class—in scenic settings and costuming, carefully co-ordinated action, choreography, and singing throughout of a high rank.
>
> The orchestra was in the hands of the experienced and admirable Mr. Reiner. The whole production had been supervised directly by Stravinsky himself. . . .
>
> It is, in fact, reasonable to say, in the light of all reliable evidence, that the Met performance comes nearer the ideal representation of the opera than any production the work has received in lyric theatres of European cities . . . in succeeding years.[8]

What could possibly have gone wrong? In Downes's view, only the opera itself. Though extreme, his judgment would become, at least for the time being, the prevailing opinion. A sample of the reviews:

> Much of the vocal line, with its strides up and down which have no particular musical or other justification, is essentially unvocal, and very difficult to sing. The whole score is in very short fragments, in a dozen different styles, which do not cohere, or do much but remind of many different works which other composers were thoughtless enough to write before Mr. Stravinsky made his appearance. . . . The moments of real feeling and inspiration are very few. (Downes, *New York Times*, February 15, 1953)

> No doubt the gifted Auden and his associate set out with a determination to avoid all the operatic banalities of the past, but they perpetrated a host of absurdities at least as damaging. The text of "the Rake" is an epic of high-sounding emptiness, over-written and hard to understand, mating pretentious language with a bearded lady as a precious kind of love interest. (Irving Kolodin, *Los Angeles Times*, February 15, 1953)

> What the audience saw was an expensive series of tableaux . . . peopled by a number of over-symbolic and under-blooded characters, none of whom evoked much sympathy.
>
> What the Met audience heard was Stravinsky gone autumnal. . . . But [the music] never found anything to get excited about, and rarely attempted to follow an idea very far. (uncredited, *Time*, February 23, 1953)

Thomson, though, recognized exactly what his fellow composer was up to. Defying conventional wisdom, he defended the integrity of the music, including the much-derided vocal writing:

> *The Rake's Progress* is no eclectic score. Its style is powerfully Stravinskian. I should say that it sounds throughout more like Stravinsky than any other single piece we have heard from this master in twenty or more years. . . .

Its difference from those earlier vocal works lies in the greater freedom, variety, and expressive power of the vocal line . . . And although the present work is chock-full of good tunes, many of them more or less familiar, it is the rhythmic structure of the instrumental accompaniments—elaborate, subtle, and tense—that give the whole work its electric potential. This tension, characteristic of all Stravinsky's music, is in his stronger works the most powerful musical individuality of our time. Its permeating pressure in *The Rake's Progress* is grounds for suspicion that this work is probably among his finest.[9]

Having lavished such resources on the production, the Met scheduled performances for the following season. However, by then the excitement of the premiere had evaporated and the production itself failed to ignite further interest. Downes gloated: "The house was poorly filled when the performance started. . . . By the end of the second act people were leaving in scores, in many cases between the scenes, while a great number scarcely waited for the second act to end before gathering wraps and hats and making for the exit. It is clear that the public has tired of this opera and by no means without justification."[10]

Amusing in hindsight, such narrow-minded criticism coupled with the original recordings also allows us to gauge the limitations of that cultural moment. What immediately stands out in the live broadcast of February 14, 1953 (bootleg excerpts of which periodically show up on YouTube) is the heaviness of the performance. His other lapses in judgment notwithstanding, in this regard Stravinsky had been right in rejecting "large theaters like the Met, Covent Garden, Grand Opéra Paris, and . . . La Scala" for the world premiere.[11] To fill a large house—so went the thinking of the day—required a Straussian body of strings, doubled wind parts, and a piano for recitatives. Such had been the practice for Mozart's operas at least since Mahler conducted *Don Giovanni* in Vienna in 1904; so too for Stravinsky's new Mozartian opera. Martin Mayer recounts in the *Esquire* profile of Stravinsky published later that year: "Fritz Reiner told [Stravinsky] that a harpsichord couldn't be heard in the Met and he'd have to take a piano. He took a piano. He had written for a small, Mozart-like orchestra, with woodwinds by twos, and 'they made me take five, as though it was *Elektra*, by Strauss.' And then his fine, transparent orchestration, through which the voices cut so cleanly, became muddled by numbers, and Reiner had to hold down the volume so that the singers could be heard."[12] Given that Stravinsky himself used a piano even in the intimate Fenice (and as late as 1957 for the first performances in Santa Fe), it appears, in spite of his grumbling, he must have agreed with the necessity of some of Reiner's changes.

And, indeed, Reiner led a performance as clean and polished as any, though his prelude demonstrates right away the adverse effect of the theater's dimensions. One hears every note and rhythm but at the expense of much-needed vigor. Tempos are slow and stiff throughout; the extra singers in the chorus rendered the text almost as unintelligible as La Scala's; the fortes are generally too robust and at times overwhelming. The impression is of a *Rake's Progress* on steroids.

The size of the theater distorted nearly every aspect of the production. Conley's sturdy Tom sounds impressively heroic rather than foolishly reckless. Gueden suffered most from the heavy orchestra, which forced her to sing with more weight than her lyric coloratura could comfortably bear. Horace Armistead, Balanchine's choice over Stravinsky's friend Eugene Berman, created overlarge sets to fill the overlarge stage. Most surprising, Balanchine's staging, though initially complimented as "remarkably eloquent and integrated," in retrospect came to seem static and unimaginative.[13]

Why had one of the most rigorously creative choreographers of the twentieth century hewed so narrowly to operatic convention? He explained in an interview with *Opera News*:

> "To me the most important element is the music. This must come first. If it is necessary that the singers should face front in order to be heard, they must face front. Even the scenery has been designed so that the scene changes shall not take longer than the music that has been composed for them."
>
> Mr. Balanchine does not believe in stylized gestures. "It is not necessary for the singers to move all the time, nor to mime while they are singing," he insists.
>
> Visiting the composer several times in Hollywood, Balanchine watched the birth and development of the score from the beginning. A musician himself from earliest youth, he is glad to accept Stravinsky's conception of opera as far removed from music drama. "I prefer poor acting and good music to good acting and bad music," says Balanchine.[14]

For the official Met Program, he elaborated: "In this opera I think of myself entirely as Stravinsky's messenger. I hope to have transmitted as simply as possible the message of Wystan Auden and Chester Kallman into theatrical terms, acknowledging first of all that the soul of opera is in its voices. . . . I have tried to bring to it a maximum of orderly action as clearly demanded by book and music, without decoration, delivering its message without comment of choreography."[15]

How ironic that the artist, who had collaborated with Stravinsky in *Apollo* and *Orpheus* to create the highest expressions of the neoclassical aesthetic, would now censor himself. Yet, in deferring to his friend's expressed intent to create a narrowly defined "conventional" opera, Balanchine seems to have missed the essential spirit of the work. But the composer had considerable input in the Met's staging. "I was at Balanchine's all day yesterday," he informed his daughter Milene, "playing *The Rake* for him and discussing all the staging problems. The next days we will meet with Auden and Balanchine (maybe also with Armistead) to fix the points I made with Balanchine."[16]

The "Music Drama versus Opera" duality he sold in publicity blurbs may have conditioned Stravinsky's thinking as he first imagined and then set about composing his *Rake*, but it hardly does justice to what he and Auden ultimately created. To bring into focus the obscure merits of this peculiar new work would require distance, both temporal and physical. Luckily, the production in distant Scotland would arrive in the nick of time.

Glyndebourne (1953)

> Osbert Lancaster ... [is] going to do the Rake in Strawberry-Hill Gothic. O my God!
> —Kallman to Lincoln Kirstein[17]

Of the various early productions, the one by Glyndebourne would be the most lasting and probably closest to what Stravinsky and Ralph Hawkes had in mind when they first discussed the project. A recent DVD release of the second, even longer-lived 1975 Glyndebourne production (discussed below) includes the following appreciation of that first version: "When the Sussex company decided in 1953 to include a contemporary opera as part of its now regular visits to the Edinburgh Festival, Ebert [Glyndebourne's first director of productions] was keen to revisit *The Rake*. That, and the work's being in English, carried the day. Between then and the production's last appearance in 1963 Stravinsky's opera, still rarely seen elsewhere, became a firm Glyndebourne favorite."[18]

A relieved Anthony Gishford of Boosey & Hawkes happily reported to Stravinsky: "Carl Ebert has improved considerably on his Venice production, quite apart from the fact that the work is much better rehearsed." Ample time and planning had allowed the director to realize a more nuanced, if perhaps too detailed, staging, thus justifying the confidence that Stravinsky had placed in him originally. Gishford nonetheless echoed the now familiar complaints: "He is always apt, however, to be a fussy producer and to obscure the music by a lot of irrelevant action. He rather spoiled the auction scene, which in my opinion is the best scene of the whole opera, in just this way."[19] Such criticism throws light on Balanchine's hands-off approach at the Met. His defensive pronouncements—for example, "It is not necessary for the singers to move all the time" or "I prefer poor acting and good music to good acting and bad music"—echo the reaction of composer and librettists to Ebert's Venice staging.

Yet whereas the Met performances largely flopped, the Glyndebourne staging was a consensus success—arguably the first for the opera—with both critics and audiences. A sample of the reviews:

> For one with a considerable experience of the Met's "Rake" the one produced by the Glyndebourne team of Carl Ebert and Osbert Lancaster held a series of stimulating possibilities. Would the more suitable frame—the King's Theatre in Edinburgh is a normal-sized house, the Met decidedly abnormal—enhance the values of the picture? Could the work be "played" as well as performed? Would the directorial skill of Ebert animate what George Balanchine had left static? Was there a continuity in the score that [conductor Alfred] Wallenstein might track down more persistently than Fritz Reiner had?
>
> All these questions were answered.... The whole work seemed more right and real for an English audience than it had for a miscellaneous one in America. The more suitable theatre helped considerably, but it was plain that all the folksy

allusions ... registered much more here than in New York. Ebert's sensitivity to musical as well as dramatic values kept the action fluid throughout ...

Purely as sound, Wallenstein's exposition of the score didn't match Reiner's for precision or pointilistic values, but the steady quest for a lyric line brought about a sense of contact between performers and listeners one had never felt in New York. (Irving Kolodin, *Los Angeles Times*, undated)

> Marvelously designed by Osbert Lancaster and produced by Carl Ebert, the opera gave the Edinburgh Festival one of its most electric occasions in its seven-year history. It gave Britain the top operatic event of the year....
>
> The Glyndebourne company threw itself into its task with great gusto. When I saw *The Rake's Progress* in New York and in Paris I found the action rather drab and skimpy.
>
> Not so in Edinburgh, where the genius of Carl Ebert filled the stage with fascinating movements and real life. (Cecil Smith, unsourced clipping)

> That the score was a masterpiece, and the Auden libretto a haunting work of art, your critic has had no doubt for some time. Carl Ebert's clearly defined and intensely musical production revealed that episodes which—on paper and on the air—appeared ineffectively contrived, are in fact, striking theatre and sound art. (Andrew Porter, *The Financial Times*, July 16, 1954)

Again in stark contrast to the Met's 1954 revival, Glyndebourne's second season of *Rake* performances in the newly renovated theater in Sussex seems to have surpassed the first. This time Ernst Roth reported to Stravinsky: "Ebert ... has been worried ever since Venice, feeling that he had to make up for the deficiency of that half-improvised performance, which did not give him a fair chance to show what he could do. He has now indeed done magnificently and every character and every scene was full of life and true to the atmosphere of the work.... All the singers were excellent and the success with the public was very great and spontaneous."[20]

Twenty-first-century productions of baroque and classical opera, at Glyndebourne and throughout Europe and the United States, continue to embrace the dramatic standards Ebert imported from the spoken stage. Whether its creators liked it or not, something resembling this approach would be required to achieve lasting success for their eighteenth-century style *Rake's Progress*. Missing from Ebert's staging, though, and crucial to the production's success was the quirky sense of style that cartoonist Osbert Lancaster brought to the sets. Glyndebourne's Mike Ashman recalls:

> Moran Caplat, the company's new post-war general manager, explains how he "put in the strongest possible plea for the designs to be by a contemporary satirical cartoonist who could enter fully into the wonderfully successful amalgam of the eighteenth and twentieth centuries, treating the nineteenth as though it had never been, which both score and libretto had achieved." Carl Ebert had been unhappy with the romanticized Italian designs effectively forced on him in Venice and so,

for the Glyndebourne production, was willing to listen to Caplat's suggestion of the witty and wacky genius of Osbert Lancaster.[21]

While still referencing "Hogarth's clean lines, wit and social satire," Lancaster moved the period to the later eighteenth century. "The *haute bourgeoisie* was very comfortable with Osbert's view of English society," remembered Director of Productions John Cox. "He had made *The Rake* not only vivid, but slightly off-kilter, as is the piece."[22]

In contrast to Ratto's overblown tableaux for Venice and Armistead's bloated sets for the Met, "Lancaster worked with flat, painted surfaces, looking like book illustrations." Figures 10.1 and 10.2 showcase Tom's lavish London apartment (2.1) and the London Street where Baba reveals her beard to the fawning crowd (2.2). His subtly irreverent backdrops accommodated "tongue-in-cheek and dramatic situations as equally strong statements," making implausible plot twists like the marriage to Baba and the bread machine less out of place.[23] What now seems obvious was apparently lost on almost everyone planning those earliest productions, including Stravinsky, Auden, and Kallman: a deferential attitude like Balanchine's won't do for *The Rake's Progress*. The staging and sets should be, in Cox's words, as "off-kilter" as the piece.

It is no exaggeration to suggest the Met's performances in 1953 and 1954 came close to sinking the opera before it could set sail. Impressions left by flops at any one of the various European houses, especially in the first year, could pass without lasting consequence. However, American audiences took their cue from the Met; the only other scheduled production in the United States by Boston University's student opera theater in April, no matter how successful, could hardly overturn the impression left by a leading international company. By 1954 the American public at least seemed ready to relegate the opera, in spite of its length and pedigree, to the composer's second tier, interesting to specialists but limited and flawed—another *Mavra* rather than an *Oedipus Rex*. The 1953 Glyndebourne production told a different story: presented in an appropriate theater and actively interpreted, *The Rake's Progress* could be a lasting masterpiece.

Santa Fe (1957 and 1960)

The ongoing success of Stravinsky's opera at Glyndebourne attracted attention not only in Britain and Europe but also in distant parts of the United States (the composer's proximity in Los Angeles did not hurt, either). The same advantages and financial enticements that in 1950 had made a world premiere in Central City seem plausible could apply to any number of American venues—even just the prospect of a venue.

Such was the case for the proposed opera festival in Santa Fe. Founding artistic director John Crosby intended to open his inaugural 1957 season with a bang, and to do so he engaged Stravinsky as artistic adviser for a production of *The Rake's Progress*. (Stravinsky now limited his conducting to relatively short

Fig. 10.1. Tom (Richard Lewis) and Nick (Ma-ko Rothmüller) consider Baba's picture in act 2, scene 1; set by Osbert Lancaster (1954). (Guy Gravett/Glyndebourne Productions Ltd/ArenaPAL)

Fig. 10.2. Concluding tableau of act 2, scene 2; set by Osbert Lancaster (1954). (Guy Gravett/Glyndebourne Productions Ltd/ArenaPAL)

works after suffering a stroke in 1956; Craft would conduct the opera over the first few seasons at Santa Fe.) Stravinsky's willingness to lend his artist's cachet and Crosby's reciprocal commitment to the composer's works proved to be one of the most fruitful ongoing engagements of the composer's later years. Santa Fe Opera would go on to produce *Oedipus Rex* (1960) and present several of Stravinsky's works in concert. Crosby even sought, without success, to commission another Stravinsky opera to a proposed libretto by Eliot.

The first performances were scrappy. The beautiful outdoor setting on a Santa Fe mountainside exposed the set—and at one point Stravinsky's score—to damaging gusts of wind (the premiere, scheduled for July 17, had to be postponed a day because of rain). However, the following night the composer was able to write in his diary: "Premiere of the *Rake*. A very good performance, singers, orchestra, and staging, except horrible *light* which spoiled (stopped) each applause on its beginning."[24]

The lighting issues were ironed out and Santa Fe Opera would eventually flourish, with no small credit to *The Rake*. The growing festival even mounted a second production in 1960 to take full advantage of its new theater. Founding board chairman Paul Horgan describes the opera's growing reputation:

> This opera now entered the history of the Santa Fe Opera as a repertory piece ... Crosby's love for the work, which identified the company in its first season as an organization as much committed to contemporary operatic works as to those of the past ... began to bear fruit with the second production in terms of bringing audiences also to love the work. In the first season, the house for *The Rake's Progress* was perhaps sixty per cent sold. This second production would draw houses of perhaps eighty per cent. In its next presentation in 1962, the audience was close to ninety per cent, and in the performances of 1966 and 1970, the work played to sold-out houses.[25]

Bergman's *Rake*: Royal Swedish Opera (1961)

> "The artist has only to discover what to do and then with all his strength to purify the doing."
>
> —Ingmar Bergman[26]

Gaining a foothold in the standard repertoire would require more than a couple of successful productions. A Great work attracts and influences other Great artists—performers, conductors, designers, painters, directors—who themselves in turn shape and even transform it. The first such visionary to be so drawn to *The Rake's Progress* would be the eminent film and stage director Ingmar Bergman. "I have always felt close to Stravinsky," he explained in an interview. "His way of thinking is close to mine. His very severe, very cold-hot way of expressing himself fascinates me."[27] Bergman's 1961 production at the Royal Swedish Opera was the first to take seriously not just the opera's eighteenth-century setting but also its archaic musical and literary style. By creating a theatrical style as archaic as the music and text, the director showed Stravinsky and Auden's moral tale to be not only freshly imaginative and sharply focused but deceptively expressive as well. Years later, as part of a failed effort to persuade him to direct *The Rake* for Hamburg Staatsoper (more about that below), Stravinsky handwrote the following message: "I remember your creation of *The Rake* as the most original and beautiful realization of any of my theater pieces that I have ever seen on any stage, and I therefore beg you to do it again in Hamburg that the German and American public may have the opportunity to share my pleasure."[28]

Such was no idle compliment, coming from one who had seen his operas and ballets staged by some of the most imaginative directors and choreographers of the twentieth century. And though Stravinsky could exaggerate when trying to persuade, Craft and other confidants verify these sentiments. Critics shared his enthusiasm:

> It is one of the most compelling pieces of theatrical wizardry I have seen in any opera house. (Noel Goodwin, *Daily Express*, April 24, 1961)

> Audiences cannot avoid being fascinated by Bergman's staging of *The Rake's Progress*. It displays his intimate knowledge of the theater. His individual and group instruction, and his extreme control of the technical equipment are clearly manifested. This production is an excellent illustration of his art. (Frederic Fleisher, *Christian Science Monitor*, May 8, 1961)

> Like the hosannas of the critics, [Bergman's top billing] honors a restless creative artist of films and stage who . . . has made opera visually stunning as well. Citing Stravinsky's dislike of sentiment and his penchant for dry intellectual exercise, one critic writes in wonder of the stirring, tensely dramatic and sometimes comic production that Bergman has created. (Werner Wiskari, *New York Times*, May 19, 1961)

Stravinsky attended a special performance on September 13, 1961, and discussed the production at length with the director over dinner a few days later, which Craft generously recounts along with a detailed description of the staging (see below). The glowing reviews confirm Craft's recollection of several distinctive features that made Bergman's interpretation so effective: (1) his rationale for a two-act division (which Stravinsky would advocate for subsequent productions); (2) his re-creation, not just of an eighteenth-century setting but also of an eighteenth-century theatrical production; and (3) his strict control of distancing stage effects combined with careful attention to details of characterization and expression.

Two-Act Division

Bergman explained his division of the opera into two acts of five and four scenes each "principally because Act Two, as published, does not have a strong beginning-middle-end structure. As I see it, the play up to the unveiling of Baba's

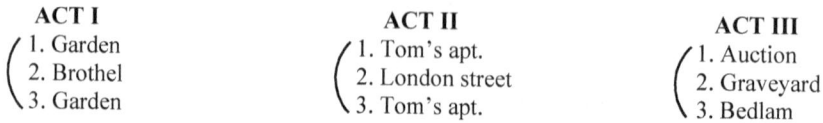

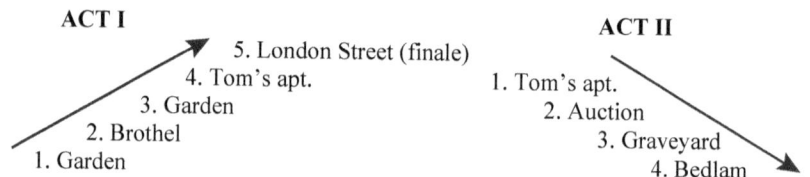

Fig. 10.3. Comparison of the original organization into three "rounded" acts with Bergman's rising and falling two-act division.

beard is one line; and not only the play but also the music: this is the protasis, the rest is the peripeteia. I was more concerned about connecting the episodes along these two lines than with rounded act-structures. I thought, too, that especially in this opera the audience's attention must not be lost for a single moment, which accounts for—please forgive me—the cuts." Bergman had shortened the orchestral march introducing act 1, scene 2, and had cut Tom's "Prepare yourselves . . ." at the beginning of the final scene. "Another reason for the two-act division," he continued, "was that I did not want the intermission to come after the bread machine and allow the audience to go out confused. This is the most difficult scene in the opera both to believe in and to stage." According to Craft, Stravinsky agreed: "the waltz music—hurdy-gurdy music, and in that sense mechanical—is deliberately indifferent."[29]

Bergman's was not the first production to impose a single intermission after act 2, scene 2. When in 1954 Glyndebourne brought the production to its Sussex home, tradition dictated a single seventy-five-minute dinner interval so that audience members could enjoy picnics on the lawn. Gustatory traditions aside, it was Bergman's dramaturgical justification that persuaded Stravinsky and most companies subsequently to adopt a two-act structure. He recognized the pressing need to articulate a single dramatic rise and fall, shown in figure 10.3, like Mozartian opera buffa.

Bergman's assertion that the Bread Machine scene is dramatically confusing and difficult to stage seems a tactful way of saying weak. Of the three wishes around which Auden and Kallman structured their plot—for pleasure (the Brothel), for happiness (the marriage to Baba), and "to become God" (the Bread Machine)—the latter was always the least grounded dramatically and emotionally. In confining this episode to the second half of a single awkward scene, even the librettists seem unconvinced. Kallman's fear that the auction would become a "parenthesis" if positioned at the end of a long act 2 betrays the fact that he and Auden had treated the Bread Machine escapade in just this way. Stravinsky's concluding brio cannot lend urgency to an under-motivated dramatic gesture.

Baroque Production

Bergman's other initial idea was that "the stage should be sufficiently long and deep to permit the actors to appear and disappear in darkness, instead of through doors."[30] Superimposed upon the wide stage of the late nineteenth-century Royal Swedish Opera House, the set, designed by Birger Bergling and shown in figure 10.4, assimilates the narrow but deep dimensions of the eighteenth-century Slottsteater (completed in 1766) at the Royal Drottningholm Palace. (In subsequent seasons the Royal Opera actually presented *The Rake's Progress* at the Slottsteater as part of its summer festival performances.) Bergman's production team took pains not just to set the opera in the eighteenth century, but to recreate aspects of an authentic eighteenth-century production: "a bare, wooden sloping stage extending over the orchestra pit and ending with a row of six oversized footlight-tins of seventeenth-century model. Wings and backdrops presented naively painted pictures in open 'changements à vue,' and two simple benches were placed symmetrically on stage as the only permanent props. The principal singers acted mainly close to the footlights and even the three typical 'knocks' from backstage, marking the beginning of each act, were revived."[31]

To recreate the intimate performance setting of an eighteenth-century court theater, Bergman went so far as to introduce a Master of Ceremonies, shown upstage center in figure 10.5, reminiscent of the major domo in Strauss's *Ariadne auf Naxos*. (The following observations are based on a washed-out archival film that has been transferred to video. Other than photographs, this is the only preserved visual record of Bergman's staging.[32]) Before the overture even begins, this elegantly dressed personage ceremoniously enters in silence. Thick wooden staff in hand, he stamps out a slow, deliberate rhythm, cues the trumpet fanfare, and then leads in a procession of six courtiers who bow before him and the audience.

Bergman adopts such baroque conventions, including the reshaped stage, not simply to assimilate an authentic eighteenth-century setting. They help reinforce and clarify the framing effect already implied by Stravinsky's prelude and epilogue. Besides announcing the beginning of each act, Bergman's Master of Ceremonies also asserts throughout a controlling presence. He organizes Tom's London household staff in the opening scene of act 2; he claps his hands to dismiss the London street revelers at the beginning of act 2, scene 2; and having stamped everyone to attention after intermission, he passes a curtain marked "Night" in front of Tom's bed to reveal the already estranged newlyweds. Finally, he leads the principals to center stage for the epilogue. Stravinsky felt Bergman's epilogue succeeded "because it did not come as a shock: the audience never loses track of the 'fable' aspect." Bergman explained: "The Epilogue is a question of preparation, for which reason I also begin each act with it, to create a frame for

282 | *The Last Opera*

Fig. 10.4. Birger Bergling's narrow but deep eighteenth-century-style set, Royal Swedish Opera (1961). (Photo by Enar Merkel Rydberg.)

the whole work.... The Epilogue should mean that 'Now the play is over and you can go home and talk about the singer's high C.'"[33]

Distancing Effect

The liminal Master of Ceremonies is just one of several carefully controlled elements Bergman introduces to create the feeling of a puppet theater. Rather than separating scenes and disguising set changes, the curtain functions as a placard to signal important stages in the plot. Scenes are changed in open view; members of the cast first take their places on the bare stage and only then are sets carried in or lowered from above. Bergling's gray settings, which subtly suggest Hogarth's engravings, are placed only on that central section of the stage behind the extension, leaving darkened areas to the sides that Bergman uses at significant moments. Lit by a special spot, Tom is the first to cross the line for his aria, "Here I stand." Shortly thereafter, Nick waits appropriately in the shadows before stepping "onstage" to explain Tom's unexpected fortune, then returns at the end of the scene to proclaim: "The PROGRESS OF A RAKE begins." Such precisely choreographed movements both onstage and offstage clarify the theatrical dimensions implicit in the music and text.

Fig. 10.5. Concluding tableau of act 2, scene 2. The "Master of Ceremonies," staff in hand, stands upstage center, Royal Swedish Opera (1961). (Photo by Enar Merkel Rydberg.)

Bergman's puppet effect is most pronounced in his handling of the chorus, whose movements are closely tied to the music. One reviewer observed, "Twice they are first seen far at the back of the stage [the Brothel and the Bedlam scenes], utterly still like a carved frieze. They spring into action with the music but relapse into stillness again when it focuses elsewhere."[34] Bergman even dictates the rhythm of their applause.

Like Balanchine, Bergman often stages set-piece ensembles—for example, the concluding quartet of act 1, scene 1, and Anne and Trulove's Duettino in Bedlam—with the singers anchored and directly facing the audience. The effect is most pronounced when Anne delivers her Cabaletta center stage, her concluding high C rounded off with a conspicuously deep bow. What makes such gestures artful, while those of Balanchine were merely static, is that Bergman uses them to compose a series of tableaux. Craft elaborates: "Bergman's groupings are 'natural' without infracting the conventions of opera: the arias and the actionless ensembles... are sung *to* the audience, stage front. The difference is that Bergman's singers act, move their bodies and use their eyes, as singers are rarely trained to do."[35]

How telling that Balanchine, the preeminent choreographer, eschewed any "comment of choreography," while the preeminent film director choreographed virtually every movement. Balanchine assumed the music and text would speak for itself, whereas Bergman understood that, as an artist and not merely facilitator, his task was "to discover what to do" and "purify the doing."[36] Although a great artist in his own right, Balanchine seemed not to know what to do on an operatic stage. Neither did Stravinsky, Auden, or Kallman. Bergman knew.

Though he surely did not intend it, Craft's observation recalls the direction of Ebert, who also demanded a standard of acting to which singers were unaccustomed. The difference is that Bergman controlled and framed their movements by imposing certain distancing effects that Craft and other critics label Brechtian, but many of which were common to the theater at least since the Renaissance. Bergman's eighteenth-century theatrical conventions, such as the deep, narrow stage and the Master of Ceremonies, both charmingly capture the period setting and maintain emotional distance, "because Stravinsky wants to tell you something. . . . The devil finds work for idle hands."[37]

Fascinated by Stravinsky's "very severe, very cold-hot way of expressing himself," Bergman sought to distance precisely because he understood that his music was at heart "ardent and personal."[38] A reviewer observes: "His method with *The Rake* has been to make the musical fable all the more real and striking through highly artificial means . . . Mr. Bergman wisely banishes naturalism. His characters are puppets whose personalities acquire life and depth through the music. But because they are presented with the breath-catching simplicity of a conjuror and the eyes of a seer, they seem twice as real and twice as human."[39]

This novel combination of controlled, stylized movement and close attention to characterization and expression created a deceptively profound experience for the audience. As if preparing for a film, Bergman went so far as to invent an individual character (and name!) for each member of the chorus; figure 10.6 displays three of the dozens of individual preparatory photographs made for the production. Indeed, a filmmaker's touch pervaded the entire production. The same interviewer summarizes its aesthetic and emotional impact:

> Bergman's attention to detail is astonishing. . . . The brilliantly hued costumes, the gray settings against a pitch-black background and a dramatic use of lights combine to achieve such rich visual effect that the music often seems to emerge from a sound track, and the singing seems a natural way of communicating. . . . "The opera has such terrible intensity," [Bergman] says, "that all are absolutely dead after it is over." But the audience also feels that it has been under strain, its emotions considerably buffeted by Bergman's Stravinsky. Few had expected to find Stravinsky so spellbinding.[40]

Fig. 10.6. Three character portraits of chorus members: Graceful Solfjader Lühert, Unreasonable Förmögne Wallskog, and "Pretty" Thighs Högstens. (Photos by Enar Merkel Rydberg.)

Stravinsky reacted similarly: "Tom's decision to marry Baba is convincing, ... and I want to thank Bergman for that. And for so much more besides. When Tom leaves for London, Anne weeps, Tom starts to go to her, and Trulove motions him back and goes to her himself: I believed in Trulove's gesture. Another thing: in the auction scene, the singing of Tom and Shadow from different places in the audience *does* bolster the idea that they are 'at large.' These small points, and many more, help establish the credibility of the play."[41]

The central scene in London culminating in the moving trio between Tom, Anne, and Baba perhaps best illustrates Stravinsky's "cold-hot" manner. As I described in chapter 7, Stravinsky and Auden struggled to find the right balance between Baba's comic interjections and the lovers' emotional exchange. Bergman carefully constructed the entire scene to set up this subtle conflict. Stravinsky singled out his staging over the haunting opening trumpet solo: "The silent movement of people in the street at the beginning of this scene is the most beautiful tableau in the opera. You have a deep feeling for music." Bergman responded: "The question for the opera director should always be, 'How much does the music tell us already?' In this scene it tells us that they are not people at all but shadows." Later a progression of cartoonesque revelers anticipates Tom and Baba's arrival; they freeze and the master of ceremonies claps his hands to dismiss them. Meanwhile Nick Shadow, who has no part in the scene, looms in the background. "That is where Shadow's work is shown in the open, and the reason I bring him on stage," the director explained. "He must look on gloatingly."[42]

Bergman's interest in *The Rake* after 1961 waxed and waned fitfully. The esteemed director could be even more sensitive to perceived slights than the thin-skinned composer. Even before their meeting, Bergman had refused to attend the special performance of the opera with Stravinsky because of the composer's apparently skeptical remark about his films to a reporter. Afterward, though, he made a point of staying in touch, reporting his continued vigilance and interest: "I keep a very close watch on the treasure we have in common, 'THE RAKE'S PROGRESS.' We rehearse carefully before each new performance. Next year I hope to produce at my own theatre "L'Histoire d'un [sic] Soldat," a play which I always loved."[43]

When in 1965 Rolf Liebermann, general director of the Hamburg Staatsoper, wanted Bergman to direct a new production of *The Rake*, he enlisted Stravinsky to send a note of encouragement (excerpted above). Liebermann later wrote back: "Bergman is completely crazy. He doesn't want to do the RAKE at all and said that he didn't like the piece anymore. Our last conversation ended when he told me: 'And what is Stravinsky doing for me'!"[44]

By 1968, the fickle Bergman cabled to Craft the following urgent appeal: "DEAR FRIEND ALL PLANS FOR MY TV VERSION OF RAKES PROGRESS SEEM TO BE GOING TO POT AS WE HAVE BEEN UNABLE TO REACH FINAL AGREEMENT WITH PUBLISHER. WHAT DO YOU SUGGEST WE DO?"[45] Why Bergman vehemently rejected the invitation to direct the opera in Hamburg only to seek the rights to film a version of it for television two years later may be attributed to his distaste for working in Germany. In any case, his insulting response did not dissuade Stravinsky from trying to help Bergman secure the film rights—far from it. He, in fact, offered to forgo his share of the $25,000 fee. "Must advise you," the composer cabled Rufina Ampenova of Boosey & Hawkes, "whatever cause of impasse I am more interested in having his superb performance seen than in realizing money myself."[46] What a loss that the parties could not reach an agreement. Knowing the director's charmingly brilliant *Magic Flute*, one can only imagine the treasure his screen version of *The Rake's Progress* might have been.

Bergman was not alone in appreciating the sometimes tentative balance between stylized gesture and disarming expressiveness in Stravinsky's opera, but he was the first director who understood how to preserve and display it. He interposed distance not because the opera is stiff and impersonal, but because he understood that Stravinsky's music is, at heart, "ardent and personal." The production struck Craft, who had followed the opera's progress nearly every step of the way, as a turning point: "At the end . . . , I. S. receives a long standing ovation. I am bursting with pride for him myself and thinking of all those terrible performances of the opera in Geneva, New York, etc."[47]

Bergman's staging would inform a flood of imaginative interpretations to follow. Thereafter, *The Rake's Progress* would be in no small part his creation as well as that of Stravinsky, Auden, and Kallman.

Postmodern Progress

"It is strange," a reviewer of the 1975 Glyndebourne production observed, "how the very attributes that agitate critics and others when a work is new often turn out to be the hallmarks of its character."[48] Indeed, by the late 1960s Baba's campiness, the ludicrous bread machine, the tongue-in-cheek epilogue, and even the stiff opening scene all suddenly seemed to match the spirit of the time. This not-so-subtle shift in how directors and audiences perceived *The Rake* would mark the larger cultural turn from modern to postmodern.

Caldwell's "Mod" Rake (1967)

The year 1967 was another bellwether for Stravinsky's opera. Not only did touring European companies from Hamburg and Sweden showcase lavish productions in New York and Montreal, but also the ambitious Sarah Caldwell would revisit the work with the Opera Company of Boston. Her "mod" setting in contemporary England presaged future versions not only of *The Rake* but of traditional operas in general.

Perhaps not surprising in retrospect, nothing about Stravinsky's eclectic neoclassicism could have anticipated Caldwell's interpolation of "leather jackets and motorcycles, psychedelic and strobe lighting, pin-ups of Allen Ginsberg and Timothy Leary in the *Rake*'s pad," as Stravinsky-Craft note, "although mutability *is* one of its themes . . . (I suppose the argument *for* them is that the music parodies and time-travels, why not the décors as well?)"⁴⁹ Yet Caldwell's time travel is far more unsettling than Stravinsky's musical anachronisms, for it disregards the eighteenth-century literary and musical foundation that the composer and librettists so lovingly crafted. Having Tom trade in his Triumph for Nick's Rolls-Royce was more than a clever gloss on Hogarth; like Bergman, Caldwell was claiming the opera for herself.

As with Bergman's production, some of Caldwell's adaptations clarified dramatic connections. "The motorcycle for Tom to tinker with and Anne to sit on" linked the lover's opening scene with their reunion in Bedlam, becoming, as Michael Steinberg describes, "something very moving when it returned white and ghostly like a Segal sculpture. Then it became a place for Adonis to enthrone Venus and also, as he hung drapes across it, the site of Tom's death. Moreover, the two scenes were further linked by the device of having their idyllic poetry sung from a book, 'the woods are green and bird and beast at play' in the Truloves' yard, and Anne's lullaby, 'Gently, little boat,' in the Bedlam scene."⁵⁰

These devices are more than useful gimmicks to tease "some life into a formality bordering on parody," as Craft grudgingly concedes.⁵¹ They set in relief and thereby justify Auden's stiff pastoral language in a way neither he nor Stravinsky quite accomplish in the opening scene. Caldwell further collapsed the theatrical space by extending much of the auction scene into the audience. Craft again provides a memorable accounting:

> Sellem—Hawaiian shirt, hippy beads, gardenia over the ear—is a combination Guru, con man, TV automobile salesman. He sits cross-legged on a Simeon-like stylite hoisted from stage level, and as he reels off the objects under the gavel, photographs of them are flashed on the curtain in the manner of a fast-moving slide lecture. The bidders, who have infiltrated the audience in Café La Mama style, move closer to the orchestra as each lot is sold, until they stand by the pit itself for the balance of promises and a better view of Baba resuscitated on TV.⁵²

Given that he did not see the production until it traveled to Tempe and Los Angeles in 1968, the reactions attributed to Stravinsky in the June 1967 issue of the *New York Review of Books*, reprinted in *Retrospective and Conclusions* (1969) and again in *Themes and Conclusions* (1982), certainly belong to Craft. (Since he also composed the anonymous questions, the entire charade is thus an elaborate interview with himself about a production that he conducted.) However, following the Los Angeles performances, the composer issued a statement defending the production against critics who thought it violated his intentions: "The Caldwell production exposes a wholly new point of view and is inventive in many, many particulars. Some critics who saw it in the East have not liked it because they are now defending the work that only a short time ago they loathed. But I like it."⁵³

The kitsch did not always wear well during moments of real emotion, as in Tom's "Love, too frequently betrayed" and "Vary the song." And, typical of Caldwell's productions, technical difficulties marred what Steinberg called a "riot of theatrical fantasy." Ambitious lighting and multimedia effects, like projecting rain during the London scene and a larger than life Baba onto the curtain during the auction (she appeared on a closed-circuit TV for the West Coast performances the following year), never quite gelled. Worst of all, at least from the composer's point of view, overly complex sets made for long changes between the scenes.

Besides the "mod" concept, Caldwell's other distinctively postmodern touches were the unsubtle references to the creator himself: Tom sporting a Stravinsky sweatshirt (after Picasso's 1917 drawing) in act 2, scene 1; and the crowning coup de théâtre, in Craft's words, "a photograph, flashed across the curtain at the end, of I. S. playing cards—of I. S. the artist, finessing his work, of I. S., indomitable."[54] How could Stravinsky not have enjoyed such a tribute? The postwar generation of Boulez, when it condescended to notice, had only sneered at his neoclassical opera. This new generation was now adopting his characters as its own and the composer as a sort of mascot. Can one imagine staging a cameo Schoenberg or Berg into a performance of *Erwartung* or *Wozzeck*? In that regard, neoclassical and postmodern play dovetails in a way expressionism cannot. That lasting image of the composer looming over the whole enterprise, later echoed in Jörg Immendorff's Salzburg production, consciously displayed what everyone had known since the Venice premiere: the clever, spritely, and elegant Artist who created this clever, moving Opera presides over every note and every theatrical gesture.

Hockney's Glyndebourne Production (1975)

Today's most widely recognizable production of *The Rake's Progress* is Glyndebourne's second, with sets and costumes designed by the English artist David Hockney. Noting the success of Ebert and Lancaster's original, last presented in 1963, producer John Cox thought the time had come to "rip it up and start again.... Hockney already knew in the early 1970s that 'if you wanted to do something spectacular in the theatre, then you went to opera.'"[55]

One might have expected the "pop" artist, like Caldwell, to impose a contemporary popular style, as he had done in his own semiautobiographical *Rake's Progress* etchings (1961–63) that first attracted Glyndebourne's producers. There, in open dialogue with Hogarth, Hockney projects himself as a starry-eyed, young, gay artist experiencing for the first time the cosmopolitan social life of New York City. And, indeed, for his operatic *Rake* Hockney would also appropriate popular images—but from Hogarth's eighteenth-century England, not twentieth-century America. A British reviewer noted the revelation: "One suddenly came to realize that there is an element of pop in Stravinsky's neo-opera. From the feigned childlike naivety of the figures and cartoon-balloons on the curtain to the clouds, trees and pieces of furniture all covered by a net of cross-hatching, one sensed a revealing parallel. Surely the painter who smuggles in representational art by the back door somewhat resembles a composer who revives the eighteenth-century form of opera . . . but will not, or not quite, use the musical idiom one associates with it."[56]

In other words, Hockney's "eighteenth-century" setting would be just as idiosyncratic as Caldwell's "mod" setting. Again he exposes the hands of the creators peeking out from the drop curtain: fragments of the composer's piano score, his own sample "swatches" of texture, even old Hogarth. Yet, through means similar to those of Bergman, this production would achieve a more stable balance between the work's farcical and heartfelt moments. Another critic observes: "Hockney's sets, less jokey than Osbert Lancaster's in the first Glyndebourne 'Rake,' but in their way as elegant and enjoyable, are full of carefully gauged alienation effects—'balloons' with moralistic tags from the libretto onto the painted backcloths, masks for the Bedlamites, whole scenes in engraver's cross-hatching (a stunningly virtuoso black and white auction scene)."[57]

Time attests to the success of his sturdy production. Having staged it five times since 1975, the Glyndebourne company has toured it throughout the United Kingdom and France and issued two video recordings (1975 and 2010). Resident companies in Salzburg, Madrid, Sydney, New York (City Opera), San Francisco, and Portland, among others, have imported its sets and costumes. If one has an image of Stravinsky's opera in mind, it likely involves playful cartoon backdrops, corseted gingham dresses, and haunting masked figures peering out of boxes. By magnifying the popular visual style of eighteenth-century London, Hockney has managed to respect both the opera's embrace of and play with the past.

Immendorff's Salzburg Production (1994)

> The opera has the quality of a mirror: a mirror that is still there for me, . . . the opera enabled me to take a detached look at my own painting.
>
> —Jörg Immendorff[58]

Just as Hockney projected his own image into his original "Rake's Progress" etchings, German artist Jörg Immendorff inserted himself into Stravinsky's opera. Out of his experience designing the curtain, set, and costumes for the Salzburg Festival, he even created a group of independent works on paper and canvas, exhibited by the Michael Werner galleries in Cologne and New York and the Salzburg Festspielhaus in 1996 and 1997. In both artworks and opera, images from the artist's personal life and work run riot alongside those of Stravinsky, Auden, and other artists and historical figures. "Basically Mr. Immendorff took the 'Rake' personally," wrote art critic Roberta Smith. "He reset the morality tale . . . into the German art world of the 1980s" with himself as the hero.[59] Edward Rothstein describes the production: "a Greek chorus of monkeys who act as stagehands, images of genitalia that appear on walls and clothing, paintings by Hogarth . . . paired with darkly rendered contemporary paintings by Mr. Immendorff, a clunky graffiti-covered airplane that shuttles Tom Rakewell from one misadventure to another, heads of great artists and poets stuck into dripping paint cans, and a setting that ignores the composer's eighteenth-century allusions and dresses up Tom and Anne as contemporary Americans."[60]

Immendorff recaptures the energy of the production in a massive, twenty-three-foot long canvas.[61] Here we view from behind the augmented cast (seven men and two women), presumably during the epilogue, on a stage crowded with, among many other objects, the bobbing heads of Stravinsky and Auden (with Freud looming behind), a portrait of the poet Arthur Rimbaud, and a hollow, Frankenstein-like figure erected from different scene sets. Over the raucous audience on the right a suspended Stravinsky hovers—like both a superman and a bee—and from the gallery to the left a portrait of Chairman Mao looms.

Like Caldwell, only more so, Immendorff imposes the personage of Stravinsky as an unsubtle puppeteer. For example, in the production poster, the composer floats behind his oblivious rake, painting finishing touches and tweaking the character's nipple. Elsewhere he appropriates the image of Irving Penn's 1948 photograph of Stravinsky standing in a corner, hand cupping his left ear, usually as a cartoon caricature, but also as a dog (still with cupped ear) pissing. The viewer gets the point, but can a performance of the opera bear this overload of images and ideas? Rothstein, to his surprise, affirms:

> The staging then succeeded by taking the opera's playfulness seriously . . . Mr. Immendorff sees it as an allegory about the education of an artist.
>
> Tom's wishes . . . are the Faustian yearnings of an aspiring artist. They often lead to kitsch. When the auctioneer smashes down his gavel, selling off Tom's bankrupt estate, he ends up demolishing plaster images from Tom's enterprise.
>
> It seems as if Tom is getting a series of lessons in esthetic sensibility. Mr. Immendorff's Ibsenesque allegory risks becoming trite, and is full of private allusions, but ends up taking on a disturbing power with the opera's concluding act. . . . In the darkest regions of Bedlam, Mr. Immendorff seems to suggest, Tom completes his education. And then at the moment of death, Tom is loaded into a plane that tilts upward toward the sky; its wings are revealed to be artist's palettes. Mr. Immendorff is in a long European tradition that sees the artist reaching transcendence through self-knowledge and madness.[62]

Immendorff essentially dramatized, in his own words, "the opera behind the opera,"[63] that is, the constellations of habitus (his, Stravinsky's, Auden's, even Hogarth's) and field (painting, music, opera) that intersect in this production, in this cultural moment. His is a truly postmodern *Rake*, in which the work (music, libretto, setting, set, costumes) and the environments that produced it (artistic, musical, literary, political, psychological) all crowd together onto the same stage and canvas. Of course, the chaos threatens to engulf the characters and story, just as Nick engulfs Tom, just as the world threatens to engulf Immendorff, Stravinsky, Auden, Kallman, and Hogarth. Nonetheless, the opera's emotional core somehow shines through.

* * *

If there is one crucial lesson to be learned from *The Rake*'s reception history, it is that a successful staging should be as conscious of the opera itself as Stravinsky and Auden were of their classical models. A work so aware of its musical and theatrical heritage invites knowing winks and open references. The multireferential productions by Immendorff, Hockney, and Caldwell stand out as extreme examples of the numerous versions that place the creators within their creation.[64] The composer and librettists may have recognized this dimension but could never admit they were dramatizing a part of themselves in these characters. That artists like Hockney and Immendorff shamelessly do so marks our postmodern age; that Stravinsky and Auden conceal themselves just as assuredly marks their modern sensibilities.

These high modernists acknowledged and even proclaimed they were playing a ritualized game. But to remove their artists' masks would mean betraying themselves and their art. It would take equally imaginative, playful, even irreverent interpreters to realize the opera's true nature. We glimpse as much in the review of the Hamburg premiere above. The penetrating mind and firm hands of Bergman wrung from the work even greater substance. Postmodern directors and designers stripped off the clotted layers of "tradition" and painted their own wildly contemporary visions, presided over by cartoon Stravinskys and Audens. That *The Rake's Progress* has inspired such bursts of creativity not only signals the profound shift in late twentieth-century arts, but also it confirms the opera's forward-looking qualities. Indeed, its first half century transformed *The Rake* from a seemingly misguided restoration into a glorious apotheosis of the genre its creators had come to love.

Notes

1. Quoted in "I don't like it" (uncredited). Craft describes the Geneva performance as "very provincial, underprepared ... [At intermission] a collection is taken up, like passing the plate in a church, to help pay the orchestra" in *Stravinsky: The Chronicle of a Friendship: 1948/1971*, revised and expanded (Nashville: Vanderbilt University Press, 1994), 75.

2. Heinz Joachim, "Stravinskij contra Sartre—Der respektvolle 'Wüstling,'" *Die Welt* (Hamburg), November 15, 1951 (translated from German).

3. Glyndebourne presented the first performances on an English stage the following July at the festival's home in Sussex. Griffiths mistakenly cites the 1956 performance by the Cambridge University Opera Group as the first English staging in *Igor Stravinsky: The Rake's Progress* (New York: Cambridge University Press, 1982), 51. Those same principals presented the London stage premiere as the New Opera Company at Sadler's Wells Theater in 1957.

4. Letter to Roth of February 9, 1951, Paul Sacher Foundation. Webster was in Los Angeles in late January.

5. Stravinsky was addressing the prospect of a concert performance by the American Opera Society in 1962. Undated letter (ca. 1961) from Stravinsky to Lincoln Kirstein, Paul Sacher Foundation.

6. An audio record of the Met production is preserved in the studio recording conducted by Stravinsky (Columbia Records, SL 125).

7. Craft, *Chronicle* (1994), 96. Elizabeth Schwarzkopf reminded Stravinsky of his request that she be his "first Anne in America" (letter of January 1, 1952, Paul Sacher Foundation), after which the composer enthusiastically endorsed what would have been her American debut (letter of January 14, 1952, Paul Sacher Foundation). General manager Rudolf Bing responded cryptically: "I am afraid that for reasons I would rather not discuss in writing, the lady you mention cannot be considered for the Metropolitan Opera" (January 16, 1952, Paul Sacher Foundation). What he preferred not to discuss was Schwarzkopf's affiliation with the Nazi Party, which she joined in 1940 as a requirement of her contract with the Deutsches Opernhaus. She would not debut at the Met until 1964 in the role of the Marschallin in *Der Rosenkavalier*.

In an ironic contrast, the Austrian Gueden was expelled from Germany in 1943 because of her mixed Jewish ancestry; see Alan E. Steinweis, *Art, Ideology, and Economics in Nazi Germany* (Chapel Hill: University of North Carolina Press, 1993), 118–20.

8. Olin Downes, "'Rake's Progress' has U.S. Premiere," *New York Times*, February 15, 1953.

9. Virgil Thomson, *A Virgil Thomson Reader* (Boston: Houghton Mifflin, 1981), 356–57. See chapter 5, note 12, for his defense of Stravinsky's text settings.

10. Olin Downes, "'Rake's Progress' of Stravinsky Makes Season's Debut at 'Met,'" *New York Times*, January 27, 1954.

11. Letter to Hawkes in Robert Craft, ed., *Stravinsky: Selected Correspondence*, vol. 3 (New York: Alfred A. Knopf, 1985), 331.

12. Excerpted in Vera Stravinsky and Robert Craft, *Stravinsky in Pictures and Documents* (New York: Simon and Schuster, 1978), 416.

13. Downes, "'Rake's Progress' of Stravinsky Makes Season's Debut." An example of the emerging contrary consensus is Winthrop Sargent's review of Menotti's 1967 staging for the Hamburg Staatsoper, which "showed me again how crude the Metropolitan's production of 1953 had been." See also Irving Kolodin's review of the Glyndebourne production.

14. "Balanchine—Theory of the Staging," *Opera News*, February 9, 1953, 11.

15. George Balanchine, "The Met at Work—Directing a Rake," *Metropolitan Opera Program* (1953).

16. Letter of December 18, 1951, Paul Sacher Foundation; quoted in V. Stravinsky and Craft, *Pictures and Documents*, 416.

17. Courtesy Kallman Estate and Chester Kallman Collection of Papers, The Henry W. and Albert A. Berg Collection of English and American Literature, The New York Public Library, Astor, Lenox and Tilden Foundations.

18. Mike Ashman, "Notes for *The Rake's Progress*." DVD. Glyndebourne Festival Production. Opus Arte 1062D (2010): 4–5.

19. Letter of August 28, 1953, Paul Sacher Foundation.

20. Letter of July 16, 1954, Paul Sacher Foundation.

21. Ashman, "Notes," 5.

22. Ibid.

23. Peter Ebert, *In This Theatre of Man's Life* (Sussex: The Book Guild, 1999), 201.

24. Robert Craft, ed., *A Stravinsky Scrapbook 1940–1971* (London: Thames and Hudson, 1983), 160. The three principals had sung Tom, Anne, and Nick in the first student performance at Boston University in 1953.

25. Paul Horgan, *Encounters with Stravinsky* (New York: Farrar, Straus, and Giroux, 1972), 189–90.

26. Quoted in Craft, *Stravinsky: Chronicle of a Friendship*. Used courtesy of Vanderbilt University Press.

27. Quoted in Werner Wiskari, "Ingmar Bergman's Way with 'The Rake,'" *New York Times*, May 19, 1961.
28. Letter of September 12, 1965, Paul Sacher Foundation.
29. Quoted in Craft, *Chronicle* (1994), 245. That Stravinsky tolerated Bergman's cuts and still professed such admiration speaks volumes. Indicative of his typical response is the following directive to his publisher: "A recent performance of my opera THE RAKE'S PROGRESS at the STATE OPERA in VIENNA, where it was done with an incredible number of cuts without my knowledge or my permission, compels me to ask you to take the following measures: Whenever any of my operas are performed it must be clearly stipulated ... that my works must be performed as they are published, and should my wishes not be respected I would ask you to stop the performances, have the material returned and obtain a payment for damages which should not be less than at least three times the amount of the original hire fee" (letter of June 16, 1966, Paul Sacher Foundation).
30. Craft, *Chronicle* (1994), 245.
31. Eva Sundler Malmnäs, "Art as Inspiration," In *Ingmar Bergman and the Arts. Nordic Theatre Studies* 11 (1998): 40. Bergman had created similar "baroque" productions for Molière's *Don Juan* and *The Misanthrope* at Malmö Stadsteater, as he would later for his film *The Magic Flute* (1975).
32. An uncatalogued copy of the video is preserved in the archives of the Royal Swedish Opera House.
33. Quoted in Craft, *Chronicle* (1994), 246.
34. Noel Goodwin, "So-Shy Film Genius Brings New Magic to the Opera Stage," *Daily Express*, April 24, 1961.
35. Craft, *Chronicle* (1994), 244.
36. Ibid., 245.
37. Wiskari, "Bergman's Way."
38. Malmnäs, "Art as Inspiration," 38.
39. Goodwin, "So-Shy Film Genius."
40. Wiskari, "Bergman's Way."
41. *Chronicle* (94), 244. Craft concludes: "As we part, he asks me to keep in touch with him, I think because he wants to film the opera" (248).
42. Quoted in Craft, *Chronicle* (1994), 246.
43. Letter of June 17, 1963, Paul Sacher Foundation.
44. Undated letter, Paul Sacher Foundation.
45. Cable of January 15, 1968, Paul Sacher Foundation.
46. Craft, *Chronicle* (1994), 477.
47. Ibid., 244.
48. Peter Heyworth, "The Rake's Triumph," *Observer Review*, June 29, 1975.
49. Igor Stravinsky, *Themes and Conclusions* (Berkeley: University of California Press, 1972), 103.
50. Michael Steinberg, "Re-Raking the Rake: Best Sort of Caldwell," *Boston Globe*, April 9, 1967, A31. Caldwell's biographer explains: "In the first scene, Tom was seen working on his motorcycle in the backyard of a dreary Midlands row house. Later, Baba the Turk arrived in a Rolls Royce hearse with an entourage of transvestite groupies in leather riding motorbikes. Sarah had been loaned six black-and-white Triumphs that were quite stunning in appearance.... However, for the Bedlam scene, Sarah decided she wanted a white bike, so one of her prop men spent all day covering one of the Triumphs in white athletic tape"; see Daniel Kessler, *Sarah Caldwell: The First Woman of Opera*. Lanham, MD: Scarecrow Press, 2008), 74.

51. Robert Craft, *Stravinsky: The Chronicle of a Friendship: 1948/1971* (New York: Vintage Books, 1972), 354. In the 1972 edition, Craft took the occasion of his performances with Caldwell's touring production to vent his feelings about the opera, most of which he removed from his otherwise more detailed 1994 account.

52. Ibid., 354–55.

53. Kessler, *Sarah Caldwell*, 76.

54. Craft, *Chronicle* (1972), 355.

55. Ashman, "Notes," 4.

56. Peter Stadlen, "Element of Pop in 'Rake's Progress,'" *Daily Telegraph*, June 23, 1975.

57. David Cairns, "Two Moral Comedies," *Sunday* Times, July 6, 1975. For images of the drop curtain and other scenes from Hockney's production, see hockneypictures.com.

58. "Jörg Immendorff to My Studio Ghosts in The Rake's Progress—Salzburg," Salzburg Festival, 1996.© The Estate of Jörg Immendorff, Courtesy Galerie Michael Werner Märkisch Wilmersdorf, Köln & New York.

59. Roberta Smith, "Melding Figures Real and Imagined to Fill a Tableau," *New York Times*, January 10, 1997, A24.

60. Edward Rothstein, "Jerry Hadley Is Stravinsky's 'Rake' in a New Production at Salzburg," *New York Times*, August 3, 1994. In his paintings Immendorff superimposes a cartoon mask of his own face onto that of the rake.

61. See color image at https//wikiart.org/en/jorg-immendorff/the-rake-s-progress-1993.

62. Rothsein, "Jerry Hadley."

63. "Jörg Immendorff to My Studio Ghosts," IV.

64. The 1979 Covent Garden production, the company's first and only (see note 4 above), recast Tom as a young Auden (Griffiths, *Rake's Progress*, 57).

PART 5

AFTER *THE RAKE*

11

"GOOD PEOPLE, JUST A MOMENT"

When, at the moment Tom dies, Stravinsky transitions gracefully, if uncharacteristically, from the world of mythic illusion to the reality of his rake's demise, he is setting us up for his greatest disjunction of all. Like a slap on the back, the orchestra's heavy-handed A major resurrects the deceased hero, and the chordal third completes the grand background <–2,+1> shown in example 8.13c. House lights go up, and the performers step out of character and step before the curtain, represented by the horizontal dotted line in figure 8.4.

Perhaps Tom's moving death is just another way of displacing our expectations, of shocking us at a higher dramaturgical level. Roland Barthes, referring to Brecht, claims the creator "does not want us to fall under the spell of another smooth surface . . . : the shock is distinct, discrete (*and* discreet), swift, repeated if need be, but never *established*."[1] The magical glow with which Stravinsky frames Tom's death is washed out by the bright house lights that once illuminated opera audiences before Wagner reformed them. The winking epilogue is *The Rake*'s final seismic displacement—in this case it is an aftershock.

Craft disliked the epilogue, recalled Donald Gramm (who played Nick Shadow in Caldwell's "mod" production), "and suggested dropping it, but Stravinsky always fought to have it retained. He believed that it balanced the opera between the emotional and the philosophical."[2] Though the conductor claimed that the final chord, shown in example 11.1, "would be less out of place in a Coca-Cola jingle," perhaps what really disturbed him was that it so perfectly caps off the opera.[3] The embedded trichord (A, B, E) recalls the introduction to act 1, scene 1; the fused tonic and dominant—$I^+\hat{2}/V^+\hat{1}$—typifies his harmonic practice throughout; the five-beat segments imposed over five 2/4 measures are quintessentially Stravinskian.

Without Tom's expressive death, the garish ending would be just the last of a series of expected tremors like the repetitious plot of *Histoire du Soldat*. Deprived of its expressive moments, *The Rake*'s artificiality would be intellectually clear, as Brecht would have it, but emotionally muddled.

Yet such expressiveness made it impossible for Stravinsky, and perhaps any serious composer, to write another opera like *The Rake*. This *ne plus ultra* of

a. [A, B, E] in the epilogue and act 1, scene 1.

b. Mixed I's and V's and five-beat displacement.

Example 11.1. Final chord of the epilogue.

neoclassicism too readily appeals to its audience, the "*ne plus ultra* of elegance." Its creator was not disinterested enough; the opera risks being middlebrow. How could it not? Real Opera *is* middlebrow—a "bastard art-form" as Auden was brought up to believe. "We will not be sentimental (à la Verdi) or sensational (à la Strauss) or emotionally manipulative (à la Puccini), the creators appear to have tacitly agreed," observes David Schiff. "But these manifestations of good taste have little to do with the compelling elements in the opera—which are precisely sentimental, sensational, and manipulative."[4]

For that matter, so is neoclassicism middlebrow. Nabokov, for all his ranting, could be just as kitschy as Shostakovich and not nearly as inventive. Stravinsky, himself, had composed the most sublime *kitsch*: he—or was it Craft?—admitted "some of *The Rake* is close to Broadway, Baba's music especially"; "I love all of [the music of *Oedipus*], even the Messenger's fanfares, which remind me of the now badly tarnished trumpets of early Twentieth-Century Fox."[5] Schoenberg had been right all along; those insolent young Parisians, too, who tried to drown out my *Four Norwegian Moods* . . . "Do you think such tricks promise you much pleasure and greatness?"[6] One imagines such thoughts raining like blows upon Stravinsky's ego on the way back from Palmdale that day in 1952, an episode Craft would later connect to his first serious encounters with twelve-tone music:

> On 24 February 1952, . . . I conducted a performance of Schoenberg's *Septet-Suite* (in a program with Webern's Quartet, Opus 22), with Stravinsky present at all the rehearsals as well as the concert. This event was the turning point in his later musical evolution.
>
> On 8 March, he asked to go for a drive to Palmdale, at that time a small Mojave Desert town . . . On the way home he startled us, saying that he was afraid he could no longer compose and did not know what to do. For a moment he broke down and actually wept . . . He referred obliquely to the powerful impression that the Schoenberg piece had made on him, and when he said that he wanted to learn more, I knew that the crisis was over; so far from being defeated, Stravinsky would emerge a new composer.[7]

But for the moment, Stravinsky was adrift artistically. He "could not continue in the same strain."[8]

As I describe in chapter 1, Schoenberg and his school represented an "other side" against which the musical world and, to some extent, Stravinsky had defined his musical identity since the 1920s. Whether the Austrian composer's death in July 1951 had a lasting personal effect, from a professional standpoint it undermined Stravinsky's artistic sense of self. That very month, he was showing subtle signs of an aesthetic shift. Having just finished editing the hundreds of pages of proofs for the opera, he apparently still had an appetite for setting archaic English verse. Even before embarking for Europe, he completed "The Maidens Came," one of several poems Auden had recommended from his new anthology and the first setting for what would eventually become his *Cantata*. The metrical counterpoint shares some of the subtlety of the "Elysium" duet and the playfulness of "Lanterloo"; indeed, it is no great leap from *The Rake* to some of Stravinsky's later complex interplay with rhythm and meter. Nonetheless, subtle differences begin to appear: a change in beaming for vocal lines and the almost systematic displacement of stressed syllables.[9] The Elizabethan lyrics further remove Stravinsky from the musical and poetic language of the opera, as if Auden's parody of the Augustan poets was not archaic enough. The composer had to go back 150 years earlier to establish the desired aesthetic distance.

Planning Another Collaboration

The English Renaissance texts dovetailed nicely with the new project Stravinsky was planning with Auden, who described it to his colibrettist:

> His idea is as follows: a one-act opera lasting about 50 minutes, capable of being performed by amateurs (i.e., colleges) all over the states. Orchestra of 18, also amateur. After talking with him, I see that he wants a Jonsonian Masque, (I have lent him the Masques to read) and the subject I have suggested to him which he likes very much is the wedding of Art and Science performed by the goddess of Wisdom. The comic antimasque will, of course, present some of our bugaboos like Twelve-Toners, Sociologists etc. He's very impatient to start it, so for God's sake get back just as quickly as you can. We ought to be able to do it in a month.[10]

As Auden notes, the composer at this point seemed eager and enthusiastic, reporting to Bean both the artistic and practical benefits and keeping ever in mind the hard lessons learned from trying to recoup a commission for *The Rake*:

> I had time before leaving New York to fix with Auden the main lines of an opera in one act calling for a chamber ensemble. After its launching, such a work should come very handy to fill the needs of universities, schools and organizations whose means do not allow them to monkey with a work of larger scope.
>
> But in order to avoid driving ourselves into the same nearly-dead-end-street from which we had a difficult escape on the last days before the *Rake* was born, I would like to have the work fully commissioned before starting my composition. . . . Here are some more informative details:
>   1. Auden is "blueprinting"—so to say—the libretto and he will complete it with Kallman when the latter (whose collaboration is very valuable) will be back.
>   2. The theme is—as I remember telling you—a kind of celebration of Wisdom in a manner comparable to Ben Johnson's masks. Nevertheless we will not stick to any set style musically or otherwise
>   3. Such opera will require:
>   About 6 characters;
>   A small chorus;
>   A chamber ensemble of about 18;
>   Several "tableaux" but easy-to-make sets.
>
> My commission should be $10,000, not including my conducting the premiere (of course) which should be made compulsory and the subject of a separate contract and fee. Naturally another contract will have to be drawn and concluded with Auden and Kallman for their libretto.
>
> Don't you think the first doorbell to ring should be Aspen [Festival director Walter] Paepcke as the work could be completed for their 1953 summer season and its size and scope would be even more convenient for them than the *Rake*'s[?][11]

Hoping to avoid another disappointing fee, the librettists were now insisting on a share (suggested at 33 percent) of a commission combining the libretti and music, leading Bean to propose $15,000 to the director of the Aspen Festival, "a good deal higher than their expectations."[12] Accessing the librettists' position from a practical (dare one say sociological) point of view, Stravinsky's son-in-law and sometime secretary, André Marion, explained his objection:

> I am affraid [sic] that Messrs Auden & Kallman's eyes have been so brightly stricken by the figure of $20,000. . . . Now if [they] also want to be commissioned this should be another matter, completely independent from Mr. Stravinsky's commission. Messrs. Auden & Kallman's work is a literary one and this, plus their standing and name, should result in certain figures which, anyhow, cannot exceed the ceiling in their field. But these figures have no relation whatsoever with Mr. Stravinsky's own estimate.
> . . . In consequence the most logical attitude would be to negotiate both commissions independently. Nevertheless I understand quite well the difficulty . . . Therefore, to be practical and sensible, it might be a lesser evil to give you the means of approaching the commissioning party with a "package deal." This implicates that a global commission would be asked. For the one act opera we are contemplating, as far as Mr. Stravinsky is concerned, his commission should definitely be set at $10,000. Now, what the librettists want is up to them and I am totally opposed to see their figures being pro-rated to Mr. Stravinsky's. If they want to make it so big that no deal is possible they should be left to blame themselves alone.[13]

Meanwhile, to his long letter protesting the proposed shift of the auction scene, Kallman added a teaser: "Wystan and I have already started that terrible and exciting work of getting our ideas in order for the new libretto; but until things are much clearer in our minds, we're maintaining a mysterious and, we hope intriguing, silence."[14] On March 28, they proudly telegraphed: "Libretto finished this instant. Love, Wystan and Chester."[15]

In the end, their mystery and intrigue backfired. What arrived in the mail on April 9 was *Delia, a Masque of the Night*, suggested by George Peele's 1595 play, *The Old Wives' Tale*, not the Allegory celebrating Wisdom that Stravinsky and Auden had discussed. Unimpressed, Craft "read it aloud to I. S. Six characters—Sacrapant (Sarastro, Klingsor), Delia (a tame Kundry), Orlando (Tamino, Parsifal), Bungay (Papageno), Xantippe (Baba the Turk), Old Crone (the goddess in disguise)—are in search of I do not know what. The libretto is too involved for a fairy tale, too prolix for musical setting and dramatically static; it contains a sizable quintet, perhaps to atone for the absence of ensembles in the *Rake*, a diverting round (the owl and the mouse), and, in the pageant of Time (Death and Mutability), beautiful poetry."[16]

For a composer who "always chose his own subjects and collaborated in the scenarios," this fait accompli could be only accepted as is or declined.[17] Craft certainly counseled against setting it, but the lack of any prospect for a commission was also a factor. Had the Aspen Festival found a Maecenas willing to pay $15,000, Stravinsky may well have enclosed himself in an incubator long enough to compose an accessible hour-long masque. But, as we know, the composer was becoming less and less interested in appealing to middlebrow audiences. The

Rake's Progress would be his last attempt to satisfy them. "The music will be very easy to listen to," he assured Ralph Hawkes, "but making this easiness is very expensive with my time."[18] After that, he was finished.

An Icon of Freedom

The concentric orbits influencing Stravinsky's artistic life extended well beyond his close circle of friends and associates and even beyond his distant, and now deceased, counterpart Schoenberg. Out of practical financial considerations and concern for his family abroad, the composer kept tabs on the European musical scene and foreign political developments. Little did he suspect the extent to which he would become caught up in or the impact he would have on world politics and culture. By setting up his friend's lucrative return to Europe for the premiere of *The Rake*, Nabokov helped facilitate one of the most prestigious musical events in over a generation. Within a decade, he would usher Stravinsky around the world, seeing to it he was paid handsomely nearly everywhere he went and for much he wished to compose. Never before had Stravinsky traveled in such luxury and created with so few conditions. Apparently he had achieved nearly unparalleled freedom to express himself; indeed, Nabokov promoted this Great Artist as an icon of Freedom.

As Bourdieu explains, "The position of 'pure' writer or artist . . . is an institution of freedom, constructed against the 'bourgeoisie' (in the artists' sense) and against institutions—in particular against the state bureaucracies, academies, salons, etc." Thus, by channeling, wittingly or not, CIA money to fund his festivals, Nabokov was "diverting the resources of the state" to prop up the position of "pure" artist. Furthermore, the "work of real emancipation, of which the 'post' of artist or poet is the culmination can be performed and pursued only if the post encounters the appropriate dispositions, such as disinterestedness and daring."[19] That Stravinsky's serial music alienated most of his listeners was not incidental; he embraced an ascetic style in order to alienate them.

"Une Fete Americaine"

Thanks to his half-century-old reputation as a "free-thinking" artist, Stravinsky's very presence lent more cachet to Nabokov's festivals than the festivals bestowed upon him (or his bank account). For every major event he organized—*Masterpieces of the Twentieth Century* (Paris 1952), *Music in the Twentieth Century* (Rome 1954), *Tradition and Change in Music* (Venice 1958), *East-West Musical Encounter* (Toyko 1961), and the Berlin Arts Festivals (1964–66)—Nabokov invariably first secured and usually sought to feature Stravinsky before planning the rest of the program.[20]

For that first and most lavish festival, Nabokov programmed nine mostly major works by his old friend, but he had dreamed of an even more ambitious showcase, including a *Rite of Spring* choreographed by Balanchine and the French premiere of *The Rake* at the Paris Opéra. His compatriots did not share his dream. The classicist Balanchine was "stupefied" by the proposition, though he entertained the idea of a "non-Russian version and with someone like Picasso" designing the sets.[21] "Comrade Picasso" was "out of the question" for the Congress for Cultural Freedom (CCF), though, and the New York City Ballet instead presented Balanchine's acclaimed *Firebird* and *Orpheus*, with Stravinsky conducting. Another acclaimed American ensemble, the Boston Symphony Orchestra, would perform *The Rite of Spring* in concert under Pierre Monteux, the man who conducted the premiere in the same Théâtre de Champs-Élysées thirty-nine years earlier. The Opéra management agreed in principle to produce *The Rake* if Stravinsky would conduct, for which he demanded $5,000. Apparently they did not want him that badly and the Paris premiere would have to wait until June 1953 at the Opéra Comique. Ernst Roth detected in the management's rejection a whiff of suspicion surrounding Nabokov's "*fete Americaine*." He wrote the composer:

> Concerning the *Rake* in Paris, I have a feeling that Mr. Nabokov's diplomacy has not been very helpful. . . . Your suspicion that [Maurice] Lehmann and Bondeville do not want to be tied to the American business of the Festival is certainly correct. . . . Their idea seems to be that Nabokov's Festival is some sort of a venture which may go wrong and they, as a State Institution, are afraid to be involved in any unpleasantness which, if nothing else, would cost them their jobs. However, perhaps it is the general political background of the Festival, which is not so much due to any official advertisement but to a lot of rumor and backchat, which makes them hesitate to take part.[22]

Instead of *The Rake*, Stravinsky would conduct *Oedipus* at the familiar Théâtre de Champs-Élysées.

The composer was much less pleased with the *Oedipus-Erwartung* double bill than he later claimed. Craft noted in his diary: "With I. S. to [Hans] Rosbaud's *Erwartung* rehearsal. I. S. does not like the music."[23] Knowing another piece would attract a mixed audience and hence potential antagonists, Stravinsky months before had made it clear he did not want his opera-oratorio to be paired with another work, let alone Schoenberg's monodrama. Nabokov, though, felt the festival required a fuller program, so the composer conducted his own *Scènes de ballet* to open the first performance on May 19, which, aside from twitters at Jean Cocteau's strangely disconnected tableaux, was well received. Those who attended the second performance, conducted by Rosbaud, to see *Erwartung* were less polite. Craft recalls: "After *Erwartung*, the younger audience retreats. During Cocteau's last *Oedipus* speech, the upper balcony explodes with boos, whistles, hissing, shouts of 'Assez avec Cocteau.' When the protest subsides, Cocteau shrewdly asks the public to show respect for *Stravinsky's* work, at which point I. S., in the seat next to me, heads for the hotel. The request provokes applause, followed by more boos and counter-applause, and the war between the claques resumes at the end of the performance."[24] Elsewhere, Craft embellished the account by quoting the composer's parting words: "I'm going to the hotel and wait there; I know my way out of this theatre."[25]

The unpleasantness of the second *Oedipus* performance failed to mar what most recognized as a spectacular return for Stravinsky. However, he was probably relieved his *Rake* had not received its French premiere that month, lest it have been upstaged by the Vienna State Opera's *Wozzeck*. The inevitable comparisons of two works composed from extreme ends of the modernist spectrum would have only highlighted the prevailing sense that Stravinsky's cultural moment had passed. Opera as a genre, though, looked anything but dead. Besides *Wozzeck*, *Oedipus*, and *Erwartung*, the festival presented the Royal Opera's premier production of *Billy Budd* and a revival of Thomson's *Four Saints in Three Acts*, the latter featuring the international debut of twenty-five-year-old soprano, Leontyne Price.

"I Loathe Festivals"

By the following fall, Nabokov was already imploring Stravinsky "to accept the presidency of the Music Advisory Board" for his next big congress, *Music in the Twentieth Century*. The latter replied, "The 'presidency' that you propose does not interest me at all. A trip to Rome and a holiday there are always agreeable, but I cannot lose the time and would come only if I had a small concert tour."[26] Nabokov met each of Stravinsky's demands (including booking the tour himself), so the composer agreed at least to show up and lend his name to the proceeding.

Though professionally and socially more intertwined than ever, Nabokov and Stravinsky no longer shared their previously intimate musical bond. The former's motivations are perhaps less transparent than his effusive correspondence would indicate. On the one hand, he voices justifiable concern over Stravinsky's health: "What disturbs me is the huge overload of concerts that you have in America. Bob wrote to me that you had the flu twice but still must do about fifteen concerts before you leave for July." After Stravinsky suffered a stroke in October 1956, Nabokov begged him to stop exerting himself: "We all need you so much."[27]

That last statement rings truer than he perhaps intended. Nabokov desperately needed an artist of Stravinsky's reputation to promote the CCF's ambitious, if rather fuzzy, agenda. His motivations got even fuzzier when, in 1962, he accepted Mayor Willy Brandt's appointment as director of Berlin's annual arts festivals. Of course, he turned to Stravinsky, this time with an invitation of which most artists could only dream:

> Would you *please* come and spend a month or two (or even three if you want) here in Berlin, . . . Vera will have her studio and you yours to work in . . . Bob will have recordings for both Berlin radio stations.
>
> . . . I have already arranged with my friends of the Ford Foundation that your round trip air or boat passage from American to Europe (for the three of you) will be paid by the Foundation. Berlin will pay all the expenses of your sojourn here, *free of any kind of tax*.
>
> In addition to this, I am proposing a fee of DM 10,000 [$2,600] for your appearance as conductor of one concert during the Festwochen and a fee of DM 4,000 [$1,100] for Bob, for the same concert.

> ... The Festival next year [1964] is dedicated to the contribution or rather the symbiosis of the Negro art with Western art of the 20th century. . . . And now comes my unexpected and rash question: would it be possible for you to consider making an orchestral arrangement, or rather a transformation and adaptation for voice and orchestra . . . of two, three, or four Negro spirituals? I have just returned from Salzburg, where I heard and saw my dear old friend Leontyne Price. She would be delighted and honored to sing these adaptations of Negro spirituals here, either under your direction or under somebody else's. I would like to commission you to do this. Thus we would have *"eine Uraufführung"* of a work of yours in our program. Thus, too, you would, I think, greatly help the cause of emancipation of the American Negro and at the same time earn the gratitude of the Negro people all over the world.
>
> I will scramble out of my Festival budget the sum of $5,000 to which Leontyne Price will add another $5,000 . . . I say this very humbly, that what I ask you to do is immense personal favor to me. I know also that if you write this kind of adaptations, it will find enormous response in Russia particularly among the younger generation.[28]

Feeling even more isolated by the recently constructed Berlin Wall, the West Berlin leadership, just as in 1950, wanted to make a major cultural statement to the world. But why was Nabokov trying to score points for the American civil rights struggle? Because covertly through its new conduit, the Ford Foundation, the State Department and the CIA were attempting to present to the world an image counter to the bigotry and violence at home.[29] Just as he had imagined the CCF's "East-meets-West festivals" in India and Japan with the global Cold War in mind, Nabokov now conceived a festival devoted to the "symbiosis of the Negro art with Western art of the twentieth century." He imagined that a set of Stravinsky "spirituals" premiered by the world-famous American Negro soprano might blunt the sharp criticism the United States was receiving for its treatment of blacks. (The same thinking had driven him to program *Four Saints in Three Acts* with an all-black cast a decade earlier.) However, little in Stravinsky's oeuvre—and nothing he had composed in the previous decade—would indicate his receptiveness to such an idea. If he at least pretended to consider the project, he held back none of his feelings about the proposed Stravinsky program:

> Though your festivals have always been the most intelligently planned and the most capably executed, and though they have always shown the greatest devotion to me and my work, I loathe festivals. Even more, I loathe most of the people they draw, the Stuckenschmidts, the Bornoffs and the thousand other *cons* from Italy to everywhere. Therefore, please reserve our concert for the end of the festival, or for a time when the white trash will have cleared out.
>
> . . . For the rest, we would like to come in August and stay as long as we find convenient . . . I don't know what I can do with a "spiritual" . . . I will study the "spirituals" when they come, and I am attracted by the idea.[30]

Reading Stravinsky's complaints one glimpses the conflicting interests Nabokov had to negotiate in planning his festivals. Cocteau had vented similar bile about the production of *Oedipus* at the Paris festival: "No one can understand better than you how impossible it is for us to acquiesce in the stupidity of an audience to which we are condemned by 'galas.'"[31] From the political side, critics were no less reticent in second-guessing Nabokov for not voicing a clearer anti-Soviet political agenda. As head of the American Committee for Cultural Freedom, Sydney Hook assessed the 1952 Paris festival: "Although there were efforts at desperate rationalization to show that all of these activities had something to do with the defense of the free world, actually it did more to further Nabokov's career and reputation that to further cultural freedom."[32]

Conversely, to fill his festival programs, Nabokov turned to numerous other artists with whom he had personal and professional connections. He especially looked to (and looked after) his Russian circle friends. In producing the continental debut of Balanchine's New York City Ballet, featuring Maria Tallchief dancing Euridice and the title role in his sensational new *Firebird*, Nabokov recreated on an international stage that intimate Christmas gathering in Hollywood over four years earlier (see fig. 1.5). Obviously, Stravinsky benefitted financially, and Craft professionally, from his connections. For the Paris festival alone the former received $4,500 for conducting *Oedipus* and *Orpheus* and $2,000 for travel. More importantly, Nabokov took a hand in arranging several major commissions—namely, *Canticum Sacrum* (1956), *Threni* (1958), *Movements* for piano and orchestra (1959), and *Abraham and Isaac* (1964)—either through the CCF, the Berlin Arts Festival, his network of contacts, or a combination thereof (his letter detailing the proposed commission of *Threni*, reproduced by Shreffler, is indicative of the way he used his position as secretary-general to make such connections[33]).

However, the more appearance money and publicity he received, the more Stravinsky resented being used as a publicity prop. He became increasingly cynical toward his patrons. Of the commissions that came through Nabokov, only *Movements* was funded without indirect CIA support, and the composer was suspicious even of that offer. In March 1958, Nabokov informed him of a commission "for piano and orchestra . . . for an excellent young Swiss pianist . . . by a Swiss industrialist who owns several hotels in Arosa. His name is [Hans] Weber. If you were interested, this gentleman would be prepared to pay $15,000 for exclusive rights during a season."[34] Stravinsky agreed to consider the proposal but, assuming the pianist was male, he bizarrely jumped to the conclusion: "He must presumably be a pansy if Weber is taking on such serious expenses."[35]

In fact, the pianist was Weber's wife, Margrit, and the arrangement was exactly as Nabokov described. Why did Stravinsky presume an ulterior sexual relationship? Perhaps he thought this "Swiss industrialist" was another Julius "Junkie" Fleischmann, the heir to the gin and yeast fortune who, as "president" of the Farfield Foundation, was supposedly the chief patron of the CCF. Writing from Venice, Mary McCarthy fills in the picture: "There was a whole overflow of people from the Congress [for Cultural Freedom] here: Nabokoff and [Melvin] Lasky . . . and Fleischman [sic] himself, who is homosexual, it seems, and is traveling with a young doctor."[36] Nabokov privately referred to the "plutocratic Junkie" as "Queen Juliana Fleischmann."[37] No wonder Stravinsky assumed Weber was just another rich, inflated prop. The thought of a wealthy person spending money solely to support artists had grown foreign to him.

With commissions coming easily and with few conditions, Stravinsky became even less willing to compromise artistically. Indicative of his aloof, even antagonistic, attitude is his unapologetic quip about *Threni*: "I'm afraid it's a big bore, but it will be good to bore my enemies."[38] One is tempted to attribute the extreme asceticism of his late style as much to this growing alienation as to any personal aesthetic concerns or the influence of Webern or Schoenberg. A disconcerting gap had opened between the product Stravinsky was delivering—that is, himself and his music—and the European "*ne plus ultra* of elegance" that had so eagerly celebrated him since the premiere of *The Rake*. In the perverse economy of disinterestedness, the composer had come to expect perversity.

That gap also interposed itself between Stravinsky and the man who was facilitating his new commissions. After his friend died, Nabokov confessed:

> We rarely discussed his new music, nor did he show me, as he used to before, his "work in progress." He never again spoke to me about my own music. We talked about a million things, we laughed together, ate and drank together, I listened to most of his new music at rehearsal, but he never asked my opinion of it. It was as if we had tacitly agreed to avoid some corpse in the closet.
>
> I did not, I could not, at least not fast enough, and not as whole-heartedly as I would have wished to, learn to love Stravinsky's new "serial" compositions, whereas I did spontaneously and instinctively love *all* of his music up until *The Rake's Progress* and *Agon*.[39]

Cultural Détente

The United States was not the only government looking to exploit Stravinsky's reputation. In the summer of 1961, a trio of Soviet cultural liaisons, including the president of the Composers' Union, Tikhon Khrennikov, traveled to Los Angeles for an international music festival and while there invited Stravinsky to celebrate his eightieth birthday in Russia the following year. The composer was deeply torn; even as the Soviet cultural climate was thawing, the political atmosphere was heating up to a degree not experienced since the Second World War.

Nabokov tried to dissuade him from accepting the invitation but others, including Craft and Charles Bohlen, felt he should not refuse the overture, however politically motivated.[40] Acting quickly, Nabokov prompted his old friend Arthur Schlesinger, now a White House adviser, to arrange for the president to officially celebrate the Russian American composer. First Lady Jacqueline Kennedy issued the invitation: "Dear Mr. Stravinsky, The President and I would so like to have you here for a dinner in your honor on or around your 80th birthday next June 5th. It would give us great pleasure to have you with us on such an important occasion. We send our very best wishes and will await your answer."[41]

When the unimpressed Stravinsky curtly declined, pointing to unspecified engagements, Schlesinger turned back to Nabokov: "This is not a very satisfactory exchange. He might at least have said that his concert engagements were out of the country. Can you get him to amplify his response by mail and raise the possibility of his coming to the White House on some other occasion than June

5?"⁴² As shocking (not to say rude) as his rejection seems, Stravinsky saw dinner with the President and Mrs. Kennedy as no different from the other tedious functions Nabokov pestered him to attend. He vented:

> The White House question is settled—going there for dinner on the 18th January. But I don't see anything wrong with my telegram to Mrs. Kennedy. Am I a man of almost 80 years to fly all alone (notice, she did *not* invite my wife) to Washington on the one day I would like to be with my family and friends. I want to add, too, that the Casals business there nauseated me—all publicity seeking and social climbing on the part of you know which American composers and conductors and violinists and . . . *No one* in Washington has any real regard for my music—it is all for my name.⁴³

He was not wrong. Stravinsky had become a political football; his eightieth year would coincide with the tensest period of the Cold War. The previous September he had witnessed the wall in newly divided Berlin; he would soon visit his Russian homeland at the very moment Soviet engineers were secretly constructing missile sites in Cuba. For most of the world, Stravinsky's name, like that of Picasso and Casals, was only shorthand for Great Artist; the Soviets and the White House were simply exploiting it as a cultural sideshow to their much more serious confrontations.

Stravinsky and the president passably carried out their uncomfortable charade. Craft, at his narrative best, recorded the highlights:

> The president toasts I. S.; and at two rather shaky moments in her spouse's speech, twinges of anxiety show in "Jackie's" eyes. "We have been honored to have had two great artists here with us in recent months," he begins, and I am wondering if I. S. realizes that Casals is meant by the other. "When my wife was a student in Paris, she wrote an essay on Baudelaire, Oscar Wilde, and Diaghilev." (I. S. later: "I was afraid he was going to say his wife had made a study of homosexuality.") "Now, I understand that you, Mr. Stravinsky, were a friend of Diaghilev. And I have just been told that rocks and tomatoes were thrown at you in your youth."
>
> Later, "cigars and cognac are passed around" and the President asked, "How do you feel now, Mr. Stravinsky?" "Quite drunk, thank you, Mr. President."⁴⁴

Stravinsky later described his hosts to Souvtchinsky: "She is very striking and charming, he very quick on the uptake, but they both have very little connection with art, and I think they invited me less for my music than for my age, and to steal a march on the Russians, *to whom, I shall not go.*"⁴⁵ But he would go. As with his refusal to sign the welcome greeting to Shostakovich in 1949, media leaks of the invitation put Stravinsky in the awkward position of having to make and, therefore, defend his decision publically. Besides, he could not deny his feelings for his country of birth. His response to what, in essence, was a diversionary move in a global chess game would be deeply personal.

Nabokov remained director of the Berlin festivals and nominally associated with the CCF until 1966, when the CIA's involvement began to unravel in reports published in the *New York Times* and the magazine *Ramparts*. Feigning ignorance and indignation, he and the CCF executive board condemned the subterfuge and voted to disband the organization. A new International Association for Cultural Freedom (IACF), openly funded by the Ford Foundation without CIA help, attempted to resume its mission, but without Nabokov, the IACF would withdraw from the musical world.

The Individual and Freedom

Stravinsky left no record of his reaction to these revelations, and little evidence suggests CIA money influenced, either directly or indirectly, his embrace of serialism.[46] The true source and lasting power of his artistry at this and every other point in his long career was the driving need to engage with music, people, and ideas. Walsh notes an ironic juxtaposition, in the first edition of *Conversations*, of the old composer's observations, influenced by a lively discussion with Boulez, with a photograph of the young composer sitting next to his wife and his teacher, Rimsky-Korsakov: "It is impossible not to be struck by the thought that Stravinsky was as impressionable at seventy-five as he had been at twenty-five."[47]

Schoenberg, by contrast, appeared to preserve his authenticity by developing the very technique—that is, dodecaphonicism—that some argue cost Stravinsky his. But Schoenberg's too came at a cost, which Mann, as we know, imagined as a Faustian pact. To his fictionalized Schoenberg the devil pronounces: "Love is forbidden you, in so far as it warms. Thy life shall be cold, therefore thou shalt love no human being. . . . Cold we want you to be, that the fires of creation shall be hot enough to warm yourself in. Into them you will flee out of the cold of your life."[48] The voice behind that devil, Adorno, states the matter less dramatically but just as clearly: "What radical music perceives is the untransfigured suffering of man. His impotence has increased to the point that it no longer permits illusion and play."[49]

Schoenberg's renunciation of the playful illusion in which composers like Stravinsky indulge, while "honest," guarantees only loneliness, the romantic affectation of individuality, the flip side of disinterestedness. About the preserial *Erwartung* Adorno writes, "The Expressionistic . . . movement originated in illusion—in the illusion of individuality itself. Expressionism remains—against its will—that which art had openly professed around 1900: loneliness as style."[50] Such stylized loneliness is a defining trope of romanticism. (Stravinsky describes "modern" as "'romantic,' of course, and it suffers . . . for it cannot accept the world as it is.")[51] Caught in the trap of unending illusions, the authentic composer's only recourse is the total organization of the elements of music, which, thus self-contained, shuts out the audience completely.

From Adorno's Marxist view, the historical imperative driving modernist music—indeed, the driving force behind modernity—paradoxically, but necessarily, consumes the foundation upon which it is built: the individual subject. On one side this inescapable truth weighs as the totalitarian monolith pressing down upon Eastern Europe and, on the other, hangs as the smog of consumerism over the West. Adorno detests Stravinsky for thinking he could escape these social forces by indulging an insufferable elite's taste for eighteenth-century confections, but he knows Schoenberg's loneliness too is an affectation. Viewed as a dispositional strategy, the perpetually revolutionary music about which Leibowitz was so enthusiastic—again paradoxically—could be only a rear-guard tactic. It would soon exhaust itself. No wonder both Schoenberg and Stravinsky rejected Adorno's *Philosophy*. Though admiring, the philosopher's pessimism especially disturbed Schoenberg, perhaps because he too had accepted the historical necessity of his role. To a superior officer's imperious inquiry, "So you are the notorious Schoenberg," the composer claims to have responded: "Beg to report sir, yes. Nobody wanted to be. Someone had to be, so I let it be me."[52]

Schoenberg's anecdote is generally understood as a reference to himself as the "emancipator" of dissonance; yet another paradox in that, in order to "liberate" sound, he had to obey the imperative of musical development. This notion of musical freedom, expressed in the language of political revolution, became the defining frame for understanding modernist music. Yet, having freed itself from social and commercial demands, musical sound could not escape its own immutable laws. The onerous task of discovering—not developing or inventing—but discovering, like Kepler, these laws would again fall upon the long-suffering Schoenberg. What the Marxist radical Adorno understood as the inevitable result of socioeconomic forces, the Hegelian conservative Schoenberg saw as a commitment to musical history. Regardless, the serious artist had no choice but to follow the command of what Mann imagined as a devil-musicologist, the embodiment of tormenting self-consciousness.

The Russian Swiss French American Stravinsky recognized no such imperative. Free of "history," he committed himself to tradition selectively and adopted conventions arbitrarily. To him freedom never meant having complete autonomy as much as being able to choose one's master. Expressed in terms reminiscent of a hellish encounter, the composer's defining manifesto rings true to the end of his life's work:

> I experience a sort of terror when, at the moment of setting to work and finding myself before the infinitude of possibilities that present themselves, I have the feeling that everything is permissible to me. If everything is permissible to me, the best and the worst; if nothing offers me any resistance, then any effort is inconceivable, and I cannot use anything as a basis, and consequently every undertaking becomes futile.
>
> Will I then have to lose myself in this abyss of freedom? To what shall I cling in order to escape the dizziness that seizes me before the virtuality of this infinitude? . . . In art as in everything else, one can build only upon a resisting foundation: whatever constantly gives way to pressure, constantly renders movement impossible.
>
> My freedom thus consists in my moving about with the narrow frame that I have assigned myself for each of my undertakings.
>
> I shall go even further: my freedom will be so much the greater and more meaningful the more narrowly I limit my field of action and the more I surround myself with obstacles. Whatever diminishes constraint diminishes strength. The more constraints one imposes, the more one frees one's self of the chains that shackle the spirit.[53]

Stravinsky's devil is the "infinitude of possibilities" that passes as autonomy; his hell is the "abyss of freedom." If we imagine his story as a Faustian pact, it would not be Nick Shadow misleading the gullible Tom. His devil is the crafty old man of *Histoire du Soldat*, who names his price, and Stravinsky the wily Soldier, who trades his fiddle for worldly riches only to win it back by renouncing them. Except Igor Fedorovich managed to take the devil's money and keep his soul.

Great Artists and the Greater World

The composer of *The Rake's Progress* never lost his soul, but he perpetually risked unsettling it by exposing himself and his music to the greater world. Near the end, his driving energy inevitably dissipated. No longer curious about contemporary music, the composer immersed himself in Handel and Mendelssohn, the *Well-Tempered Clavier*, and Beethoven's late quartets. His new discoveries were the songs of Hugo Wolf, not the works of Stockhausen or Boulez. He picked up his pencils and stylus only to arrange Bach fugues. He could not even join Vera, Bob, Wystan, or Nika and his new (and last) wife, Dominique, for dinner.

"One of the last times I saw Stravinsky," Nabokov remembered, "he was sitting in his little wheelchair at the Essex House in New York, thin and transparent, his profile of an extraordinary ancient Oriental beauty. He was holding my hand and whispering. 'Nika, don't go away. Stay with me. Don't leave me *avec les femmes de chambres.*' . . . That took place, as far as I remember, on February 12, 1971, less than two months before Stravinsky died."[54] Ascribing Nabokov's recollection to another occasion, Craft shares Vera's diary entry: "Nabokov comes in the afternoon to say goodbye to Igor—before going to Berlin—but makes the mistake of asking him how he is. 'You can see how I am, miserable,' he shouts at him, and so angrily that N. leaves with tears in his eyes. Igor tells him to get out."[55]

History, like the decrepit Stravinsky, has been unkind to Nicolas Nabokov. He, Auden, and Kallman, perhaps for old time's sake, would attempt to recreate the magic of that heady collaboration of over twenty years earlier by adapting the one Shakespeare play Auden thought suitable for opera: *Love's Labour's Lost*. The Deutsche Oper of Berlin premiered it in Brussels in 1973, then put it aside, as have other opera and ballet companies and orchestras that used to perform his music. Auden, "finding life absurd, wanting to get out of it, . . . waiting for the end," died the following fall.[56] Kallman, only fifty-four, followed in 1975. Nabokov joined them in 1978, his funeral—as dramatic as his life—was attended by all four previous wives.

Nabokov has fallen through the cracks of cultural history. However, his life with the momentous events he witnessed, the fascinating people he knew, and his unique and evolving perspectives on the world testifies to that mid-twentieth-century moment as does few others. If the Cultural Cold War was a chess game, then Nabokov was a Knight. What he lacked in range and depth, he made up for by thinking and moving around corners and jumping over obstacles. He possessed an agile and imaginative intellect that allowed him to see connections,

Fig. 11.1. *Clockwise from far left*: George Balanchine, Robert Craft, Lincoln Kirstein, W. H. Auden, Vera Stravinsky, and Igor Stravinsky dine at the Stravinskys' New York City apartment, ca. 1969. (Igor Stravinsky Collection, Paul Sacher Foundation)

meet people, and go places others overlooked. He had a keen feel for the game of music and culture in the mid-twentieth century.

Stravinsky, though, remains with Auden in the pantheon of modernists. More than that, he stands, like Picasso and Einstein, astride his era as an iconic "genius." He understood the label was an affectation: "A 'pathetic' term strictly; or, in literature, a propaganda word used by people who do not deserve rational opposition," he answered Craft. "I detest it literarily and cannot read it in descriptive works without pain. If it doesn't already appear in the *Dictionnaire des Idées Reçues*, it should be put there, with, as its automatic responses, 'Michelangelo' and 'Beethoven.'"[57] He could have added his own name as a last living example, for even as they played out their fascinating game of question and answer, he and Craft were exploiting Stravinsky's "genius" status for all it was worth. We should not blame them, though. As long as an educated class still recognized and valued independent "geniuses" and "masterworks," a select few could prosper in the upside-down economy of disinterestedness. That era passed away, though, with Opera and the last Great Artist, one chilly spring morning in the mid-to-late twentieth century.

The Great Artist Dies

"This is the first time since Guillaume de Machaut that the world is without a great composer," wrote George Perle in one among hundreds of messages of condolence sent to Stravinsky's family after his death on April 6, 1971.[58] One might debate his choice of the first, but there is little disagreement about the last.

Great music has been written since Stravinsky's death and memorable premieres of lasting works continue to fill the pages of music histories, but the media and adoring crowds no longer clamor to greet arriving composers at airports. Composer-conductors lead orchestras, but none receive a handsome fee just to appear and conduct half a concert. For perhaps the final time, every news agency and television network announced the death of someone known solely as an inventor of music.

For most people, to the extent they knew it at all, the name Igor Stravinsky signaled some fuzzy notion of a famous artist (was he a composer?) who "knew Diaghilev" (who is that?) and had "rocks and tomatoes thrown at him in his youth." Such was the personage President Kennedy toasted. The picture of the man was more vivid to the First Lady who, after all, had written a college essay "on Baudelaire, Oscar Wilde, and Diaghilev." She had at least heard his music, maybe even seen Balanchine's sensational *Firebird* at City Center.

I imagine the narratives of Stravinsky's aesthetic change—a return to his "classical" attitude, release from his opposition to Schoenberg, Craft's expanding influence, unconditional (covert) funding facilitated by Nabokov—as ever-widening perspectives that together form a composite "Stravinsky." The seeming disconnection explains his and other artists' irritation at having to attend celebratory festivals and dinners. The persona being "celebrated" is inevitably one they have little control over and may even feel alienated from. Stravinsky knew full well the White House invited him only "to steal a march on the Russians" (see note 45). When he complains, "*No one* in Washington has any real regard for my music—it is all for my name," he assumes the two can be separated (see note 43). He even distrusted those who flattered his music, like Souvtchinsky and Nabokov, whom he allowed to manipulate him in return for, respectively, cultural and financial cachet. Those seeking the "true" Stravinsky suspect even Craft's influence. We dig deeper for the chain linking his early, middle, and late works that anchors the artist amid the turbulence of times, places, and people. And we discover—or perhaps imagine—that, too.

The degrees to which we may "know" artists and their work range from such distant, vague notions to whatever level of detail we choose as our focus, telescoping down from the president's superficial toast all the way to Milton Babbitt's weighty "Remarks on Recent Stravinsky." At every level, the observer attempts to "make something" of Stravinsky, and the "Stravinskys" thus made cohabitate. The point is not that President Kennedy construed a superficial "Stravinsky" and that Babbitt or Stephen Walsh or Richard Taruskin or Robert Craft presents a richer, authentic one. The notion that the more we analyze, the further we penetrate, the closer we come to the true subject is a modern act of faith. Superficial and profound observations may not reveal equally, but they are equally real and interact to form the composite identity we recognize as Stravinsky and his music—a lot to cram into a five-foot-three-inch frame.

The persona of the Great Artist, like the Masterwork he creates, is a collaboration between composer and audience. Strictly speaking, the label describes a sociological phenomenon, not a person; an affectation rather than artistic merit (the latter being assumed). Nor should one confuse adulation for appreciation; the adoring are as affected as the adored. The day may come when our relationship to music is so central to our cultural identity that we again worship composers, but it would be a mixed blessing. As professional servants, Mozart and Bach received no such attention during their lifetimes. Machaut may have been the first musician to compose great music, but Beethoven was the first Great Composer, and he was ambivalent about it. Disinterestedness is part of the Great Artist's act. To desire adoration—like Leonard Bernstein, whose antics Stravinsky despised—is decidedly middlebrow. The Great Artist is inclined to turn his back, like Schoenberg or Miles Davis; or a deaf ear, like Beethoven, whose emblematic moment was neglecting to notice the audience's ovation at the premiere of his Ninth Symphony.

If the history of the modern age is the collective stories of such men, then its end is theirs as well. We need not lament its passing. Women, composers of color, and other so-called "lesser" artists may well be relieved to see the elitist, racist, undemocratic Old Man pass into history. Besides, his spritely image lives on perpetually in our collective imagination, ready to spring up again like dead Tom Rakewell.

After the Last Opera

The same may be said of Opera, no more or less dead than the city of Venice. After all, composers still write them. *Billy Budd* premiered only two months later in the theater his publishers had planned for Stravinsky's opera and has fared almost as well. With Henze, Auden and Kallman twice more hit upon success.[59]

By 1953, even Stravinsky seemed ready to take on another, if more modest, operatic venture. So motivated was he by the prospect of collaborating with Dylan Thomas that he added a room to his house to accommodate the poet's expected visit. In their preliminary meeting in Boston, he explained "what he requires in a libretto. Thomas says he has a science fiction idea . . . 'It is about the rediscovery of the planet after an atomic misadventure; and about the recreation of language: a person, an object, a word.'"[60] The poet's untimely death left Stravinsky, then mired in the second crisis of his career, without a clear creative direction, although he and Craft would revisit the apocalyptic theme in *The Flood* (1962). We can only imagine what Thomas and Stravinsky might have created.

The success of *The Rake* at Santa Fe inspired Paul Horgan to propose a collaboration between Stravinsky and T. S. Eliot, with a commission of $20,000 for each. Whether he could have raised the money ceased to be an issue when Eliot declined, feeling he lacked any proficiency in music. In any case, Stravinsky admitted, "I am not very attracted by the operatic form at present and I would certainly not undertake to write an opera like *The Rake's Progress* for any fee. . . . Perhaps I counter-propose another kind of work, a cantata, or static piece (genre my *Oedipus Rex*), a shorter work than an opera and one more suitable to my present non-operatic musical thought."[61]

By then, the nearly eighty-year-old composer preferred the efficient asceticism of abstract ballet (*Agon*) and hybrid religious drama (*The Flood*) to the time-consuming extravagance of Opera. The idea of this exotic and irrational entertainment would nonetheless entertain the weakening composer's imagination to the end of his creative life. His final diary entry from April 23, 1968, gests (I presume): "Asked Bob to compose opera libretto for me. He agreed."[62]

Religious Drama Reawakens

Stravinsky would not be the only composer to turn—or return, as it were—to religious drama. In content and setting, Britten's church parables, including his own *Noye's Fludde* (1958), harken back to a long dormant tradition of sung religious plays. The humanist intellectual concerns and aesthetic goals that spawned opera simultaneously rejected the ritual mysticism of medieval drama. One could say early opera defined itself against medieval drama; church and opera house would remain largely separate and distinct for three hundred fifty years. The decline of traditional opera, though, has opened up the operatic stage to a virtual procession of religious and spiritual figures: Messiaen's *Saint François d'Assise* (1983); the angels Lucifer, Eve, and Michael from Stockhausen's megacycle *Licht* (1977–2003); Glass's *Satyagraha* (1979) and *Ahknaten* (1983); and Kaija Saariaho's *Le Passione de Simone* (2006). Though on a grander, more "operatic" scale, these works nonetheless mark a reawakening of spiritual drama that both precedes and supersedes the modern subject.

Anti-Opera

The avant-garde that snubbed *The Rake* took a different tact: it sought to kill Opera once and for all. "I cannot, will not, compose a traditional 'opera,'" pronounced György Ligeti. "For me the operatic genre is irrelevant today, it belongs to a historical period utterly different from the present compositional situation. Yet by that I do not mean that I cannot compose a work for the facilities an opera house offers."[63] Ligeti would indeed compose for the "facilities of an opera house" *Le Grand Macabre* (1975–76; revised 1996), a work that critiques not only traditional opera but also the efforts of his fellow iconoclasts (labeled *Musiktheater*): among them Luigi Nono's *Intolleranza 1960* (1961), Henri Pousseur's *Votre Faust* (1967), Luciano Berio's *Opera* (1970), and Mauricio Kagel's *Staatstheater* (1971). These "anti-operas" essentially adopt the strategy of the young Stravinsky and choreographer Vaslav Nijinsky, who in *The Rite of Spring* sought to upend conventional ballet. But the spectacular end of the world prophesized by Ligeti's character Necrotzar fizzles, leaving his pastoral lovers Amanda and Amando to sing on.

The Tradition Continues

And several mostly Anglo-American composers have sung on as well. Britten, Menotti, Michael Tippett, Carlisle Floyd, Thea Musgrave, and Dominick Argento have each written several more or less traditional operas, arguably fulfilling the New Opera Group's goal to revive English opera. And by "traditional" I mean not only works that preserve operatic conventions but also those that carry on opera's "general function of envoicing subjectivity through song."[64] Here I use the term broadly to describe works created for and that generally accede to the assumptions of established houses—what Brecht derisively called the "apparatus" of opera. The category is broad enough to encompass Britten's airy *A Midsummer Night's Dream* (1960) and Bernd Alois Zimmerman's hyper-expressionist *Die Soldaten* (1958–64). As long as the music expresses thinking, feeling beings—no matter how shattered or debased—it extends the tradition. Traditional opera even seemed to enjoy a comeback in the 1990s when major houses like the Met, Chicago Lyric, and San Francisco commissioned marketable titles, usually based on recognizable literary works or films, from accessible composers like John Corigliano (*The Ghosts of Versailles*, 1991), André Previn (*A Streetcar Named Desire*, 1998), William Bolcom (*A View from the Bridge*, 1999), John Harbison (*The Great Gatsby*, 2000), and Jake Heggie (*Dead Man Walking*, 2000).[65]

Post-Opera

Experimental American artists have enjoyed some lasting success by ignoring, rather than attacking or emulating, conventional opera. Glass recounts his and designer-director Robert Wilson's conception of *Einstein on the Beach*: "We knew from the beginning that the piece would have to be presented . . . in a modern theater or opera house. Besides that, . . . it never occurred to us that *Einstein on the Beach* would have a story or contain anything like an ordinary plot."[66] Whereas modernist opera clings to the subject in crisis, Glass's solfege and numbers and Wilson's dreamscapes erase the grime of expressionist subjectivity and clutter of neoclassical pastiche.

Sung drama has even become a defining form for experimental composers seeking to expand the dramatic potential of the human voice: Meredith Monk has turned wordless vocalism into dramatic expression; Robert Ashley transformed dramatic speech into music. In *Hopscotch: A Mobile Opera for 24 Cars* (2015), director Yuval Sharon flings wide the doors of music drama to a team of creators and the roadways of Los Angeles. These artists discard even basic assumptions about singing, musical expression, and story to create new forms of music theater. Determinedly independent of established institutions, they also create new artistic selves and, by necessity, new audiences.

The major difference between these American experimenters and composers of anti-opera depends on their relationship to Opera. Essentially irrelevant to Glass, Monk, and Ashley, conventional opera was the first place John Cage turned to create *Europeras* (1987). He explained the title: "For two hundred years the Europeans have been sending us their operas. Now I'm sending them back." Commissioned by Frankfurt Opera, he immediately set about "to ransack the repertoire of traditional (i.e., European) operas that were no longer protected by copyright. . . . To get these fragments, Cage and his assistant . . . went to the basement library of the Metropolitan Opera, where they pulled pages at random to be photocopied."[67] The rest of the material including costumes, props, and even stage sets was similarly chosen for random assignments in each performance.

Appropriating material also defines postmodern opera (and, of course, Stravinsky). If anti-operas launch parodistic assaults, then eclectic works like Thomas Adès's *Powder Her Face* (1995) and *Exterminating Angel* (2016) and Mark Anthony Turnage's *Anna Nicole* (2011) engage in intertextual play. Jonathan Kramer likens postmodernists to adolescents who have outgrown their oedipal conflicts and now "feel they that they can be whatever they wish. Their music can happily acknowledge the past, without having to demonstrate superiority to it."[68]

Postmodern culture doesn't necessarily erase the lines defining high, middle, and low; it's that creators and consumers now feel free to cross them at will. "Freedom" and "autonomy" in a postmodern world mean not being tied to a fixed identity. A gratuitous act is one unbound by lines of influence or historical narrative. What postmodernists are attempting to dismantle, though, is that imaginary wall protecting the "sacred island of art" from the "profane world of production." They and the host of experimenters, pop artists, and virtually all other creators of music theater no longer apologize for appealing to their audience. In that, Stravinsky and his *Rake* are their exemplar.

Apotheosis

"Imagine a woodsman . . . in the Sahara desert," poses Ortega y Gasset. "What good are his bulging muscles and his sharp ax? A woodsman without woods is an abstraction. And the same applies to artists."[69] The seismic cultural shifts of the 1960s have transformed utterly the field of cultural production and, for once, the sociological perspective may reveal a single work and artist to be unique. Far from heralding a rebirth of conventional Opera, as far as new works are concerned, *The Rake's Progress* represents the final word. Who now seriously dares to write a bel canto style "number"?[70] To the genre of vocal roulades, secco recitatives, glittering premieres, and showstopping bravos, Stravinsky delivered the coup de grace.

Yet the creation and in many cases the quality of sung dramas continue unabated. Perhaps the most successful new opera composed in the past half century is John Adams's *Nixon in China* (1987), a work that fits wholly in none of my narratives. Its minimalist repetitions, amplified voices, and stiff, iconic characters defy operatic tradition. Even the "expressive" moments, like Pat Nixon's aria in act 2, are more surreal than personal. Yet the adventurous Houston Grand Opera commissioned the work, which has since been embraced by established houses across America and around the world.

Contemporary composers are as talented as ever. If certain musical and dramatic skills dissipate in favor of others, if traditions become stale, it is because they outlast their appeal; audiences no longer respond. That companies every year commission and produce new works does not mean the genre thrives. Cultural institutions have a self-perpetuating mission; they don't die willingly or easily. Stravinsky's observation about the "hopelessly non-actual" demand for new symphonies applies equally to new operas:

> Probably the most significant difference between the role of the commission today and in the past is the question of utility. Or, at any rate, I imagine that music was

commissioned in the past to satisfy an *actual* need. The commissions of a Renaissance duke, of the Church, of an Esterházy or Diaghilev, were of this sort. . . . In the main, . . . the [present] need for new cantatas, string quartets, symphonies, is wholly imaginary, and commissioning organizations, like the Ford, and the Rockefeller, are really only buying up surplus symphonies as the government buys up surplus corn. In fact, the need for such music is so hopelessly non-actual that the commissioners are now obliged to try to buy the need for the symphony as well as the symphony.[71]

I live in a city in which one of two major companies recently folded and the other—the Met—still struggles to balance annual budgets. Yet I suspect New York City will not let this cultural symbol die. Is that what Opera has come to? A monument preserved in the municipal landscape, a glittering memorial to a bygone heritage? Do we cling to Opera like some idealized but antiquated Penn Station, averse to demolishing it out of a sense of history, but no longer valuing it for its intended purpose? Comparing the old terminal to its inglorious successor, architectural historian Vincent Scully lamented, "One entered the city like a god. One scuttles in now like a rat."[72] If ever a dramatic genre made its audience feel like gods, it was Opera. But do we still long for such a feeling?

Consider again Kallman's analogy that *The Rake* "is a tribute to opera in much the same way that *Apollon musagète* is a tribute to the dance."[73] The comparison fits, but perhaps not as he intended, for Stravinsky and Balanchine's trilogy of *Apollo*, *Orpheus*, and *Agon* also represents ballet's apotheosis. Modern dance proliferates and even flourishes, but classical Ballet, like Opera, is dead. Dance critic Jennifer Homans laments:

> Today we no longer believe in ballet's ideals. We are skeptical of elitism and skill, which seem to us exclusionary and divisive. . . . Ballet's fine manners and implicitly aristocratic airs, its white swans, regal splendor, and beautiful women on pointe (pedestals), seem woefully outmoded, the province of dead white men and society ladies in long-ago places. . . .
>
> For classical ballet to recover its standing as a major art would thus require more than resources and talent (the 'next genius'). Honor and decorum, civility and taste would have to make a comeback. We would have to *admire* ballet again, not only as an impressive athletic display but as a set of ethical principles.[74]

If democracies are to continue preserving noncommercial culture, then producers and artists must better understand how they serve the larger society. Does opera still entertain? Edify? Enrich? Or just mark the status of an elite? But then, have not opera and ballet always been status symbols? No single response can answer these questions; pluralistic societies require a variety of responses. Divergent visions of what (or whether) sung drama is or should be need not signal its decline. That after four centuries the operatic stage remains such a contested space may even testify to its power, range, and sheer adaptability. Despite the perverse cultural economy that tries to support it, seemingly every artist—composer, director, dramatist, and filmmaker; conservative and avant-garde; modernist and postmodernist; "high" and "low"—wants to create some form of music theater. No wonder the genre seems to be going in several directions at once. No single attitude or context can contain this complex, multifaceted form. But that multiplicity is also bewildering, and not just to audiences. Witness Stravinsky's frustration with trying to stage *The Rake*.

Here again, a sociological perspective helps clarify the muddled state. By pioneering a new path to success, *Einstein on the Beach* helped form a new, if still unstable, habitus for sung drama. Compare Glass and Wilson's experience at the Met to that of Stravinsky. In 1976 their production easily filled the huge theater for several performances, but without subsidies, they hemorrhaged money and had to cancel further shows. By contrast, in 1954 Stravinsky earned a handsome royalty even as *The Rake* played to empty seats.

Habitus, of course, entails much more than the example of a single opera or composer. It involves the entire apparatus of companies, producers, funders, directors, composers, performers, critics, and audiences. The handful of successful postoperas has done little to reform that 200-year-old tradition. To be relevant and viable, the culture of sung drama and new music must re-join the "right-side-up" economy, where aesthetic and economic values aren't regarded as mutually exclusive. Otherwise, it risks shrinking into hidden recesses as a *musica reservata*.

About the end of opera I have fewer regrets than does Homans about ballet. To the 125-year period "between Gluck's *Orpheus* and Verdi's *Othello*" that Auden favorably compared to the seventy-five years of Athenian drama, *The Rake's Progress* stands as a glorious and touching apotheosis. That explains why he and Stravinsky preferred, against all practical sense, a Venetian premiere. A Hogarthian opera in English should have played first in London, but Opera's epilogue belonged to Venice. I can offer no better conclusion than to repeat Auden's: "That age is over.... New operas may and, let us hope, will be written, but their composers cannot carry on from where their predecessors left off, but must start anew from the beginning."[75]

Notes

1. Roland Barthes, *The Rustle of Language*, trans. Richard Howard (New York: Hill and Wang, 1986), 214.
2. Quoted in "Moral View of 'The Rake,'" *The Times*, June 16, 1975.
3. Robert Craft, *Stravinsky: The Chronicle of a Friendship: 1948/1971* (Nashville: Vanderbilt University Press, 1994), 46.
4. David Schiff, "Redeeming the Rake," *Atlantic Monthly* (November 1997): 137.
5. Igor Stravinsky and Robert Craft, *Dialogues and a Diary* (Garden City, NY: Doubleday, 1963), 110 (see chapter 1, note 6, for context); ibid., 14.
6. Thomas Mann, *Doctor Faustus: The Life of the German Composer Adrian Leverkühn, as Told by a Friend*, trans. John E. Woods (New York: Alfred A. Knopf, 1997), 257; see chapter 1, note 68, for context.
7. Robert Craft, *Stravinsky: Glimpses of a Life* (New York: St. Martin's Press, 1992), 38–39. Craft failed to mention this episode in earlier accounts of the composer's first encounters with twelve-tone music; see Robert Craft, "A Personal Preface," *Score* 20 (1957): 12 and Vera

Stravinsky and Robert Craft, *Stravinsky in Pictures and Documents* (New York: Simon and Schuster, 1978), 422. I discuss the influence of Schoenberg on Stravinsky's Ricercar II ("Tomorrow shall be my dancing day") in Chandler Carter, "The Rake's Progress and Stravinsky's Return: The Composer's Evolving Approach to Setting Text," *Journal of the American Musicological Society* 63, no. 3 (2010): 629–33.

8. Igor Stravinsky and Robert Craft, *Themes and Episodes* (New York: Alfred A. Knopf, 1966), 23; see prelude, note 34, for context.

9. For my analysis of Ricercar I and discussion of Stravinsky's aesthetic shift, see Carter, "Rake's Progress and Stravinsky's Return," 625–28, 633–34.

10. Letter of December 24, 1951, quoted in W. H. Auden and Chester Kallman, *Libretti and Other Dramatic Writings: 1939–1973*, ed. Edward Mendelson (London: Faber and Faber, 1993), 630.

11. Letter of January 8, 1952, Paul Sacher Foundation; excerpted in V. Stravinsky and Craft, *Pictures and Documents*, 204–5 and Robert Craft, ed., *Stravinsky: Selected Correspondence*, vol. 3 (New York: Alfred A. Knopf, 1985), 353.

12. Letter of January 28, 1952, Paul Sacher Foundation.

13. Letter to Bean of January 31, 1952, Paul Sacher Foundation.

14. Letter of January 27, 1952, Paul Sacher Foundation.

15. Craft, *Correspondence*, vol. 1, 321.

16. Craft, *Chronicle* (1994), 74.

17. Craft, *Glimpses*, 54.

18. V. Stravinsky and Craft, *Pictures and Documents*, 401.

19. Pierre Bourdieu, *The Field of Cultural Production: Essays on Art and Literature*, ed. and introduced by Randal Johnson (Cambridge, MA: Polity Press, 1993), 62–63.

20. Anne Shreffler provides an overview of the CCF's mission and Nabokov's support of Stravinsky's work in "Ideologies of Serialism, Stravinsky's *Threni* and the Congress for Cultural Freedom," in *Music and the Aesthetics of Modernity*, ed. Karol Berger and Anthony Newcomb (Cambridge, MA: Harvard University Press, 2005), esp. 225–29. For more on the genesis and critical reception of the CCF festivals, see Ian Wellens, *Music on the Frontline: Nicolas Nabokov's Struggle against Communism and Middlebrow Culture* (Burlington, VT: Ashgate, 2002), 45–62; Frances Stonor Saunders, *The Cultural Cold War* (New York: New Press, 2013), 95–107; and Vincent Giroud, *Nicolas Nabokov: A Life in Freedom and Music* (New York: Oxford University Press, 2015), 250–69.

21. Letter of June 27, 1951, Paul Sacher Foundation; excerpted in Craft, *Correspondence*, vol. 2, 381.

22. Letter of March 6, 1952, Paul Sacher Foundation. Given his pivotal role in arranging the Venice premiere of *The Rake*, which infuriated Leslie Boosey (Nabokov, "The Gracious Master," 181), Stravinsky's publishers were generally suspicious of Nabokov's enterprise.

23. Craft, *Chronicle* (1994), 82. By contrast, Stravinsky presented a thoughtful, even admiring recollection of his relationship with Schoenberg, concluding: "Less than a year [after Schoenberg's death], his *Erwartung* and my *Oedipus Rex*—an unthinkable juxtaposition a few years before—were performed together in Paris . . . as a double bill. I hope Schoenberg would have been pleased. I know I was," in Igor Stravinsky and Robert Craft, *Dialogues and a Diary* (Garden City, NY: Doubleday, 1963), 56.

24. Craft, *Chronicle* (1994), 82. Images of Cocteau's tableaux are reproduced in *Stravinsky: The Rake's Progress—Oedipus Rex* (New York: Riverrun Press, 1991), 23–27.

25. Craft, *Correspondence*, vol. 3, 131, note 40.

26. Letters of November 25 and December 3, 1952, Paul Sacher Foundation; excerpted in Craft, *Correspondence*, vol. 2, 384, 386.

27. Letters of January 21, 1954, and November 26, 1956, in Craft, *Correspondence*, vol. 2, 389, 392.

28. Letter of September 2, 1963, Paul Sacher Foundation; excerpted in Craft, *Correspondence*, vol. 2, 407–8. Nabokov had initiated a "program of long-term fellowships allowing writers and creative artists from all over the world to spend as long as a year in the German city at the Ford Foundation's expense" (Giroud, *Nicolas Nabokov*, 344). Several prominent younger composers took advantage of this generous offer, including Elliot Carter, Roger Sessions, Gilbert Amy, Luciano Berio, and Iannis Xenakis. Auden would spend 1964 in Berlin as an artist-in-residence.

29. Nicolas Nabokov, *Bagázh: Memoirs of a Russian Cosmopolitan* (New York: Atheneum, 1975), 257. Through the Ford Foundation, the CIA helped fund the Berlin Festival and, I suspect, Price's share of the proposed commission. The State Department was concurrently sending jazz musicians abroad with a similar message.

30. Letter of October 6, 1963, Paul Sacher Foundation; excerpted in Craft, *Correspondence*, vol. 2, 409. Despite Stravinsky's professed openness, Craft wrote Nabokov "that you don't want to touch Negro Spirituals. I quite well understand, so let us drop the matter" (letter of October 24, 1963, Paul Sacher Foundation). In the end, the Stravinskys resided in the Kempinski Hotel, the entire bill of which was "paid by the office of the Mayor of Berlin" (letter of December 14, 1963, Paul Sacher Foundation).

31. Letter of March 21, 1952, quoted in Stephen Walsh, *Stravinsky—The Second Exile: France and America, 1934–1971* (New York: Alfred A. Knopf, 2006), 286.

32. Sydney Hook, *Out of Step: An Unquiet Life in the Twentieth Century* (New York: Harper, 1987), 445. There is some truth to Hook's statement. While he never programmed his own music, Nabokov admitted using CCF contacts to promote his personal projects. "Thanks to two international musical festivals, [he] knew a few VIPs of the European opera world," specifically, Oscar Fritz Schuh of Cologne Opera, to whom he successfully promoted *Rasputin's End* (1959), written in collaboration with Stephen Spender, editor of the CCF magazine *Encounter* (Nabokov, *Bagázh*, 251).

33. Shreffler, "Ideologies of Serialism," 230. Nabokov explained: "Hamburg would offer you a fee of $5,000 for the commission—that is for the rights of the "Urauffuehrung" of the new work [*Threni*] and $2,500 as a conducting fee. I am confident . . . that I will obtain for you an additional $2,500 for the rights covering the first performance of your work in Japan" (letter of June 17, 1957, Paul Sacher Foundation).

34. Letter of March 11, 1958, in Craft, *Correspondence*, vol. 2, 397.

35. Letter of March 16, 1958, quoted in Walsh, *Second Exile*, 641, note 34 (see Craft, *Correspondence*, vol. 2, 397, for Craft's misleading translation).

36. Letter of September 29, 1955, to Hannah Arendt in Mary McCarthy, *Between Friends: The Correspondence of Hannah Arendt and Mary McCarthy 1949–1975* (New York: Harcourt Brace, 1995), 36.

37. Saunders, *Cultural Cold War*, 107.

38. Quoted in Walsh, *Second Exile*, 384. Shreffler describes the thirty-five-minute serial cantata as "stringent, ascetic, and decidedly unspectacular" ("Ideologies of Serialism," 236).

39. Nabokov, *Bagázh*, 178–79.

40. Lillian Libman, *Music at the Close* (New York: Norton, 1972), 151. Ross misinterprets Nabokov's inquiry about a rumor (see Walsh, *Second Exile*, 440) for evidence that he, "playing his usual rainmaker role," had instigated the visit; Alex Ross, *The Rest Is Noise: Listening to the Twentieth Century* (New York: Picador, 2007), 424.

41. Letter of November 21, 1961, quoted in V. Stravinsky and Craft, *Pictures and Documents*, 653, note 122.

42. Letter of December 12, 1961, Paul Sacher Foundation.
43. Letter of January 3, 1962, quoted in Walsh, *Second Exile*, 447.
44. Craft, *Chronicle* (1994), 285.
45. Letter of February 4, 1962, quoted in Walsh, *Second Exile*, 451 (author's emphasis).
46. The commissions he received from CIA front organizations for *Threni* and *Abraham and Isaac* represented only a fraction of his income during his final two decades. Most of his earnings came from royalties, conducting engagements, recording contracts, record and book sales, the sale of manuscripts, and other commissions.
47. Walsh, *Second Exile*, 372.
48. Mann, *Doctor Faustus*, 249.
49. Theodor W. Adorno, *Philosophy of Modern Music*, trans. Anne G. Mitchell and Wesley V. Blomster (New York: Seaburg, 1973), 41–42.
50. Ibid., 46.
51. Igor Stravinsky and Robert Craft, *Memories and Commentaries* (Garden City, NY: Doubleday, 1960), 109. Isaiah Berlin admitted to Craft, "*Erwartung*... seems to me a marvelously gifted piece of super-Kitsch" (quoted in Craft, *Glimpses*, 232).
52. Arnold Schoenberg, *Style and Idea* (Berkeley: University of California Press, 1984), 104.
53. Igor Stravinsky, *Poetics of Music*, trans. Arthur Knodel and Ingolf Dahl (Cambridge, MA: Harvard University Press, 1970), 63–65. Gide expressed a strikingly similar sentiment: "Art is always the result of constraint.... Whenever it (art) feels vigorous, it seeks struggle and obstacle." See André Gide, "The Evolution of the Theater," trans. Jackson Mathews, in *My Theater: Five Plays and an Essay*, 259–74 (New York: Alfred A. Knopf, 1952). Carr traces this attitude of artistic restraint in the writings of Gide, Maritain, and Valéry and links it to the broader notion of aesthetic distance, in Maureen Carr, *Multiple Masks: Neoclassicism in Stravinsky's Works on Greek Subjects* (Lincoln: University of Nebraska Press, 2002), 7. See also chapter 6, note 12.
54. Nabokov, *Bagázh*, 180.
55. V. Stravinsky and Craft, *Pictures and Documents*, 498. Craft later softened the telling: "he shouts, and so angrily that N., who loves him more than anyone, leaves with wet eyes," in Craft, *Chronicle* (1994), 536.
56. Nabokov, *Bagázh*, 231.
57. Igor Stravinsky and Robert Craft, *Conversations with Stravinsky* (Garden City, NY: Doubleday, 1959), 119.
58. Quoted in Craft, *Chronicle* (1994), 548.
59. Carolyn Abbate and Roger Parker briefly survey a few representative operas composed after 1945 in *A History of Opera* (New York: Norton, 2015), 543–48.
60. Craft, *Chronicle* (1994), 100.
61. Letter to Eliot of April 8, 1959, quoted in Robert Craft, *An Improbable Life* (Nashville: Vanderbilt University Press, 2002), 212.
62. Robert Craft, ed., *A Stravinsky Scrapbook 1940–1971* (London: Thames and Hudson, 1983), 179.
63. Quoted in Paul Griffiths, *Modern Music: The Avant Garde Since 1945* (New York: George Braziller, 1981), 248. Incensed by his experience conducting a revival of *Wozzeck* in Frankfurt, Boulez pronounced: "The most expensive solution would be to blow up the opera houses. But don't you think this would be the most elegant?" in "Blow up the Opera Houses!" Interview in *Der Spiegel*, September 25, 1967.
64. Gary Tomlinson, *Metaphysical Song: An Essay on Opera* (Princeton, NJ: Princeton University Press, 1999), 6.

65. Richard Taruskin, *Oxford History of Western Music*, vol. 5 (New York: Oxford University Press, 2005), 515–16.
66. Philip Glass, *Music by Philip Glass* (New York: Harper and Row, 1987), 31–32.
67. Richard Kostelanetz, *John Cage Ex(plain)ed* (New York: Schirmer Books, 1996), 133.
68. Jonathan Kramer, "The Nature and Origins of Musical Postmodernism," in *Postmodern Music/Postmodern Thought*, eds. Judy Lochhead and Joseph Auner (New York: Routledge, 2002), 18.
69. "Notes on the Novel" in José Ortega y Gasset, *"The Dehumanization of Art" and Other Writings on Art and Culture* (Garden City, NY: Doubleday, 1956), 58.
70. John Corigliano so dared in *Ghosts of Versailles* to mixed results. Kirke Mechem's more modest *Tartuffe* (1980), having been presented internationally in scores of productions, resembles *The Rake*'s neoclassical success, but its reputation seems too isolated to leave a lasting impact.
71. I. Stravinsky and Craft, *Memories*, 86–87.
72. Quoted in Anne-Marie Cantwell and Diana diZerega Wall, *Unearthing Gotham: The Archaeology of New York City* (New Haven, CT: Yale University Press, 2001), 10.
73. See prelude, note 25.
74. Jennifer Homans, "Is Ballet Over?" *New Republic*, October 13, 2010.
75. See prelude, note 4.

BIBLIOGRAPHY

Abbate, Carolyn, and Roger Parker. *A History of Opera*. New York: W. W. Norton, 2015.
Abbiati, Franco. "La 'Carriera del libertino' di Strawinski accolta con successo al Festival musicale." *Corriere della sera*, September 12, 1951.
Adorno, Theodor W. *Philosophy of Modern Music*. Translated by Anne G. Mitchell and Wesley V. Blomster. New York: Seaburg, 1973.
Andriessen, Louis, and Elmer Schönberger. *The Apollonian Clockwork on Stravinsky*. Translated by Jeff Hamburg. New York: Oxford University Press, 1989.
Ansen, Alan. *The Table Talk of W. H. Auden*. Princeton, NJ: Ontario Review, 1990.
Ashman, Mike. Notes for *The Rake's Progress*. DVD. Glyndebourne Festival Production. Opus Arte 1062D (2010): 4–5.
Auden, W. H. "Craftsman, Artist, Genius." *The Observer*, April 11, 1971.
———. *The Dyer's Hand*. New York: Vintage International, 1989.
———. "The Ironic Hero: Some Reflections on Don Quixote." *Horizon* 20 (1949): 86–94.
———, ed. *The Living Thoughts of Kierkegaard*. Bloomington: Indiana University Press, 1952.
———. "Opera Addict: At the Root of the Addiction Is an Understanding of Willfulness." *Vogue*, July 1948.
———, ed. *Poets of the English Language*. 5 vols. New York: Viking Press, 1950.
Auden, W. H., and Chester Kallman. *Libretti and Other Dramatic Writings: 1939–1973*. Edited by Edward Mendelson. London: Faber and Faber, 1993.
Austin, William. "Stravinsky's 'Fortunate Continuities' and 'Legitimate Accidents,' 1882-1982." In *Stravinsky Retrospectives*, eds. Ethan Haimo and Paul Johnson, 1-14. Lincoln: University of Nebraska, 1987.
Babbitt, Milton. "Remarks on Recent Stravinsky." *Perspectives of New Music* 2 (1964): 35–55.
Balanchine, George. "The Met at Work—Directing a Rake." *Metropolitan Opera Program* (1953).
Barthes, Roland. *The Rustle of Language*. Translated by Richard Howard. New York: Hill and Wang, 1986.
Becker, Howard S. *Art Worlds*. Berkeley: University of California Press, 1982.
Beal, Amy C. *New Music, New Allies: American Experimental Music in Germany from Zero Hour to Reunification*. Berkeley: University of California Press, 2006.
Ben Chaim, Daphna. *Distance in the Theater: The Aesthetics of Audience Response*. Ann Arbor: UMI Research Press, 1984.
Benjamin, Walter. "The Work of Art in the Age of Mechanical Reproduction." In *Illuminations*, edited by Hannah Arendt, 217-51. New York: Schocken Books, 1968.
Berlin, Isaiah. *The Hedgehog and the Fox: An Essay on Tolstoy's View of History*. London: Weidenfeld & Nicolson, 1953.
Bindman, David. *Hogarth and His Times*. Berkeley: University of California Press, 1997.
Blair, John G. *The Poetic Art of W. H. Auden*. Princeton, NJ: Princeton University Press, 1965.
Bouchourechliev, Andre. *Stravinsky*. Translated by Martin Cooper. New York: Holmes and Meier, 1987.

Boulez, Pierre. "Blow up the Opera Houses!" Interview in *Der Spiegel*, September 25, 1967.
———. "Éventuellement . . . ," *La Revue musicale* 212 (May1952). Translated as "Possibly . . ." in *Stocktakings of an Apprentice*. Translated by Stephen Walsh, 111–40. New York: Oxford University Press, 1991.
Bourdieu, Pierre. *Distinction: A Social Critique of the Judgment of Taste*. Translated by Richard Nice. Cambridge, MA: Harvard University Press, 1984.
———. *The Field of Cultural Production: Essays on Art and Literature*. Edited and introduced by Randal Johnson. Cambridge, MA: Polity Press, 1993.
———. *Outline of a Theory of Practice*. Translated by Richard Nice. New York: Cambridge University Press, 1977.
———. *The Rules of Art: Genesis and Structure of the Literary Field*. Translated by Susan Emanuel. Stanford, CA: Stanford University Press, 1995.
Brecht, Bertolt. *Brecht on Theater: The Development of an Aesthetic*. Edited and translated by John Willett. New York: Hill and Wang, 1964.
Briggs, John. "Recording of 'Rake.'" *New York Times*, November 15, 1953.
Cairns, David. "Two Moral Comedies." *Sunday Times*, July 6, 1975.
Cantwell, Anne-Marie, and Diana diZerega Wall. *Unearthing Gotham: The Archaeology of New York City*. New Haven, CT: Yale University Press, 2001.
Caplat, Moran. *Dinghies to Divas*. New York: Harper Collins, 1985.
Carpenter, Humphrey. *W. H. Auden: A Biography*. Boston: Houghton Mifflin, 1981.
Carr, Maureen. *Multiple Masks: Neoclassicism in Stravinsky's Works on Greek Subjects*. Lincoln: University of Nebraska Press, 2002.
Carter, Chandler. "The Progress in *The Rake's* Return." PhD diss., Graduate Center of the City University of New York, 1995.
———. "*The Rake's Progress* and Stravinsky's Return: The Composer's Evolving Approach to Setting Text." *Journal of the American Musicological Society* 63, no. 3 (2010): 553–640.
———. "Stravinsky's 'Special Sense': The Rhetorical Use of Tonality in *The Rake's Progress*." *Music Theory Spectrum* 19, no. 1 (1997): 55–80.
———. "Stravinsky's Truth and Mozart's Lies: Composers' Use of Musical Signs to Manipulate Theatrical Distance." *European Journal for Semiotic Studies* 13 (2001): 601–22.
Chew, Geoffrey. "Pastoral and Neoclassicism: A Reinterpretation of Auden's and Stravinsky's *Rake's Progress*." *Cambridge Opera Journal* 5 (1993): 239–63.
Clark, Thekla. *Wystan and Chester*. New York: Columbia University Press, 1997.
Coleman, Peter. *The Liberal Conspiracy: The Congress for Cultural Freedom and the Struggle for the Mind of Postwar Europe*. New York: Free Press, 1989.
Cone, Edward T. "Stravinsky: The Progress of a Method." *Perspectives of New Music* 1, no. 1 (1962): 18–26.
Conrad, Peter. "The Libertine's Progress." In *Don Giovanni: Myths of Seduction and Betrayal*, edited by Jonathan Miller, 81–92. New York: Schocken Books, 1990.
Cooke, Deryck. "'The Rake' and the 18th Century." *Musical Times* 103 (1962): 20–23.
Craft, Robert. "An Appreciation of the Music." In liner notes for *Igor Stravinsky: The Rake's Progress*. Columbia Records SL 125 (1953): 2–4.
———, ed. *Dearest Bubushkin: The Correspondence of Vera and Igor Stravinsky, 1921–1954, with Excerpts from Vera Stravinsky's Diaries, 1922–1971*. London: Thames and Hudson, 1985.
———. *An Improbable Life*. Nashville: Vanderbilt University Press, 2002.
———. "A Note on the Sketches and Two Versions of the Libretto." In Paul Griffiths, *Igor Stravinsky: The Rake's Progress*, 18–30.
———. "On a Misunderstood Collaboration: Assisting Stravinsky." *Atlantic Monthly* (December 1982): 68, 70–74.

———. "A Personal Preface." *Score* 20 (1957): 7–13.
———. "Reflections on 'The Rake's Progress.'" *Score and I.M.A. Magazine* 9 (1954): 24–30.
———. "Robert Craft on Stephen Walsh's *Stravinsky: The Second Exile*." Naxos.com (2006).
———. "Roland-Manuel and the *Poetics of Music*." *Perspectives of New Music* 21, no. 1–2 (1982–83): 487–505.
———. *Stravinsky: The Chronicle of a Friendship: 1948/1971*. New York: Vintage Books, 1972; revised and expanded Nashville: Vanderbilt University Press, 1994.
———. *Stravinsky: Glimpses of a Life*. New York: St. Martin's Press, 1992.
———, ed. *A Stravinsky Scrapbook, 1940–1971*. London: Thames and Hudson, 1983.
———, ed. *Stravinsky: Selected Correspondence*. 3 vols. New York: Alfred A. Knopf, 1982–85.
———. "Words for Music Perhaps." Review of *The Complete Works of W. H. Auden: Libretti and Other Dramatic Writings (1939–1973)*. *The New York Review of Books* 41, no. 18 (1994): 54–58.
Cumming, Naomi. "The Subjectivities of 'Erbarme Dich.'" *Music Analysis* 16 (1997): 5–44.
Daily Mail. "'I Don't Like It, Says Founder of Glyndebourne.'" August 28, 1953.
Davenport-Hines, Richard. *Auden*. New York: Pantheon, 1995.
Dent, Edward. *Mozart's Operas: A Critical Study*. New York: Oxford University Press, 1947.
Downes, Olin. "'Rake's Progress' Has U.S. Premiere." *New York Times*, February 15, 1953.
———. "'Rake's Progress' of Stravinsky Makes Season's Debut at 'Met.'" *New York Times*, January 27, 1954.
Drushkin, Mikhail. *Igor Stravinsky: His Personality, Works and Views*. Translated by Martin Cooper. New York: Cambridge University Press, 1983.
Ebert, Peter. *In This Theatre of Man's Life*. Sussex: The Book Guild, 1999.
Engelhardt, Jürgen. *Gestus und Verfremdung: Studien zum Musiktheater bei Stravinsky und Brecht/Weill*. Munich: Katzbichler, 1984.
Flanner, Janet (writing as "Gênet"). "Letter from Paris." *New Yorker*, May 31, 1952.
Fleisher, Frederic. Untitled Review. *Christian Science Monitor*, May 8, 1961.
Gide, André. "The Evolution of the Theater." Translated by Jackson Mathews. In *My Theater: Five Plays and an Essay*, 259–74. New York: Alfred A. Knopf, 1952.
Giroud, Vincent. *Nicolas Nabokov: A Life in Freedom and Music*. New York: Oxford University Press, 2015.
Glass, Philip. "Keynote Speech at 2003 *Opera America* Conference." *Opera America Newsline* 12 (September 2002): 15.
———. *Music by Philip Glass*. New York: Harper & Row, 1987.
Goethe, Johann Wolfgang von. *Goethe's Faust*. Translated by Walter Kaufman. New York: Vintage, 1961.
Goléa, Antoine. *Rencontres avec Pierre Boulez*. Paris: Julliard, 1958.
Goodwin, Noel. "So-Shy Film Genius Brings New Magic to the Opera Stage." *Daily Express*, April 24, 1961.
Greenberg, Clement. "Avant Garde and Kitsch." *Partisan Review* 6, no. 5 (1939): 34–49.
Griffiths, Paul. *Igor Stravinsky: The Rake's Progress*. New York: Cambridge University Press, 1982.
———. *Modern Music: The Avant Garde since 1945*. New York: George Braziller, 1981.
Grünbacher, Armin. "Cold-War Economics: The Use of Marshall Plan Counterpart Funds in Germany, 1948–1960." *Central European History* 45 (2012): 697–716.
Habermas, Jürgen. *The Structural Transformation of the Public Sphere: An Inquiry into a Category of Bourgeois Society*. Cambridge, MA: MIT Press, 1989.
Hatten, Robert. *Musical Meaning in Beethoven: Markedness, Correlation, and Interpretation*. Bloomington: Indiana University Press, 1994.

Henze, Hans Werner. *Bohemian Fifths*. Princeton, NJ: Princeton University Press, 1999.
Heyworth, Peter. "The Rake's Triumph." *Observer Review*, June 29, 1975.
"Hockney to Hogarth: A Rake's Progress." Whitworth Art Gallery: University of Manchester, n.d.
Homans, Jennifer. "Is Ballet Over?" *New Republic*, October 13, 2010.
Hook, Sydney. *Out of Step: An Unquiet Life in the Twentieth Century*. New York: Harper, 1987.
Hope-Wallace, Phillip. "'Rake's Progress' at Glyndebourne." *Manchester Guardian*, July 18, 1954.
Horgan, Paul. *Encounters with Stravinsky*. New York: Farrar, Straus and Giroux, 1972.
Horlacher, Gretchen. "Metric Irregularity in *Les noces*: The Problem of Periodicity." *Journal of Music Theory* 39 (1995): 285-309.
Hulme, Thomas Ernest. *The Collected Writings of T. E. Hulme*. Edited by Karen Csengeri. Oxford: Clarendon Press, 1994.
———. *Speculations: Essays on Humanism and the Philosophy of Art*. Edited by Herbert Read. New York: Harcourt Brace, 1924.
Hunter, Mary. "Igor and Tom: History and Destiny in *The Rake's Progress*," *Opera Quarterly* 7, no. 4 (1990/91): 38-52.
Immendorff, Jörg. "Jörg Immendorff to My Studio Ghosts," in *The Rake's Progress—Salzburg*. Salzburg Festival, 1996.
Jameson, Frederic. *Brecht and Method*. New York: Verso, 1998.
Joachim, Heinz. "Stravinskij contra Sartre—Der respektvolle 'Wüstling.'" *Die Welt* (Hamburg), November 15, 1951.
Joseph, Charles M. *Stravinsky Inside Out*. New Haven, CT: Yale University Press, 2001.
Jung, Carl S. *The Collected Works of C. G. Jung*. Translated by R. F. C. Hull. Princeton, NJ: Princeton University Press, 1969.
———. *The Portable Jung*. Edited by Joseph Campbell. New York: Penguin Books, 1971.
Karlinsky, Simon. "Igor Stravinsky and Russian Preliterate Theater." In Pasler, *Confronting Stravinsky: Man, Musician and Modernist*, 3-15. Berkeley: University of California Press, 1986.
Kerman, Joseph. "Opera à la mode." *Hudson Review* (Winter 1954): 560-77. Revised and incorporated into *Opera as Drama*, 190-202. Berkeley: University of California Press, 1988.
Kessler, Daniel. *Sarah Caldwell: The First Woman of Opera*. Lanham, MD: Scarecrow Press, 2008.
Kierkegaard, Søren. *Either/Or*, Part I. Edited and translated by Howard V. Hong and Edna H. Hong. Princeton, NJ: Princeton University Press, 1987.
Koestenbaum, Wayne. *The Queen's Throat: Opera, Homosexuality, and the Mystery of Desire*. New York: Simon and Schuster, 1993.
Kolodin, Irving. "Huge Crowd Greets Stravinsky's Opera." *Los Angeles Times*, February 15, 1953.
———. "Stravinsky in the 'King's' English." *Los Angeles Times*, n.d. (Paul Sacher Foundation).
Kostelanetz, Richard. *John Cage Ex(plain)ed*. New York: Schirmer Books, 1996.
Kramer, Jonathan. "The Nature and Origins of Musical Postmodernism." In *Postmodern Music/Postmodern Thought*, eds. Judy Lochhead and Joseph Auner. New York: Routledge, 2002.
Kramer, Lawrence. *Opera and Modern Culture: Wagner and Strauss*. Berkeley: University of California Press, 2004.
Leibowitz, René. "Béla Bartók, ou la possibilité du compromise dans la musique contemporaine." *Les Temps Modernes* 3, no. 25 (1947): 705-34.

———. "Music Chronicle—Two Composers: A Letter from Hollywood." *Partisan Review* 15, no. 3 (1948): 361–65.
———. *Schoenberg and His School.* Translated by Dika Newlin. New York: Philosophical Library, 1949.
———. "Stravinsky ou le choix de la misère musicale." *Les Temps Modernes* 1 (1946): 1320–36.
Lessem, Alan. "Schoenberg, Stravinsky, and Neoclassicism." *Musical Quarterly* 68 (1982): 527–42.
Levitz, Tamara. *Modernist Mysteries: Perséphone.* New York: Oxford University Press, 2012.
Libman, Lillian. *Music at the Close.* New York: Norton, 1972.
Loney, Glenn. "Elegy for a Bacchic Rake." *Opera Monthly* 4, no. 11 (1992): 9–16.
Lupishko, Marina. "'Rejoicing Discovery' Revisited: Re-accentuation in Russian Folklore and Stravinsky's Music." *Ex-tempore* 13, no. 2 (2007): 1–36.
McCarthy, Mary. *Between Friends: The Correspondence of Hannah Arendt and Mary McCarthy, 1949–1975.* New York: Harcourt Brace, 1995.
McFadden, George. "*The Rake's Progress*: A Note on the Libretto." *Hudson Review* 8, no. 1 (1955): 105–12.
Malmnäs, Eva Sundler. "Art as Inspiration." In *Ingmar Bergman and the Arts. Nordic Theatre Studies* 11 (1998): 34–45.
Mann, Thomas. *Doctor Faustus: The Life of the German Composer Adrian Leverkühn, as Told by a Friend.* Translated by John E. Woods. New York: Alfred A. Knopf, 1997.
———. *The Story of a Novel.* New York: Alfred A. Knopf, 1961.
Mason, Colin. "Stravinsky's Opera." *Music and Letters* 33 (1952): 1–9.
"Masterpieces of English Painting: William Hogarth, John Constable, J.M.W. Turner." Exhibition catalogue. Chicago: The Art Institute of Chicago, 1946.
Mayer, Martin. "Igor Makes a Record." *Esquire* (December 1953): 145, 209–13; excerpted in *SPD*, 416–18.
Mendelson, Edward. *Early Auden.* New York: Farrar, Straus and Giroux, 1981.
———. *Later Auden.* New York: Farrar, Straus and Giroux, 1999.
Messing, Scott. *Neoclassicism in Music: From the Genesis of the Concept through the Schoenberg/Stravinsky Polemic.* Ann Arbor, MI: University Microfilms International, 1988.
Milward, Alan S. *The Reconstruction of Western Europe, 1945–51.* Berkeley: University of California Press, 1984.
Mitchell, Donald. *The Language of Modern Music.* London: Faber and Faber, 1963.
Nabokov, Nicolas. "The Atonal Trail: A Communication." *Partisan Review* 15 (1948): 580–81.
———. *Bagázh: Memoirs of a Russian Cosmopolitan.* New York: Atheneum, 1975.
———. "The Case of Dmitri Shostakovich." *Harper's Bazaar* (March 1943).
———. "The Gracious Master." Typescript. Nicolas Nabokov Papers, Beineke Rare Book and Manuscript Library, Yale University.
———. "Igor Stravinsky." *Atlantic Monthly* (November 1949): 21–7; expanded and reprinted as the chapters "Christmas with Stravinsky" and "Stravinsky in Hollywood" in *Old Friends and New Music.*
———. "The Music Purge." *Politics* 5, no. 2 (1948).
———. "Music under Dictatorship," *Atlantic Monthly* (January 1942).
———. *Old Friends and New Music.* Boston: Little, Brown, 1951.
———. "Russian Music after the Purge." *Partisan Review* 16, no. 8 (1949).
———. "Sergei Prokofiev." *Atlantic Monthly* (July 1942).
———. "Stravinsky's 'Rake' Has Its Surprises." *New York Herald Tribune*, November 30, 1951.
Nattiez, Jean-Jacques, ed. *The Boulez-Cage Correspondence.* Translated and edited by Robert Samuels. New York: Cambridge University Press, 1993.

Newcomb, Anthony. "Sound and Feeling." *Critical Inquiry* 10, no. 4 (1984): 614–43.
Newman, Ernst. Untitled review. *Sunday Times*, August 30, 1953.
Opera News. "Balanchine—Theory of the Staging." February 9, 1953, 11.
Oppenheim, Hans. "Carl Ebert." *Glyndebourne Festival Program* (1953): 26–30.
Ortega y Gasset, José. *"The Dehumanization of Art" and Other Writings on Art and Culture*. Garden City, NY: Doubleday, 1956.
Palmer, Tony. Transcribed outtakes from documentary film *Aspects of Stravinsky* (1982). Paul Sacher Foundation.
Parmenter, Ross. "The World of Music: Stravinsky Plans Opera." *New York Times*, December 7, 1947.
Pasler, Jann, ed. *Confronting Stravinsky: Man, Musician and Modernist*. Berkeley: University of California Press, 1986.
Peyser, Joan. "Stravinsky-Craft, Inc." *American Scholar* 52, no. 4 (1983): 513–18.
Porter, Andrew. "Glyndebourne: The Rake's Progress by Stravinsky." *Financial Times*, July 16, 1954.
Raftopoulos, Rigas. "Italian Economic Reconstruction and the Marshall Plan: A Reassessment." *Politische Italien-Forschung Occasional Papers* 3 (2009): 5–29.
Robinson, Paul. "The Opera Queen: A Voice from the Closet." *Cambridge Opera Journal* 6, no. 3 (1994): 283–91.
Rogers, Lynne. "Stravinsky's Alternative Approach to Counterpoint." PhD diss., Princeton University, 1989.
Roose, Henk, and Alexander Vander Stichele. "Living Room vs. Concert Hall: Patterns of Music Consumption in Flanders." *Social Forces* 89, no. 1 (2010): 185–207.
Ross, Alex. *The Rest Is Noise: Listening to the Twentieth Century*. New York: Picador, 2007.
Rothstein, Edward. "Jerry Hadley Is Stravinsky's 'Rake' in a New Production at Salzburg." *New York Times*, August 3, 1994.
Sargent, Wintrop. Untitled review. *New Yorker*, July 15, 1967.
Sartre, Jean-Paul. *The Emotions*. Translated by Bernard Frechtman. New York: Philosophical Library, 1948.
Saunders, Frances Stonor. *The Cultural Cold War*. New York: New Press, 2013.
Schain, Martin A., ed. *The Marshall Plan: Fifty Years After*. New York: Palgrave Macmillan, 2001.
Scherliess, Volker. "Inspiration und fabrication: Beobachten zu Igor Strawinsky's Arbeit an 'The Rake's Progress.'" In *Quellen Studien II: Zwölf Komponisten des 20. Jahrhunderts*, edited by Felix Meyer, 39–72. Winterthur: Amadeus Verlag, 1993.
Schiff, David. "Redeeming the Rake." *Atlantic Monthly* (November 1997): 136–39.
Schlesinger, Arthur Jr. *The Vital Center: The Politics of Freedom*. Boston: Houghton Mifflin, 1949.
Schoenberg, Arnold. *Drei Satiren*. Vienna: Universal Edition, 1926.
———. *A Schoenberg Reader: Documents of a Life*. Edited by Joseph Auner. New Haven, CT: Yale University Press, 2003.
———. *Style and Idea*. Berkeley: University of California Press, 1984.
Scholl, Tim. *From Petipa to Balanchine: Classical Revival and the Modernization of Ballet*. New York: Routledge, 1994.
Scull, Christina. *The Soane Hogarths*. London: Sir John Soane's Museum, 1991.
Scruton, Roger. *Art and Imagination: A Study in the Philosophy of Mind*. London: Methuen, 1974.
Shesgren, Sean, ed. *Engravings by Hogarth*. New York: Dover, 1973.
Shestov, Lev. *Kierkegaard et la philosophie existentielle*. Paris: Librarie J. Vrin, 1936.

Shreffler, Anne C. "Ideologies of Serialism: Stravinsky's *Threni* and the Congress for Cultural Freedom." In *Music and the Aesthetics of Modernity*, edited by Karol Berger and Anthony Newcomb, 217–45. Cambridge, MA: Harvard University Press, 2005.
Smith, Roberta. "Melding Figures Real and Imagined to Fill a Tableau." *New York Times*, January 10, 1997, A24.
Sprouts, Leslie A. "The 1945 Stravinsky Debates: Nigg, Messiaen, and the Early Cold War in France." *The Journal of Musicology* 26, no. 1 (2009): 85–131.
Smith, Cecil. "This Is an Electric Progress." (PSS).
Stadlen, Peter. "Element of Pop in 'Rake's Progress.'" *Daily Telegraph*, June 23, 1975.
Stephan, Rudolf. "Zur Deutung von Strawinskys Neoklassizismus." In *Vom musikalischen Denken: Gesammelte Vorträge*. Mainz: Schott, 1985, 243–48.
Stein, Leonard. "Schoenberg and 'Kleine Modernsky.'" In *Confronting Stravinsky: Man, Musician, and Modernist*, edited by Jann Pasler, 310–24. Berkeley: University of California Press, 1988.
Steinberg, Michael. "Mod 'Rake' Bold, Fantastic." *Boston Globe*, March 31, 1967, 18.
———. "Re-Raking the Rake: Best Sort of Caldwell." *Boston Globe*, April 9, 1967, A29.
Steinweis, Alan E. *Art, Ideology, and Economics in Nazi Germany*. Chapel Hill: University of North Carolina Press, 1993.
Steptoe, Andrew. *The Mozart-Da Ponte Operas: The Cultural and Musical Background to Le Nozze di Figaro, Don Giovanni, and Così fan tutte*. New York: Oxford University Press, 1988.
Sternfeld, F. W. *The Birth of Opera*. New York: Oxford University Press, 1995.
Straus, Joseph N. "Harmony and Voice Leading in the Music of Stravinsky." *Music Theory Spectrum* 36, no. 1 (2014): 1–33.
———. *Introduction to Post-Tonal Theory*, 4th Ed. New York: Norton, 2016.
———. "The Progress of a Motive in Stravinsky's *The Rake's Progress*." *Journal of Musicology* 9, no. 2 (1991): 165–85.
———. *Remaking the Past*. Cambridge, MA: Harvard University Press, 1992.
———. *Stravinsky's Late Music*. New York: Cambridge University Press, 2001.
———. "Three Stravinsky Analyses." *Music Theory Online* (2012): 18.4.6.
Stravinsky, Igor. *An Autobiography*. New York: Norton, 1962.
———. *Cantata*. New York: Boosey & Hawkes, 1952.
———. "The Composer's View." In Griffiths, *The Rake's Progress*, 2–4. Part I, "A programme note" originally published in liner notes, *Igor Stravinsky: The Rake's Progress*. Sony Classical SM2K 46 299 (1964).
———. *Poetics of Music*. Translated by Arthur Knodel and Ingolf Dahl. Cambridge, MA: Harvard University Press, 1970.
———. *The Rake's Progress*. Libretto by W. H. Auden and Chester Kallman. New York: Boosey & Hawkes, 1951.
———. *The Rake's Progress*, Chorus and Orchestra of the Teatro alla Scala; Igor Stravinsky, conductor. Fonit Cetra (DOC 29) 1982.
———. "Reflections on the *Rake*: Stravinsky—The Origin of the Music." *Opera News*, 9 (February 1953): 8. Originally published in Italian translation from the typescript "About *The Rake's Progress*" as "Como ho composto *The Rake's Progress*" in *La Biennale di Venezia* (1951): 8.
———. *Themes and Conclusions*. Berkeley: University of California Press, 1972.
Stravinsky, Igor, and Robert Craft. *Conservations with Stravinsky*. Garden City, NY: Doubleday, 1959. Reprint, Berkeley: University of California Press, 1980. Citations refer to the Doubleday edition.

Stravinsky, Igor, and Robert Craft. "'Dear Bob[sky]' (Stravinsky's Letters to Robert Craft, 1944–1949)." *Musical Quarterly* 65, no. 3 (1959): 392–439.

———. *Dialogues and a Diary*. Garden City, NY: Doubleday, 1963.

Stravinsky, Igor, and Robert Craft. *Expositions and Developments*. Garden City, NY: Doubleday, 1962. Reprint, Berkeley: University of California Press, 1981. Citations refer to the Doubleday edition.

Stravinsky, Igor, and Robert Craft. *Memories and Commentaries*. Garden City, NY: Doubleday, 1960. Reprint, Berkeley: University of California Press, 1981. Citations refer to the Doubleday edition.

Stravinsky, Igor, and Robert Craft. *Retrospectives and Conclusions*. New York: Alfred A. Knopf, 1969.

Stravinsky, Igor, and Robert Craft. *Themes and Episodes*. New York: Alfred A. Knopf, 1966.

Stravinsky, Vera, and Robert Craft. *Stravinsky in Pictures and Documents*. New York: Simon and Schuster, 1978.

Stravinsky: The Rake's Progress—Oedipus Rex. New York: Riverrun Press, 1991.

Striggio, Alessandro. *L'Orfeo*. Translated by Nigel Rogers. London: EMI Records Ltd, 1993.

Taruskin, Richard. "Back to Whom? Neoclassicism as Ideology." *19th-Century Music* 16 (1992–3): 286–302.

———. *The Danger of Music and Other Anti-Utopian Essays*. Berkeley: University of California Press, 2008.

———. "In From the Cold." *Times Literary Supplement*, August 5, 2016, 3–5.

———. *Oxford History of Western Music*, 6 vols. New York: Oxford University Press, 2005.

———. *Stravinsky and the Russian Traditions: A Biography of the Works through Mavra*, 2 vols. Berkeley: University of California Press, 1996.

———. "Stravinsky and the Subhuman—A Myth of the Twentieth Century: 'The Rite of Spring,' the Tradition of the New, and 'The Music Itself.'" In *Defining Russian Musically*, 360–467. Princeton, NJ: Princeton University Press, 1997.

———. "Stravinsky's 'Rejoicing Discovery' and What It Meant: In Defense of His Notorious Text Setting." In *Stravinsky Retrospectives*, edited by Ethan Haimo and Paul Johnson, 162–99. Lincoln: University of Nebraska, 1987.

Thomson, Virgil. *A Virgil Thomson Reader*. Boston: Houghton Mifflin, 1981.

Time. "The Rite of Autumn." February 23, 1953.

The Times. "Moral View of 'The Rake.'" June 16, 1975.

Tippins, Sherill. *February House*. New York: Houghton Mifflin, 2005.

Tomlinson, Gary. *Metaphysical Song: An Essay on Opera*. Princeton, NJ: Princeton University Press, 1999.

Van den Toorn, Pieter C. *The Music of Igor Stravinsky*. New Haven, CT: Yale University Press, 1983.

———. *Music, Politics and the Academy*. Berkeley: University of California Press, 1995.

———. "Stravinsky, Adorno, and the Art of Displacement." *Musical Quarterly* 87, no. 3 (2004): 468–509.

———. *Stravinsky and "The Rite of Spring": The Beginnings of a Musical Language*. Berkeley: University of California Press, 1987.

———. "Stravinsky, *Les Noces*, and the Prohibition against Expressive Timing." *Journal of Musicology* 20, no. 2 (2003): 285–304.

———. "Stravinsky Re-Barred." *Music Analysis* 7, no. 2 (1988): 165–95.

Van den Toorn, Pieter C., and John McGinness. *Stravinsky and the Russian Period: Sound and Legacy of a Musical Idiom*. New York: Cambridge University Press, 2012.

Von Franz, Marie-Louise. "The Process of Individuation." In *Man and His Symbols*, edited by C. G. Jung, 157–254. Garden City, NY: Laurel, 1964.
Wagner, Richard. *Wagner on Music and Drama*. Selected and arranged by Albert Goldman and Evert Sprinchon. Translated by H. Ashton Ellis. New York: Da Capo, 1988.
Walsh, Stephen. *Stravinsky—A Creative Spring: Russia and France, 1882–1934*. New York: Alfred A. Knopf, 1999.
———. *Stravinsky—The Second Exile: France and America, 1934–1971*. New York: Alfred A. Knopf, 2006.
Watkins, Glenn. "Canon and Stravinsky's Late Style." In Pasler, *Confronting Stravinsky: Man, Musician and Modernist*, 217–46. Berkeley: University of California Press, 1986.
———. *Pyramids at the Louvre: Music, Culture and Collage from Stravinsky to the Postmodernists*. Cambridge, MA: Harvard University Press, 1994.
Weiher-Waege, H. "'The Rake's Progress': The New Stravinsky Gleamingly Staged by Dr. Günther Rennert." *Hamburg Free Press*, November 15, 1951.
Wellens, Ian. *Music on the Frontline: Nicolas Nabokov's Struggle against Communism and Middlebrow Culture*. Burlington, VT: Ashgate, 2002.
Wilson, Edmund. *The Fifties: From Notebooks and Diaries of the Period*. New York: Farrar, Straus and Giroux, 1986.
Wiskari, Werner. "Ingmar Bergman's Way with 'The Rake.'" *New York Times*, May 19, 1961.
Yates, Peter. "The Rake's Progress." *Arts and Architecture* (June 1953): 37–40.
Žižek, Slavoj, and Mladen Dolar. *Opera's Second Death*. New York: Routledge, 2002.

INDEX

Adams, John: *Nixon in China*, 319
Adès, Thomas, 319
Adorno, Theodor, 13, 33, 41–43, 311–12; Mann, as character model for, 41–42, 311; *Philosophy of Modern Music*, 34, 43
agape (Christian love), 85–86, 94
Altman, Georges, 253
American Federation of Labor (AFL), 248
American Intellectuals for Freedom (AIF), 245, 247
American Opera Society, 292n5
Ampenova, Rufina, 287
analysis: formal, 12–13, 100 (*see also* close reading); pluralistic, 102, 119; stratified, 118–19, 122n18
Ansen, Alan, 62
Argento, Dominick, 317
Armistead, Horace, 272, 275
Art Institute of Chicago, ix, 23–24, 30, 45n9, 57, 59
artist. *See* freedom: artistic ("free" artist); Great Artist
Ashman, Mike, 274
Ashley, Robert, 318
Aspen Music Festival, 302, 303
Atlantic Monthly, 34, 39
Auden, Wystan H., 22, 51, 263, 314; as conceptualizer, 56–57, 76, 79; death of, 313; *Delia*, 7, 15, 50, 54; *Delia*, planning for, 302–3; disillusionment with politics, 43, 53; on expressiveness of art, 55–56; hygiene, 40, 56, 73n17; image in productions, 291, 295n64; Kallman, collaboration with, 4, 6–7, 50, 65–69, 71, 78, 238; Kallman, relationship with, 53, 69–72, 75n55; on opera: as expression of free will, 3, 5, 7, 83, 93, 180; on opera: as immediate, 53–54; opera, love of, 4, 53, 69–70; sociologists, dislike of, 13, 15, 43, 302; as versifier, stylized or ritual, 52–53, 54–55, 67, 156; Wagner, affection for, 20, 55, 73n16. *See also under* Kierkegaard; Nabokov; and under *Rake's Progress*: collaboration with Stravinsky; premiere of
Auden, Wystan H., works of: *Age of Anxiety*, 53, 71, 79; "Anthem for St. Cecilia's Day," 54, 73n12; *The Ascent of F6*, 53, 95n31; "Balaam and his Ass," 79; *Dance of Death*, 53; *The Dog Beneath the Skin*, 53; *Elegy J. F. K.*, 50; *For the Time Being*, 54; "The Ironic Hero" 88, 90–92; *Living Thoughts of Kierkegaard* (introduction), 78, 88–89; "New Year Letter," 79; *Night Mail*, 52, 54; "Opera Addict," 4, 15, 70, 321; *The Orators* 79; *Poets of the English Language* (editor), 50, 301; "The Sea and Mirror" 79, 85–86, 90–91. *See also* Henze: *Bassarids, Elegy for Young Lovers*; Nabokov: *Love's Labour's Lost*; and *Rake's Progress*: libretto
authenticity, 35, 311, 315

Babbitt, Milton, 315
Bach, J. S., 149, 316; *Art of the Fugue*, 122n11; *Well-Tempered Clavier*, 313
Balanchine, George, 6, 13, 39, 40, 54, 97, 123, 162, 314; as choreographer, 40, 50, 304–5, 308, 320; as stage director, 41, 231n4, 270, 272, 273, 275, 283–84
ballet, 152, 316, 317; "death" of, 5, 320
Ballets Russes, 32, 52, 170n10
Ballets Russes de Monte Carlo, 32
Ballo, Ferdinando, 256, 257–58
Balthus, Balthasar, 259
Barnes, Dr. Albert, 32
Barthes, Roland, 299
Bartok, Bela, 34, 47n50, 102, 124
Bean, Betty, 242, 251, 255–56, 257, 302
Becker, Howard, 17n32
Beethoven, Ludwig van, 35, 314, 316; late quartets, 313
Beggar's Opera, The (John Gay), 8, 27, 58
Bellini, Vincenzo, 178

337

Benjamin, Walter, 33, 35, 58
Benois, Alexandre, 152
Bérard, Christian, 201
Berg, Alban, 10, 29, 34, 124; *Lulu*, 5, 253; *Wozzeck*, 5, 94, 289, 306, 324n63
Bergling, Birger, 281, 282, 282-83
Bergman, Ingmar, 155, 202, 278-87, 292, 294n29, 294n41; *Magic Flute* (film), 287, 294n31
Berio, Luciano, 7, 317, 323n28
Berlin (city): Arts Festival, 254, 304, 306-8, 310, 323nn28-30; Congress for Cultural Freedom (1950), 38, 247-48, 250-51; Deutsch Oper, 313; "peace" conference, 245; Wall, 307, 310
Berlin, Isaiah, 32, 34, 251, 324n51
Berman, Eugene, 39-40, 259, 272
Bernstein, Leonard, 265n28, 316; *Candide*, 267n69
La Biennale. *See* Venice International Festival of Contemporary Music
Bing, Rudolph, 269, 293n7
Blake (Nabokov), Patricia, 6, 40, 123, 245, 247; on Brothel scene, 162-63, 168, 169
Bohlen, Charles, 32, 34, 244, 248, 309
Bolcom, William, 318
Bondy, François, 253
Boosey & Hawkes, 24, 25, 123, 238, 242, 258, 264n10, 266n57, 322n22; formal agreement with Stravinsky, 27, 241; *Rake's Progress* libretto commission, 27, 61-62, 74n27, 256. *See also* Ampenova; Bean; Gishford; Hawkes; Roth
Boston Symphony Orchestra, 248, 305
Boston University, 275, 293n24
Bouchourechliev, Andre, 152
Boulanger, Nadia, 19, 30-31, 39, 44, 46n36, 130
Boulez, Pierre, 5, 15, 30, 48n67, 150, 289, 311, 313, 324n63
Bourdieu, Pierre, 12-13, 37-38, 98-99, 304. *See also* disinterestedness, disposition, "feel for the game," habitus and field
bourgeois culture, 8, 34, 42, 57, 59, 72n9, 216; bourgeoisie, 58, 275, 304. *See also* middlebrow
Braden, Tom, 253
Brandt, Willy, 306, 323n30

Brecht, Bertolt, 53, 318; alienation/distance, 150-52, 156, 170n12, 284, 299; *Die Dreigroschenoper*, 58, 70, 169n8
Britten, Benjamin, 26, 45n11, 54; *Billy Budd*, 240, 264n10, 306, 316; church parables, 317; *Hymn to St. Cecilia*, 54, 73n12; *Midsummer Night's Dream*, 318; *Noye's Fludde*, 317; *Paul Bunyan*, 54; *Rape of Lucretia*, 26, 46n20
Brooklyn College, 69, 71
Brown, Irving, 248-49, 250
Bugs Bunny, 201
Bunyan, John, *Pilgrim's Progress*, 89
Burnham, James, 244, 248, 249, 250
Byrd, William, 27

Cage, John, 15; *Europeras*, 318
Caldwell, Sarah, 201, 202, 232n16, 287-89, 292, 294n50, 295n51, 299
Cambridge University, 292n3
Camus, Albert, 244
Caplat, Moran, 274-75
Carr, Maureen, 73n16, 324n53
Carter, Elliot, 7, 32, 323n28
Casals, Pablo, 310
CCF. *See* Congress for Cultural Freedom
Central City Opera, 238, 241, 243, 258, 264n10, 269, 275
Central Intelligence Agency (CIA), 244, 247, 248-50, 265n32, 304, 308, 311; use of "fronts," 245, 249, 253, 266n44, 307, 323n29, 324n46
Chamber Art Society, 123-24
Chew, Geoffrey, 89-90, 95n47
Christie, John, 268
"classical" attitude, 128-29, 147n14, 315
close reading, 12, 98-99
Cocteau, Jean, 266n60, 305, 307, 322n24. *See also* Stravinsky: *Oedipus Rex*
Colciaghi, Ebe, 259
Cold War, 14, 32-34, 38, 244, 307, 310, 313
Cologne Opera, 323n32
Cone, Edward, 122n18
Congress for Cultural Freedom (CCF), 14, 247-51, 253-54, 308, 310-11, 322n20; festivals: *East-West Musical Encounter*, 304, 307; *Masterpieces of the 20th Century*, 34, 248, 250, 253, 304-6, 308;

Music in the Twentieth Century, 304, 306; *Tradition and Change in Music*, 304, 308; resistance to, 307–8, 315; suspicion of, 305;
Conley, Eugene, 269, 272
consumerism, 33, 35, 37, 43–44, 98–99, 311
Cooke, Deryck, 149, 163, 169, 192
Cooper, Christiane, 261
Copland, Aaron, 246, 265n28
Corigliano, John, *Ghosts of Versailles*, 318, 325n70
counterpart funds, 247–48, 250, 253, 258
Covent Garden. *See* Royal Opera House
Cowles, Chandler, 241
Cox, John, 275, 289
Craft, Robert (Bob), *314*; as author/memoirist, 11, 65–66, 245; as conductor, 50, 123–24, 278, 306; contradictions/revisions of, 17n24, 18n37, 23, 29, 44n2, 45n13, 50, 52, 125, 142, 239, 267n75, 295n51, 305, 321n7, 323n35, 324n55; "Craft–Igor," 25, 45n13, 287–88, 301; diary accounts, 6, 19–20, 254–55, 260–62, 266n56, 279–80, 284, 287–89, 292n1, 294n41, 305, 310; mistakes of, 24, 35, 46n27, 74n41, 147n23, 194n1, 265n30; as protégé/assistant, 13, 20, 26, 33, 162, 314, 315, 316; Stravinskys, relationship with, 40–41, 44n2, 56, 73n17, 123, 124, 146n3, 259, 264n1. Critical responses of: *See under* Auden: *Delia*; under *Rake's Progress*: libretto, text settings.
Crosby, John, 275–77
Cuenod, Hugues, 262, 269
cultural acts, 99
cultural capital, 38, 99. *See also* highbrow culture
cultural moment, 3, 11, 13, 33–34, 306, 313
Cumming, Naomi, 155–56

Dahl, Ingolf, 239
Davenport-Hines, Richard, 72
De Neufville, Lawrence, 248
Diaghilev, Serge, 3, 32, 47n43, 128, 201, 237, 310, 315, 320; "World of Art" circle, 152, 170n10
disinterestedness, 300, 304, 311, 316; perverse economy of, 38, 309, 314, 320–21

distance (theatrical): defined, 150–52, 324n53; in comic opera, 153–55, 156–61; in music, 152–56, (diminished) 168, 170n22; in *Rake's Progress*, 191–92, 198, 212, (*Cantata*) 301 (see also *Rake's Progress*, productions: "pop"; puppet theater effect). *See also* Brecht, alienation; play; sincere vs. insincere; Stravinsky: expressiveness.
disposition (Bourdieu), 12, 72n9, 98, 101, 304, 312
Dolar, Mladen, 5
Don Quixote, Auden's interpretation of, 88, 90–92, 94. See also *Rake's Progress*: Tom as Ironic Hero
Donizetti, Gaetano, 144, 178; *Don Pasquale*, 181, 184–85
Downes, Olin, 245, 246, 270, 271
Dubinsky, David, 245, 248

Ebert, Carl, 41, 232n4, 238, 239, 260–62, 273–74, 284
Economic Recovery Program (ERP, Marshall Plan), 248, 250, 253. *See also* counterpart funds
Edinburgh (Festival), 232n4, 238–39, 240, 256, 258, 264n8. *See also* Glyndebourne, British premiere
Eliot, T. S., 78, 92, 278, 316
English Opera Group, 26–27, 45n11, 46n20, 317
Erlanger, Baroness Catherine d', 259
Esquire, 271
Europe-America Groups (EAG), 244
"Evenings on the Roof" concerts, 56, 124
existential state: aimlessness, 56, 81, 86; despair, 94, 99; suffering, 53. *See also* Kierkegaard; Sartre
expressionism, 289, 311; hyper-, 318

Faust legend, references to: 56, 63, 87, 162, 291; Faustian pact, 78, 124, 311, 313; Goethe's *Faust* (redemption), 82–83, 87, 90, 92–93, 216; Mephistopheles, 10, 20, 28, 80–81 (see also *Rake's Progress*, characters: Nick Shadow). *See also* Mann, *Doctor Faustus*
Farrell, Anthony Brady, 241

Farfield Foundation, 253, 266n44, 308. *See also* Congress for Cultural Freedom
La Fenice: Teatro, 19, 21, 41, 237, 239, 254, 256, 258, 263, 271; Taverna, 22, 44, 262. *See also* Venice
"feel for the game," 12, 20, 313–14
field. *See* habitus and field
Fleischmann, Julius, 248, 308. *See also* Farfield Foundation
Floyd, Carlisle, 317
Ford Foundation, 306, 307, 311, 320, 323nn28–29
Frankfurt Opera, 318, 324n63
freedom, 34, 37–38, 41, 225; artistic ("free artist"), 99, 244, 245, 312; icon of, 304; postmodern, 319; Stravinsky's terror of, 312–13. *See also* Auden: on opera as expression of free will
Freud, Sigmund, 5; image, 291; influence on Auden, 43, 56, 78–81, 95n14. *See also* *Rake's Progress*: allegorical meaning

Gabarain, Marina de, *60*, 276
Geneva, 287, 292n1
Ghirighelli, Antonio, 239, 257–58
Gide, André, 16n3, 87, 95n37, 126, 170n12, 266n60, 324n53. *See also* Stravinsky, *Perséphone*
Gishford, Anthony, 273
Glass, Philip, 317; *Einstein on the Beach*, 318, 321
Gluck, Christoph Willibald, 4, 10, 181; *Orpheus and Euridice*, 5, 156, 321
Glyndebourne Opera, ix, 238, 239, 268; British premiere (1953), 232n4, 262, 269, 273–75, *276–77*; English premiere (1954), 280, 292; (1975), 287, 289–90
Gramm, Donald, 299
Great artist ("genius"), 3, 14, 33, 289, 314–16; and Great work, 278; "pure" artist, 304
Greenberg, Clement, 33, 35, 38, 43, 58, 244
Griffiths, Paul, 74n41, 98, 117, 122n17, 163, 205, 292n3
Gueden, Hilde, 269, 272, 293n7

Habermas, Jürgen, 57
habitus and field, 12–13, 20, 98, 321; dramatized, 291

Hamburg Staatsoper, 77, 268–69, 279, 286, 287, 292, 293n13, 323n33
Handel, Georg Friedrich, 8, 27, 130, 313; *Semele*, 20
Harbison, John, 318
Harper's Bazaar, 34
Harrell, Mack, 269
Hartford, Huntington, 241, 264n11
Hatten, Robert, 154–55
Hawkes, Ralph, 13, 24, 26–28, 45n11, 61, 238–39, 240, 264n8, 273, 304; death of, 242, 255
Heggie, Jake, 318
Henze, Han Werner, 316; operas by, 7
highbrow (elitist) culture, 35, 37–38, 58, 98, 311, 320
Hindemith, Paul, 102, 244, 246
Hockney, David, 289–90, 292, 295n57
Hoffman, E. T. A., 93
Hogarth, William, 23, 27, 45nn8–9, 269, 275; "bourgeois cautionary tales," 57–58, 216; image in productions, 290; works of: *A Harlot's Progress*, 57; *Idleness and Industry*, 57, 58, 88; *Marriage A-la-Mode*, 23–24, 57, 61; "The Tête à Tête," 59, *60*, 73n25. *See also A Rake's Progress*
Homan, Jennifer, 320–21
Hook, Sydney, 244, 245, 308, 323n32
Horgan, Paul, 278, 316
Houston Grand Opera, 319
Hulme, T. E., 129, 147n17
humanism (liberal), 5, 7, 43, 317
Huxley, Aldous, 49, 52, 62

Immendorff, Jörg, 243, 289, 290–92, 295n60
individuality. *See* subject
Isherwood, Christopher, 53, 69

Jaffe, Rhoda, 71–72
James, Henry, 146n3, 201
Jonson, Ben, 302; *The Alchemist*, 59
Joseph, Charles, 24, 45n13, 267n67
Josselson, Michael, 253, 265n32
Juilliard School, 123, 242; Quartet, 40
Jung, Carl: individuation (shadow, anima), 80–82, 95n24, 95n30; Auden, influence on, 56, 79, 80, 95n31. *See also Rake's Progress*: allegorical meaning

Kagel, Mauricio, 317
Kallman, Chester, 263, 273; on Baba, 201, 269; death of, 313; defense of act breaks, 196–98; as manic-depressive, 71; outline of Auction duet, 46n27, 202, 203, 205. See also Auden: collaboration with; relationship with; *Delia. See also* under *Rake's Progress*: interpretation; as Opera, tribute to; libretto; notes (1964); scenario, criticism of. *See also* under Stravinsky
Kendall, Raymond, 239–40
Kennan, George, 32, 244, 248
Kennedy, Jacqueline, 309–10, 315
Kennedy, John F., 50, 310, 315
Kerman, Joseph, 52, 83, 87–88, 92–93, 225
Khrennikov, Tikhon, 309
Kierkegaard, Søren: on Don Giovanni, 82–83, 89, 93; influence on Auden, 56, 78–79, 92; "leap into the absurd," 88, 216, 224; "sensuous genius," 73n10, 83; state of anxiety, 89, 94, 232n24. *See also* existential state; *Rake's Progress*: allegorical meaning
Kirstein, Lincoln, 4, 13, 54, 70, 123, 201, 240–41, *314*
kitsch, 35, 70, 291, 301, 324n51. *See also* Greenberg, Clement
Klemperer, Otto, 239
Koestenbaum, Wayne, 70
Kolodin, Irving, 270, 273–74
Kramer, Jonathan, 319
Kramer, Lawrence, 7
Kristol, Irving, 244

Labroca, Mario, 239, 243, 249, 251–53, 254, 258
Lancaster, Osbert, 273–75, *276*, 290
Lasky, Melvin, 247, 308
Leibowitz, Rene, 13, 30–31, 39, 41, 46n33, 47n39, 48n67, 100, 312
Leitner, Ferdinand, 196, 255, 259, 261, 262
Levitz, Tamara, 16n3
Lewis, Richard, *60*, 276
Lieberman, Rolf, 286
Life (magazine), 34
Ligiti, György, 7; *Le Grand Macabre*, 317
London. *See* Royal Opera House

Los Angeles, culture of European émigrés in, 42–43
Los Angeles Times, 82
Love's Labour's Lost (Shakespeare), 17n18, 44. *See also* Nabokov, works of
Lupishko, Marina, 147n14

MacDonald, Dwight, 244
Machaut, Guillaume de, 314, 316
MacLeish, Archibald, 32
Maggio Musicale Fiorentino (Florence Music Festival), 251, 254, 256
Mahler, Gustav, 271
Mann, Erika, 43
Mann, Klaus, 43, 53
Mann, Thomas, 13, 29, 237; *Doctor Faustus*, 8, 17n18, 41–44, 84, 87, 94, 225, 301, 311–12
Marion, André, 303
Marshall Plan. *See* Economic Recovery Program
Marxism (Marx), 43–44; Adorno's, 34, 311–12; Brecht's, 150
mass culture, 35, 41, 44, 244. *See also* consumerism; totalitarianism
Mayer, Elizabeth, 70, 255, 260
Mayer, Martin, 271
McCarthy, Mary, 244–45, 248, 308
McFadden, George, 67, 85, 88–90, 95n9
Mechem, Kirk, *Tartuffe*, 325n70
Mendelson, Edward, 54, 71, 201
Menotti, Giancarlo, 241, 293n13, 317; operas by, 240
Messiaen, Olivier, 7, 30, 317
Metropolitan Opera, The, 62, 70, 196, 201, 238, 258, 318, 320, 321; American premiere, 41, 262, 269–72, 273–74, 275, 293n7, 293n13
Meyerhold, Vsevolod, 152, 260
middlebrow culture, 37–38; 47n60, 241, 300–1, 303–4, 316. *See also* bourgeois, kitsch
Milan. *See* La Scala
Mitchell, Donald, 101–2
modern era, 4, 5, 7, 11, 16, 34, 37, 80, 287, 316; act of faith, 315; condition, 98; ears, 153; hero, 93; sensibilities, 292; society, 43
modernism (twentieth-century), 7, 11, 15, 37, 44; as antipopular, 35; as antirealist, 128, 153; Stravinskian, 129

modernist crisis, 3–4, 29, 53, 95n9, 99; hero, 88, 94; music, 28, 41–42, 101–2, 306, 311–12, (Soviet condemnation of) 244, 246; opera, 10, 25, 318; theater, 150–52
modernity, 35, 311
Monk, Meredith, 318
Monteverdi, Claudio, 225, 228; *L'Orfeo*, 8, 152–53, 163; "La Musica," 212
Monteux, Pierre, 305
Mozart, Wolfgang Amadeus, 4, 5, 26, 144, 169, 185, 271, 316 (see also *Rake's Progress*, as model for); Works of: *Così fan tutte*, 82, 150, 153–55, 166, 168, 170n19; "Di scrivermi," 156–61, 166, 191; "Di scrivermi," performances of, 28, 238; *Don Giovanni*, 23, 82, 87, 90, 95n28, 97, 150, 181, 232n23; *Don Giovanni*, enlarged orchestra for, 271; *Don Giovanni*, Kierkegaard on, 73n10, 82–83, 89, 93; *Die Entführung aus dem Seraglio*, 23; *Le Nozze di Figaro*, 70, 181; *Die Zauberflöte*, 8, 95n24; film, 287, 294n31. See also *Rake's Progress*: intertextural references
Musgrave, Thea, 317
"music (work) itself," 11–12, 98
mythology. See *Rake's Progress*: allegorical meaning

Nabokov, Nicolas (Nika or "Nicky"): Auden, relationship with, 32, 62, 78; "bohemian" private life, 244, 265n31; as cosmopolitan, 34, 38; death, 313; as elitist, 34–35, 38, 43; as "kitschy," 35, 301; opposition to Soviet Union, 34, 244–48; *Rake's Progress*, interest in, 4, 6, 15, 19–20, 22, 40, 44n2; *Rake's Progress*, as liaison for premiere, 33, 237, 243–44, 253–54; *Rake's Progress*, letter of December 1950, 78, 239, 249, 251, 252, 266n48; as secretary-general of CCF, 33, 266n44, 323n32 (see also Berlin Arts Festival; Congress for Cultural Freedom); Stravinsky, relationship with, 13, 32, 47n44; Stravinsky, as friend, 39, 40, 41, 306–7, 309, 313; Stravinsky, as defender/promoter, 31, 33–34, 304, 308, 309, 315, 322n20, 323n33;

unreliability of, 32–33, 250. See also "feel for the game"
Nabokov, Nicolas (Nika or "Nicky"), works of: *Love's Labour's Lost*, 7, 17n18, 313; *Ode*, 32, 47n43; *Rasputin's End*, 323n32; *Return of Pushkin*, 40; *Union Pacific*, 32, 35; writings of: "The Atonal Trail," 31, 38, 47n41; *Bagázh*, 32, 250
Nabokov, Vladimir, 32
Nazi Germany (Nazis), 30, 42–43, 53; de-Nazification, 32
neoclassicism, 12, 15–16, 29, 44, 101, 128, 272, 300–1; neoclassical clutter, 318; play, 289. See also under Stravinsky: periods
New York City Ballet (Ballet Society), 40, 240, 305, 308, 320
New York Intellectuals, 244
New York Times, 19, 24, 26, 162, 245, 310
Nietszche, Friedrich, 42, 73n16, 78
Nijinsky, Vaslav, 317
Non-Communist Left (NCL), 34, 244
Nono, Luigi, 317
Nouvel, Walter, 25, 45n15

Offenbach, Jacques: *Les Contes d'Hoffman*, 202, 259
opera: "ballet opera," 152; conventional ("Opera"), 4, 7–8, 150, 169, (real) 300, 314, 316, 318 (see also *Rake's Progress* as Opera); as cultural relic, 5, 15; "death" of, 4–5, 7–8, 10, 98, 306, 317; "death" of, "non-actual" demand for, 319–21; English-language, renewal of, 26, 54; Golden Age of, 4–5, 8, 25; impracticality of, 25–26; sung drama, 7–8, 153, 192, 318, 320–21; transvestism in, 201
opera, types of, historical: ballad opera, 28; bel canto, 130, 144, 149, (multipart structure) 178, 268, 319; grand opera, 205; masque, 7, 26, 302, 303; musical theater, 8; music drama, 7, 8, 9–11, 16, 27, 56, 272; *opera buffa*, 8, 9, 15, 27–28, 44, 153, 157, (finale) 181, 280; *opera seria*, 7–8, 181; operetta, 28, 155; recitative style (Monteverdi), 225, 228; semi-opera, 7, 26, 54
opera, types of, recent: anti-opera (*Musiktheater*), 317, 318–19; neo-opera,

289; postopera, 15–16, 318, 321; religious drama, 316, 317
Opéra Comique, 305
Opera News, 272
opera queens, 14, 70, 99, 201
Ortega y Gasset, José, 37–38, 98, 319; "The Dehumanization of Art," 35, 128–30, 152, 168–69

Paris, Grand Opéra, 257, 258, 304–5
Partisan Review, 30, 41
"Peace, Cultural and Scientific Conference for," 38, 245, 248
Peabody School of Music, 249
Peele, George, *The Old Wives' Tale*, 303
Peirce, Charles, 155
Pergolesi, Giovanni Battista, 62
Perle, George, 314
Picasso, Pablo, 12, 289, 269, 305, 310, 314
Piovesan, Alessandro, 252
Piper, John, 46n20, 259
Pirandello, Luigi, 35, 152
play, 150; parody, 154–55, 161, ("camp") 201; "seeing as," 156. *See also* distance; sincere vs. insincere; *Rake's Progress*, as parody
postmodern: age, 5, 7, 292; culture (postmodernism), 99, 201, 287, 289, 319; *Rake's Progress* as, 15–16, 291; scholars, 3. *See also under* opera, recent types of
Poulenc, Francis, 30, 46n36
Pousseur, Henri, 317
Previn, Andre, 318
Price, Leontyne, 306, 307, 323n29
Prokofieff, Serge, 32, 34, 47n50, 244
Puccini, Giacomo, 5, 300; *Turandot*, 238
Purcell, Henry, 26–27, 130, 163, 228; *King Arthur*, 54; *The Fairy Queen*, 149–51

Radio Audizioni Italiane (RAI), 251, 253, 262, 267n78
Rake's Progress, A (Hogarth), 23–24, 28, 35–37, 57–58, 61, 83; as catabasis, 56, 92–93; Hockney's, 289; "Sarah Young" in, 36, 57, 83, 225; images of: "The Heir," (print) 36, (painting) 37; "The Levee," 8, 9, 36; "The Orgy," 58, 59; "The Marriage," 61; "The Gaming House," 63; "The Madhouse," 63, 64, 83, 87, 224
Rake's Progress, The (Stravinsky)
  act breaks: Stravinsky's frustration with stops, 196–97, 231n4, 262; two-act division, 232n4, 279–81
  allegorical meaning: as artist (Immendorff), 291, 295n60; as Auden/Kallman relationship, 71–72, 75n54; as classical myth, 56, 84–87, 90, 92–93; as Freudian self/super-ego/volition, 79–80, 83 (*see also* Freud); as Jungian shadow/anima, 80–81, 83, 90, 92–93, 224 (*see also* Jung); as Kierkegaardian ascent (redemption), 81, 88–90, 92–94, 201, 216, 224 (*see also* Kierkegaard); as Opera, 11, 29; as Progress/Return, 28–29, 65, 82, 87, 93, 212, 215, 224; as Progress, three-stage (wishes), 63–64, 76–78, 79, 88, 280; as seasonal cycle, 85–87
  Auden/Stravinsky collaboration, 6, 8–9, 20, 40, 51, 50–53, 61, 190; November 1947 meeting, 28, 54–55, 62–63, 74n34, 94 (*see also under* Auden: Delia; *Rake's Progress*: scenario; Stravinsky: Auden)
  Broadway, potential for, 23, 54, 240–41, 301
  chords, favorite, 104–5, 110, 119, 162, 163, 181, 188, 189, 192, 194n7, 212, 232n21
  choric parabasis, 62, 155, 231
  chronology, 194n1
  cuts to, 280, 294n29
  "dolce" markings, 152–53, 212, 214
  initial ideas, abandoned, 55, 61–63, 76–77, 85, 196, 198, 201
  interpretation/rationale: Auden's, 71, 76, 80; Kallman's, 63
  intertextural references, 20–23, 103; *Les Contes d'Hoffman*, 202; *Così*, 20, 161, 163, 166, 181, 184; *Don Giovanni*, 23, 232n23; *Don Pasquale*, 181, 184–85; "Dove sono," 178–80; *L'Orfeo*, 152–53
  libretto, 50; commissioning of, 27, 61–62, 74n27, 256; critical responses to, 50, 52, 56–57, 77, 299; exact attribution, 66–67; revisions to, 6, 78, 87, 147n10, 189–91; Stravinsky's reaction to, 40, 74n39 (*see also* Auden: Kallman, collaboration with)

Rake's Progress, The (Stravinsky) *(cont.)*
  libretto, as parody (critique) of: "*l'acte gratuit*," 34, 37, 77, 89, 225 (see also Sartre); Augustan poets, 301; Christian tragic hero, 92; enlightened thought, 58–59, 89; "grand" theater, 197; nursery rhyme, 55, 135
  metronome markings, 126, 210–12
  Mozart, as model for, 9, 15, 19, 27–28, 98, 130, 144, 150, 189, 192
  off-stage voices, 198, 202, 286
  as Opera: conventional (vs. Music Drama), 7, 9–11, 15, 23, (pure) 50, 130, 153, 237, 272, 300; apotheosis of, 98, 319–21; "number," 9, 27–28, 69, 135, 180; tribute to, 11, 29
  orchestration: winds (reeds), 152, 175, 212, 216–17, 224; harpsichord (cembalo), 149, 210–12, 215, 271; string harmonics, 207
  program (liner) notes: (1951) 23, 26; (1953) 9, 11, 23, 45n8, 50, 52; (1964) 9–10, 11, 66
  productions, stylized: baroque, 281, 284, 282–83; "mod," 287–89; "pop," 289–90; postmodern, 290–91; puppet theater effect, 282–83, 284, 286, 291; "off-kilter," 273, 274–75, 276–77. See also Bergman, Caldwell, Geneva, Glyndebourne, Hamburg, Hockney, Immendorff, Metropolitan, Opéra Comique, Royal Opera, Santa Fe, Vienna
  reuse of melodies, 90, 174, 210, 207–9, 216
  reviews: Boston, 288; Glyndebourne, 149, 273–74, 287, 289–90; Hamburg, 77, 78; Metropolitan, 270–71; Royal Swedish, 279, 284; Salzburg, 290–91; Venice, 11, 19. See also text settings, critical reactions to
  scenario (outline), 28, 46n27, 63–65, 84, 161, 198; Kallman's criticism of, 66, 76, 78. See also initial ideas
  sketches: (1.1) 126–27, 130; (1.2) 138–40, *139*, *165*; (1.3) 140–45, *142–43*; (2.2) 187–88, *192*; (3.1) 198, 132, *133–34*, 198; (3.2) 30, 103–4, 110–11, 172, *173*, 217, 220; (3.3) 109
  Stravinsky's artistic crisis, as prompting, 14–15, 301, 304
  Stravinsky's assessment of staging: Bergman's, 279, 286; Caldwell's, 288; Ebert's, 41, 261–62

  Stravinsky's preference for small theater, 238–39, 258, 271–72
  synopsis, 10
  text settings: approach to, 124–25, 129–30; critical reactions to, 125–26, 130, 142, 147n10; heightened, 140–46, 185, 207, 228–31; natural, 129–35; subverted, 135–40, 185
  text settings, English: as determining factor, 26–27, 254; timidity about, 28
  time: suspension of, (Graveyard) 64–65, 88, 210, 214–15; timelessness, sense of, 89, 216, 221–24; turning back of (Brothel), 161–62
  tonal symbolism, 118, 122n17, 163, 168, 172, 174–75, 178, 198; in *Così*, 170n19; "sharps vs. flats," 205; tonal illusion/posttonal reality, 118–19, 166, 189, 194, 224–31, 299
Rake's Progress, The (Stravinsky), characters
  Anne, 10; as determined, 81, 175, 185, 194; as doubtful, 181, 185, 192; as faithful Girl, 28, 63; "goodness" of, 68, 80 (see also Jung: anima; as "Venus," 29, 83, 84–87
  Baba, 10, 23, 50, 52, 76, 181, 189–90; as "Artist," 201; depth of, 81, 169, 205; as "homosexual joke," 200–1; as "mechanical," 202
  Mother Goose, 55, 81, 85
  Nick, 50, 52, 55; as actor, 80, 168; as Mephistopheles, 10, 78–81, 161–2 (see also Jung: shadow); as preacher, 90; as puppeteer, 168, 198, 286; as Villain, 28, 63–65
  Sellem, 55, 198, 288
  Tom, 10, 55, 194; as "Adonis," 65, 84–87, 216–17; death of, 231, 299; as Faust, 83, 87; as Hero, 28, 63–65; as Ironic Hero, 88, 90–94; as manic-depressive, 71, 76; as static, 29, 178
Rake's Progress, The (Stravinsky), motives
  (+1, –2): (1.2) 163–64; (1.3) 178–80; (2.2) 181–83, 187, 189, 192–93, 194; (3.1) 205–6; (3.2) 106, 110–11; (3.3) 119–21, 299
  "B-A-C-H," 106, 110, 122n11
  "C-C#/Db," 111, 126, 165, 172–74, 188, 212;
  "Db-D§," 224–25, 231

motivic spans, 180, 192–94, 212–13, 225, 228
"trill," 174, 216–20, 221–23
Rake's Progress, The (Stravinsky), premiere of, 21, 263
  Auden's disgruntlement with: accommodations, 260; Ebert's staging, 260–61; fee/royalties, 255–56, 266n60, 302; Stravinsky's conducting, 255
  Auden's wish to direct, 238, 260, 261–62
  celebration, 20, 22, 29, 44
  Stravinsky's efforts to "cash in on," 240–42, 251, 252, 254–55, 259
  See also La Fenice, Venice Festival of Contemporary Music
Rake's Progress, The (Stravinsky), specific scenes and numbers
  (1.1) prelude, 152–53, 174; introduction, 212–14; duet, 85, 126–27, 155, 174; aria, 58, 71, 79–80, 89; arioso, 20, 68; duettino, 174; terzetto, 20, 23
  (1.2) opening chorus, 85, 147n10, 280; catechism, 55, 80–81, 156–59; cavatina, 20, 71, 89, 146, 149–50, 161–69; "Lanterloo," 135–40, 174; whores' chorus, 20, 166, 168
  (1.3) 81, 175–78; introduction, 212–14, aria, 68, 117–18, 130, 140–46, 146, 178; prayer, 174, 178; cabaletta, 5–6, 71, 174, 178–80
  (2.1) Tom's aria, 67, 72, 82, 84, 90, 162, 178; Nick's aria, 77, 80, 89, 131, 162, 276; duet, 90
  (2.2) 180–83; introduction, 181–85, 286; arioso, 82, 174, 185–88, 215; duet, 188–89; trio, 146, 189–93; finale, 190, 192–94; 277, 283
  (2.3) aria, 60, 131, 155; Bread machine, 59, 89–90, 92, 154, 280–80; prayer, 90, 162, 174
  (3.1) 172, 196–99, 204; opening chorus, 198–200; aria, 55, 58, 125, 131–35, 198; Baba's awakening, 202; ballad tune, 67, 172, 202, 207–10, 286; duet with chorus, 69, 81, 202–6
  (3.2) 63–65, 210–11, 213; prelude, 40, 103–7, 110–16, 172; duet 67–68, 174, 216–18; ballad tune, 207–9; card-guessing game, 55, 82, 87, 89, 94, 131, 212–15;

Anne's appearance, 174, 207, 210, 215; Nick's descent, 162; Tom as "Adonis," 174, 216, 218
  (3.3) 221, 224–27; arioso, 20, 85, 280; duet, 84, 89, 146, 149, 174, 221–24; lullaby, 102–3, 107–11; duettino, 87, 117–19, 225; Tom's death, 225–31; "mourning" chorus, 155, 231
  epilogue, 23, 52, 79, 80, 82–83, 281–82, 299–300
Ramparts (magazine), 310
Ratto, Gianni, 259, 260, 275
Ravel, Maurice: *L'Heure espagnole*, 23
Reiner, Fritz, 264n8, 269–70, 271, 273–74
Reinhardt, Max, 260
Rennert, Günther, 78, 268
Ricketson, Frank, 241–42, 258
Rimsky-Korsakov, Nicolai: *Sadko*, 103, 311
Robinson, Paul, 70
Roland-Manuel, Alexis, 25
romanticism, 129, 311
Rosbaud, Hans, 305
Rose, Billy, 241
Rosenthal, Manuel, 30
Ross, Alex, 323n40
Roth, Ernst, 242–43, 255, 256–58, 266n57, 274, 305
Rothmüller, Marko, 276
Rothstein, Edward, 290, 291
Rounseville, Robert, 259–62, 267n69
Rossini, Gioachino, 8, 26
Royal Opera House (Covent Garden, London), 27, 238, 241–42, 257, 258, 264n10, 269, 295n64
Royal Swedish Opera, ix, 278, 281, 282–83, 285, 287. *See also* Bergman
Rubinstein, Ida, 16n3
Russian formalists, 102, 169n8, 170n12

Saariaho, Kaija, 317
St. John's College, 32
St. Petersburg, 264n1
Sadler's Wells Theater, New Opera Company at, 292n3
Salzburg Festival, 256, 307. *See also* Immendorff
Santa Fe Opera, ix, 271, 275–77, 316
Sapiro, Aaron, 200–1, 238, 266n60

Sargent, Wintrop, 293n13
Sartre, Jean-Paul: "*l'acte gratuite*," 37, 77, 225; on emotion, 150, 155, 168–69; as existentialist 33–34, 35, 43, 77–78, 94
Saunders, Frances Stonor, 244
La Scala (Milan), 196, 238, 239, 241–43, 254–55, 256–62
Schaeffner, André, 30–31, 47n41
Schiff, David, 300
Schlesinger, Arthur Jr., 33, 244, 309; *The Vital Center*, 34
Schoenberg, Arnold, 12–13, 34, 43, 100, 124, 244, 246, 316; as character model for Mann, 42, 44, 311; influence on Stravinsky, 301, 322n7; loneliness of, 311–12. *See also* Stravinsky: dualism with
Schoenberg, Arnold, works of: *Erwartung*, 5, 289, 305, 311, 324n51; operas, 11; *Pierrot Lunaire*, 12, 124; *Serenade*, 124; *Septet-Suite*, 124, 301; "Vielseitigkeit" from *Drei Satiren*, 29
Schwarzkopf, Elizabeth, 262, 263, 293n7
Scruton, Roger, 150, 156
semiotics: sign/signified, 149, 153–54; interpreter/interpretant, 155–56
Sharon, Yuval, 318
Shestov, Lev, 78
Shreffler, Anne, 322n20
sincere (real) vs. insincere (feigned, artificial), 153–62, 168–69; in *Così fan tutte*, 170n19
Shostakovich, Dimitri, 34–35, 244, 245–47, 301, 310; 7th Symphony, 35, 47n50. *See also* Stravinsky: dualism with
Slottsteater (Drottningholm), 281
Smith, Roberta, 290
Soane's Museum, Sir John, 24, 36–37
sociological perspective, 15, 17n32, 43, 98, 303, 319, 321; effect, 35; factors, 99; phenomenon, 315. *See also* Auden: sociologists, dislike of; Bourdieu
Southern California, University of (USC), 239, 242
Souvtchinsky, Pierre, 30–31, 45n15, 46n37, 232n24, 310, 315
Soviet Union (Russia), 33, 309–10; Bolsheviks, 14, 78, 246; *Red Star* (newspaper), 245; Soviet music, 35, 39; stranglehold on culture, 34, 40, 244, 246–47, 309. *See also* Cold War; Nabokov, opposition to; "Peace, Cultural and Scientific Conference for"
Spender, Stephen, 146n3, 323n32
State Department, US, 247–48, 254, 259, 307, 323n29. *See also* Bohlen; Kennan
Steinberg, Michael, 288
Steptoe, Andrew, 155, 170n19
Stockhausen, Karlheinz, 7, 313, 317
Stravinsky, Igor, 22, 40, 51, 263, 314
  aesthetic change, 25, 315. *See also Rake's Progress*: Stravinsky's artistic crisis
  Auden: affinity/contrast with, 54–56; respect for, 7, 53, 135, 256. *See also* under *Rake's Progress*
  audience, attempts to please, 15, 304
  conducting, 254–55; Cuba tour, 243, 259
  death, 44, 314–15; burial, 237, 264n1
  eightieth birthday celebration, 254, 309–10
  expressiveness ("cold-hot" manner), 278, 284, 286, 287; embrace of, 15–16, 126–28, 129–30, 168–69 (see also *Rake's Progress*: (1.2) cavatina, (1.3) aria, (3.2) Anne's appearance, (3.3) Tom's death); resistance to, 55, 152, 155 (*see also under* distance. *See also* under *Rake's Progress*, scenes: (2.3) bread machine; (3.1) ballad tune; (3.2) card-guessing game; epilogue)
  family responsibilities, 25, 304
  health of, 39, 45n13, 278, 306; decline, 313
  image of in productions, 289, 291
  income: commissions, 252, 302–3, 307, 308, 316, 323n33; conducting, 15, 252, 253, 305, 306; other sources, 324n46. *See also* Boosey & Hawkes, formal agreement with; *Rake's Progress*: premiere, efforts to "cash in on"
  influence, susceptibility to, 3, 311. *See also under* Schoenberg
  Kallman, respect for, 65–66, 302
  Mann, as character model for, 8, 41, 44
  opera, feelings about, 4, 9, 169n4
  periods: Russian, 14, 126, 128–29, 217; neoclassical, 11, 14–15, 38, 101, 126, 129, 147n14; serial, 14, 304, 309, 311

proposed works (unrealized): Negro spirituals, 307, 323n30; operas: with Auden (*Delia*), 7, 50, 54, 302–3; with T. S. Eliot, 278, 316; with Dylan Thomas, 316

Stravinsky's revisionism, 322n23; suspicion of, 25, 46n29

Russian circle, 39–40, *40*, 308

Shostakovich, dualism with, 38

Schoenberg, dualism with, 11, 13, 15, 29–31, 34, 38, 41, 101, 301, 304, 315. See also Schoenberg, influence

world events, effect of on, 3, 25; Cold War, 304, 309–10; Russian revolution, 14, 101; World War II, 30, 33. See also Cold War

Stravinsky, Igor, compositional practices of
chord transformations, 104, 106, 117–18, 205–6
disjunction/stratification (bitonality), 118–19, 166, 188, 194
metrical counterpoint (polymeter), 135–40, 299, 301
modal mixture, 178–80; conflict, 212; shift, 232n23
modulation, 163–66, 231
octatonic scale, 119, 122n19, 162
rhythmic displacement, 107–9, 111, 122n13, 126, 135, 138, 144, 156, 216–21, 228, 301; radical/conservative barring, 135–38
recomposition (collage), 102, 181
tonality, rhetorical use of, 101–2
tonal/posttonal interplay, 107–21, 188, 194 (see also under *Rake's Progress*: tonal illusion)

Stravinsky, Igor, works of
Abraham and Isaac, 308, 324n46
Agon, 14, 50, 309, 316, 320
Apollo (Apollon musagète) 11, 32, 50, 129, 268, 272, 320
Cantata, 14; "Ricercar I," 301, 322n9, "Ricercar II," 322n7
Canticum Sacrum, 14, 237, 252, 308
Circus Polka, 38
Danses concertantes, 30, 123
Ebony Concerto, 38, 237
Firebird, 305, 308
The Flood, 316
Four Norwegian Moods, 30, 33, 301

Histoire du Soldat (The Soldier's Tale), 27, 38, 268, 286; as distant (cartoonish), 128, 152, 168, 299, 170n10; as Faust story, 63, 313; use of polymeter in, 138, 140
Jeu de Cartes, 50
Mass, 38, 40, 239, 254, 268
Mavra, 9, 26, 130, 201, 268, 275
Movements, 308
Les Noces (The Wedding), 9, 14, 26, 32, 38, 124, 126–28, 135
Oedipus Rex, 14, 27, 35, 266n60, 275, 278; as collage, 181, 301; as distant (masked), 128; as hybrid form, 9, 129, 316; as Latin setting, 26, 128, 147n14; double bill with *Erwartung*, 305–6, 307
Orpheus, 40, 50, 123, 129, 240, 272, 305, 308, 320
Perséphone, 16n3, 27, 87, 96n37, 124, 129, 254, 266n60; as French setting 26, 147n14, 147n21; as hybrid form, 9, 130
Petrushka, 32, 35, 43, 152, 155, 254
Pulcinella, 3, 9, 61, 124, 128
Renard, 128, 152, 170n10
Le Rossignol (The Nightingale), 9, 26, 152, 215, 254
Le Sacre du Printemps (The Rite of Spring), 12, 13, 304–5, 317
Scènes de ballet, 33, 305
Symphonies of Wind Instruments, 123, 210, 232n20
Symphony in C, 124
Symphony in Three Movements, 31
Symphony of Psalms, 26, 38, 147n14
Threni, 308, 309, 323n33, 323n38, 324n46
Violin Concerto, 122n13, 129

Stravinsky, Igor, writings of: autobiography, 8, 25, 45n15; conversation books, 24–25, 45n13, 138, 288, 311, 314 (*see also under* Craft: "Craft-Igor"; revisions of); *Poetics of Music*, 25, 45n15, 101, 312

Stravinsky, Theodore, 268

Stravinsky, Vera, 19, 20, 22, 40, 73n13, 123–24, 237, 254, 259, 260, 306, *314*; diary entries, 23–24, 45n9, 45n12, 313; "La Prima Assoluta," 44n2, 129, 225. See also Craft: Stravinskys', relationship with

Straus, Joseph N., ix, 109, 111, 118, 165, 172, 212, 232n21, 232n23

Strauss, Richard, 4–5, 8, 10, 20, 55, 300; *Ariadne* 268, 281; *Der Rosenkavalier*, 70; *Elektra*, 271
subject (subjectivity), 5, 8, 33, 41, 43, 315, 318; individuated (individual), 34, 35, 37–38, 42, 44, 129, 155–56, (illusion of) 311; postmodern, 99. *See also* Jung, individuation
Swarthmore College, 79, 95n31

Tallchief, Maria, 39, 308
Tangeman, Nell, 263
Taruskin, Richard, 12, 25, 45n13, 46n29, 163, 201; "Rejoicing Discovery," 126, 129–30, 142, 147n10
Taubman, Howard, 19, 44n2
Tchaikovsky, Pyotr Ilyich, 20, 23
Thayer, Charles, 244
Thebom, Blanche, 201, 269
Thomas, Dylan, 316
Tippett, Michael, 317
Tomlinson, Gary, 5
totalitarianism, 33, 35, 37, 99, 311
Tourel, Jennie, 261, 262
Théâtre de Champs-Elysées, 305
thematic reminiscence, 174, 210
Thomson, Virgil, 25, 125–26, 270–71; *Four Saints in Three Acts*, 306, 307
trajectory (Bourdieu), 12–13, 15
Trevor-Roper, Hugh, 247
Turnage, Mark Anthony, 319
Twelve-tone method (dodecaphonicism, serialism), 14, 31, 38, 41–42, 47n41, 311; music, 301; "twelve-toners," 15, 302

USC. *See* Southern California, University of

Van den Toorn, Pieter C., 12, 122n19, 147n14, 147n25–27
Varèse, Edgar, 124
Venice, 14, 67, 197, 237, 243, 264n1, 308, 316; International Festival of Contemporary Music (La Biennale), 238, 251–52, 253, 255–58, 259, 261, 269, 274–75; as venue for premiere, criticism of, 256–57; as venue for premiere, justification for, 239, 258–59, 321
Verdi, Giuseppe, 4, 101, 178, 300; *Falstaff*, 70; *Otello*, 5, 88, 321; *La Traviata*, 202; "Willow Song," 103
Vienna State Opera, 294n29, 306
Vogue, 4, 15
Volga Boat Song, 20
Voltaire, *Candide*, 58
Von Franz, Marie Louise, 81

Wagner, Richard, 4, 20, 55, 57, 87, 169n4, 197, 237, 299; *Gesamtkunstwerk* (anti-), 152; leitmotif, 174; *Das Rheingold*, 89. *See also under* opera, types: music drama. *See also under Rake's Progress*, as Opera: conventional (vs. Music Drama)
Waldorf "Peace" Conference. *See* "Peace, Cultural and Scientific Conference for"
Wallenstein, Alfred, 273–74
Walsh, Stephen, 24, 45n13, 126, 311
Watkins, Glenn, 102
Weber, Hans, 308
Weber, Margrit, 308
Webern, Anton, 29, 124; Quartet, op. 22, 301
Webster, David, 238, 240, 255, 269
Webster, John: *Duchess of Malfi*, 53
Weill, Kurt, 152. *See also* Brecht, *Die Dreigroschenoper*
Weissberger, Arnold, 241–42
Werner galleries, Michael, 290
Wilder, Thornton: *Our Town*, 168
Wilson, Edmund, 70
Wilson, Robert, 318, 321
Wolf, Hugo, 313

Yates Peter, 56

Zhdanov, Andrei, 244
Zimmerman, Bernd Alois, *Die Soldaten*, 318
Žižek, Slavoj, 5

CHANDLER CARTER is Professor of Music at Hofstra University. Besides Stravinsky and opera, his scholarly interests include semiotics and modernist culture. He recently received a prestigious Opera for All Voices commission to compose *This Little Light of Mine*, based on the life of civil rights activist Fannie Lou Hamer.

www.ingramcontent.com/pod-product-compliance
Lightning Source LLC
Chambersburg PA
CBHW071359300426
44114CB00016B/2115